COGNITIVE DISSONANCE

SECOND EDITION

COGNITIVE DISSONANCE

Reexamining a Pivotal Theory in Psychology

EDITED BY
EDDIE HARMON-JONES

AMERICAN PSYCHOLOGICAL ASSOCIATION
Washington, DC

Copyright © 2019 by the American Psychological Association. All rights reserved. Except as permitted under the United States Copyright Act of 1976, no part of this publication may be reproduced or distributed in any form or by any means, including, but not limited to, the process of scanning and digitization, or stored in a database or retrieval system, without the prior written permission of the publisher.

The opinions and statements published are the responsibility of the authors, and such opinions and statements do not necessarily represent the policies of the American Psychological Association.

Published by
American Psychological Association
750 First Street, NE
Washington, DC 20002
www.apa.org

APA Order Department
P.O. Box 92984
Washington, DC 20090-2984
Phone: (800) 374-2721; Direct: (202) 336-5510
Fax: (202) 336-5502; TDD/TTY: (202) 336-6123
Online: http://www.apa.org/pubs/books
E-mail: order@apa.org

In the U.K., Europe, Africa, and the Middle East, copies may be ordered from
Eurospan Group
c/o Turpin Distribution
Pegasus Drive
Stratton Business Park
Biggleswade, Bedfordshire
SG18 8TQ United Kingdom
Phone: +44 (0) 1767 604972
Fax: +44 (0) 1767 601640
Online: https://www.eurospanbookstore.com/apa
E-mail: eurospan@turpin-distribution.com

Typeset in Meridien and Ortodoxa by Circle Graphics, Inc., Reisterstown, MD

Printer: Sheridan Books, Chelsea, MI
Cover Designer: Beth Schlenoff, Bethesda, MD
Cover Art: Mossy Bikoni, b. 1970, One Way (Sens Unique), 2010, mixed media

Library of Congress Cataloging-in-Publication Data
Names: Harmon-Jones, Eddie, editor.
Title: Cognitive dissonance : reexamining a pivotal theory in psychology / edited by Eddie Harmon-Jones.
Description: Second edition. | Washington, DC : American Psychological Association, [2019] | Includes bibliographical references and index.
Identifiers: LCCN 2018043486 (print) | LCCN 2018044132 (ebook) | ISBN 9781433830778 (eBook) | ISBN 1433830779 (eBook) | ISBN 9781433830105 (pbk.) | ISBN 1433830108 (pbk.)
Subjects: LCSH: Cognitive dissonance—Congresses.
Classification: LCC BF337.C63 (ebook) | LCC BF337.C63 C64 2019 (print) | DDC 153.4—dc23

British Library Cataloguing-in-Publication Data
A CIP record is available from the British Library.

Printed in the United States of America

http://dx.doi.org/10.1037/0000135-000

10 9 8 7 6 5 4 3 2 1

CONTENTS

Contributors   vii
Foreword to the First Edition   ix
Foreword to the Second Edition   xi
Preface   xv

1. **An Introduction to Cognitive Dissonance Theory and an Overview of Current Perspectives on the Theory**   3
   Eddie Harmon-Jones and Judson Mills

I. PERSPECTIVES EMPLOYING THE ORIGINAL VERSION OF THE THEORY   25

2. **Improving the 1957 Version of Dissonance Theory**   27
   Judson Mills

3. **A Radical Point of View on Dissonance Theory**   41
   Jean-Leon Beauvois and Robert-Vincent Joule

4. **Understanding the Motivation Underlying Dissonance Effects: The Action-Based Model**   63
   Eddie Harmon-Jones and Cindy Harmon-Jones

5. **What Is Cognitive Consistency, and Why Does It Matter?**   91
   Bertram Gawronski and Skylar M. Brannon

6. **Dissonance Now: How Accessible Discrepancies Moderate Distress and Diverse Defenses**   117
   Ian McGregor, Ian R. Newby-Clark, and Mark P. Zanna

II. THE ROLE OF THE SELF IN DISSONANCE — 139

7. Dissonance, Hypocrisy, and the Self-Concept — 141
   Elliot Aronson

8. Self-Affirmation Theory: An Update and Appraisal — 159
   Joshua Aronson, Geoffrey Cohen, and Paul R. Nail

9. In Search of the Motivation for Dissonance Reduction: The Drive to Lessen Aversive Consequences — 175
   Joel Cooper

III. MATHEMATICAL MODELS, NEURAL ACTIVATIONS, AND AFFECTIVE RESPONSES — 195

10. Modeling Cognitive Dissonance as a Parallel Constraint Satisfaction Network With Learning — 197
    Stephen J. Read and Brian M. Monroe

11. Neural Basis of Cognitive Dissonance — 227
    Keise Izuma and Kou Murayama

12. Moving Beyond Attitude Change in the Study of Dissonance-Related Processes: An Update on the Role of Discomfort — 247
    Patricia G. Devine, John M. Tauer, Kenneth E. Barron, Andrew J. Elliot, Kristen M. Vance, and Eddie Harmon-Jones

Appendix A: Social Communication and Cognition: A Very Preliminary and Highly Tentative Draft — 271
Leon Festinger (1954)

Appendix B: Reflections on Cognitive Dissonance: 30 Years Later — 289
Leon Festinger (1987)

Appendix C: Historical Note on Festinger's Tests of Dissonance Theory — 293
Judson Mills

Index — 295
About the Editor — 303

CONTRIBUTORS

Elliot Aronson, University of California, Santa Cruz
Joshua Aronson, New York University, New York
Kenneth E. Barron, James Madison University, Harrisonburg, VA
Jean-Leon Beauvois, Université de Nice, France
Skylar M. Brannon, University of Texas at Austin
Geoffrey Cohen, Stanford University, Stanford, CA
Joel Cooper, Princeton University, Princeton, NJ
Patricia G. Devine, University of Wisconsin–Madison
Andrew J. Elliot, University of Rochester, Rochester, NY
Bertram Gawronski, University of Texas at Austin
Cindy Harmon-Jones, The University of New South Wales, Australia
Eddie Harmon-Jones, The University of New South Wales, Australia
Keise Izuma, University of Southampton, United Kingdom
Robert-Vincent Joule, Universite de Provence, France
Ian McGregor, University of Waterloo, Canada
Judson Mills, University of Maryland, College Park (deceased)
Brian M. Monroe, University of Alabama, Tuscaloosa
Kou Murayama, University of Reading, United Kingdom, and Kochi University of Technology, Japan
Paul R. Nail, University of Central Arkansas, Conway
Ian R. Newby-Clark, University of Guelph, Canada
Stephen J. Read, University of Southern California, Los Angeles
John M. Tauer, University of St. Thomas, St. Paul, MN
Kristen M. Vance, United States Air Force (retired)
Mark P. Zanna, University of Waterloo, Canada

FOREWORD TO THE FIRST EDITION

"This is more like what I had in mind" could easily be what Leon L. Festinger would have said about this volume had he lived to see it. He would not have been referring to the two appendices that report his own words—the first being his early, unpublished formulation of dissonance theory, the second, his comments on the state of dissonance theory 30 years after its publication. In earlier comments about the state of social psychology, after having been away from the field for several years, he had said, in effect, "It's not exactly what I had in mind."

This is a volume that Leon Festinger surely would have loved to see. It presents a variety of ideas and clever research from a collection of investigators located in Canada, France, and Japan, as well as in the United States, and almost all intended to produce a better understanding of the phenomena of cognitive dissonance. Whereas the common thread is dissonance theory as first stated by Festinger, the common concern starts with the assumption that the theory must be taken seriously. From that point, these chapters fan out into a diverse array of suggestions, propositions, qualifications, and additions for the original theory.

This book contains the medication required for all those people who, quite rightly, became bored with dissonance theory in the later 1960s or early 1970s. The present collection demonstrates clearly and convincingly that the problem was not with the theory but rather with the research that was largely confined to conceptual replications of some of the major implications of the theory. Although the issues addressed in some of the chapters have been around for several years (e.g., the role of the self in the instigation of dissonance and the role of aversive consequences), even in those cases there are new and revealing programs of research reported.

What we also find in this new volume are attempts to make the theory more precise in certain respects, a summary of an ambitious research program centered on the justification of behavior, and a report of carefully crafted research to reveal dissonance arousal due to discrepancy between perception and behavior in the absence of negative consequences. There is as well a contribution that takes up the issue of multiple modes of dissonance reduction and how they are determined and interact, and then, for more formal and general points of view, there are two contributions on mathematical formulations that help to place dissonance processes in a larger conceptual context.

Finally, there are contributions that address dissonance as an affective state; one emphasizes the advantage of measuring the feeling of dissonance in pinning down how dissonance processes work, whereas the other attempts to demonstrate the connection between dissonance and ambivalence and how that connection promises to give us a much broader understanding of dissonance effects. All of these reports are preceded by a concise history of the early supporting research as well as of the theoretical and methodological controversies stirred up by the original publication of the theory.

In 1976, in his Foreword to the Wicklund and Brehm, *Perspectives on Cognitive Dissonance*, Edward E. Jones wrote, "We may now have reached a less flamboyant stage of tidying of loose ends and charting out relations between dissonance theory and other psychological conceptions. . . ." Twenty years later, what this volume demonstrates is not a neat, tidy, theoretical and empirical package to which the practitioner can turn for help, but rather a remarkably exciting and growing set of research questions about how the human mind works. It is a most enticing invitation to behavioral scientists of all kinds to explore the expanding frontiers of cognitive dissonance.

—*Jack W. Brehm*
University of Kansas

FOREWORD TO THE SECOND EDITION

Every science has a defining moment—and a defining theory that signifies that it has truly come of age. Arguably for our discipline, social psychology, the development of cognitive dissonance theory over 60 years ago represents that critical moment, as confirmed by the voluminous research this theory has stimulated ever since. The outstanding collection in this book reviews the most recent developments in this dynamic field and, at the same time, provides a timely and welcome reminder of the profound debt our field owes to dissonance theory.

The modern discipline of psychology would be unimaginable without the theory of cognitive dissonance. Dissonance theory, and the experiments it stimulated, is responsible for some of the most significant, exciting, and enduring findings in our discipline. Classic dissonance experiments remain the mainstay of contemporary psychology textbooks, and every year, new generations of students continue to be stimulated and challenged by these findings.

The theory of cognitive dissonance has been a trailblazer in our field in at least three different ways. By postulating that an internal, cognitive, and motivational conflict state can play a determining and often counterintuitive role in the production of manifest behaviors, cognitive dissonance and the theoretical thinking it triggered were the first attempts to focus attention on the complex internal processes of the person. In a fundamental sense, dissonance theory was the first truly influential cognitive paradigm and, as such, the harbinger of the later "cognitive revolution" that so profoundly altered all of psychology.

Dissonance theory and research also played a pioneering role in a second way. By highlighting the often paradoxical and even self-defeating ways that humans frequently deal with the world, dissonance theory was the first comprehensive model to focus our attention on the landscape of human irrationality and the genesis of suboptimal judgments and behaviors. The voluminous modern literature on judgmental errors and heuristics, subliminal processes, fluency and priming effects, and motivated distortions in the way the world is represented owes a great deal to the kind of thinking first pioneered and later developed by dissonance researchers, as contributions to this book amply demonstrate.

Although not widely appreciated, the early demonstration of dissonance processes also paved the way for the emerging focus on the role of universal adaptive and evolutionary mechanisms in life. The kind of cognitive and motivational processes producing dissonance effects can now also be seen as part of a larger domain of evolutionarily determined and universal "mind modules" that characterize our species.

These mechanisms are broadly adaptive in many circumstances, but they can also produce manifestly incorrect and even dysfunctional reactions in some situations. Contemporary evolutionary models, such as error management theory, show a great deal of affinity with the ideas first developed by dissonance researchers six decades ago. It is becoming apparent that dissonance research anticipated and stimulated many of the insights later systematized in evolutionary theorizing about the development and fundamental characteristics of the "social mind."

There is no doubt that dissonance research has given rise to a rich and thriving paradigm that continues to define our field. The first edition of this book has made a landmark contribution to our understanding of dissonance research. With the passage of almost two decades, the present volume offers a welcome and much-needed revision and an update featuring the latest developments in dissonance research.

Some of the classic chapters included in the first edition are reproduced here, as their relevance is as great today as it was then. Part I of the book deals with research that is based on the classical formulations of dissonance theory. Chapters in Part II discuss the crucial role of the self in dissonance processes. Part III takes dissonance theory to a new level, by focusing on neural processes, mathematical models, and the role of affective processes in dissonance mechanisms.

The contributors are internationally renowned researchers, and the new chapters present the most recent theoretical ideas and findings. The structure of the book has also been substantially revised to take better account of how research has evolved in the past two decades. All chapters deal with either classical work, or describe important theoretical advances in dissonance theory, and the book provides a comprehensive overview of the most recent empirical discoveries in this area.

Interest in dissonance theories has continued unabated for over 60 years now, and the influence of this paradigm remains undiminished in a variety of fields of social psychology. A theory as important as cognitive dissonance does require the periodic publication of integrative reviews and summaries, and this is precisely what this book provides. Researchers, students, and practitioners interested in all aspects of thinking and behavior will welcome this book as a definitive summary of the current status of dissonance research. As was the case with the first edition, this book is also destined to become an essential reference work for years to come.

—Joseph P. Forgas, AM, DPhil, Dsc (Oxford), FASSA
Scientia Professor
The University of New South Wales
Sydney, Australia

PREFACE

Over 60 years ago, Leon Festinger (1957) published the book *A Theory of Cognitive Dissonance*. Festinger's book outlined a theory that has had a tremendous impact in psychological science and beyond. Then, over 20 years ago, Judson Mills and I coedited the first edition of this book to assess the state of research and theory on cognitive dissonance. That book was a landmark title in the APA Science Volumes series.

Since then, much has happened in relation to the theory of cognitive dissonance. For example, research has delved into the minimal conditions necessary to evoke dissonance, how dissonance processes relate to large bodies of psychological research that may have previously seemed unrelated, and the neural correlates of dissonance processes. Chapters in this second edition expand on these important issues. Moreover, the theory continues to generate interest in empirical, theoretical, and practical ways. This new edition highlights those advances (e.g., E. Harmon-Jones & C. Harmon-Jones, Chapter 4; Gawronski & Brannon, Chapter 5; Read & Monroe, Chapter 10; Izuma & Murayama, Chapter 11; McGregor, Newby-Clark, & Zanna, Chapter 6). In addition, other chapters that already presented important advances in the first edition have been updated with coverage of more recent research supporting these original advances (J. Aronson, Cohen, & Nail, Chapter 8; Cooper, Chapter 9; Devine et al., Chapter 12). Finally, some chapters were reproduced verbatim from the first edition—these chapters were either written by authors who are now deceased (Mills, Chapter 2) or have since retired (Beauvois & Joule, Chapter 3; E. Aronson, Chapter 7). Thus, the book provides an important assessment of the current status of the theory, and it presents the theoretical controversies and the recent research on important questions about the dissonance process.

For this book, we are fortunate to have contributions from the prominent scientists who have made major contributions to research and theory on cognitive dissonance We feel honored to be able include unpublished material by Leon Festinger (which was also included in the first edition). These works present his earliest version of the theory and his final public comment on the theory. Festinger's first paper on the theory, "Social Communication and Cognition: A Very Preliminary and Highly Tentative Draft" (Appendix A, this volume), was distributed to students in his University of Minnesota winter quarter 1954 graduate seminar, which included Jack Brehm and Judson Mills. Festinger's last words on dissonance theory (Appendix B, this volume) were transcribed from a tape recording of comments he made as a discussant in "Reflections on Cognitive Dissonance: *30 Years Later*," a symposium conducted at the 95th Annual Convention of the American Psychological Association (APA) in 1987. We would like to thank Trudy Festinger for giving us permission to publish these important materials.

Part of the inspiration for the first edition of this book came from a conference held at the University of Texas at Arlington (UTA) in the winter of 1997 (organized by Eddie Harmon-Jones and Judson Mills). This conference, designed to discuss the current status of cognitive dissonance theory and research, included an international group of researchers and was attended by approximately 70 faculty, graduate students, and undergraduate students. Although the first edition of this book did not represent the proceedings of the conference, it was an outgrowth of the conference.

The first edition of this book and the conference were aided immensely by UTA and the Science Directorate of APA. We would like to thank the staff at APA who were involved with the project. We also would like to thank UTA Dean Vern Cox and Psychology Department Chair Roger Mellgren for financial support and assistance with the logistics of organizing the conference. Additionally, we received assistance with the conference from UTA staff members Pauline Gregory, Susan Sterling, and Karen Twohey; UTA students Bruce Frankel, Victoria Swanson, and Tracy West; and Professor Bob Schatz from Texas A & M University–Corpus Christi. Further, we received assistance with the book from Todor Gerdjikov and Cindy Harmon-Jones, who helped in numerous ways. We are most grateful for their generous assistance. Others were invaluable and contributed to the success of the conference, and their efforts are greatly appreciated.

On a more personal note, since the publication of the first edition, two legends and mentors of mine have passed away. Judson Mills, who made several important contributions to the theory and coedited the first edition, died in May 2008. Jack Brehm, who also made several important contributions to the theory and wrote the Foreword for the first edition, died in August 2009. They are both sorely missed and fondly remembered. This second edition is dedicated to their memories.

SECOND EDITION

COGNITIVE DISSONANCE

An Introduction to Cognitive Dissonance Theory and an Overview of Current Perspectives on the Theory

Eddie Harmon-Jones and Judson Mills

A little more than 60 years ago, Leon Festinger published *A Theory of Cognitive Dissonance* (1957). Festinger's theory of cognitive dissonance has been one of the most influential theories in social psychology (Jones, 1985). It has generated hundreds and hundreds of studies, from which much has been learned about the determinants of attitudes and beliefs, the internalization of values, the consequences of decisions, the effects of disagreement among persons, and other important psychological processes.

As presented by Festinger in 1957, dissonance theory began by postulating that pairs of cognitions (elements of knowledge) can be relevant or irrelevant to one another. If two cognitions are relevant to one another, they are either consonant or dissonant. Two cognitions are *consonant* if one follows from the other, and they are *dissonant* if the obverse (opposite) of one cognition follows from the other. The existence of dissonance, being psychologically uncomfortable, motivates the person to reduce the dissonance and leads to avoidance of information likely to increase the dissonance. The greater the magnitude of the dissonance, the greater is the pressure to reduce dissonance.

Festinger used the same term, dissonance, to refer to the discrepancy between cognitions and to psychological discomfort. These two concepts are theoretically distinct and the first is now referred to as cognitive inconsistency

---

This chapter is a revision of the chapter that appeared in 1999. Judson Mills passed away in 2008 and did not contribute to this revision. Because of his contributions to the earlier version, he is listed as an author of this version.

http://dx.doi.org/10.1037/0000135-001
Cognitive Dissonance, Second Edition: Reexamining a Pivotal Theory in Psychology,
E. Harmon-Jones (Editor)
Copyright © 2019 by the American Psychological Association. All rights reserved.

or cognitive discrepancy, whereas the second is referred to as dissonance or dissonance discomfort.

The magnitude of dissonance between one cognitive element and the remainder of the person's cognitions depends on the number and importance of cognitions that are consonant and dissonant with the one in question. Formally speaking, the magnitude of dissonance equals the number of dissonant cognitions divided by the number of consonant cognitions plus the number of dissonant cognitions. This is referred to as the *dissonance ratio*. Holding the number and importance of consonant cognitions constant, as the number or importance of dissonant cognitions increases, the magnitude of dissonance increases. Holding the number and importance of dissonant cognitions constant, as the number or importance of consonant cognitions increases, the magnitude of dissonance decreases.

Dissonance can be reduced by removing dissonant cognitions, adding new consonant cognitions, reducing the importance of dissonant cognitions, or increasing the importance of consonant cognitions.[1] The likelihood that a particular cognition will change to reduce dissonance is determined by the resistance to change of the cognition. Cognitions that are less resistant to change will change more readily than cognitions that are more resistant to change. Resistance to change is based on the responsiveness of the cognition to reality and on the extent to which the cognition is consonant with many other cognitions. Resistance to change of a behavioral cognitive element depends on the extent of pain or loss that must be endured and the satisfaction obtained from the behavior.

An example used by Festinger (1957) may assist in elucidating the theory. A habitual smoker who learns that smoking is bad for health will experience dissonance because the knowledge that smoking is bad for health is dissonant with the cognition that he continues to smoke. He can reduce the dissonance by changing his behavior, that is, he could stop smoking, which would be consonant with the cognition that smoking is bad for health. Alternatively, the smoker could reduce dissonance by changing his cognition about the effect of smoking on health and believe that smoking does not have a harmful effect on health (eliminating the dissonant cognition). He might look for positive effects of smoking and believe that smoking reduces tension and keeps him from gaining weight (adding consonant cognitions). Or he might believe that the risk to health from smoking is negligible compared with the danger of automobile accidents (reducing the importance of the dissonant cognition). In addition, he might consider the enjoyment he gets from smoking to be a very important part of his life (increasing the importance of consonant cognitions).

Since it was presented by Festinger over 60 years ago, cognitive dissonance theory has continued to generate research, revision, and controversy. Part of

---

[1] Increasing the importance of consonant cognitions was not specified by Festinger as a way to reduce dissonance, although it follows logically from consideration of the dissonance ratio that is used to calculate the magnitude of dissonance and Festinger's (1957) statement that "the magnitude of dissonance (and consonance) increases as the importance or value of the elements increases" (p. 18).

the reason it has been so generative is that the theory was stated in very general, highly abstract terms. As a consequence, it can be applied to a wide variety of psychological topics involving the interplay of cognition, motivation, and emotion. A person can have cognitions about behaviors, perceptions, attitudes, beliefs, and feelings. Cognitions can be about oneself, another person or group, or about things in the environment. Rather than being relevant to a single topic, the theory is relevant to many different topics.

RESEARCH PARADIGMS IN DISSONANCE RESEARCH

We now review briefly the common paradigms used in dissonance research. Important research generated by the theory has been concerned with what happens after individuals make decisions, the consequences of exposure to information inconsistent with a prior belief, the effects of effort expenditure, and what happens after persons act in ways that are discrepant with their beliefs and attitudes.

The Free-Choice Paradigm

Once a decision is made, dissonance is likely to be aroused. After the person makes a decision, each of the negative aspects of the chosen alternative and positive aspects of the rejected alternative is dissonant with the decision. On the other hand, each of the positive aspects of the chosen alternative and negative aspects of the rejected alternative is consonant with the decision. Difficult decisions should arouse more dissonance than easy decisions, because there will be a greater proportion of dissonant cognitions after a difficult decision than there will be after an easy one. Because of this, there will be greater motivation to reduce the dissonance after a difficult decision. Dissonance following a decision can be reduced by removing negative aspects of the chosen alternative or positive aspects of the rejected alternative, and it can also be reduced by adding positive aspects to the chosen alternative or negative aspects to the rejected alternative. Altering the aspects of the decision alternatives to reduce dissonance will lead to viewing the chosen alternative as more desirable and the rejected alternative as less desirable. This effect has been termed *spreading of alternatives*, and the experimental paradigm has been termed the *free-choice paradigm*.

J. W. Brehm (1956) conducted the first experiment using the free-choice paradigm to test predictions derived from dissonance theory. In his experiment, which was presented as market research, he had women rate how desirable they found eight different products (e.g., toaster, coffeemaker) and then gave each of them a choice between two products that were close in desirability (difficult decision) or between two products that were not close in desirability (easy decision). After choosing which of the two products they would keep, the women rerated the desirability of the products. Results indicated that the women who made a difficult decision changed their evaluations of the products to be more positive about the chosen product and less positive about the rejected product. Spreading of alternatives was less for the women who made an easy decision. The free-choice paradigm continues to be used to gain insights into dissonance processes (e.g., E. Harmon-Jones, Harmon-Jones, Fearn, Sigelman, & Johnson, 2008; Shultz & Lepper, 1996).

The Belief-Disconfirmation Paradigm

Dissonance is aroused when people are exposed to information that is inconsistent with their beliefs. If the dissonance is not reduced by changing one's belief, the dissonance can lead to misperception or misinterpretation of the information, rejection or refutation of the information, seeking support from those who agree with one's belief, and attempting to persuade others to accept one's belief. In a study of the effect of belief disconfirmation on proselytizing, Festinger, Riecken, and Schachter (1956) acted as participant observers in a group that had become committed to an important belief that was specific enough to be capable of unequivocal disconfirmation. The group believed a prophecy that a flood would engulf the continent. The prophecy was supposedly transmitted by beings from outer space to a woman in the group. The group members also believed that they had been chosen to be saved from the flood and would be evacuated in a flying saucer.

Festinger et al. (1956) described what happened when the flood did not occur. Members of the group who were alone at that time did not maintain their beliefs. Members who were waiting with other group members maintained their faith. The woman (who was "receiving transmissions from outer space") reported receiving a message that indicated that the flood had been prevented by God because of the group's existence as a force for good. Before the disconfirmation of the belief about the flood, the group engaged in little proselytizing. After the disconfirmation, they engaged in substantial proselytizing. The group members sought to persuade others of their beliefs, which would add cognitions consonant with those beliefs. This paradigm, referred to as the *belief-disconfirmation paradigm*, continues to generate insight into dissonance processes (e.g., Burris, Harmon-Jones, & Tarpley, 1997; Gawronski, Ye, Rydell, & De Houwer, 2014; E. Harmon-Jones & Harmon-Jones, Chapter 4, this volume).

The Effort-Justification Paradigm

Dissonance is aroused whenever a person engages in an unpleasant activity to obtain some desirable outcome. From the cognition that the activity is unpleasant, it follows that one would not engage in the activity; the cognition that the activity is unpleasant is dissonant with engaging in the activity. Dissonance should be greater, the greater the unpleasant effort required to obtain the outcome. Dissonance can be reduced by exaggerating the desirability of the outcome, which would add consonant cognitions.

In the first experiment designed to test these theoretical ideas, Aronson and Mills (1959) had women undergo a severe or mild "initiation" to become a member of a group. In the severe-initiation condition, the women engaged in an embarrassing activity to join the group, whereas in the mild-initiation condition, the women engaged in an activity that was not very embarrassing to join the group. The group turned out to be rather dull and boring. The women in the severe-initiation condition evaluated the group more favorably than the women in the mild-initiation condition. This paradigm is referred to as the *effort-justification paradigm,* and it continues to be used fruitfully in research (e.g., Beauvois & Joule, 1996; E. Harmon-Jones, Price, & Harmon-Jones, 2015).

The Induced-Compliance Paradigm

Dissonance is aroused when a person does or says something that is contrary to a prior belief or attitude. From the cognition of the prior belief or attitude, it would follow that one would not engage in such behavior. On the other hand, inducements to engage in such behavior, promises of reward or threats of punishment, provide cognitions that are consonant with the behavior. Such cognitions provide justifications for the behavior. The greater the number and importance of the cognitions justifying the behavior, the less the dissonance aroused. Dissonance can be reduced by changing the belief or attitude to correspond more closely to what was said. Instead of using Festinger's original term, *forced compliance,* this paradigm is now called the *induced-compliance paradigm.*

The first experiment using the induced-compliance paradigm was the groundbreaking study by Festinger and Carlsmith (1959). They tested the hypothesis derived from dissonance theory that the smaller the reward for saying something that one does not believe, the greater the opinion changes to agree with what one has said. In their experiment, men performed boring tasks for 1 hour. Then each was told by the experimenter that there were two groups in the experiment: the one the participant was in, which received no introduction, and a second group, which was told the tasks were enjoyable by a person who had supposedly just completed them. The experimenter asked the participant to substitute for the person who usually said the tasks were enjoyable, and the participant was given $1 or $20 to tell the next person (actually a female accomplice of the experimenter) that the tasks were enjoyable and to remain on call in the future. The participants were then asked to evaluate the tasks by an interviewer from the psychology department, who ostensibly had nothing to do with the experiment. Results indicated that those paid $1 rated the tasks as more enjoyable than did those paid $20 or those who merely performed the tasks and were not asked to describe them to another person.

The participants in the experiment by Festinger and Carlsmith (1959) engaged in what is referred to as *counterattitudinal behavior.* The finding that the less money received for engaging in the counterattitudinal behavior, the more positive the attitude has been labeled the *negative-incentive effect*. The reason that term is used is that there is a negative relationship between the amount of incentive (money) and the amount of attitude change in the direction of the counterattitudinal behavior.[2] Later research by Linder, Cooper, and Jones (1967) showed that the negative-incentive effect occurs when the person feels free to decide about engaging in the counterattitudinal behavior, but when there is no perceived freedom to engage in the counterattitudinal behavior, the opposite effect occurs, that is, the more incentive, the more positive the attitude. When there is no choice about engaging in the behavior, dissonance is minimal, because there is sufficient justification for the behavior (see Festinger, Appendix B, this volume).

Other dissonance theorists have given different reasons why perceived choice is a crucial factor in dissonance effects (Beauvois & Joule, 1996; J. W. Brehm & Cohen, 1962; Cooper & Fazio, 1984; Wicklund & Brehm, 1976). However, Festinger's original theory can easily explain why perceived choice is an important variable. Low choice (i.e., being forced) to engage in counterattitudinal behavior is a cognition consonant with the counterattitudinal behavior (e.g., the person is essentially being forced to behave in that manner by the experiment). In contrast, high choice manipulations lack this consonant cognition (or at least have less of it). In layperson terms, low choice justifies the counterattitudinal behavior more than high choice does. Experiments using this choice manipulation often subtly encourage participants to engage in the counterattitudinal behavior but still feel like they chose to engage in that behavior. Research has revealed that participants given high choice, as opposed to low choice, to write counterattitudinal essays change their attitudes to be more consistent with their behavior.

A variant of the induced-compliance paradigm that involves threat of punishment rather than promise of reward is known as the *forbidden-toy paradigm*. In the forbidden-toy paradigm (Aronson & Carlsmith, 1963), young children were given the opportunity to play with toys and were threatened with severe or mild punishment if they played with a very attractive toy. The threatened punishment was sufficient to prevent the children from playing with the attractive toy. When asked at a later time to evaluate the attractive toy, children who were threatened with mild punishment evaluated the toy less positively than children who were threatened with severe punishment. The induced-compliance paradigm and the forbidden-toy paradigm continue to be used to address questions about dissonance processes (e.g., J. Aronson, Cohen, & Nail, Chapter 8; Beauvois & Joule, Chapter 3; Cooper, Chapter 9; Devine et al., Chapter 12; E. Harmon-Jones & Harmon-Jones, Chapter 4, all in this volume).

---

[2] As in many attitude-change studies, there was no measure of attitude before the experimental treatment. The measure of attitude was taken only after the experimental treatment. This type of design is referred to as an after-only design. In an after-only design, attitude change is shown by differences between the experimental conditions on the measure of attitude taken after the experimental treatment.

Other Paradigms

The paradigms reviewed above are the ones that have been used most frequently in tests of dissonance theory. However, other paradigms have been used and they illustrate the large array of situations in which dissonance occurs. In one early experiment testing the theory, Mills (1958) used dissonance theory to test how behaving in an honest or dishonest (cheating) manner would influence attitudes toward honesty. In the experiment, sixth-grade students first completed a measure of attitudes toward cheating. A day later, the students were given some tasks that provided an opportunity to be honest or cheat (e.g., counting dots within squares on piece of paper). On the next day, the students completed the attitudes measure again. To analyze the results, Mills first removed about 15% of participants who were initially extremely opposed to cheating and thus could not change their attitudes to become more extreme. With these extreme responders removed, the results revealed, consistent with predictions derived from dissonance theory, that students who behaved honestly changed their attitudes to be more opposed to cheating than those who cheated. More recent experiments have found other ways individuals reduce dissonance over cheating, such as motivated forgetting (Shu, Gino, & Bazerman, 2011).

Dissonance can also be evoked when individuals engage in other behaviors that might be inconsistent with their values or moral concerns. One example that has received research attention is meat eating, which may evoke dissonance because eating meat is inconsistent with having concern for the welfare for animals. To reduce dissonance over eating meat, individuals may reduce their concern for animals and deny that animals have the capacity to suffer. In one experiment testing these ideas (Loughnan, Haslam, & Bastian, 2010), participants were induced to eat dried beef or dried nuts. Then, participants reported their moral concerns for animals and cattle. As predicted by dissonance theory, participants who ate meat had less moral concern for animals and for cattle (for review of other evidence, see Loughnan, Bastian, & Haslam, 2014).

ALTERNATIVE ACCOUNTS OF DISSONANCE PHENOMENA

Over the years, various alternative theoretical accounts have been advanced to explain the effects found in dissonance experiments. The alternative accounts of dissonance have provoked considerable controversy. In some cases, the controversy has led to important empirical and theoretical advances. We briefly review the major alternative accounts and the controversy they generated.

Alternatives to Dissonance Theory

Self-Perception Theory
Self-perception theory (Bem, 1967, 1972) argues that dissonance effects were not the result of motivation to reduce the psychological discomfort produced by cognitive dissonance but were due to a nonmotivational process whereby

persons merely inferred their attitudes from their behavior and the circumstances under which the behavior occurred. The self-perception theory explanation for the negative-incentive effect found by Festinger and Carlsmith (1959) assumes that persons use their overt behavior to judge their attitudes if external cues (such as an incentive) are not seen as controlling the behavior, but they do not use their overt behavior to judge their attitudes if external cues are seen as controlling the behavior. The explanation assumes that a small incentive is not seen as controlling the behavior, whereas a large incentive is seen as controlling the behavior.

One of the consequences of the controversy generated by the self-perception account was research testing the implications of dissonance theory using the *misattribution paradigm*. In the misattribution paradigm, participants are exposed to an extraneous stimulus (e.g., a pill) that is said to have a certain effect on the person's internal state (e.g., produces tenseness). If the supposed effect of the extraneous stimulus is the same as the actual internal state the person is experiencing, the person may misattribute the internal state to the extraneous stimulus rather than attribute it to the actual cause. If this misattribution occurs, the person may not respond to the internal state in the same way (e.g., will not change cognitions to reduce dissonance, to eliminate the negative affect or arousal).

Zanna and Cooper (1974) were the first to use the misattribution paradigm to show that the attitude change found in the induced-compliance paradigm is motivated by the need to reduce negative affect or arousal, as assumed in the dissonance interpretation. In their experiment, under the guise of a study of the effects of a drug on memory, participants were given a pill to ingest that was actually a placebo with no real effect. The pill was said to cause tenseness, to cause relaxation, or to have no side effects. The participants then took part in a supposedly unrelated experiment in which they wrote a counterattitudinal message under high or low choice. If the pill was said to have no side effects, participants changed their attitudes to be more consistent with the counterattitudinal essay when choice was high but not when choice was low, in keeping with the results of other dissonance research. However, if the pill was said to cause tenseness, participants did not change their attitudes in either the low- or high-choice condition.

Zanna and Cooper (1974) reasoned that the feeling of tenseness that was experienced due to the dissonance created by writing the counterattitudinal message under high choice was misattributed to the pill when the pill was said to cause tenseness. With the tenseness misattributed to the pill, there was no need to reduce the dissonance that was the true cause of the feeling and thus no need for attitude change to reduce the dissonance.[3] Bem's (1967, 1972)

---

[3] High-choice participants given the pill that was said to cause relaxation changed their attitudes more than did high-choice participants given the pill said to cause no side effects. Zanna and Cooper (1974) reasoned that when the pill was said to cause relaxation, the participants deduced the amount of their tenseness by combining the amount of tenseness actually experienced and the amount of tenseness the pill supposedly reduced.

self-perception account of dissonance phenomena is unable to explain the findings of the study by Zanna and Cooper. If, as assumed by the self-perception account, attitude change was not the result of motivation to reduce the discomfort produced by cognitive dissonance, then the extraneous stimulus to which the discomfort could be misattributed would have no influence on attitude change.

Prompted in part by the controversy engendered by the self-perception account, additional research has been carried out to assess the motivational and emotional nature of dissonance. By showing that dissonance is associated with physiological arousal and psychological discomfort and that the cognitive changes that occur are motivated by this discomfort, research has demonstrated that self-perception processes cannot account for all effects produced in dissonance experiments (Elliot & Devine, 1994; Fazio, Zanna, & Cooper, 1977; Gerard, 1967; E. Harmon-Jones, Brehm, Greenberg, Simon, & Nelson, 1996; Losch & Cacioppo, 1990; Zanna & Cooper, 1974). Beauvois and Joule (Chapter 3, this volume), Devine et al. (Chapter 12, this volume), and E. Harmon-Jones and Harmon-Jones (Chapter 4, this volume) present further experimental evidence that is consistent with dissonance theory but cannot be explained by self-perception theory.

Impression-Management Theory

Another alternative theoretical account that has been offered for the effects obtained in dissonance experiments is impression-management theory (Tedeschi, Schlenker, & Bonoma, 1971). According to this interpretation, attitudes appear to change because persons want to manage the impressions others have of them. They try to create a favorable impression or avoid an unfavorable impression by appearing to have attitudes that are consistent with their behavior. This alternative theoretical account assumes that the attitude change that occurs in dissonance experiments is not genuine and that participants in experiments only appear to change their attitudes after counterattitudinal behavior to avoid being viewed unfavorably by the experimenter.

In contrast to the assumption of the impression-management account, dissonance processes do produce genuine cognitive changes. Results supporting the dissonance interpretation have been obtained in experiments in which the attitude measure was taken by someone who did not appear connected with the experimenter that observed the participant's behavior (Festinger & Carlsmith, 1959; Linder et al., 1967) and in experiments using extremely private situations (E. Harmon-Jones, 2000a; E. Harmon-Jones et al., 1996). Impression-management theory has difficulty accounting for findings that show that dissonance processes that justify recent behavior can produce physiological changes (M. L. Brehm, Back, & Bogdonoff, 1964; E. Harmon-Jones, Harmon-Jones, Serra, & Gable, 2011), and it has problems explaining results obtained in paradigms other than the induced-compliance paradigm, for example, the free-choice paradigm (Wicklund & Brehm, 1976).

Does Dissonance Reduction Only Occur in Certain Types of Cultures?

Heine and Lehman (1997) conducted a free-choice study that provided evidence that has been interpreted to suggest that individuals from some cultures may not engage in dissonance reduction. In their study, individuals who were recent immigrants to Canada from Japan and China did not show significant spreading of alternatives, whereas individuals from Canada did. Heine and Lehman posited that "a reasonable working assumption is that dissonance effects are, at least in some important ways, culturally constructed" (p. 397). Asian cultures (e.g., Japan, China) are generally more collectivistic, and Western cultures (e.g., United States, Canada) are generally more individualistic (e.g., Markus & Kitayama, 1991). In collectivistic cultures, individuals have an interdependent self, and are thus more likely to be influenced by social roles, positions, and relationships, rather internal attributes, such as their own attitudes. In individualistic cultures, individuals are more likely to be influenced by their internal attributes rather than social roles. Consequently, individuals from collectivistic cultures, who are more sensitive to social role requirements, may be more likely to attribute cognitive discrepancies to the situation. Doing so would result in less or no dissonance.

Although these results fit with theories on psychological differences between interdependent and individualistic cultures, the study of Heine and Lehman (1997) contained methodological problems that may explain the lack of spreading of alternatives in their Asian participants. That is, prior to the decision, the Canadian participants desired the decision alternatives more than the Asian participants did. These differences in desirability of the decision alternatives would likely influence the difficulty and importance of the decision, with Asian participants regarding the decision as less difficult and important than Canadian participants did. Spreading of alternatives is more likely to occur following difficult and important decisions.

Moreover, older studies conducted in collectivistic cultures had provided evidence of dissonance-related attitude change in standard dissonance paradigms (Sakai, 1981; Sakai & Andow, 1980). More recent studies have also found that individuals from collectivistic cultures show evidence of discrepancy reduction. For example, a significant amount of spreading of alternatives in the free-choice paradigm has been found in Japanese individuals (Izuma et al., 2010) and in Chinese individuals (Qin et al., 2011). These results suggest that most persons likely experience dissonance and reduce it in ways predicted by Festinger's theory.

However, situational and cultural variables may moderate the arousal and reduction of dissonance, as Festinger (1957) predicted:

> Dissonance could arise because of cultural mores. If a person at a formal dinner uses his hands to pick up a recalcitrant chicken bone, the knowledge of what he is doing is dissonant with the knowledge of formal dinner etiquette. The dissonance exists simply because the culture defines what is consonant and what is not. In some other culture those two cognitions might not be dissonant at all. (p. 14)

Consistent with Festinger's idea that culture may moderate dissonance responses, Japanese individuals show more discrepancy reduction when they viewed a counterattitudinal behavior from the perspective of others (Kitayama, Snibbe, Markus, & Suzuki, 2004). Moreover, Asian Canadians who identify strongly with being Asian showed more spreading of alternatives when they made the difficult decision for a close friend as compared with when they made it for themselves. On the other hand, European Canadians showed more spreading of alternatives when they made the difficult decision for themselves as compared with when they made it for a close friend (Hoshino-Browne et al., 2005). These results are in accord with Festinger's prediction that culture will "define what is consonant and what is not" (1957, p. 14). Taken together, research has revealed that dissonance processes occur in many cultures, although culture may moderate what causes dissonance and how individuals reduce dissonance. It is unlikely that dissonance processes are entirely culturally constructed, as dissonance processes have been found to occur in a wide range of animal species, including pigeons (Zentall, 2016), white rats (Lawrence & Festinger, 1962), and capuchin monkeys (Egan, Bloom, & Santos, 2010; Egan, Santos, & Bloom, 2007). Although some have challenged this research on theoretical (Zentall, 2016) and methodological grounds (Chen & Risen, 2010), these criticisms are unfounded and have been addressed (Egan et al., 2010; C. Harmon-Jones, Haslam, & Bastian, 2017; E. Harmon-Jones, 2017).

Methodological Criticisms

In the early years of dissonance theory research, some researchers expressed concerns about the methods of some dissonance experiments and suggested that methodological problems accounted for the observed effects that were attributed to dissonance (Chapanis & Chapanis, 1964). Researchers responded to these criticisms and they were all addressed (Wicklund & Brehm, 1976).

More recently, some researchers have suggested that the spreading of alternatives effect is an artifact (Chen & Risen, 2010). They have argued that the attitude ratings (or rankings) are a function of the true attitude and measurement error, and that measurement error can fluctuate from predecision to postdecision. Furthermore, they have argued that predecision attitude ratings of the decision options may appear to be similar because of measurement error, but that the true attitudes may already be different. They have contended that, in a free-choice paradigm, participants are more likely to choose the item that they already preferred, that therefore this item's true rating is likely already higher than that of the rejected item, and that the apparent spreading of alternatives reflects these prior preferences, not attitude change. Chen and Risen (2010) reported two experiments testing this hypothesis. Participants viewed and then ranked 15 postcard-sized art prints (by artists such as Monet, van Gogh, and Kandinsky) according to their preferences. Then, they made six decisions (choices) between art prints; five of the decisions were between novel art prints and one decision was between art prints previously ranked seventh and ninth. The order of rankings and decisions varied as a function of condition. Some participants ranked, then chose, and then reranked the posters (R-C-R); this is a standard dissonance experiment. Other participants ranked, then re-ranked, and then chose between posters (R-R-C); this order of events should not have evoked dissonance because no decision was made. In both conditions, spreading of alternatives occurred from the first to the second ranking. However, the degree of spreading was greater in the R-C-R condition than the other condition, as would be predicted by dissonance theory. This difference was not statistically significant in the first experiment, but it was marginally significant in the second experiment.

The spreading of alternatives may have only weakly supported dissonance theory in these experiments because the decisions may have not been sufficiently difficult or important to evoke much dissonance or much dissonance reduction. Indeed, participants in these experiments made six decisions between art prints, and they were informed they would receive only one of the art prints they chose. Thus, most of their decisions had no action implications as they did not expect to receive the chosen option for most of their decisions (see the discussion of the action-based model that follows; E. Harmon-Jones & C. Harmon-Jones, Chapter 4, this volume). In a typical free-choice dissonance experiment, participants make only one decision and they expect to receive what they choose. Thus, this decision is likely more important to participants, and they are more likely to remember the option they chose. In addition, in the experiments by Chen and Risen (2010), participants chose between the seventh and ninth ranked options (out of 15). This further reduces the difficulty and importance of the decision, as many past dissonance experiments had participants decide between options that were rated or ranked more highly.

The results of Chen and Risen (2010) do suggest that measurement error may contribute to the spreading of alternatives effect (but as noted above, dissonance may produce more spreading as well). Kitayama, Tompson, and Chua (2014) suggested that several features of the experiment might create more measurement error of the predecision attitudes, which would lead to the effect observed by Chen and Risen. These features, which were all present in Chen and Risen's experiment, are: having participants make a large number of ratings; presenting participants with a large number of decisions; and rushing participants through their ratings. In contrast, J. W. Brehm's (1956) participants rated eight options rather than 15 (Chen & Risen, 2010), made one decision rather than six (Chen & Risen, 2010), and spent on average 15 minutes evaluating the eight options (no time information was presented by Chen & Risen, 2010). The methods used by J. W. Brehm are more typical of dissonance experiments (e.g., C. Harmon-Jones, Schmeichel, Inzlicht, & Harmon-Jones, 2011; E. Harmon-Jones & Harmon-Jones, 2002; E. Harmon-Jones et al., 2008; E. Harmon-Jones, Price, et al., 2015).

Since the research of Chen and Risen (2010) was published, several studies have been conducted to evaluate this alternative interpretation against the dissonance theory interpretation, and these studies have found evidence consistent with the dissonance theory prediction. For instance, experiments have revealed that when participants make decisions without seeing the decision alternatives ("a blind choice"), they still show spreading of alternatives (Egan et al., 2010; Nakamura & Kawabata, 2013; Sharot, Velasquez, & Dolan, 2010). If postdecision spreading of alternatives were due to measurement error of predecision attitudes, then this type of experimental design should not reveal spreading of alternatives. Thus, like the early criticisms advanced by Chapanis and Chapanis (1964), these methodological criticisms have been addressed.

Revisions of Dissonance Theory

Several versions of dissonance theory assume, along with the original version, that situations evoking dissonance produce a motivation that results in genuine cognitive changes. However, these revisions offer somewhat different theoretical interpretations for the phenomena observed in dissonance experiments. The revisions differ in what they posit to be the underlying motivation for dissonance effects. Those differences are a source of controversy about dissonance. The different theoretical positions are covered extensively in the present volume by authors who have been intimately involved in the development of the revisions and the controversy they have generated.

Self-Consistency

One of the first revisions proposed was the *self-consistency* interpretation of dissonance (Aronson, 1968, 1992). It is based on the idea that situations that evoke dissonance do so because they create inconsistency between the self-concept and a behavior. Because most persons have a positive self-concept, persons are likely to experience dissonance when they behave in a way that they view as incompetent, immoral, or irrational. This revision interprets the effects observed in the Festinger and Carlsmith (1959) experiment as resulting from an inconsistency between the person's self-concept as a moral person and the person's behavior of telling a lie to another person. This revision has led to an examination of the way in which variables related to the self, such as self-esteem, are involved in dissonance processes and to the generation of new research paradigms. This revision is presented by Elliot Aronson in Chapter 7, this volume.

The New Look

Another revision has proposed that the effects observed in dissonance studies are the result of feeling personally responsible for producing foreseeable aversive consequences (Cooper & Fazio, 1984; Scher & Cooper, 1989). This revision, often referred to the *new look* version of dissonance, proposes that the attitude change observed in the Festinger and Carlsmith (1959) experiment resulted from the desire to avoid feeling personally responsible for producing the aversive consequence of having harmed the other participant by leading them to believe that a boring task was enjoyable. This revision has generated research concerned with identifying necessary and sufficient conditions for the production of dissonance and with the role of arousal and its interpretation in dissonance processes. Controversy about this revision has spurred empirical and theoretical advances. For example, research has tested whether dissonance can occur when individuals produce positive consequences but act in a hypocritical manner (see E. Aronson, Chapter 7, this volume) or whether dissonance can occur when an individual's behavior produces no aversive consequences (E. Harmon-Jones & Harmon-Jones, Chapter 4, this volume). This revision is presented by Joel Cooper in Chapter 9, this volume.

Self-Affirmation
Self-affirmation theory proposes that dissonance effects are not the result of cognitive inconsistency, self-inconsistency, or feeling personally responsible for producing aversive consequences, but of behaving in a manner that threatens one's sense of moral and adaptive integrity (Steele, 1988; Steele, Spencer, & Lynch, 1993). This revision interprets Festinger and Carlsmith's (1959) results by assuming that the participants in that experiment changed their attitudes about the task because saying that the tasks were enjoyable when they knew they were boring made them feel foolish and threatened their sense of self-worth. The self-affirmation revision also has generated much controversy that has led to empirical and theoretical advances, such as how self-affirmation may decrease as well as increase discrepancy reduction (e.g., Cooper, Chapter 9, this volume). This revision is presented by Joshua Aronson, Geoffrey Cohen, and Paul Nail in Chapter 8 of this volume.

The Original Version Reaffirmed
Although the revisions of dissonance theory have produced serious challenges to the original version of the theory, other theorists maintain that the original version continues to be viable and that it can explain the evidence generated by the revisions (Beauvois & Joule, 1996; Mills, Chapter 2; Beauvois & Joule, Chapter 3; E. Harmon-Jones & Harmon-Jones, Chapter 4; Gawronski & Brannon, Chapter 5; McGregor, Newby-Clark, & Zanna, Chapter 6, all in this volume). The resurgence of the original version has generated new experimental paradigms and conceptual advances.

The Action-Based Model
One recent conceptual model is based on this reaffirmation of Festinger's (1957) original theory. It accepts the premise that cognitive inconsistency has the potential to cause the negative affective state of dissonance and the motivation to reduce dissonance, but goes further to explain why cognitive inconsistency causes dissonance and dissonance reduction. According to this action-based model (E. Harmon-Jones, 1999; E. Harmon-Jones, Amodio, & Harmon-Jones, 2009; E. Harmon-Jones, Harmon-Jones, & Levy, 2015), cognitions usually have implications for behavior, and when these cognitions with action implications are inconsistent with one another, dissonance occurs because unconflicted and effective action cannot occur. That is, the affective state of dissonance signals a problem and dissonance is reduced so that effective action can occur. To state

these ideas less abstractly, consider that most dissonance situations involve a commitment to a chosen course of action. Once an individual commits to a given action, any information inconsistent with that commitment is likely to arouse dissonance and prevent the action from occurring. To maintain the commitment in the face of this inconsistent information, the individual selectively enhances the value of the chosen course of action and reduces the value of the unchosen course of action. Doing so makes effective execution of the chosen action more likely (for a more complete review, see E. Harmon-Jones & Harmon-Jones, Chapter 4, this volume).

Areas of Agreement and Disagreement and a Possible Integration
Although the above revisions disagree about the specific underlying motivation for dissonance effects, dissonance theorists agree that genuine cognitive changes occur as a results of dissonance processes. They also agree that these cognitive changes are motivated in nature and that the source of this motivation is a form of psychological discomfort. Over the last 20 years, research has provided additional support for Festinger's original version of the theory, thereby suggesting that the revisions are not necessary (e.g., E. Harmon-Jones & Harmon-Jones, Chapter 4, this volume; Gawronski & Brannon, Chapter 5, this volume). For example, dissonance occurs in non-human animals (e.g., Egan, Bloom, et al., 2010; Egan, Santos, et al., 2007), suggesting that the metacognitive structure of self is not necessary. Moreover, dissonance-evoking situations have been found to evoke a general negative affect without also evoking increased self-directed negative affect (Elliot & Devine, 1994) or decreased state self-esteem (E. Harmon-Jones, 2000a). Other results have challenged the aversive consequences or "new look" revision (e.g., E. Harmon-Jones & Harmon-Jones, Chapter 4, this volume).

Although these results may suggest that the revisions are unnecessary for dissonance to occur, they do not suggest that the revisions have not offered useful information. In fact, the revisions have identified cognitions that are often important in influencing the magnitude of dissonance and they have also identified alternative ways of reducing dissonance. For example, the self-consistency version has suggested that dissonance is increased when individuals compare their dissonance-evoking behavior to their positive self-concept (E. Aronson, Chapter 7, this volume), and self-affirmation theory has suggested that dissonance is decreased when individuals focus on important self-related cognitions that are irrelevant to the dissonance-evoking event (J. Aronson, Cohen, & Nail, Chapter 8, this volume). However, the results obtained by the revisions do not indicate that dissonance will not occur as a result of a simple cognitive inconsistency.

The various results revealed by proponents of Festinger's original theory and later revisions can be integrated by appealing to the level of abstraction at which the cognitions are mentally represented. Along the lines of other theories (e.g., Carver & Scheier, 1981; Vallacher & Wegner, 1987), cognitions can range from being very concrete (e.g., "My index finger just pressed the 'e' key") to being very abstract (e.g., "I am writing this article to fulfill my need for competence"). The lower level, concrete cognitions likely do not involve self-conceptions, whereas higher level, abstract cognitions likely do (Carver & Scheier, 1981). Discrepancies between concrete cognitions can evoke dissonance (e.g., E. Harmon-Jones & Harmon-Jones, Chapter 4, this volume; Gawronski & Brannon, Chapter 5, this volume), though this dissonance might be of lower magnitude and of a different affective quality than discrepancies between abstract, self-related cognitions. Such would likely occur because of differences in the importance of concrete versus abstract cognitions. For example, the discrepancy between the concrete attitude toward a bitter-tasting beverage and verbal behavior opposite to that attitude evokes discomfort but not self-directed negative affect (E. Harmon-Jones et al., 1996), whereas the discrepancy between the self-concept of honesty and lying to another person may evoke discomfort as well as self-directed negative affect. In other words, the motivational, affective, cognitive, and behavioral consequences of discrepancies between concrete versus abstract cognitions may differ greatly but dissonance occurs with both types of cognitions (see also, E. Harmon-Jones, 2000b). Future research is needed to examine these speculations.

OVERVIEW OF THE PRESENT VOLUME

The first edition of this book was published in 1999. Since then, several theoretical and empirical advances have occurred for dissonance theory. This second edition highlights those advances. For example, one chapter presents a new extension of dissonance theory, referred to as the action-based model (E. Harmon-Jones & Harmon-Jones, Chapter 4), while an additional chapter considers the connections between dissonance processes and other motivational processes (McGregor, Newby-Clark, & Zanna, Chapter 6). Another chapter illustrates how dissonance processes play a fundamental role in a broad array of information processes and how the theory then contributes valuable insights into a wide range of phenomena (Gawronski & Brannon, Chapter 5). A new mathematical model of dissonance processes is presented in one chapter (Read & Monroe, Chapter 10), and evidence on the neural correlates of dissonance processes is presented in another chapter (Izuma & Murayama, Chapter 11). In addition, other chapters that already presented important advances in the first edition have been updated with coverage of more recent research supporting these original advances (J. Aronson, Cohen, & Nail, Chapter 8; Cooper, Chapter 9; Devine et al., Chapter 12). Finally, some chapters were reproduced verbatim from the first edition; this occurred for chapters written by authors who are deceased (Mills, Chapter 2) or who have retired (Beauvois & Joule, Chapter 3; E. Aronson, Chapter 7). Also reproduced from the first edition are two chapters by Festinger (Appendix A, Appendix B) and a chapter by Mills (Appendix C). One chapter by Festinger contains his first draft of the theory of cognitive dissonance, which he presented to his graduate student class in 1954; the other chapter by Festinger contains his last public speech about the theory, which he delivered in 1987 at the American Psychological Association conference. The chapter from Mills contains his recollections of how the Festinger and Carlsmith (1959) experiment was conducted, and it addresses an important misunderstanding of how it was conducted.

The chapters included in the second edition have been grouped into three parts, organized on the basis of themes shared by the chapters. The placement of the chapters into different parts should not be taken to mean that what is included in the chapters in one part is not relevant to the material contained in the chapters in a different part. Each of the chapters shares the common theme of dealing with issues of importance for the continued development of theory and research on dissonance processes.

Part One, "Perspectives Employing the Original Version of the Theory," consists of chapters discussing work that uses the original version of dissonance theory. In Chapter 2, Judson Mills presents suggestions for improving the original version. He contends that the magnitude of avoidance of new dissonance is not influenced by the amount of existing dissonance and that spreading of alternatives occurs before a choice. He proposes changing the definition of dissonance to include the degree to which a behavior will lead to a consequence and the desirability of the consequence.

Jean-Leon Beauvois and Robert-Vincent Joule present their radical dissonance theory in Chapter 3. They suggest that dissonance theory is a theory concerned with rationalization of behavior and that as such, it is not a theory of cognitive consistency, the management of personal responsibility, or the management of one's moral worth. They review experiments supporting their viewpoint and describe two new paradigms for dissonance research.

In Chapter 4, Eddie Harmon-Jones and Cindy Harmon-Jones present arguments and evidence suggesting, in contrast to the "new look" version of dissonance, that feeling personally responsible for the production of aversive consequences is not necessary to create cognitive dissonance and that dissonance will occur even when aversive consequences are not produced. After considering how the "new look" and other revisions cannot explain all of the evidence produced by dissonance theory, they present the action-based model of dissonance theory and review evidence supporting it.

In Chapter 5, Bertram Gawronski and Skylar M. Brannon posit that cognitive consistency plays a vital role in information processing and that the breadth of processes associated with cognitive consistency suggests that an even wider range of phenomena should be considered within Festinger's theory of dissonance. In support, they review several lines of evidence on processes in areas such as impression formation and stereotyping/prejudice that they argue should be united under the cognitive dissonance theory.

In Chapter 6, Ian McGregor, Ian R. Newby-Clark, and Mark P. Zanna review research on two phenomena related to Festinger's original theory of dissonance—ambivalence and discrepancy detection. Research on these topics support the original theory by demonstrating that a mere cognitive inconsistency evokes psychological discomfort. By considering these topics together with research on the simultaneous accessibility of cognitive elements, McGregor et al. illustrate dissonance theory's relevance to contemporary issues.

Part Two, "The Role of the Self in Dissonance," comprises chapters that discuss the revisions of cognitive dissonance theory that use the self as a crucial factor in dissonance processes. In Chapter 7, Elliot Aronson presents his self-consistency interpretation of dissonance and describes a new paradigm for dissonance theory, the *hypocrisy paradigm*, that makes persons mindful of the fact that they are not practicing what they are preaching. He argues that evidence obtained in this paradigm indicates that the production of aversive consequences is not essential for the creation of dissonance.

Joshua Aronson, Geoffrey Cohen, and Paul R. Nail present the self-affirmation reformulation of dissonance theory in Chapter 8. They describe research derived from self-affirmation theory that was used to challenge the original version of dissonance theory and discuss evidence that poses challenges for a self-affirmation theory account of dissonance research.

In Chapter 9, Joel Cooper presents the new look version of dissonance theory and discusses recent research on how the self is implicated in dissonance processes. Proposing an interpretation different from self-consistency and self-affirmation theories, he reviews evidence showing that the self is multiply involved in dissonance processes.

Part Three, "Mathematical Models, Neural Activations, and Affective Responses," includes a chapter that reviews several mathematical models of dissonance processes and then presents a novel one. This section also includes a chapter that reviews research on neural activations involved in dissonance processes and a chapter that reviews research on the role of affective responses in dissonance processes.

In Chapter 10, Stephen J. Read and Brian M. Monroe suggest that cognitive dissonance processes can be mathematically modelled in a connectionist model. They provide a recurrent- or feedback-network-with-learning model that integrates the strengths (and avoids the weaknesses) of previous connectionist models. They then use this mathematical model to successfully model classic cognitive dissonance experiments based on the free-choice, forbidden-toy, induced-compliance, and effort justification paradigms.

In Chapter 11, Keise Izuma and Kou Murayama review research that has revealed several brain regions involved in various cognitive dissonance processes and suggest what functional roles those brain activations reveal about dissonance processes. They also discuss how neuroscience methods can advance the understanding of the psychological processes in cognitive dissonance in ways not revealed by other methods.

Patricia G. Devine, John M. Tauer, Kenneth E. Barron, Andrew J. Elliot, Kristen M. Vance, and Eddie Harmon-Jones argue in Chapter 12 that attitude change, the most commonly used dependent variable in dissonance research, is limited in what it can reveal about the nature of dissonance motivation and dissonance reduction. They describe research demonstrating the value of measures of self-reported affect in dissonance studies.

As editors of the book, we encouraged the authors to present their own personal views on the important issues in cognitive dissonance research and theory. We hoped to encourage a free and open exchange of ideas relevant to the theory. As expected, differing viewpoints about dissonance are expressed in the different chapters. Also as expected, the differences are not resolved within the book. We hope that the debate about the differences and the controversy about the nature of dissonance will stimulate theoretical development and lead to new insights and findings. We believe that the future of dissonance research promises to be as exciting and valuable as the past 60 years of work on the theory.

REFERENCES

Aronson, E. (1968). Dissonance theory: Progress and problems. In R. P. Abelson, E. Aronson, W. J. McGuire, T. M. Newcomb, M. J. Rosenberg, & P. H. Tannenbaum (Eds.), *Theories of cognitive consistency: A sourcebook* (pp. 5–27). Chicago, IL: Rand McNally.

Aronson, E. (1992). The return of the repressed: Dissonance theory makes a comeback. *Psychological Inquiry, 3,* 303–311. http://dx.doi.org/10.1207/s15327965pli0304_1

Aronson, E., & Carlsmith, J. M. (1963). Effect of the severity of threat on the devaluation of forbidden behavior. *Journal of Abnormal and Social Psychology, 66,* 584–588. http://dx.doi.org/10.1037/h0039901

Aronson, E., & Mills, J. (1959). The effect of severity of initiation on liking for a group. *Journal of Abnormal and Social Psychology, 59,* 177–181. http://dx.doi.org/10.1037/h0047195

Beauvois, J.-L., & Joule, R.-V. (1996). *A radical dissonance theory.* London, England: Taylor & Francis.

Bem, D. J. (1967). Self-perception: An alternative interpretation of cognitive dissonance phenomena. *Psychological Review, 74,* 183–200. http://dx.doi.org/10.1037/h0024835

Bem, D. J. (1972). Self-perception theory. In L. Berkowitz (Ed.), *Advances in experimental social psychology* (Vol. 6, pp. 1–62). New York, NY: Academic Press.

Brehm, J. W. (1956). Postdecision changes in the desirability of alternatives. *Journal of Abnormal and Social Psychology, 52,* 384–389. http://dx.doi.org/10.1037/h0041006

Brehm, J. W., & Cohen, A. R. (1962). *Explorations in cognitive dissonance.* New York, NY: Wiley. http://dx.doi.org/10.1037/11622-000

Brehm, M. L., Back, K. W., & Bogdonoff, M. D. (1964). A physiological effect of cognitive dissonance under stress and deprivation. *Journal of Abnormal and Social Psychology, 69,* 303–310. http://dx.doi.org/10.1037/h0041671

Burris, C. T., Harmon-Jones, E., & Tarpley, W. R. (1997). "By faith alone": Religious agitation and cognitive dissonance. *Basic and Applied Social Psychology, 19,* 17–31. http://dx.doi.org/10.1207/s15324834basp1901_2

Carver, C. S., & Scheier, M. F. (1981). *Attention and self-regulation: A control-theory approach to human behavior.* New York, NY: Springer-Verlag. http://dx.doi.org/10.1007/978-1-4612-5887-2

Chapanis, N. P., & Chapanis, A. (1964). Cognitive dissonance: Five years later. *Psychological Bulletin, 61,* 1–22. http://dx.doi.org/10.1037/h0043457

Chen, M. K., & Risen, J. L. (2010). How choice affects and reflects preferences: Revisiting the free-choice paradigm. *Journal of Personality and Social Psychology, 99,* 573–594. http://dx.doi.org/10.1037/a0020217

Cooper, J., & Fazio, R. H. (1984). A new look at dissonance theory. In L. Berkowitz (Ed.), *Advances in experimental social psychology* (Vol. 17, pp. 229–266). Orlando, FL: Academic Press.

Egan, L. C., Bloom, P., & Santos, L. R. (2010). Choice-induced preferences in the absence of choice: Evidence from a blind two choice paradigm with young children and capuchin monkeys. *Journal of Experimental Social Psychology, 46,* 204–207. http://dx.doi.org/10.1016/j.jesp.2009.08.014

Egan, L. C., Santos, L. R., & Bloom, P. (2007). The origins of cognitive dissonance: Evidence from children and monkeys. *Psychological Science, 18,* 978–983. http://dx.doi.org/10.1111/j.1467-9280.2007.02012.x

Elliot, A. J., & Devine, P. G. (1994). On the motivational nature of cognitive dissonance: Dissonance as psychological discomfort. *Journal of Personality and Social Psychology, 67,* 382–394. http://dx.doi.org/10.1037/0022-3514.67.3.382

Fazio, R. H., Zanna, M. P., & Cooper, J. (1977). Dissonance and self-perception: An integrative view of each theory's proper domain of application. *Journal of Experimental Social Psychology, 13,* 464–479. http://dx.doi.org/10.1016/0022-1031(77)90031-2

Festinger, L. (1957). *A theory of cognitive dissonance.* Evanston, IL: Row, Peterson.

Festinger, L., & Carlsmith, J. M. (1959). Cognitive consequences of forced compliance. *Journal of Abnormal and Social Psychology, 58,* 203–210. http://dx.doi.org/10.1037/h0041593

Festinger, L., Riecken, H. W., & Schachter, S. (1956). *When prophecy fails.* Minneapolis, MN: University of Minnesota Press. http://dx.doi.org/10.1037/10030-000

Gawronski, B., Ye, Y., Rydell, R. J., & De Houwer, J. (2014). Formation, representation, and activation of contextualized attitudes. *Journal of Experimental Social Psychology, 54,* 188–203. http://dx.doi.org/10.1016/j.jesp.2014.05.010

Gerard, H. B. (1967). Choice difficulty, dissonance, and the decision sequence. *Journal of Personality, 35,* 91–108. http://dx.doi.org/10.1111/j.1467-6494.1967.tb01417.x

Harmon-Jones, C., Haslam, N., & Bastian, B. (2017). Dissonance reduction in nonhuman animals: Implications for cognitive dissonance theory. *Animal Sentience, 12*(4). Retrieved from https://animalstudiesrepository.org/cgi/viewcontent.cgi?referer=&httpsredir=1&article=1191&context=animsent

Harmon-Jones, C., Schmeichel, B. J., Inzlicht, M., & Harmon-Jones, E. (2011). Trait approach motivation relates to dissonance reduction. *Social Psychological & Personality Science, 2,* 21–28. http://dx.doi.org/10.1177/1948550610379425

Harmon-Jones, E. (1999). Toward an understanding of the motivation underlying dissonance effects: Is the production of aversive consequences necessary? In E. Harmon-Jones, & J. Mills (Eds.), *Cognitive dissonance: Perspectives on a pivotal theory in social psychology* (pp. 71–99). Washington, DC: American Psychological Association. http://dx.doi.org/10.1037/10318-004

Harmon-Jones, E. (2000a). Cognitive dissonance and experienced negative affect: Evidence that dissonance increases experienced negative affect even in the absence of aversive consequences. *Personality and Social Psychology Bulletin, 26,* 1490–1501. http://dx.doi.org/10.1177/01461672002612004

Harmon-Jones, E. (2000b). An update on cognitive dissonance theory, with a focus on the self. In A. Tesser, R. B. Felson, & J. M. Suls (Eds.), *Psychological perspectives on self and identity* (pp. 119–144). Washington, DC: American Psychological Association. http://dx.doi.org/10.1037/10357-005

Harmon-Jones, E. (2017). Clarifying concepts in cognitive dissonance theory. *Animal Sentience, 12*(5). Retrieved from https://animalstudiesrepository.org/animsent/vol1/iss12/5/

Harmon-Jones, E., Amodio, D. M., & Harmon-Jones, C. (2009). Action-based model of dissonance: A review, integration, and expansion of conceptions of cognitive conflict. In M. P. Zanna (Ed.), *Advances in experimental social psychology* (Vol. 41, pp. 119–166). San Diego, CA: Academic Press.

Harmon-Jones, E., Brehm, J. W., Greenberg, J., Simon, L., & Nelson, D. E. (1996). Evidence that the production of aversive consequences is not necessary to create cognitive dissonance. *Journal of Personality and Social Psychology, 70,* 5–16. http://dx.doi.org/10.1037/0022-3514.70.1.5

Harmon-Jones, E., & Harmon-Jones, C. (2002). Testing the action-based model of cognitive dissonance: The effect of action orientation on postdecisional attitudes. *Personality and Social Psychology Bulletin, 28,* 711–723. http://dx.doi.org/10.1177/0146167202289001

Harmon-Jones, E., Harmon-Jones, C., Fearn, M., Sigelman, J. D., & Johnson, P. (2008). Left frontal cortical activation and spreading of alternatives: Tests of the action-based model of dissonance. *Journal of Personality and Social Psychology, 94,* 1–15. http://dx.doi.org/10.1037/0022-3514.94.1.1

Harmon-Jones, E., Harmon-Jones, C., & Levy, N. (2015). An action-based model of cognitive-dissonance processes. *Current Directions in Psychological Science, 24,* 184–189. http://dx.doi.org/10.1177/0963721414566449

Harmon-Jones, E., Harmon-Jones, C., Serra, R., & Gable, P. A. (2011). The effect of commitment on relative left frontal cortical activity: Tests of the action-based model of dissonance. *Personality and Social Psychology Bulletin, 37,* 395–408.

Harmon-Jones, E., Price, T. F., & Harmon-Jones, C. (2015). Supine body posture decreases rationalizations: Testing the action-based model of dissonance. *Journal of Experimental Social Psychology, 56,* 228–234. http://dx.doi.org/10.1016/j.jesp.2014.10.007

Heine, S. J., & Lehman, D. R. (1997). Culture, dissonance, and self-affirmation. *Personality and Social Psychology Bulletin, 23,* 389–400. http://dx.doi.org/10.1177/0146167297234005

Hoshino-Browne, E., Zanna, A. S., Spencer, S. J., Zanna, M. P., Kitayama, S., & Lackenbauer, S. (2005). On the cultural guises of cognitive dissonance: The case of Easterners and Westerners. *Journal of Personality and Social Psychology, 89,* 294–310. http://dx.doi.org/10.1037/0022-3514.89.3.294

Izuma, K., Matsumoto, M., Murayama, K., Samejima, K., Sadato, N., & Matsumoto, K. (2010). Neural correlates of cognitive dissonance and choice-induced preference change. *Proceedings of the National Academy of Sciences of the United States of America, 107,* 22014–22019. http://dx.doi.org/10.1073/pnas.1011879108

Jones, E. E. (1985). Major developments in social psychology during the past five decades. In G. Lindzey & E. Aronson (Eds.), *The handbook of social psychology* (3rd ed., pp. 47–108). New York, NY: Random House.

Kitayama, S., Snibbe, A. C., Markus, H. R., & Suzuki, T. (2004). Is there any "free" choice? Self and dissonance in two cultures. *Psychological Science, 15,* 527–533. http://dx.doi.org/10.1111/j.0956-7976.2004.00714.x

Kitayama, S., Tompson, S., & Chua, H. F. (2014). Cultural neuroscience of choice justification. In J. Forgas, & E. Harmon-Jones (Eds.), *Control within: Motivation and its regulation* (pp. 313–330). New York, NY: Psychology Press.

Lawrence, D. H., & Festinger, L. (1962). *Deterrents and reinforcement: The psychology of insufficient reward.* Palo Alto, CA: Stanford University Press.

Linder, D. E., Cooper, J., & Jones, E. E. (1967). Decision freedom as a determinant of the role of incentive magnitude in attitude change. *Journal of Personality and Social Psychology, 6,* 245–254. http://dx.doi.org/10.1037/h0021220

Losch, M. E., & Cacioppo, J. T. (1990). Cognitive dissonance may enhance sympathetic tonus, but attitudes are changed to reduce negative affect rather than arousal. *Journal of Experimental Social Psychology, 26,* 289–304. http://dx.doi.org/10.1016/0022-1031(90)90040-S

Loughnan, S., Bastian, B., & Haslam, N. (2014). The psychology of eating animals. *Current Directions in Psychological Science, 23,* 104–108. http://dx.doi.org/10.1177/0963721414525781

Loughnan, S., Haslam, N., & Bastian, B. (2010). The role of meat consumption in the denial of moral status and mind to meat animals. *Appetite, 55,* 156–159. http://dx.doi.org/10.1016/j.appet.2010.05.043

Markus, H. R., & Kitayama, S. (1991). Culture and the self: Implications for cognition, emotion, and motivation. *Psychological Review, 98,* 224–253. http://dx.doi.org/10.1037/0033-295X.98.2.224

Mills, J. (1958). Changes in moral attitudes following temptation. *Journal of Personality, 26,* 517–531. http://dx.doi.org/10.1111/j.1467-6494.1958.tb02349.x

Nakamura, K., & Kawabata, H. (2013). I choose, therefore I like: Preference for faces induced by arbitrary choice. *PLoS One, 8,* e72071. http://dx.doi.org/10.1371/journal.pone.0072071

Qin, J., Kimel, S., Kitayama, S., Wang, X., Yang, X., & Han, S. (2011). How choice modifies preference: Neural correlates of choice justification. *NeuroImage, 55,* 240–246. http://dx.doi.org/10.1016/j.neuroimage.2010.11.076

Sakai, H. (1981). Induced compliance and opinion change. *The Japanese Psychological Research, 22,* 32–41. http://dx.doi.org/10.4992/psycholres1954.22.32

Sakai, H., & Andow, K. (1980). Attribution of personal responsibility and dissonance reduction. *Japanese Psychological Research, 22,* 32–41. http://dx.doi.org/10.4992/psycholres1954.22.32

Scher, S. J., & Cooper, J. (1989). Motivational basis of dissonance: The singular role of behavioral consequences. *Journal of Personality and Social Psychology, 56,* 899–906. http://dx.doi.org/10.1037/0022-3514.56.6.899

Sharot, T., Velasquez, C. M., & Dolan, R. J. (2010). Do decisions shape preference? Evidence from blind choice. *Psychological Science, 21,* 1231–1235. http://dx.doi.org/10.1177/0956797610379235

Shu, L. L., Gino, F., & Bazerman, M. H. (2011). Dishonest deed, clear conscience: When cheating leads to moral disengagement and motivated forgetting. *Personality and Social Psychology Bulletin, 37,* 330–349. http://dx.doi.org/10.1177/0146167211398138

Shultz, T. R., & Lepper, M. R. (1996). Cognitive dissonance reduction as constraint satisfaction. *Psychological Review, 103,* 219–240. http://dx.doi.org/10.1037/0033-295X.103.2.219

Steele, C. M. (1988). The psychology of self-affirmation: Sustaining the integrity of the self. In L. Berkowitz (Ed.), *Advances in experimental social psychology* (Vol. 21, pp. 261–302). San Diego, CA: Academic Press. http://dx.doi.org/10.1016/S0065-2601(08)60229-4

Steele, C. M., Spencer, S. J., & Lynch, M. (1993). Self-image resilience and dissonance: The role of affirmational resources. *Journal of Personality and Social Psychology, 64,* 885–896. http://dx.doi.org/10.1037/0022-3514.64.6.885

Tedeschi, J. T., Schlenker, B. R., & Bonoma, T. V. (1971). Cognitive dissonance: Private ratiocination or public spectacle? *American Psychologist, 26,* 685–695. http://dx.doi.org/10.1037/h0032110

Vallacher, R. R., & Wegner, D. M. (1987). What do people think they're doing? Action identification and human behavior. *Psychological Review, 94,* 3–15. http://dx.doi.org/10.1037/0033-295X.94.1.3

Wicklund, R. A., & Brehm, J. W. (1976). *Perspectives on cognitive dissonance.* Hillsdale, NJ: Lawrence Erlbaum.

Zanna, M. P., & Cooper, J. (1974). Dissonance and the pill: An attribution approach to studying the arousal properties of dissonance. *Journal of Personality and Social Psychology, 29,* 703–709. http://dx.doi.org/10.1037/h0036651

Zentall, T. R. (2016). Cognitive dissonance or contrast? *Animal Sentience, 12*(1). Retrieved from https://animalstudiesrepository.org/animsent/vol1/iss12/1/

I

PERSPECTIVES EMPLOYING THE ORIGINAL VERSION OF THE THEORY

Improving the 1957 Version of Dissonance Theory

Judson Mills

In this chapter, I am going to do something audacious. I am going to propose some improvements in Leon Festinger's most important contribution to psychology, his 1957 theory of cognitive dissonance. Some of the proposed changes have to do with Festinger's assumptions about the magnitude of avoidance of dissonance and about what occurs before a choice. A major proposed change is concerned with how dissonance is determined by desired consequences and importance of cognitions.

In Festinger's last public reflections on dissonance theory made at the symposium, *Reflections on Cognitive Dissonance: 30 Years Later*, conducted at the 95th Annual Convention of the American Psychological Association (1987; see Appendix B, this volume), he described why he left social psychology: "I left and stopped doing research on the theory of dissonance because I was in a total rut. The only thing I could think about was how correct the original statement had been" (Appendix B, this volume, p. 290). If Festinger, the master theoretician, could not improve dissonance theory, what hope is there?

However, in his remarks, Festinger also said, "If a theory is at all testable it will not remain unchanged. It has to change. All theories are wrong. One doesn't ask about theories, can I show they are wrong or can I show they are right, but rather one asks, how much of the empirical realm can it handle and how must it be modified and changed as it matures?" (Appendix B, this volume, p. 290).

---

http://dx.doi.org/10.1037/0000135-002
Cognitive Dissonance, Second Edition: Reexamining a Pivotal Theory in Psychology,
E. Harmon-Jones (Editor)
Copyright © 2019 by the American Psychological Association. All rights reserved.

Referring to dissonance theory, Festinger said, "I am quite sure that there is enough validity to the theory, and as changes are made, emendations are made, there will be even more validity to the theory, that research on it will continue, and a lot will get clarified" (Appendix B, this volume, p. 291). So although Festinger felt unable to improve the theory and left dissonance research and social psychology in 1964, his retrospection gives us hope and encouragement to develop and improve the theory.

As is well known, dissonance theory has been extremely fruitful and has stimulated an enormous amount of research. Beyond that, as I noted when moderating the 1987 symposium on dissonance, Festinger's theorizing about dissonance has had repercussions far outside the field of social psychology. It has changed the meaning of the word *dissonance*. No longer do educated people immediately think of music when the word dissonance is mentioned. *Cognitive dissonance* has become a part of the language. For example, the term has appeared in articles on the op-ed page of the *Washington Post*.

Why was dissonance theory, and specifically the 1957 version, so fruitful and important? One answer to that question emphasizes Festinger's unique research style. In the obituary for Festinger in the *American Psychologist*, Zajonc (1990) likened Festinger to Dostoyevsky and Picasso. Zajonc wrote, "Like Dostoyevsky and like Picasso, Festinger set in motion a *style* of research and theory in the social sciences that is now the common property of all creative workers in the field," (p. 661). Zajonc said about Festinger, "Leon is to social psychology what Freud is to clinical psychology and Piaget to developmental psychology," (p. 661). Such a statement made by a Festinger advisee such as myself would be viewed as biased and possibly self-serving, but Zajonc, who is a very distinguished psychologist, was not a Festinger advisee.

I prefer to answer the question about why the theory became so important in terms of the content of the theory. I believe that it has been so important because it has uncovered a large number of new and interesting phenomena. These phenomena dealt primarily with the effect of actions on beliefs and attitudes. The theory went far beyond the simple idea that saying is believing. It specified the conditions under which saying is believing and doing is valuing. The concern with the effect of behavior on cognition that is the hallmark of dissonance theory can be seen in the earliest version of the theory, in an unpublished paper Festinger distributed in his seminar in 1954 (see Appendix A, this volume). In that first version of dissonance theory, Festinger hypothesized that there exists a tendency to make one's cognition and one's behavior consonant, to reduce dissonance between behavior and cognition.

I am going to concentrate on the 1957 version of dissonance theory, which has been, and I believe continues to be, a very useful theoretical statement. The 1957 version started with a (seemingly) simple definition of dissonance. "Two elements are in dissonant relationship if, considering these two alone, the obverse of one element would follow from the other. To state it a bit more formally, x and y are dissonant if not-x follows from y" (Festinger, 1957, p. 13).

I prefer to focus on the second sentence of the definition because it avoids the obscure term *obverse*.[1]

The key element of dissonance theory that made the theory so useful was, I believe, the assumption that dissonance varies in magnitude, that the total amount of dissonance depends on the proportion of relevant elements that are dissonant with the one in question. The focal element was typically a behavior or what Festinger called a *behavioral element*. The assumption concerning the magnitude of the dissonance, with the assumptions that dissonance was uncomfortable and that the pressure to reduce dissonance was a function of the magnitude of the dissonance, allowed the derivation of many interesting predictions, for example, the prediction that the less money one receives for convincing someone that a boring task is enjoyable, the more positive one's attitude toward the boring task will be (Festinger & Carlsmith, 1959).

Festinger's assumption about the magnitude of dissonance was very different than what was assumed in the other theories of cognitive consistency common in the 1950s and 1960s. It allowed not only derivations about when dissonance would be more likely to be created and thus when tendencies to reduce dissonance would be stronger but predictions about how dissonance would be reduced. The assumption that dissonance was a function of the proportion of dissonant elements enabled predictions concerning the reduction of dissonance by adding consonant cognitions as well as by removing dissonant cognitions. Those predictions were not made by the other cognitive consistency theories, which did not make assumptions about degrees of inconsistency or alleviating an inconsistency by adding a different consistency.

THE MAGNITUDE OF AVOIDANCE OF DISSONANCE

There are some assumptions in the 1957 version of dissonance theory that have received insufficient attention and are in need of revision. One is Festinger's assumption that the greater the magnitude of existing dissonance, the greater will be the magnitude of avoidance of new information expected to increase dissonance (up to an extreme point; p. 130).

Some of the earliest research on dissonance theory examined the implications of the theory for selectivity in exposure to information. It was known in the 1950s that the mass media were generally ineffective in changing socially significant attitudes and that one prominent reason for this was self-selection of mass media audiences (Hovland, 1959). Dissonance theory was particularly useful in understanding bias in voluntary exposure to information because it

---

[1] The term *obverse* does not seem to have been used in accord with the dictionary definition of *obverse* as a proposition inferred immediately from another by denying the opposite of that which the given proposition affirms, for example, the obverse of "all *a* is *b*" is "no *a* is not *b*."

specified conditions under which persons will seek out or avoid information. It predicted that persons will seek out information expected to increase consonance (*consonant* information) and avoid information expected to increase dissonance (*dissonant* information). It also predicted that the greater the existing dissonance, the stronger will be the tendencies to seek out consonant information and to avoid dissonant information.

The early dissonance studies of selective exposure to information showed that there was a preference for consonant information (Ehrlich, Guttman, Schonbach, & Mills, 1957; Mills, Aronson, & Robinson, 1959). However, the fact that people prefer consonant information does not provide evidence of avoidance of dissonant information, because such a preference can be due solely to the seeking of consonant information. To show actual avoidance of dissonant information, it is necessary to make comparisons against a neutral baseline.

Later experiments on interest in consonant and dissonant information had a neutral baseline, and evidence of avoidance of dissonant information was found (Mills, 1965a). The effect of the amount of existing dissonance on interest in consonant and dissonant information was tested (Mills, 1965b). Evidence was found that the greater the postdecision dissonance, the greater the interest in consonant information. Interest in information favoring the chosen alternative was stronger when the chosen and rejected alternatives were closer in attractiveness. However, it was not found that avoidance of dissonant information was greater, the greater the postdecision dissonance. Avoidance of information favoring the rejected alternative was not stronger when the chosen and rejected alternatives were closer in attractiveness.

The failure to find that the magnitude of avoidance of dissonance was influenced by the amount of existing dissonance in the experiment by Mills (1965b) cannot be explained away on the basis of inadequate procedures. It cannot be attributed to inadequate manipulation of amount of dissonance or inadequate measurement of interest in information. The reason is that, in the same experimental situation using the same manipulation of amount of dissonance and the same measure of interest in information, it was found that interest in consonant information was greater, the greater the amount of existing dissonance. The positive result for interest in consonant information would not have occurred unless the manipulation of amount of dissonance and the measurement of interest in information had been adequate in that experiment. That positive result provides evidence that the negative result for the effect of amount of existing dissonance on the magnitude of avoidance of dissonance was not due to inadequate procedures.

The experiment on the effect of amount of existing dissonance on interest in consonant and dissonant information (Mills, 1965b) is the only one I am aware of that has tested Festinger's assumption about the effect of existing dissonance on the magnitude of avoidance of new dissonance. There is no evidence that I know of that supports the assumption that avoidance of new dissonance is greater, the greater the amount of existing dissonance. On the basis of what little research there is on the topic, I conclude that the assumption in the 1957 version that the magnitude of avoidance of dissonance is influenced by the amount of existing dissonance is in need of revision.

WHAT HAPPENS BEFORE A CHOICE

Another aspect of the 1957 version that is in need of revision is Festinger's assumption about what happens before a choice. Festinger assumed that there is no cognitive bias in the prechoice situation. Festinger took the position, which, strictly speaking, was not integral to the theory, that "the preaction or predecision situation will be characterized by nonselective seeking of relevant information" and "there will be a lack of resistance to accepting and cognizing any relevant information" (p. 126).

Contrary to what Festinger assumed, research on the topic of exposure to information before a choice has found evidence of selective exposure to information. When people are not committed to a position, the more certain they are that their position is the best one, the more they prefer information supporting their position (Mills & Ross, 1964), whereas the opposite occurs when commitment is high. Before a choice, people who are certain that an alternative is not the best are less interested in information favoring that alternative than people uncertain about which alternative is best (Mills, 1965c). People certain that an alternative is not the best before a choice show evidence of avoidance of information favoring that alternative by displaying less interest in it than people who can not even choose that alternative (Mills & Jellison, 1968).

The research on selective exposure before commitment has been based on the assumption that people want to be certain when they take an action that it is better than the alternatives. That conception was termed *choice certainty theory* (Mills, 1968). Another line of research based on choice certainty theory found evidence of cognitive bias before a choice. The anticipation of making a choice about other people increases the halo effect in the impressions of those other people on positive traits, reflecting a greater difference in evaluations of those other people (Mills & O'Neal, 1971; O'Neal, 1971; O'Neal & Mills, 1969). When a prospective choice is nearer in time, there is greater difference in private evaluations of the alternatives (Brounstein, Ostrove, & Mills, 1979) but smaller difference in public evaluations of the alternatives.

The effects of importance of a prospective choice on private and public evaluations of the alternatives were tested in a recent experiment (Mills & Ford, 1995). It found that the more important the prospective choice, the greater the difference in private evaluations of the alternatives and the less the difference in public evaluations of the alternatives. Those results can be interpreted in terms of dissonance, specifically, avoidance of dissonance expected to occur after the choice.[2]

---

[2] The interpretation in terms of dissonance was relegated to a footnote in the article by Mills and Ford, in accordance with the wishes of the article's editor.

The greater difference in private evaluations of the alternatives when the prospective choice was more important can be interpreted in terms of greater motivation to avoid the dissonance that would otherwise be expected to occur after the choice. Spreading the attractiveness of the alternatives in private before a choice will reduce dissonance that might otherwise be expected after the choice. The dissonance expected after the choice should be greater, the more important the choice, and so spreading the attractiveness of the alternatives in private to avoid dissonance after the choice should be greater, the more important the choice.[3] The finding that the more important the choice, the less the difference in public evaluations of the alternatives provides evidence that the private and public evaluations were made in a prechoice situation. If the evaluations were made in a postchoice situation, opposite effects for private and public evaluations should not have occurred.

The smaller difference in public evaluations of the alternatives when the prospective choice is more important can be explained in terms of the assumption Festinger (1957) made that the fear of dissonance may lead to a reluctance to commit oneself (p. 30). The explanation involves the assumption that the public expression of a preference for one alternative before a choice is regarded as involving commitment to choose that alternative. Commitment can be avoided by minimizing the difference in public evaluations of the alternatives. The greater the importance of the prospective choice, the greater the fear of dissonance and of the minimizing of the difference in public evaluations.

In *Conflict, Decision, and Dissonance*, Festinger (1964) emphasized that dissonance does not occur until after a choice. However, in discussing the consequences of the anticipation of postdecision dissonance for predecision behavior, Festinger (1964) stated, "If a person anticipates dissonance as a consequence of making a decision, he would be expected to react by attempting to minimize, or to avoid completely, the anticipated dissonance" (1964, pp. 144–145). If the need to be certain about the correctness of a prospective choice is construed in terms of the need to avoid dissonance that would otherwise be expected to occur after the choice, the research based on *choice-certainty* theory (which found bias in information seeking and evaluations before a choice) can be interpreted in terms of dissonance. As mentioned in the article by Mills and Ford (1995), choice-certainty theory can be integrated with dissonance theory.[4]

On the basis of a fair amount of research dealing with the issue, I conclude that when faced with a prospective choice, people will be motivated to avoid dissonance anticipated as a consequence of making a decision. They will avoid information expected to increase dissonance after the decision, and they will spread the attractiveness of the alternatives, in private, to avoid the dissonance that would otherwise be expected to occur after the choice. That is contrary to

---

[3] The assumption that the magnitude of avoidance of dissonance is determined by the amount of dissonance otherwise expected to occur is separate and distinct from the assumption questioned earlier that the magnitude of avoidance of dissonance is determined by the amount of existing dissonance.

[4] The mention occurred in a footnote about the dissonance interpretation.

what Festinger assumed. The avoidance of dissonance is an important aspect of the theory, which has been neglected in most recent work on dissonance. It needs to be addressed in any revision of the theory.

HOW DISSONANCE IS DETERMINED BY DESIRED CONSEQUENCES AND IMPORTANCE OF COGNITIONS

There are some other important aspects of the 1957 version that I feel have been ignored or have not received sufficient attention. One is that Festinger said that "motivations and desired consequences may also be factors in determining whether or not two elements are dissonant" (p. 13). Another is Festinger's assumption that if two elements are dissonant, the magnitude of dissonance will be a function of the importance of the elements (p. 16). Those neglected aspects of the theory are involved in a proposal I make for a change in the definition of *dissonance*.[5] The change I will propose also stems from some aspects of the theory that have concerned me for a long time, ever since the time I was working as Festinger's research assistant in the period 1954–1957, when he was developing the theory.

One thing about the 1957 version that has always troubled me is that the definition of dissonance disregards the existence of all the other cognitive elements that are relevant to either or both of the two under consideration and simply deals with those two alone (p. 13). For a long time, I have thought that if motivations and desired consequences determine whether there is dissonance, then one would not simply consider the two cognitive elements alone. Desired consequences would seem to constitute a third cognition that must be taken into account.

Immediately after Festinger (1957) made the statement about the role of desired consequences in determining whether cognitions are dissonant, he gave the following example:

> A person in a card game might continue playing and losing money while knowing that the others in the game are professional gamblers. This latter knowledge would be dissonant with his cognition about his behavior, namely, continuing to play. But it should be clear that to specify the relation as dissonant is to assume (plausibly enough) that the person involved wants to win. If for some strange reason this person wants to lose, this relation would be consonant. (p. 13)

In the situation in Festinger's example, it would seem reasonable to assume that if the person wants to win, there would be a cognition that the person

---

[5] I was stimulated to consider the role of importance in dissonance by conversations with Haruki Sakai when he visited Maryland during the summer of 1995. Readers can find an essay by Sakai in the first edition of this volume (Chapter 11, "A Multiplicative Power-Function Model of Cognitive Dissonance: Toward an Integrated Theory of Cognition, Emotion, and Behavior After Leon Festinger").

wants to win. If the person wants to win but for some strange reason does not have the cognition that he wants to win, it would seem that the playing the game would not be dissonant with the knowledge that the others in the game are professional gamblers. Taking desired consequences into account when determining the presence of dissonance seems to require considering more than just two cognitive elements alone.

Another aspect of the theory that has long bothered me has to do with the assumption that elements either follow or do not follow from one another but that there is no variation in the degree to which one element follows from another. I recall an argument with Festinger about that issue. It occurred when I was working on the study that was to be my doctoral dissertation. That study examined the effect of resistance to temptation on changes in attitudes toward cheating (Mills, 1958). One aspect of that study varied restraints against cheating by making it seem highly likely that cheating would be detected or very unlikely that cheating would be detected.

I suggested to Festinger that the cognition that there was a high likelihood of being caught was more dissonant with cheating than the cognition that there was a low likelihood of being caught, and I went further than that and suggested that a 95% chance of being caught was more dissonant with cheating than a 55% chance of being caught. Festinger maintained that dissonance was either/or, that there was no degree to which a behavior followed from a cognition. He took the position that there were a larger number of cognitions dissonant with cheating if there was a 95% chance of being caught than if there was a 55% chance. As with every argument I ever had with Festinger, I did not win that argument.

Festinger did make an assumption in the 1957 version about degrees of dissonance between two cognitions, when he assumed that the magnitude of the dissonance between two cognitions depends on the importance of the cognitions. Unfortunately, the variable of importance of cognitions has not been given much emphasis in research and theorizing about dissonance. One possible reason is that Festinger (1957) did not say much about what he meant by importance beyond saying that "the more these elements are important to, or valued by the person, the greater will be the magnitude of a dissonant relation between them" (p. 16). Another possible reason, perhaps more consequential, is that Festinger did not do any studies varying importance.

Festinger often made his points by giving examples, which he was a master at constructing. He gave an example of reducing dissonance by reducing importance, when a habitual cigarette smoker has the belief that smoking is bad for health:

> Our smoker, for example, could find out all about accidents and death rates in automobiles. Having then added the cognition that the danger of smoking is negligible compared to the danger he runs driving a car, his dissonance would also have been somewhat reduced. Here the total dissonance is reduced by reducing the *importance* of the existing dissonance. (Festinger, 1957, p. 22)

Like most of Festinger's examples, this one seems clear, but it does not provide a general conceptualization of the variable of importance.

The variable of importance seems to be involved with the consequences of the behavior for things that are valued or desired or with the consequences of the behavior for things regarded as undesirable. Now that appears similar to the idea that motivation and desired consequences determine dissonance, except that the variable of importance varies the magnitude of the dissonance. It seems reasonable to assume that a behavior follows from a cognition about a consequence of the behavior, if there is a desire for that consequence, and that the obverse (or opposite) of the behavior follows from a cognition about a consequence of the behavior, if there is a desire to avoid that consequence. Such a formulation would incorporate desired (and undesired) consequences within the definition of dissonance.

One result of incorporating the desirability (or undesirability) of consequences of the behavior within the definition of dissonance is that the determination of dissonance would involve three cognitions: (a) a cognition about the behavior, (b) a cognition about a consequence of the behavior, and (c) a cognition about the desirability (or undesirability) of the consequence. Using three cognitions when specifying dissonance would make dissonance theory more like *balance* theory. Some years ago, Insko and collaborators (Insko, Worchel, Folger, & Kutkus, 1975) proposed a balance theory interpretation of dissonance, although in somewhat different terms. In their recent constraint-satisfaction neural network model of dissonance, Shultz and Lepper (1996) made assumptions that they noted were reminiscent of cognitive balance theory.

Sticking as closely as possible to the language of the 1957 version, my suggestion for specifying dissonance is that a behavior follows from (is consonant with) a cognition about a consequence of the behavior, if the consequence is desirable, and a behavior does not follow from (is dissonant with) a cognition about a consequence of the behavior, if the consequence is undesirable. Thinking about dissonance in terms of three cognitions clarifies why dissonance is sometimes reduced by changing an attitude and sometimes by changing a belief. A smoker can reduce dissonance by believing there is no evidence smoking causes cancer or by downplaying the undesirability of having cancer, although the latter is less likely because negative attitudes toward cancer are very strong and resistant to change. Most dissonance research has focused on reducing dissonance by changing an attitude (e.g., disliking someone to whom one has made disparaging comments; Davis & Jones, 1960) and has used situations in which it was very difficult to reduce dissonance by changing a belief (e.g., by denying that one's comments were disparaging to the other).

The idea that a behavior is dissonant with a cognition about a consequence of the behavior if there is a desire to avoid the consequence sounds very similar to the assumption of Cooper and Fazio (1984) about the necessity of aversive consequences for the arousal of dissonance. However, the similarity is not quite so clear when one looks at their definition of an aversive event as "an event that blocks one's self-interest or an event that one would rather not have occur" (Cooper & Fazio, 1984, p. 232). Their definition of an aversive event has two distinct aspects. An event may be one that one would rather not have occur, but it may not be an event that blocks one's self-interest.

It seems clear that the consequence of the behavior has to be undesirable, something the person is motivated to avoid, for dissonance to be aroused. Using ideas similar to the general version of balance proposed by Rosenberg and Abelson (1960), it is possible to state in general terms what constitutes a desirable or undesirable consequence. A consequence is desirable if it has a positive effect on or promotes something that is positively evaluated or if it has a negative effect on or negates something that is negatively evaluated. A consequence is undesirable if it promotes something that is negatively evaluated or if it negates something that is positively evaluated.

As Brehm and Cohen (1962) emphasized, dissonance trades on the frustration of other motives. But whether the self has to be involved is another matter. The recent research by Harmon-Jones, Brehm, Greenberg, Simon, and Nelson (1996), showing that a public statement of one's position is not necessary for the arousal of dissonance, indicates that blocking one's self-interest or harming another person is not required for dissonance arousal. The way in which the self is involved in dissonance is an important matter that I return to later.

Explicitly including desired (and undesired) consequences in the definition of dissonance has other advantages. It includes importance or value directly in the specification of dissonance. In addition, it makes it easy to take the next step of allowing for degrees of dissonance between cognitions, depending on the strength of the motivation to avoid the particular consequence. What determines importance is not just that a behavior has consequences for something that is desirable or undesirable but also the degree of likelihood that a behavior has the consequence and the degree to which the consequence is desirable or undesirable.

I propose that the degree to which the obverse (or opposite) of a behavior follows from a cognition about a consequence depends on the amount of the desire to avoid the consequence. Dissonance should depend on the degree of certainty that a behavior will lead to a consequence and on the degree to which the consequence is desirable or undesirable. To give some examples, there should be more dissonance if a smoker thinks there is a 100% probability that smoking causes cancer than if she or he thinks the chance that smoking causes cancer is only 1%. There should be more dissonance if a smoker believes that smoking will cause cancer within 5 years than if she or he believes smoking will cause cancer within 50 years. There should be more dissonance if a smoker believes smoking will cause large inoperable tumors than if she or he thinks it will cause only very small tumors that are easily removed. And, of course, there should be more dissonance for a smoker to believe that smoking causes cancer than to believe that smoking causes something less undesirable, such as discolored teeth.

This formulation of dissonance in terms of the degree to which a behavior follows from a consequence and the desirability of the consequence has another advantage. It avoids the awkwardness of the original version that requires that degrees of dissonance always be described in terms of the number of consonant and dissonant cognitions. In some cases, such as the amount of money received for convincing someone a boring task is enjoyable (Festinger & Carlsmith, 1959), it is not unreasonable to talk about a person receiving $20 as having a larger number of consonant cognitions than a person receiving $1. But in other cases, such as the amount of effort involved in engaging in an action, it is rather awkward to talk in terms of number of cognitions. It is strained to say that a highly effortful action involves more cognitions than one involving moderate effort. That kind of awkward usage can be avoided if one thinks of dissonance in terms of the strength of the relationship between the cognitive elements as opposed to simply counting the number of consonant versus dissonant elements.

The formulation which I propose which explicitly takes into account the desirability of consequences and thus, in effect, the importance of the elements, has another potential advantage. It could help to reconcile the current theories that place emphasis on the role of the self in dissonance processes (Thibodeau & Aronson, 1992) with the formulation of dissonance in the original 1957 version. When considering the role of the self, I am going to assume that there is a distinction between the motivation of the person and the role of the self. If lower animals such as rats have dissonance and reduce dissonance as Festinger believed (Lawrence & Festinger, 1962), then the self does not have to be involved for dissonance to occur. We do not assume that rats have self-concepts. But, of course, rats do have motivations. For rats, there are desired and undesired consequences, such as the presence of food or electric shock.

In the case of humans, in addition to motives that do not require invoking the concept of the self, there are, of course, self-concepts, self-esteem, self-beliefs, and self-attitudes. All of these self-aspects have important implications for motivation. In my interpretation of dissonance, the engagement of the self may increase desired consequences or undesired consequences. If we use the definition of dissonance that allows for degrees of dissonance depending on the degree of the consequences and the degree of the desirability or undesirability of the consequences, we can unify the current thinking about the role of the self in dissonance with the general framework of the original version of the theory.

In some cases, self-relevance may increase dissonance by increasing the motivation to avoid certain consequences and, in other cases, a focus on the self may reduce dissonance by reducing the motivation to avoid the consequences. Some important work recently by Simon, Greenberg, and Brehm (1995) has provided evidence that the self-affirmation manipulation of Steele and Liu (1983), which has been shown to reduce dissonance, can be explained in terms of the lowering of the importance of the dissonant action. The present formulation, which explicitly includes importance in the definition of dissonance, can explain why sometimes dissonance is greater when the self is involved and also why it is less under other circumstances when the self is involved.

Obviously, my proposal (that the degree of dissonance depends on the degree to which the opposite of the behavior follows from the cognitions about the degree of the consequences of the behavior and the degree of desirability or undesirability of the consequences) is something that goes beyond Festinger's original definition of dissonance. However, I feel it is within the spirit of Festinger's original 1957 version and fits with many of the examples that he gave. There are many complexities in this formulation that need to be addressed, which could pose formidable problems. How does one measure the degree to which a behavior follows from a consequence? How does one measure the degree of desirability or undesirability of a consequence? A number of important issues need to be considered.

CONCLUSION

I am frequently reminded of the statement attributed to Einstein that everything should be made as simple as possible, but no simpler. This formulation of dissonance is not as simple as the 1957 version, which I believe was deceptively simple. However, I believe it provides a more precise and accurate account of the domain of dissonance research. If that is true, it should prove useful in providing new insights. Hopefully, it will promote the continued development of dissonance theory. I believe we honor Festinger's contribution by continuing to develop the theory.

REFERENCES

Brehm, J. W., & Cohen, A. R. (1962). *Explorations in cognitive dissonance*. New York, NY: Wiley. http://dx.doi.org/10.1037/11622-000

Brounstein, R. J., Ostrove, N., & Mills, J. (1979). Divergence of private evaluations of alternatives prior to a choice. *Journal of Personality and Social Psychology, 37*, 1957–1965. http://dx.doi.org/10.1037/0022-3514.37.11.1957

Cooper, J., & Fazio, R. H. (1984). A new look at dissonance theory. In L. Berkowitz (Ed.), *Advances in experimental social psychology* (Vol. 17, pp. 220–262). New York, NY: Academic Press.

Davis, K. E., & Jones, E. E. (1960). Changes in interpersonal perception as a means of reducing cognitive dissonance. *Journal of Abnormal and Social Psychology, 61*, 402–410. http://dx.doi.org/10.1037/h0044214

Ehrlich, D., Guttman, I., Schonbach, P., & Mills, J. (1957). Postdecision exposure to relevant information. *Journal of Abnormal and Social Psychology, 54*, 98–102. http://dx.doi.org/10.1037/h0042740

Festinger, L. (1957). *A theory of cognitive dissonance*. Evanston, IL: Row, Peterson.

Festinger, L. (1964). *Conflict, decision, and dissonance*. Palo Alto, CA: Stanford University Press.

Festinger, L., & Carlsmith, J. M. (1959). Cognitive consequences of forced compliance. *Journal of Abnormal and Social Psychology, 58*, 203–210. http://dx.doi.org/10.1037/h0041593

Harmon-Jones, E., Brehm, J., Greenberg, J., Simon, L., & Nelson, D. E. (1996). Evidence that the production of aversive consequences is not necessary to create cognitive dissonance. *Journal of Personality and Social Psychology, 70*, 5–16. http://dx.doi.org/10.1037/0022-3514.70.1.5

Hovland, C. I. (1959). Reconciling conflicting results derived from experimental and survey studies of attitude change. *American Psychologist, 14*, 8–17. http://dx.doi.org/10.1037/h0042210

Insko, C. A., Worchel, S., Folger, R., & Kutkus, A. (1975). A balance theory interpretation of dissonance. *Psychological Review, 82*, 169–183. http://dx.doi.org/10.1037/0033-295X.82.3.169

Lawrence, D. F. I., & Festinger, L. (1962). *Deterrents and reinforcement*. Palo Alto, CA: Stanford University Press.

Mills, J. (1958). Changes in moral attitudes following temptation. *Journal of Personality, 26*, 517–531. http://dx.doi.org/10.1111/j.1467-6494.1958.tb02349.x

Mills, J. (1965a). Avoidance of dissonant information. *Journal of Personality and Social Psychology, 2*, 589–593. http://dx.doi.org/10.1037/h0022523

Mills, J. (1965b). Effect of certainty about a decision upon postdecision exposure to consonant and dissonant information. *Journal of Personality and Social Psychology, 2*, 749–752. http://dx.doi.org/10.1037/h0022676

Mills, J. (1965c). The effect of certainty on exposure to information prior to commitment. *Journal of Experimental Social Psychology, 1*, 348–355. http://dx.doi.org/10.1016/0022-1031(65)90014-4

Mills, J. (1968). Interest in supporting and discrepant information. In R. P. Abelson, E. Aronson, W. J. McGuire, T. M. Newcomb, M. J. Rosenberg, & P. H. Tannenbaum (Eds.), *Theories of cognitive consistency: A source book*. Skokie, IL: Rand McNally.

Mills, J., Aronson, E., & Robinson, H. (1959). Selectivity in exposure to information. *Journal of Abnormal and Social Psychology, 59*, 250–253. http://dx.doi.org/10.1037/h0042162

Mills, J., & Ford, T. E. (1995). Effects of importance of a prospective choice on private and public evaluations of the alternatives. *Personality and Social Psychology Bulletin, 21*, 256–266. http://dx.doi.org/10.1177/0146167295213007

Mills, J., & Jellison, J. M. (1968). Avoidance of discrepant information prior to commitment. *Journal of Personality and Social Psychology, 8*, 59–62. http://dx.doi.org/10.1037/h0025319

Mills, J., & O'Neal, E. (1971). Anticipated choice, attention, and halo effect. *Psychonomic Science, 22*, 231–233. http://dx.doi.org/10.3758/BF03332586

Mills, J., & Ross, A. (1964). Effects of commitment and certainty upon interest in supporting information. *Journal of Abnormal and Social Psychology, 68*, 552–555. http://dx.doi.org/10.1037/h0043278

O'Neal, E. (1971). Influence of future choice importance and arousal upon the halo effect. *Journal of Personality and Social Psychology, 19*, 334–340. http://dx.doi.org/10.1037/h0031466

O'Neal, E., & Mills, J. (1969). The influence of anticipated choice on the halo effect. *Journal of Experimental Social Psychology, 5*, 347–351. http://dx.doi.org/10.1016/0022-1031(69)90059-6

Rosenberg, M. J., & Abelson, R. R. (1960). An analysis of cognitive balancing. In C. I. Hovland & M. J. Rosenberg (Eds.), *Attitude organization and change* (pp. 112–163). New Haven, CT: Yale University Press.

Shultz, T. R., & Lepper, M. R. (1996). Cognitive dissonance reduction as constraint satisfaction. *Psychological Review, 103*, 219–240. http://dx.doi.org/10.1037/0033-295X.103.2.219

Simon, L., Greenberg, J., & Brehm, J. (1995). Trivialization: The forgotten mode of dissonance reduction. *Journal of Personality and Social Psychology, 68*, 247–260. http://dx.doi.org/10.1037/0022-3514.68.2.247

Steele, C. M., & Liu, T. J. (1983). Dissonance processes as self-affirmation. *Journal of Personality and Social Psychology, 45*, 5–19. http://dx.doi.org/10.1037/0022-3514.45.1.5

Thibodeau, R., & Aronson, E. (1992). Taking a closer look: Reasserting the role of the self-concept in dissonance theory. *Personality and Social Psychology Bulletin, 18*, 591–602. http://dx.doi.org/10.1177/0146167292185010

Zajonc, R. B. (1990). Obituary: Leon Festinger (1919–1989). *American Psychologist, 45*, 661–662. http://dx.doi.org/10.1037/h0091620

3

A Radical Point of View on Dissonance Theory

Jean-Leon Beauvois and Robert-Vincent Joule

In 1957, Leon Festinger put forth the theory of cognitive dissonance (Festinger, 1957). His book described research and proposed a theory that explained the experimental results presented. It also contained a metatheory that borrowed from the Zeitgeist of the period and incited Festinger to make various generalizations, including one that made a connection between his theory and cognitive-consistency theories. In fact, extracted from the metatheory, the central element of Festinger's theory boils down to this: A person can experience an unpleasant state of arousal (state of dissonance) that can be quantified by a ratio (the *dissonance* ratio; see Chapter 2, this volume, for further explanation) and is reduced when this ratio decreases. Cognitions are relevant and taken into consideration only to the degree that they allow for composing this ratio. Further, in 1962, Brehm and Cohen stated that everything nontrivial that this theory offers relates to the dissonance ratio. When we speak below of the "theory of '57," we are referring to this central element of Festinger's presentation.

After functioning on this basis for about 10 years and producing the experimental results and classical paradigms that made its reputation, the theory was revised. These revisions consisted of the introduction of new propositions (assumptions?) that were supposed to explain why the state of dissonance existed. These propositions pulled the theory of dissonance toward a theory of the ego, and in fact, researchers neglected the rate of dissonance ratio and

---

This chapter is reprinted from the first edition of this book. The editor added some citations to relevant studies that have occurred since the original publication.

http://dx.doi.org/10.1037/0000135-003
Cognitive Dissonance, Second Edition: Reexamining a Pivotal Theory in Psychology,
E. Harmon-Jones (Editor)
Copyright © 2019 by the American Psychological Association. All rights reserved.

its theoretical implications,[1] to deal with a new kind of cognition that Festinger had not foreseen (e.g., I was free to accept or to refuse). In spite of the interest of these revisions and the experimental work that they inspired, we believe that in abandoning the dissonance ratio, these revisions broke with the theory of '57. The conception that we propose rests, on the contrary, on the idea that we must stick as close as possible to the theory of '57, which was never disproven and produced the most fascinating products of dissonance theory. Thus, all hypotheses must be derived from the dissonance ratio.

Does this mean that the revisions were ill timed? Of course not! They had a genuine problem as their origin: The effects of dissonance are observed only in certain conditions (e.g., free choice or weighing consequences of the performed behavior). To deal with this problem, we favored a course other than revising the theory.[1,2] In fact, we strove to resolve this problem without altering the theory of '57 but rather by adding to it a single proposition, which was faithful, moreover, to Brehm and Cohen (1962): An act induces a state of dissonance only when there is commitment. Accepting this proposition amounts to making an important theoretical decision. It actually amounts to inserting dissonance theory into a more general theoretical framework, that of the psychology of commitment (Kiesler, 1971). However, this framework does not have affinities with that of ego theories. In fact, the same situation applies to Kiesler's book as to Festinger's. It contains a theory packaged within a metatheory. When one takes it out of the metatheory, Kiesler's theory looks like a theory of *external* commitment (rather than the person committing to the act, the situation commits the person to the act), and this external commitment is rather incompatible with an ego theory.

This option, which implies the careful distinction between theory and metatheory,[3] led us to propose a *radical dissonance theory* (Beauvois & Joule, 1996), which conserves only the central element of Festinger's (1957) work, and a *theory of external commitment* (Joule & Beauvois, 1998), which conserves only the central element of Kiesler's (1971) book. It goes without saying that returning to the central element of a theory does not mean that one is sticking to a theoretical status quo. It also goes without saying that giving up the metatheories of Festinger and Kiesler can result in new theoretical developments likely to astonish Festinger and Kiesler themselves.

---

[1] For example, in establishing a dissonance ratio and putting the relevant, considered perceptions in the numerator or denominator, one can consider only the psychological implications of two perceptions at a time.

[2] Further, this course was more or less suggested by Brehm and Cohen (1962), who were the first to introduce the idea of commitment. Similar to Kiesler (1971), *we* think that the concept of commitment was a throwaway construct for dissonance theorists.

[3] Experimental practice is a good criterion. One needs a theory to explain experimental practice and experimental results.

The goal of this chapter is twofold. On the one hand, we want to show how our theoretical developments result in original hypotheses and even in new experimental paradigms. On the other hand, we want to present the particularities of the radical view relative to other versions of dissonance theory. For this, we select from the experimental work on which this radical view is based, and we describe several experimental results that, although compatible with the theory of '57, seem quite incompatible with the other versions of the theory. Thus, we show that, within the experimental framework of forced compliance: (a) dissonance theory is not a theory of consistency, (b) the reduction of dissonance is not to serve a morally good ego, and (c) dissonance arousal does not necessarily imply personal responsibility for the act. Finally, we show that this radical view allows for the proposal of new experimental paradigms.

DISSONANCE REDUCTION VERSUS INCONSISTENCIES REDUCTION

Two basic features of the theory of '57 are important here:

1. The dissonance ratio, the reduction of which corresponds to the dissonance-reduction process, is defined with reference to one and only one cognition. This cognition appears in neither the numerator nor the denominator of the ratio. It represents the participant's behavior.

    Shortly before Festinger decided to quantify the state of dissonance, structural balance theorists had proposed a measure of structure imbalance (Cartwright & Harary, 1956), which derived from a fundamentally different conception. This measure was the ratio of the unbalanced triads to the total number of triads implied by the structure. It was, therefore, a measure relating to the whole structure under consideration and accorded no particular status to any of the cognitions involved. This type of measure was in perfect conformity with Heider's premises, which viewed the cognitive universe as a scene contemplated by the perceiver and that satisfied, to a greater or lesser degree, his or her preference for balance (Heider, 1958).

    Festinger chose a different approach. In effect, for him, the evaluation of the total amount of dissonance requires that one define a special element that makes it possible to assign the status of consonant or dissonant to the other cognitions. Therefore, this measure is oriented by a special cognition. We call it the *generative* cognition (Mills, Chapter 2, this volume, calls it the *focal* element). Formal and experimental arguments do at least suggest that this cognition is behavioral in nature. Several experiments (see Beauvois & Joule, 1996) allowed us to develop two types of hypotheses: one in which the behavioral cognition was generative, and one in which it was attitudinal. All the results indicate that the generative cognition is provided by the representation of behavior. This is the case of Experiment 1, which we report below.

2. Decreasing the dissonance ratio is compatible with the emergence of inconsistent relations between certain cognitions implicated by the dissonance ratio. The reason for this is that cognitions in the ratio are determined solely by their relation with the generative cognition. So, if the generative cognition is behavioral, the goal of the dissonance-reduction process is not the production of cognitive consistency, but rather the rationalization of the behavior that produced the generative cognition. That is why the dissonance-reduction process may result in greater inconsistency among other cognitions. Therefore, the reduction of the ratio, which for us remains the unconditional objective of the dissonance-reduction process, in no way implies that there is consistency among the cognitions that it contains. These two basic features come into play in the following experiment (Experiment 1).

Festinger and Carlsmith (1959) realized that the condition that produced the greatest attitude change also produced less argumentation about the position being defended. Rabbie, Brehm, and Cohen (1959) observed incidentally that in a counterattitudinal role-playing situation, participants who had produced the greatest number of arguments in favor of the position being defended were also the ones whose attitudes changed the least. These observations suggested an inverse relationship between the elaborateness of argumentation and attitude change. In fact, these findings were never formalized by dissonance theorists, who, on the contrary, mentioned them as mere curiosities. Yet they clearly fit quite well into the strict (let us say "radical") view of the theory of '57: The counterattitudinal arguments that participants produce furnish cognitions that are consistent with the counterattitudinal behavior precisely because it consists of defending the argued viewpoint. There is nothing shocking about this statement to a dissonance theorist, who "naturally" recognizes that arguments consistent with the initial private attitude imply defending it by writing an attitudinal essay. As such, every argument that psychologically implies the viewpoint being defended must be regarded as a consonant cognition and, as such, is a dissonance-reducing cognition. It is thus easy to see why, in a counterattitudinal role-playing situation, the more arguments participants find supporting the attitude that they defend and against their initial attitude, the less dissonance they experience, and consequently, the less they change their mind to reduce dissonance. We would, therefore, expect an inverse relation between argumentation and attitude change. Beauvois, Ghiglione, and Joule (1976) obtained results supporting this hypothesis. For participants who were free to choose, as opposed to those with no choice, the more time allotted to supporting the counterattitudinal position, the less the participants' attitudes changed. Joule and Levèque (1993) tested this hypothesis more recently with a 2 × 3 factorial design, with participants in a classical counterattitudinal roleplaying situation (individual training).

In the Joule and Levèque (1993) experiment, 120 participants (literature students at the University of Provence) had to write a persuasive essay favoring the counterattitudinal position that "leisure activities are a waste of time for students." All participants had volunteered to participate in what was said to be a study on persuasion. Half were told that they were free to accept or refuse to write the essay (free-choice instructions), whereas the other half heard no such statement (Independent Variable 1). A third of the participants were given 20 min to write the advocacy essay before assessing their attitude. Another third were given 5 min before assessing their attitude, and the final third expressed their attitudes immediately, before beginning to write (Independent Variable 2). The postexperimental attitude was measured on a 21-point scale, where the participants rated their degree of agreement with the position they were asked to defend (Dependent Variable 1). Of course, the arguments produced by the participants in the 20-min condition significantly outnumbered those generated in the 5-min condition (Dependent Variable 2). The results are given in Table 3.1.

As for the postexperimental attitude, the expected interaction between the two independent variables was significant and did indeed exhibit the predicted pattern: In the free-choice condition, the more time the participants had to find arguments, the further away their postexperimental attitudes were from the position being defended (i.e., less attitude change). The opposite pattern was obtained in the no-choice condition.

As in the Beauvois et al. (1976) study, the results observed in the free-choice condition support the hypothesis that producing more arguments reduces the dissonance generated by the behavior executed during the counterattitudinal role-playing. Note that these results are incompatible with self-perception theory: No self-perception view could possibly be used to derive the idea that participants are less likely to adhere to the position they are defending as the number of arguments they produce increases.

These results fit fully with the theory of '57, with the arguments found being cognitions that implicate psychologically the counterattitudinal behavior and that therefore increase the denominator of the dissonance ratio (i.e., add consonant

TABLE 3.1. Effects of Counterattitudinal Advocacy on Attitude

Assessment	Free-choice condition			No-choice condition		
	0 min	5 min	20 min	0 min	5 min	20 min
Arguments	0.00	2.85	5.05	0.00	2.80	5.40
Attitude	6.20	3.40	2.50	1.30	2.90	8.00

Note. For attitude, the higher the figure, the more closely the measured attitude conforms to the counterattitudinal act. In a control group (n = 20), the mean attitude was 2.60. Judges who were unaware of conditions were asked to assess the arguments furnished by the participants. The arguments given in the 5-min conditions were found also in the 20-min conditions, along with new arguments deemed acceptable by the judges. From "Quelques Limites des Reinterpretations Commodes des Effets de Dissonance [Some Limitations of Convenient Reinterpretations of Dissonance Affects]," by J.-L. Beauvois, R. Ghiglione, and R.-V. Joule, 1976, *Bulletin de Psychologie, 29*, p. 760. Copyright 1976 by *Bulletin de Psychologie*. Reprinted with permission.

cognitions). They support the view that the behavioral cognition functions as the generative cognition in the evaluation of the total amount of dissonance. It is self-evident that taking the private attitude as the generative cognition would force us to the opposite expectation, with participants experiencing more dissonance, the more time they had to find arguments opposed to their private attitude. Results do not support this expectation. Moreover, results go against the widely accepted idea (see the classical presentations of dissonance theory: Feldman, 1966; and especially, Zajonc, 1968) that dissonance theory is a theory of consistency. It is indeed difficult to see how there could be a consistency effect in the fact that participants change their attitude even less when they come up with numerous arguments against it. Brehm and Cohen (1962) even judged dissonance theory to be ambiguous in this respect, claiming that another hypothesis opposing the one we have just set forth was just as compatible with the theory and, needless to say, more compatible with the consistency axiom ("the higher the quality of the participant's arguments, the more dissonance there should be, assuming an initial disagreement with the advocated position," p. 34). But as we have already seen, the inverse relationship between argument quantity and attitude change is not ambiguous from the standpoint of dissonance theory.

THE DISSONANCE IN TELLING THE TRUTH

The principal reformulations of dissonance theory (Aronson, 1968, 1969; Cooper & Fazio, 1984; Wicklund & Brehm, 1976) have gradually turned the original theory into a cognitive-defense theory, describing the mechanisms used by responsible participants concerned about their own morality. These reformulations date back, as we noted previously, to the discovery in the sixties of factors that Kiesler (1971) considered to be the conditions for commitment (e.g., free choice, irrevocability, and consequences). We would now like to demonstrate that even if one agrees that commitment is necessary, it does not have to be interpreted in terms of the morally good self. Let us begin by showing that we can derive hypotheses from dissonance theory that are incompatible with this interpretation. Contrary to what the versions based on the morally good self and centered around the idea of lying would lead us to expect, dissonance can be increased by a perfectly moral act: telling the truth.

But first, let us analyze this situation used in Festinger and Carlsmith's (1959) classic experiment. Participants were induced to perform two consecutive behaviors likely to generate dissonance. The first behavior consisted of accomplishing a particularly boring and mindless task. Thus, the cognition, "This task is boring" would imply the opposite psychologically of the cognition "I will do this work," just as the cognition "I'm thirsty" implied the opposite psychologically of "I do not drink." The second behavior consisted of telling a peer that the task was interesting (counterattitudinal advocacy). Joule and Girandola (1995) demonstrated that this situation would be regarded as one of *double compliance* (Joule, 1991), making it necessary to consider the relationship between the two behavioral cognitions. This relationship would be obviously consonant if we confined ourselves to dual relationships involving two cognitions only, as required by the 1957 definition of psychological implication and dissonance relations. Dissonance theory treats relationships two at a time, and psychological implication indeed only looks at relationships between two cognitions. Saying that a task is interesting goes quite well (is consonant) with having carried out that task. This is true regardless of one's attitude toward the task, and the attitude constitutes a third cognition. In short, the actual accomplishment of the task provided Festinger and Carlsmith's participants who said the task was interesting with a consonant cognition. They would thus experience less dissonance than participants who said the same thing but had not been required to carry out the task.

What happens when participants are led to tell the truth, namely, to say that the task is uninteresting? This time, the two acts are inconsistent with each other. The requested statement, which involves telling the truth, should thus increase the dissonance induced by task execution. In short, once they have executed the tedious task, participants having "lied" should experience less dissonance than participants having told the truth. These conjectures have been confirmed by the experiment conducted by Joule and Girandola (1995), described next (Experiment 2).

The participants, all volunteers, were 80 female literature students at the University of Provence, assigned to the four cells of a 2 × 2 design. They were asked to take part in unpaid research ostensibly concerning the effects of concentration on performance. Half had to accomplish a tedious task (turning knobs on a board for 13 min). The other half simply had the task described to them and were clearly told that they would not have to perform it (Independent Variable 1). Then all participants described the task to a peer, either positively (counter attitudinal role playing) or negatively (attitudinal role playing; Independent Variable 2), using arguments supplied by the experimenter (e.g., "It was very enjoyable" or "I had a lot of fun" vs. "It was tedious" or "I got bored"). Finally, the participants rated their attitude toward the task on an 11-point scale (dependent variable). This scale was strictly identical to the one used by Festinger and Carlsmith (1959; the scale that produced the most significant findings). The results are given in Table 3.2.

TABLE 3.2. Attitude Toward a Tedious Task

Condition	Positive presentation	Negative presentation
With Task	−0.5	1.5
Without Task	1.4	−1.3

Note. Entries are participant ratings of the task on an 11-point scale ranging from −5 (not at all interesting) to 5 (very interesting). In Control Situation 1 of simple compliance (task execution only), the participants' mean rating of the task was −0.2. In Control Situation 2 of simple task assessment, the mean rating by the participants who neither executed nor presented the task was −2.1. From "Tâche Fastidieuse et Jeu de Rôle dans le Paradigme de la Double Soumission [Tedious Task and Role-Playing in the Double Compliance Paradigm]," by R.-V. Joule and F. Girandola, 1995, *Revue Internationale de Psychologie Sociale, 8*, p. 109. Copyright 1995 by Presses Universitaires de Grenoble. Reprinted with permission.

Festinger and Carlsmith's (1959) main finding was replicated: Participants who had to accomplish and positively present the task had a better attitude toward it than Control Group 2 participants, who only had to rate the task (−0.5 vs. −2.1). But what these results showed above all was that participants who performed the tedious task found it more interesting after telling a peer it was boring than after telling a peer it was interesting (1.5 vs. −0.5). In addition, participants who performed the task and negatively described it found it more interesting than Control Condition 1 participants, who only had to perform the task (1.5 vs. −0.2). This last result was absolutely incompatible with a self-perception view of dissonance phenomena.

Thus, the immorality of the "lie" was not behind the dissonance experienced by the Festinger and Carlsmith (1959) participants, nor was the fact that they had tricked their peer. Joule and Girandola's (1995) results showed that participants would have felt even more dissonance, had the researchers asked them to tell the truth. Thus, counterattitudinal advocacy does not evoke dissonance because it is immoral but, from a theoretical perspective, because there are some cognitions that would have implied doing the opposite. From this same theoretical perspective, it is possible that the same would apply to proattitudinal advocacy. We have just seen, for example, that having previously performed the task sufficed for the participant to experience more dissonance for telling the truth than for telling a lie. This double-forced compliance effect has been replicated and extended in other research (Joule & Azdia, 2003).

This conclusion prompts us to think about the role played by the consequences of the act. Indeed, it is probably because they shared this somewhat moral interpretation of dissonance that certain researchers (in particular, Cooper & Fazio, 1984) insisted so strongly on the importance of what they called the act's *aversive* consequences (here, tricking a peer), to the point of making it the core of their "new look." Granted, we are not questioning the necessity of the commitment, and even less so the importance of the act's consequences as a commitment factor. Nevertheless, having shown in this situation that telling the truth to a peer (and in doing so, suggesting that he or she not agree to perform the tedious task) leads to an increase in dissonance compels us to reconsider the theoretical role sometimes ascribed to these consequences. As we have just seen (see also Harmon-Jones, Brehm, Greenberg, Simon, & Nelson, 1996), they need not be morally aversive at all for dissonance to be generated. Note once again that we have adhered strictly to the stipulations of the theory of '57.

COMMITMENT TO COMPLIANCE

Since Brehm and Cohen (1962), dissonance theorists accepted the idea that the simple presence of relations of inconsistency among cognitions is not a sufficient condition for the arousal of dissonance. In fact, the 1960s were to prove a rich source of experiments showing that the primary reward effect of dissonance in forced-compliance situations is observed only if the participants are allowed to choose whether to perform the requested act. When participants do not have this choice, the dissonance effect is replaced by a reinforcement effect (Holms & Strickland, 1970; Linder, Cooper, & Jones, 1967). At the same time that the critical importance of free choice was being demonstrated, researchers revealed the significance of other cognitions relating to the public or anonymous nature of the problematic behavior (Carlsmith, Collins, & Helmreich, 1966), the irrevocable or reversible nature of the act (Helmreich & Collins, 1968), and, above all, the role of cognitions concerning its consequences (Calder, Ross, & Insko, 1973; Cooper & Worchel, 1970). Like free choice, such cognitions seem to function as more or less necessary conditions for dissonance arousal. In our view, the idea of commitment, in the form proposed by Kiesler (1971), provides the best conceptual synthesis of this rich research tradition and allows us to hypothesize that the induction of a state of dissonance in a forced-compliance situation requires the participant's commitment to the problematic behavior. In fact, Kiesler treated all the cognitions that have been studied as preconditions for dissonance effects (e.g., free choice, public nature of the behavior, irrevocability, and consequences) as variables affecting a person's level of commitment. Since 1971, a number of dissonance theorists have placed at least two of the conditions of commitment (free choice and consequences) at the heart of their formulations. To the extent that they thought they had discovered the psychological reason for the arousal of dissonance in these conditions of commitment, they were led to revise Festinger's original theory, turning it into a theory of personal responsibility (Wicklund & Brehm, 1976) or a theory of the cognitive management of the consequences of behavior (Cooper & Fazio, 1984).

It is clear that for these researchers commitment to one's behavior is a key element of the revised theory. Was it really necessary to change the basic assumptions of the original theory to introduce commitment? Before addressing this question, we clarify the meaning of the most important factor of commitment: free choice.

Indeed, the traditional way to manipulate free choice (i.e., "You are entirely free to do or not to do what I ask you. It's up to you") authorizes two interpretations with very different theoretical implications. Free choice can mean that the participant agrees (or, in a few cases, refuses) to execute the particular act requested of him or her, such as writing an essay in favor of police intervention, refraining from eating or drinking, stopping smoking temporarily, or saying that a task is interesting. No one would deny that this is the traditional interpretation. In fact, this is the interpretation that allows for understanding the effects of dissonance in terms of self-perception. Yet manipulating free choice can be interpreted to mean something else, namely, that the participant agrees (or, in a few cases, refuses) to comply with the obedience relationship proposed by an experimenter in a research framework. It is obvious that this is not the same choice as above. Replying "No, I don't want to do that particular thing, but you can ask me to do some other thing" (first interpretation) is not the same as replying "I have no reason to comply with your demands" (second interpretation). In the first case, accepting means agreeing to perform a specific act (and, thus, to be held responsible for that act), as several post-Festinger theorists assume. In the second case, which is closer to our idea of what a forced compliance contract is (Beauvois & Joule, 1996, pp. 146–154), accepting means being willing to comply with the experimenter, in which case the experimenter can be held responsible for whatever happens. The following description of Experiment 3 (Beauvois, Bungert, & Mariette, 1995) shows that the commitment necessary to induce a state of dissonance corresponds to the second interpretation of free choice (for a more recent discussion of commitment, see Joule, Girandola, & Bernard, 2007).

Three independent variables were manipulated in a $2 \times 2 \times 2$ design. In every case, participants were asked in the end to write a counterattitudinal essay, for which they did or did not choose the topic (Independent Variable 1: commitment to act). Before writing the essay, they either chose to or were assigned to (Independent Variable 2: compliance commitment) an experimental situation in which they had to perform problematic behaviors. The third independent variable dealt with the problematic behaviors announced to participants before the manipulation of the second independent variable. For the first half of the participants, the stated problematic behavior was writing counterattitudinal essays, like that which they would genuinely have to write (paradigmatic-sequence condition). For the second half of the participants, these problematic behaviors consisted of doing tedious tasks (which they would never be asked to perform in reality: nonparadigmatic-sequence condition). Further details with regard to this third independent variable are described in the following paragraphs.

In the *paradigmatic-sequence condition*, the participants were either given the choice or not (Independent Variable 2) to take part in a counterattitudinal role-playing situation. Before they made their decision or, in the no-choice condition, before they were told to do the behavior, Beauvois et al. (1995) presented the participants with the topics (all counterattitudinal) that they might be asked to write about (i.e., drivers under 16 years old no longer allowed to drive when accompanied by an adult, shorter holidays, or scholarships to be limited to students achieving an average grade of 14/20, approximately a "B" in the American system, in the preceding year). In the commitment-to-compliance condition, the experimenter said that the participants were entirely free to agree or to refuse to take part in the research and asked them to make their own decision. However, they were not told which of these essays they would ultimately have to produce but that this would be decided later. In contrast, in the other condition (no commitment to compliance), the experimenter stated that the research had been requested by the government and made no mention of the possibility of refusing to take part. Independent Variable 1, commitment to the counterattitudinal act, was then manipulated. In the commitment condition, the experimenter reformulated the three topics and asked the participant which one he or she would like to write about. In the no-commitment condition, the experimenter told the participant to write about "today's topic," which were topics that matched those chosen by the participants in the commitment to the counterattitudinal act condition.

In the no-paradigmatic-sequence condition (Independent Variable 3), the participants were either given the choice or not, to take part in a tedious task experiment. Before manipulating the commitment to compliance (statement of participant's free choice to participate in the experiment), the experimenter gave examples of problematic behaviors that were very different from the ones the participants would actually have to accomplish (e.g., glue a piece of confetti on every occurrence of the letter a in a long text, copy three pages of the telephone book, or take a lengthy test involving crossing out symbols). The commitment-to-compliance manipulation was the same as the paradigmatic-sequence condition. In the commitment-to-compliance condition, the experimenter told the participants that they were entirely free to agree or to refuse to take part in the research. Then, once commitment to compliance was manipulated, the experimenter claimed she had made a mistake and told the participants that the task would be something completely different from what had just been said. Without repeating the statement that participants were free to participate, she went on to the counter-attitudinal essays paradigm and manipulated the chosen or nonchosen topic variable. In summary, all participants wrote a counterattitudinal essay for which they had chosen or not chosen the topic (commitment to act vs. no commitment to act). Before this, they either could choose to accept or were assigned to a situation (commitment to compliance vs. no commitment to compliance), with or without the knowledge of what problematic act this situation really involved (paradigmatic sequence vs. nonparadigmatic sequence). Finally, after the completion of the essays, a postexperimental questionnaire was used to assess three attitudes (vacations, driving, and scholarships).

Let us consider first the paradigmatic-sequence condition. As shown in Table 3.3, participants who changed attitudes the most, and thereby reduced dissonance the most, were the ones who had been given the choice to enter

TABLE 3.3. Commitment to Compliance and Free Choice of the Problematic Act in a Forced-Compliance Situation

Commitment to compliance	Paradigmatic sequence		Nonparadigmatic sequence	
	Choice	No choice	Choice	No choice
Choice	5.36	6.63	4.72	4.82
No choice	3.36	2.59	2.77	2.05

Note. The higher the number, the more closely the participant's attitude conforms to the position defended in the selected essay (dissonance effect). From "Forced Compliance: Commitment to Compliance and Commitment to Activity," by J.-L. Beauvois, M. Bungert, and P. Mariette, 1995, *European Journal of Social Psychology, 25*, p. 24. Copyright 1995 by John Wiley and Sons. Reprinted with permission.

or not, into the situation (commitment to compliance), but who were required to write about the topic of the day. This result has important theoretical implications.

If the traditional free choice were indeed the choice to execute or not to execute the specific behavior requested, then the choice of one particular act among three in Experiment 3 would indeed be the best approximation of this type of free choice. Yet being able to choose one of three acts did not generate dissonance in this case. On the contrary, it seemed to have reduced it when the participant was committed to compliance, and this is what we expected.[4] Imagine a participant who has just agreed to comply with the experimenter, knowing that he or she will have to execute a counterattitudinal behavior but not knowing which. Once this commitment to compliance is obtained, the participant is given the choice between various obviously counterattitudinal behaviors. In such a decision-making situation, being able to choose must reduce the dissonance ratio, compared with a classical forced-compliance situation, in which the participant is proposed one and only one act. Indeed, insofar as the chosen alternative is the least discomforting for the participant (the lesser of three evils), it must reduce the total amount of dissonance by creating consistent cognitions (the higher cost of the nonselected alternatives psychologically implies choosing the selected one). The fact that having chosen one out of three acts in Experiment 3 reduced dissonance is thus perfectly compatible with the theory of '57.

The most important point in this experiment is that commitment to compliance must be considered as the factor that aroused the dissonance in the commitment-to-compliance-nonchosen-issue situation. These results were confirmed in the nonparadigmatic-sequence condition. We discovered that participants who committed to compliance by agreeing to perform boring tasks modified their attitude in favor of the essay topic when it was imposed. Here again, the choice of one of three counterattitudinal acts did not induce dissonance per se. However, in the commitment-to-compliance condition, being able to choose a topic does not seem to have reduced the dissonance (as in the paradigmatic condition). This is probably because in the nonparadigmatic condition, the participants had been told nothing about the two nonchosen topics when they had to pick one of three, so they had not already implicitly agreed to write about them (during the commitment-to-compliance manipulation). In effect, avoiding two topics one has never heard about and therefore never agreed to write about does not provide any consonant cognitions, unlike the case in which participants could choose to write about the least problematic of three topics.

In opposition to the traditional understanding of free choice, it is indeed commitment to compliance, not commitment to a particular counterattitudinal act, that is the condition needed to induce a state of dissonance. The results of Experiment 3 point out the limitations of a view of the dissonance-reduction

---

[4] The interaction between these two independent variables was statistically significant in the paradigmatic-sequence condition.

process that reduces it to the management of responsibility. In our minds, revisions based on responsibility, the anticipation of aversive consequences, and other similar concepts stem from a faulty interpretation of what free choice really is in classic forced-compliance experiments. Of course, it is quite understandable that participants who experience the feelings involved in having chosen to perform the particular counterattitudinal act just performed have some problems about their own values and have trouble accepting that the act has aversive consequences. But these feelings have nothing to do with the state of dissonance. Note first of all, against this view, that dissonance is induced in a number of situations void of moral implications. Such is the case in situations of abstinence from smoking, for example, or in situations involving eating an unappetizing dish. Note also, and still opposing this view, that the traditional free-choice effects are not incompatible with very slight although real differences in the feeling of freedom between participants who had free choice and those given no choice: Either they all globally experience a strong feeling of constraint (Steiner, 1980), or on the contrary, they all experience a strong feeling of freedom (Beauvois, Michel, Py, Rainis, & Somat, 1996). In the studies mentioned by Steiner (1980), as well as in those described by Beauvois et al. (1996), dissonance effects are observed only in participants assigned to a free choice condition, whether they experience a strong feeling of freedom (as in Beauvois et al.) or, on the contrary, a strong feeling of obligation (as reported by Steiner).

Furthermore, for us, the key element for dissonance arousal is not the feeling of freedom, but rather whether the participant is said to have choice. In any case, the results of Experiment 3, described here, and those of another experiment described by Beauvois et al. (1995), more clearly pinpoint the limits of personal responsibility in a "morally good self" and the ideological confusion this view implies: Are participants morally responsible when they accept a condition of obedience and perform an imposed, unexpected act, which they do (no refusals observed) simply because they accept their state of compliance with the experimenter? Even if we obviously have to answer no to this question, the results show that participants nevertheless experience cognitive dissonance right from the very moment they are told they are free to comply or not to comply.

A RADICAL VIEW

In our minds, no theory other than dissonance theory can make sense out of all of the effects presented here. This also applies to the theories devised by Festinger's critics (e.g., self-perception and impression management) and even to the revised versions proposed by his followers. Yet if dissonance theory indeed remains the only theory that can make sense out of these effects, then it is not just one of many theories of dissonance. Does the radical theory really diverge that far from the theory of '57? The answer to this question is no to the extent that the radical theory conserves the key element of this theory of '57. In the remainder of this section, we discuss what is necessary for it to do so.

Strictly calculating the dissonance ratio and accepting its implications. The use of this ratio has several repercussions: Insofar as the state of dissonance is calculated from relationships (both dissonant and consonant) between cognitions, the calculation requires making the important theoretical distinction between the state of dissonance and the presence (vs. absence) of dissonant relationships between cognitions. The fact that Festinger used the word *dissonance* to refer to both of these instances may have led to the assumption that a state of dissonance exists whenever dissonant relationships between cognitions exist.

Radically calculating the total amount of dissonance means recognizing that all cognitions do not have the same status. To calculate, one of the cognitions must be designated as the generative cognition. This cognition allows us to say that the other cognitions (the ones we put in the numerator or denominator of the dissonance ratio) are consistent (whenever there is psychological implication) or inconsistent (whenever there is implication of the obverse of the generating cognition). The other cognitions enter into play only as a result of potential psychological implications that link them to the generating cognition or to its obverse.

Radically calculating the dissonance ratio also means only considering those relationships involving the generative cognition. Indeed, relationships are included in this calculation only to the extent that they link the generative cognition (or its obverse) to other cognitions. This implies that certain relationships, and in particular those between the cognitions in the numerator or denominator of the dissonance ratio, are not part of the calculation of the total amount of dissonance. For instance, anyone would agree that Festinger and Carlsmith (1959) were correct in ignoring the potential relationship between personal attitude and reward, that is, between two cognitions included in the dissonance ratio because of the relationships (inconsistency for the former and consistency for the latter) they had with the generative cognition (the counterattitudinal behavior). Note that in the present case, the relationship between these two cognitions is irrelevant. There may exist cases however, in which there is a relevant relationship between two cognitions in the dissonance ratio. If so, should it also be ignored in the calculation of total dissonance? The answer is yes. We have even seen that total dissonance could be decreased by the generation of new inconsistencies between the cognitions in the dissonance ratio. In Experiment 1, for instance, the counterattitudinal advocacy that led to the production of cognitions that were inconsistent with the participant's personal attitude was accompanied by less overall dissonance, because the total amount of dissonance was reduced by those cognitions.

Finally, radically calculating the total dissonance calculation implies considering only those relationships that link two cognitions (two-term relationships). Coming back to the role of the reward in the Festinger and Carlsmith (1959) experiment we can agree once again—because the findings support their reasoning—that Festinger and Carlsmith were quite right to call the relationship between the reward and the counterattitudinal behavior consistent. Yet it would suffice to bring a third cognition into the picture, personal attitude, for the relationship between the reward and the behavior to change in nature, because the participants might think that they were being bribed by the experimenter. In this case, the reward would become outright immoral, even aversive, and would generate dissonance. This type of reasoning is invalid, because the findings clearly show that rewards reduce dissonance. So why, then, would this reasoning become valid when we looked at other possible cases of relationships among three cognitions, in particular, when the consequences of the act were at stake? Indeed, the very idea of aversive consequences (Cooper & Fazio, 1984), presumably responsible for dissonance, relies on the consideration of three-term relationships (the relationship between one's act and its consequences being modified by one's personal attitude).

Granting a particular status to commitment cognitions. Discovery of commitment factors had a strong impact on the evolution of dissonance theory. Was it really necessary to change it? First of all, if we limit ourselves to two-term relationships, which are the only ones defined in the theory, then *commitment* cognitions (e.g., "I was told I was free to accept or refuse," "What I do will have such and such a consequence," and "I will not be able to go back on my word") do not really fall within the scope of the theory of '57. Such cognitions are obviously relevant, because they condition the dissonance-reduction process. They are definitely consistent with the act. Indeed, it makes no sense to contend that knowing one is free to do something (psychologically) implies that one does not do it. Commitment cognitions thus pose a real theoretical problem: Although relevant, they are not inconsistent with the act, even though their presence is necessary to induce a state of dissonance. This is the reason why theorists quickly veered away from the theoretical constraints of the 1957 version of dissonance theory, especially those involving the calculation of the dissonance ratio. They began to reason in a very flexible fashion by intuitively ascertaining a state of dissonance that participants experience as they engage in a sort of reasoning based on three, if not four, cognitions ("I say x, but I am against x, and yet I was free not to say x" or "I say x, but I am against x, and it is even worse because my act is going to have such and such a consequence").

We think there is an alternative, one that is in keeping with the experimental practices and data. This alternative fits into one proposition: Commitment to an act is a necessary condition (but insufficient, because the act must also be discomforting, i.e., counterattitudinal or countermotivational) for the induction of a state of dissonance. This proposition has three implications. The first goes without saying: The theory of '57 can remain unchanged. The second is that it forces us to carefully examine this mandatory dissonance-inducing commitment. Reflection about this problem should give rise to a second branch of a more complete theory (see Experiment 3 above). The third is that dissonance theory is a local theory of the psychology of commitment; more precisely, it is a theory of the effects of commitment to a problematic act. From an experimental point of view, one can imagine that there is no arousal below a certain threshold of commitment and that experimental operationalizations (declaration of free choice or the salience of consequences) ordinarily allow us to attain this threshold. This proposition allows us to distinguish two types of cognitions: cognitions generating arousal (commitment cognitions) and cognitions composing the total amount of dissonance (specific cognitions). This perspective is justified first because commitment cognitions are not consistent or inconsistent cognitions and so cannot be located in the dissonance ratio (e.g., "I was free to accept or to refuse"). It is justified also by the fact that some cognitions facilitate commitment, therefore arousal, even though they reduce the total amount of dissonance. This is the case of internal explanations. These explanations increase commitment because they reinforce the link between the individual and the behavioral act. But because they psychologically imply the act, they are consistent cognitions, which reduce the total amount of dissonance (see Beauvois et al., 1996, for experimental support).

Thus, on a formal level we can distinguish commitment cognitions, which define the committing character of the generative cognition, from specific cognitions. Both types of cognitions are represented in the dissonance ratio on either the right or the left side of the equal sign in the formula:

$$D_g - b(F, C, \ldots) = A/A + R + \ldots$$

where D is the total amount of dissonance induced by the generative cognition g relative to the behavior b and F (free choice) and C (consequences) are commitment cognitions without which there would be no dissonance arousal. Their status comes from the theory of commitment. A (attitude) and R (reward) are specific cognitions that appear in the numerator and denominator of the dissonance ratio. These cognitions allow for the quantification of the state of dissonance.

TWO NEW PARADIGMS

By focusing on the generative cognition as a behavior-related cognition and on the rationalization of behavior, the radical theory has made it possible to explore two new paradigms (for a review, see Beauvois & Joule, 1996): *double forced compliance* (see Experiment 2 above), and *act rationalization*.

In the double forced compliance paradigm, we are interested in the dissonance-reduction process after the execution of two behaviors, at least one of which is discomforting. Let us consider a participant who has produced two behaviors, B_1 and B_2. Naturally, if this participant is to experience a state of dissonance, it is necessary and sufficient for one of these behaviors to contradict the participant's attitudes or motivations A. Let us suppose that the discrepant behavior is B. If we reason on the basis of behavior B_1 alone, then we will consider the participant to be in a classic forced-compliance situation. However, if we also consider behavior B_2, we must take account not only the relations between this new behavior and the attitudes or motivations A of the participant (inconsistent, consistent, or neutral relations) but also the relations that exist between behavior B_2 and behavior B_1 (inconsistent, consistent, or neutral relations).

FIGURE 3.1. Double Compliance Situations: Relevant Relationships

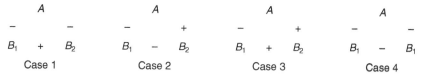

Note: — = inconsistent relationship; + = consistent relationship.

First of all, let us consider only the relevant relations that may exist among B_1, B_2, and A. If we assume the inconsistent relation between B_1 and A to be constant, then logic indicates the presence of four possible cases, as shown in Figure 3.1.

Let us now consider both the relevant and irrelevant relations among B_1, B_2, and A. If we once again assume the relation of inconsistency between B_1 and A to be constant, then logic this time presents us with 9 possible cases, namely, the 4 cases presented in Figure 3.1 and the 5 cases presented in Figure 3.2.

Of these theoretically possible cases, two have been studied in particular detail: Cases 1 and 2. These are easier to imagine than the others, possibly because they correspond to balanced triads. Festinger and Carlsmith's (1959) situation implemented Case 1 (B_1: perform a boring task; B_2: lie). Joule and Girandola's (1995) "truth situation" (Experiment 2) implemented Case 2. In a study by Joule (1991), the first behavior (B_1), produced by smokers, consisted of refraining from smoking for an evening (B_1). The second behavior consisted of writing an essay either against (B_2: Case 1) or in favor (B_2: Case 2) of smoking. As expected on the bases of radical considerations, the participants who had to write an essay against tobacco after being induced to refrain from smoking found it most difficult to go without tobacco and felt the greatest need for tobacco.

In the act rationalization paradigm, we are interested in the conditions that are likely to lead a participant who has just carried out a discomforting act to rationalize that act by carrying out another discomforting act. The dissonance

FIGURE 3.2. Double Compliance Situations: Relevant and Irrelevant Relationships

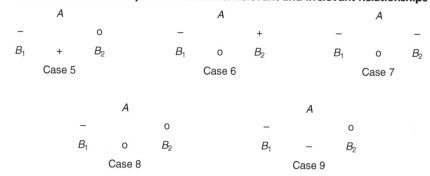

Note: — = inconsistent relationship; + = consistent relationship.

state is one of tension, which as such must be reduced. One can imagine that the participant will adopt the most convenient route or the first one available. But whatever the case may be, the arousal can only be reduced by two principal kinds of processes. These processes serve to make the act less problematic. Some processes affect the commitment to the act and reduce this commitment, and other processes reduce the total amount of dissonance by changing one or several existing cognitions or by producing new ones.

In ordinary circumstances, the behavior cannot be denied, and the easiest route available is the change of the private attitude that would have implied the contrary. This is most likely what happens in daily life, and it is natural that it was the first studied and remains the most traditional route of study. But if the participant is given the chance to trivialize his behavior and therefore make it less or even not at all problematic (to the point of no longer having commitment: a great distance between the participant and his act), it is probable that he or she will resort to this route (Simon, Greenberg, & Brehm, 1995). This route is probably less spontaneous than the preceding one (except in the case of a very polarized or salient initial attitude) because in daily life people are reluctant to say to themselves or others that they engage in trivial behaviors. But the participant can also reduce this tension by any other route that becomes available.

We have more specifically studied act rationalization. In fact, alongside the classic forms of rationalization (attitude change and trivialization), which we might term *cognitive* rationalization, we have been persuaded of the possibility of another form of rationalization. We have given the name *act* rationalization to this new type of rationalization because the problematic behavior that underlies the generative cognition is rationalized (and thereby rendered less problematic) by the production of a new, more problematic behavior rather than by cognitive realignment, which has been the classic object of investigation by dissonance theorists.

The hypothesis of the alternative nature of the cognitive path and behavioral path of dissonance reduction has received substantial support (Beauvois, Joule, & Brunetti, 1993; Joule, 1996): Act rationalization is hindered when cognitive rationalization is promoted, and in contrast, it is promoted when cognitive rationalization is blocked. For example (Beauvois et al., 1993, Experiment 1), smokers who had just accepted a first period of abstinence (18 hr without smoking) were proposed a second, much longer abstinence period (6 days without smoking), which was the final request. Before making this final request, the experimenter asked half of the participants to write down the reasons that led them to accept the first abstinence period; nothing of this sort was asked of the other half. Thus, we gave the first group, but not the second, the chance to cognitively rationalize their first abstinence. Fewer of the participants who had the chance to rationalize the first abstinence (26.1%) accepted the final request than of those who did not have this rationalization opportunity (82.6%).

Since the discovery of the conditions necessary for inducing a state of dissonance, dissonance theory has greatly evolved, to the point where previously rival theories are now considered as ways of thinking about dissonance reduction. We do not want to imply here that this evolution has been infertile or that it has not produced substantial data. It remains the case, however, that this evolution has led to the neglect of essential points of Festinger's theory and that this theory can still teach us a lot. And who knows, what it still has to teach us may contain many new surprises.

REFERENCES

Aronson, E. (1968). Dissonance theory: Progress and problems. In R. P. Abelson, E. Aronson, W. J. McGuire, T. M. Newcomb, M. J. Rosenberg, & P. H. Tannenbaum (Eds.), *Theories of cognitive consistency: A sourcebook*. Chicago, IL: Rand McNally.

Aronson, E. (1969). The theory of cognitive dissonance: A current perspective. In L. Berkowitz (Ed.), *Advances in experimental social psychology* (Vol. 4, pp. 1–34). New York, NY: Academic Press. http://dx.doi.org/10.1016/S0065-2601(08)60075-1

Beauvois, J.-L., Bungert, M., & Mariette, P. (1995). Forced compliance: Commitment to compliance and commitment to activity. *European Journal of Social Psychology, 25*, 17–26. http://dx.doi.org/10.1002/ejsp.2420250103

Beauvois, J.-L., Ghiglione, R., & Joule, R.-V. (1976). Quelques limites des reinterpretations commodes des effets de dissonance [Some limitations of convenient reinterpretations of dissonance affects]. *Bulletin de Psychologie, 29*, 758–765.

Beauvois, J.-L., & Joule, R.-V. (1996). *A radical dissonance theory*. London, England: Taylor & Francis.

Beauvois, J.-L., Joule, R.-V., & Brunetti, F. (1993). Cognitive rationalization and act rationalization in an escalation of commitment. *Basic and Applied Social Psychology, 14*, 1–17. http://dx.doi.org/10.1207/s15324834basp1401_1

Beauvois, J.-L., Michel, S., Py, J., Rainis, N., & Somat, A. (1996). Activation d'explications internes et externes du comportement problematique dans une situation de soumission forcee [Activation of internal and external explanations of problematic behavior in a forced compliance situation]. In J.-L. Beauvois, R.-V. Joule, & J.-M. Monteil (Eds.), *Perspectives cognitives et conduites sociales: 5. Contextes et contextes sociaux* [Cognitive Perspectives and social conduct: 5. Contexts and social contexts]. Neuchatel, Switzerland: Delachaux et Niestle.

Brehm, J. W., & Cohen, A. R. (1962). *Explorations in cognitive dissonance*. Hoboken, NJ: Wiley. http://dx.doi.org/10.1037/11622-000

Calder, B. J., Ross, M., & Insko, C. A. (1973). Attitude change and attitude attribution: Effects of incentive, choice, and consequences. *Journal of Personality and Social Psychology, 25*, 84–99. http://dx.doi.org/10.1037/h0034264

Carlsmith, J. M., Collins, B. E., & Helmreich, R. L. (1966). Studies in forced compliance: I. The effect of pressure for compliance on attitude change produced by face-to-face role playing and anonymous essay writing. *Journal of Personality and Social Psychology, 4*, 1–13. http://dx.doi.org/10.1037/h0023507

Cartwright, D., & Harary, F. (1956). Structural balance: A generalization of Heider's theory. *Psychological Review, 63*, 277–293. http://dx.doi.org/10.1037/h0046049

Cooper, J., & Fazio, R. H. (1984). A new look at dissonance theory. In L. Berkowitz (Ed.), *Advances in experimental social psychology* (Vol. 17, pp. 229–266). New York, NY: Academic Press.

Cooper, J., & Worchel, S. (1970). Role of undesired consequences in arousing cognitive dissonance. *Journal of Personality and Social Psychology, 16*, 199–206. http://dx.doi.org/10.1037/h0029830

Feldman, S. (1966). Motivational aspects of attitudinal elements and their place in cognitive interaction. In S. Feldman (Ed.), *Cognitive consistency* (pp. 75–108). New York, NY: Academic Press. http://dx.doi.org/10.1016/B978-1-4832-2828-0.50008-8

Festinger, L. (1957). *A theory of cognitive dissonance*. Stanford, CA: Stanford University Press.

Festinger, L., & Carlsmith, J. M. (1959). Cognitive consequences of forced compliance. *Journal of Abnormal and Social Psychology, 58*, 203–210. http://dx.doi.org/10.1037/h0041593

Harmon-Jones, E., Brehm, J. W., Greenberg, J., Simon, L., & Nelson, D. E. (1996). Evidence that the production of aversive consequences is not necessary to create cognitive dissonance. *Journal of Personality and Social Psychology, 70*, 5–16. http://dx.doi.org/10.1037/0022-3514.70.1.5

Heider, F. (1958). *The psychology of interpersonal relations*. Hoboken, NJ: Wiley. http://dx.doi.org/10.1037/10628-000

Helmreich, R., & Collins, B. E. (1968). Studies in forced compliance: Commitment and magnitude of inducement to comply as determinants of opinion change. *Journal of Personality and Social Psychology, 10*, 75–81. http://dx.doi.org/10.1037/h0026282

Holms, J. G., & Strickland, L. H. (1970). Choice freedom and confirmation of incentive expectancy as determinants of attitude change. *Journal of Personality and Social Psychology, 14*, 39–45. http://dx.doi.org/10.1037/h0028617

Joule, R.-V. (1991). Practicing and arguing for abstinence from smoking: A test of the double forced compliance paradigm. *European Journal of Social Psychology, 21*, 119–129. http://dx.doi.org/10.1002/ejsp.2420210203

Joule, R.-V. (1996). Une nouvelle voie de reduction de la dissonance: La rationalisation en acte [A new model for dissonance reduction: Act rationalization]. In J.-L. Beauvois, R.-V. Joule, & J.-M. Monteil (Eds.), *Perspectives cognitives et conduites sociales: 5. Contextes et contextes sociaux* [Cognitive Perspectives and social conduct: 5. Contexts and social contexts; pp. 293–307]. Neuchatel, Switzerland: Delachaux et Niestle.

Joule, R.-V., & Azdia, T. (2003). Cognitive dissonance, double forced compliance, and commitment. *European Journal of Social Psychology, 33*, 565–571. http://dx.doi.org/10.1002/ejsp.165

Joule, R.-V., & Beauvois, J. L. (1998). *La soumission librement consentie* [Freely granted submission]. Paris, France: Presses Universitaires.

Joule, R.-V., & Girandola, F. (1995). Tâche fastidieuse et jeu de rôle dans le paradigme de la double soumission [Tedious task and role-playing in the double compliance paradigm]. *Revue Internationale de Psychologie Sociale, 8*, 101–116.

Joule, R.-V., Girandola, F., & Bernard, F. (2007). How can people be induced to willingly change their behavior? The path from persuasive communication to binding communication. *Social and Personality Psychology Compass, 1*, 493–505. http://dx.doi.org/10.1111/j.1751-9004.2007.00018.x

Joule, R.-V., & Levèque, L. (1993). *Le changement d'attitude comme fonction du temps d'argumentation* [Attitude change as a function of argumentation length]. Unpublished manuscript, Provence University, Aix-en-Provence, France.

Kiesler, C. A. (1971). *The psychology of commitment: Experiments linking behavior to belief*. New York, NY: Academic Press.

Linder, D. E., Cooper, J., & Jones, E. E. (1967). Decision freedom as a determinant of the role of incentive magnitude in attitude change. *Journal of Personality and Social Psychology, 6*, 245–254. http://dx.doi.org/10.1037/h0021220

Rabbie, J. M., Brehm, J. W., & Cohen, A. R. (1959). Verbalization and reactions to cognitive dissonance. *Journal of Personality, 27*, 407–417. http://dx.doi.org/10.1111/j.1467-6494.1959.tb02363.x

Simon, L., Greenberg, J., & Brehm, J. (1995). Trivialization: The forgotten mode of dissonance reduction. *Journal of Personality and Social Psychology, 68*, 247–260. http://dx.doi.org/10.1037/0022-3514.68.2.247

Steiner, I. D. (1980). Attribution of choice. In M. Fishbein (Ed.), *Progress in social psychology* (pp. 1–47). Mahwah, NJ: Lawrence Erlbaum.

Wicklund, R. A., & Brehm, J. W. (1976). *Perspectives on cognitive dissonance*. New York, NY: Wiley.

Zajonc, R. B. (1968). Cognitive theories in social psychology. In G. Lindzey & E. Aronson (Eds.), *Handbook of social psychology* (Vol. 1, pp. 320–411). Reading, MA: Addison-Wesley.

4

Understanding the Motivation Underlying Dissonance Effects

The Action-Based Model

Eddie Harmon-Jones and Cindy Harmon-Jones

Starting in the 1960s, researchers began to challenge the original theory of cognitive dissonance and proposed that cognitive discrepancy (as defined by the original version of the theory; see Chapter 1, this volume) was not the cause of the cognitive and behavioral changes that were observed in experiments testing dissonance theory. Several revisions to the original theory emerged (Aronson, 1969; Cooper & Fazio, 1984; Cooper & Worchel, 1970; Steele, 1988). For the most part, these revisions aimed to address one of the most fundamental and important questions for dissonance theory and research—it concerns the underlying motivational force driving dissonance effects. In the present chapter, we provide a brief overview of the original version of the theory of cognitive dissonance (for more complete descriptions, see Festinger, 1957; Chapter 1, this volume) and one of these revisions that attracted much attention, the aversive consequences model (Cooper & Fazio, 1984). We then present our action-based model of dissonance, which proposes why dissonance and dissonance reduction occur. We then review evidence obtained in a variety of experimental paradigms that support predictions derived from this model. We conclude by suggesting that this extension of the original theory assists in understanding the function of dissonance processes.

---

http://dx.doi.org/10.1037/0000135-004
Cognitive Dissonance, Second Edition: Reexamining a Pivotal Theory in Psychology,
E. Harmon-Jones (Editor)
Copyright © 2019 by the American Psychological Association. All rights reserved.

THE ORIGINAL VERSION

The original statement of cognitive dissonance theory (Festinger, 1957) proposed that discrepancy between cognitions creates a negative affective state that motivates individuals to attempt to reduce or eliminate the discrepancy between cognitions (see Chapter 1, this volume, for a more complete description of this process). Several paradigms have been used to test predictions derived from dissonance theory. In each of these paradigms, the availability of the cognitions that serve to make the entire set of relevant cognitions more or less discrepant is manipulated. The most commonly used of these is the induced-compliance paradigm, in which participants are induced to act contrary to an attitude, and if they are provided few consonant cognitions (few reasons or little justification) for doing so, they are hypothesized to experience dissonance and reduce it, usually by changing their attitude to be more consistent with their behavior. In one of the first induced-compliance experiments, Festinger and Carlsmith (1959) paid participants either $1 (low justification) or $20 (high justification) to tell a fellow participant (confederate) that dull and boring tasks were very interesting and to remain on call to do it again in the future. After participants told this to the confederate, they were asked how interesting and enjoyable the tasks were. As predicted, participants given little justification for performing the counterattitudinal behavior rated the tasks as more interesting than did participants given much justification. Festinger and Carlsmith posited that participants provided low justification (just enough justification to say the counterattitudinal statement) experienced dissonance and changed their attitudes because of the inconsistency between their original attitude (they believed that the task was boring) and their behavior (they had said that the task was interesting). Participants provided with high justification, on the other hand, experienced little dissonance, because receiving $20 to perform the behavior justified the behavior or was consonant with the behavior.

In later research (Brehm & Cohen, 1962), the degree of dissonance was manipulated by means of perceived choice rather than by the magnitude of an incentive to engage in the counterattitudinal behavior. Having low choice (i.e., being forced) to behave counterattitudinally can be considered a cognition consonant with the counterattitudinal behavior; in contrast, the high choice induction would lack this consonant cognition (or at least have less of it). Experiments found that participants who were given high choice, as opposed to low choice, to write counterattitudinal essays changed their attitudes to be more consistent with their behavior.

REVISIONS TO THE ORIGINAL THEORY

Within the decades after the publication of the original theory of dissonance (Festinger, 1957) and its early experiments (e.g., Festinger & Carlsmith, 1959), researchers offered alternative theoretical and experimental accounts. One revision that received the most empirical attention was based on the idea that individuals needed to feel personally responsible for producing aversive consequences in order to experience dissonance and dissonance-related attitude change. We briefly review this revision below, and then review evidence that has challenged this revision. Afterward, we briefly review two other revisions and evidence that challenged those revisions.

The Aversive-Consequences Revision

The aversive-consequences revision suggested that low-justification participants in the Festinger and Carlsmith (1959) experiment changed their attitudes not because of cognitive discrepancy, but because their actions brought about an aversive event (convincing another person to expect boring tasks to be interesting). In one of the first experiments testing this explanation, Cooper and Worchel (1970) replicated and extended the Festinger and Carlsmith study. Cooper and Worchel found that low-justification participants changed their attitudes to be consistent with their behavior when the confederate believed their statement, but not when the confederate did not believe their statement.

Using a slightly different procedure, other research has suggested that, when the counterattitudinal actions do not cause aversive consequences, attitude change does not occur (e.g., Collins & Hoyt, 1972; Goethals & Cooper, 1975; Hoyt, Henley, & Collins, 1972; Scher & Cooper, 1989). According to the aversive-consequences revision, a sufficient cognitive discrepancy is neither necessary nor sufficient to cause dissonance and discrepancy reduction. Instead, feeling personally responsible for the production of foreseeable aversive consequences is necessary and sufficient. Aversive consequences are events that one would not want to occur (Cooper & Fazio, 1984).

Alternative Explanations for the Evidence Produced by the Aversive-Consequences Revision

The aversive-consequences revision was supported by evidence obtained in the induced-compliance paradigm. More specifically, the support for the aversive-consequences revision comes from the absence of measurable attitude change in the conditions in which aversive consequences were not produced. There are several explanations for the absence of this attitude-change effect in the no-aversive-consequences conditions, and these alternative explanations must prevent us from concluding that cognitive discrepancy is not necessary or sufficient to create dissonance. First, this is a null effect. It is difficult to draw clear inferences from null effects, as they may be produced by a variety of factors (e.g., failure to manipulate the constructs of interest, insufficient power to detect the effects). Had these past theorists and researchers drawn the conclusion that feeling personally responsible for producing an aversive outcome *intensifies* dissonance, we would be in complete agreement, for it is likely that feeling personally responsible for such will intensify dissonance and dissonance-produced attitude change. Feeling personally responsible for an aversive consequence is an important discrepant cognition, and importance increases the magnitude of dissonance. However, these past theorists and researchers instead proposed that feelings of personal responsibility for aversive outcomes were *necessary* to produce dissonance effects.

Two sets of alternative explanations can be offered for the lack of attitude change in the no-aversive-consequences conditions. The first set of alternative explanations argues that the level of dissonance was not large enough to generate dissonance sufficient to produce attitude change and that the addition of the production of aversive consequences was necessary to produce dissonance sufficient to cause attitude change. Several of the past induced-compliance experiments that included a no-aversive-consequences and an aversive-consequences condition used attitudinal issues that were not extremely negative or positive, that is, control-condition participants reported moderately negative or positive attitudes (e.g., Calder, Ross, & Insko, 1973; Nel, Helmreich, & Aronson, 1969). Moreover, the lack of extremity might have reflected ambivalence or a mix of positive and negative attitudes toward the issues. Because the attitudes used in past experiments were not extremely positive or negative and might have been held with ambivalence, they were likely not to arouse much dissonance when behavior counter to them occurred. In essence, the magnitude of dissonance aroused may have been too small to generate attitude change.

In the past experiments, the researchers often encouraged participants to generate lengthy counterattitudinal statements. This may increase the likelihood of finding no attitude change in the no-aversive-consequences conditions. Research has shown that the length of the counterattitudinal statement relates inversely with the amount of attitude change that occurs (e.g., Rabbie, Brehm, & Cohen, 1959; see also Chapter 3, this volume), that is, longer essays are likely to produce less attitude change. This inverse relationship between essay length and attitude change may occur because participants may provide their own justifications and hence more cognitions consonant with the behavior in these lengthy essays. As the number of consonant cognitions increases, the magnitude of dissonance decreases.

In addition, because of the salience of the audiences in these experiments, the participants' attention may have been focused more on the audience and whether they were convinced or could affect a disliked policy than on the nature of their own counterattitudinal actions or their own attitudes. As a result of this, the magnitude of dissonance may have been determined in large part by what the audience did or would do as a result of the counterattitudinal advocacy. Thus, the unconvinced audience, in contrast to the convinced audience, may have reduced the importance of the dissonant cognitions, to the point of making the counterattitudinal action seem trivial. If the perceived importance of dissonant cognitions is low, dissonance may not reach a magnitude that requires reduction.

Another possible explanation is that participants in these past experiments may have been provided too much justification (too many consonant cognitions) for producing the counterattitudinal statement, and the production of aversive consequences may have been necessary to elicit enough dissonance to produce measurable attitude change. This explanation seems very reasonable when one considers the high compliance rates observed in most if not all of this past research.[1] Typically, 100% of the participants have complied with the experimenter's request to write the counterattitudinal statement. As Festinger (1957) explained, for attitude change to result from dissonance, the person should be offered *"just enough reward or punishment to elicit the overt compliance"* (p. 95, italics in original). Thus, the past experiments on the necessity of aversive consequences may have had inducing forces (the friendliness of the experimenter, the benefits to science) that were so great that little or no dissonance was produced, and the addition of feeling personally responsible for producing aversive consequences may have been necessary to produce sufficient dissonance to cause measurable discrepancy reduction (e.g., attitude change).

Another set of alternative explanations for the lack of attitude change in the no-aversive-consequences conditions argues that dissonance may have been aroused in participants in the no-aversive-consequences conditions of the past experiments but was not detected. The sole method of detecting dissonance in the experiments testing the aversive-consequences model against the original version of the theory has been assessment of attitude change. Because no assessments of dissonance were obtained in experiments testing the aversive consequences model, it is impossible to know whether dissonance was aroused in the no-aversive-consequences conditions. The only conclusion that can safely be drawn is that measurable attitude change did not occur. On the other hand, attitude change may have occurred in the no-aversive-consequences conditions but may have been small, and it would not have been detected if one had only 10 to 12 persons per condition, as was done in much of the past research (e.g., Calder et al., 1973; Cooper & Worchel, 1970). Research has found that effects in personality and social psychological research are typically small to medium (Fraley & Marks, 2007; Richard, Bond, & Stokes-Zoota, 2003). According to power analysis using G*Power (Faul, Erdfelder, Buchner, & Lang, 2009), 139 participants per condition would be required to detect an effect of small-to-medium size (Cohen's $d = 0.3$), suggesting that these studies were seriously underpowered. In addition, the dissonance may have been reduced in a route other than attitude change. Persons whose counterattitudinal actions had no undesired effects may have reduced dissonance by reducing the importance (Simon, Greenberg, & Brehm, 1995) or the perceived effectiveness (Scheier & Carver, 1980) of the counterattitudinal behavior.

It is unlikely that one of these possible alternative explanations accounts for all of the nonsignificant effects that have been found in the past no-aversive-consequences conditions. However, given the number of plausible alternative explanations for the null effects produced in the past experiments that had

---

[1] An examination of the past experiments that manipulated whether participants produced an aversive consequence revealed extremely high compliance rates in the high-choice and low-justification conditions. These experiments are listed with the number of noncompliers indicated in parentheses after the date of publication: Nel et al., 1969 (1); Cooper and Worchel, 1970 (1); Collins and Hoyt, 1972 (0); Goethals and Cooper, 1972 (2 experiments; 0); Hoyt et al., 1972 (1); Calder et al., 1973 (1); Cooper, Zanna, and Goethals, 1974 (0); Goethals and Cooper, 1975 (1); Scher and Cooper, 1989 (1); Johnson, Kelly, and LeBlanc, 1995 (0).

been used to support the aversive-consequences revision, we thought it was premature to abandon the original version of the theory.

Induced-Compliance Experimental Results Inconsistent With the Aversive-Consequences Revision

All of the research on the aversive-consequences revision has been conducted using the *induced-compliance* paradigm, which is the focal paradigm in which predictions derived from dissonance theory and its revisions have been tested. We have conducted several induced-compliance experiments to test the hypothesis that feeling personally responsible for producing aversive consequences is not necessary to produce dissonance and that cognitive discrepancy is sufficient to produce dissonance even in the induced-compliance paradigm. In conducting these experiments, we created a situation in which participants would write counterattitudinal statements but not produce aversive consequences. We designed the experiments so that conditions present in previous induced-compliance experiments that might have prevented attitude change from occurring were not present. We took special care to ensure that the inducing force was "just barely sufficient to induce the person" to behave counterattitudinally (Festinger & Carlsmith, 1959, p. 204), to reduce the number of consonant cognitions to a bare minimum, so that the dissonance aroused after the action would be at high levels. In addition, we had participants write short counterattitudinal statements about objects toward which they held attitudes that were highly salient, strongly negative (or positive), simple, and not ambivalent. Also, in some of the experiments, we assessed negative affect and arousal, to provide measures of dissonance arousal as well as dissonance reduction.

In each experiment, under the guise of an experiment on recall, participants were exposed to a stimulus, were given low or high choice to write a counterattitudinal statement about that stimulus, threw away the statement they wrote, and then completed questionnaires that assessed their attitudes toward the stimulus. We assured participants that their counterattitudinal statements and their responses to the questionnaires would be made in private and would be anonymous. We did so to create a situation in which the counterattitudinal behavior would not lead to aversive consequences, because, as Cooper and Fazio (1984) argued, "making a statement contrary to one's attitude while in solitude does not have the potential for bringing about an aversive event" (p. 232). We predicted that participants provided high choice for engaging in the counterattitudinal behavior would change their attitudes to be more consistent with their behavior, whereas participants provided low choice would not.

Dissonance and an Unpleasant Beverage. In the first experiment testing this idea (E. Harmon-Jones, Brehm, Greenberg, Simon, & Nelson, 1996, Experiment 1), participants were told that the research concerned factors that influenced the recall of characteristics of products, and that this study would test how writing a sentence evaluating a product would affect recall of the characteristics of the product. Participants would drink one of a variety of beverages, write a sentence about it, and then recall characteristics of it. The experimenter explained that participants should not let him know what type of drink they received. He also explained that all of their responses would be anonymous and that he would not see their responses to questionnaires but that an assistant would enter them into a computer.

The experimenter gave the participant a lid-covered cup containing fruit-punch flavored Kool-Aid mixed either with the amount of sugar suggested (a pleasant-tasting drink), or with white vinegar and no sugar (an unpleasant-tasting drink). Because the experimenter was unaware of whether participants were given a pleasant- or an unpleasant-tasting drink, he was unaware of whether participants experienced dissonance.

After the participant drank some of the beverage, the experimenter returned to the participant's cubicle and induced the choice manipulation. He told participants in the low-choice condition that they were randomly assigned to write a statement saying they liked the beverage. He told participants in the high-choice condition that they could write a statement saying they liked or disliked the beverage and that it was their choice. The experimenter explained that he needed some more persons to write that they liked the beverage, and he asked the participant if she or he would write that she or he liked the beverage. Once the experimenter gained compliance from the participant, he reminded her or him that it was her or his choice.

The experimenter then asked both low-choice and high-choice participants to write one sentence saying they liked the beverage. He also told participants that he did not "need the sheet of paper you will write your sentence on; we just need for you to go through the process of writing the sentence. So when you are done, just wad it up and throw it in the wastebasket." He did this to ensure that the participants perceived that they had anonymity and that there would be no consequences to their behavior. The experimenter then left the participants alone to write the sentence.

After the participant discarded the sentence, the experimenter gave the participant an envelope and said that previous research had indicated that the characteristics a person recalls about a product may be affected by whether they liked the product and that to take this into account, he needed them to answer a questionnaire that assessed their thoughts about the drink. The questionnaire assessed how much the drink was liked. The experimenter left the participant alone to answer this questionnaire. After the participant finished with this questionnaire, the experimenter had the participant complete a questionnaire that assessed the effectiveness of the manipulation of choice. After assessing suspicion and debriefing, the experimenter collected the participants' statements from the trash can, to assess whether participants complied with the request to write the counterattitudinal statement.

Approximately 15% of the participants did not write counterattitudinal statements. This effect suggests that we had designed a situation in which there was just enough but not too much external justification to write the counterattitudinal statement. Results indicated that participants in the unpleasant-tasting drink/high-choice condition reported more positive attitudes toward the drink than did participants in the unpleasant-tasting drink/low-choice condition.

This effect was significant when both compliers and noncompliers were included in the analysis, as well as when only compliers were included. Thus, the results of the first experiment suggested that dissonance can be created in induced-compliance situations void of aversive consequences.

Dissonance, Boring Passages, and Electrodermal Activity. Subsequent experiments were designed to conceptually replicate the effects of the first experiment using a different manipulation of choice, a different attitudinal object, and measures of dissonance arousal and affect. Using similar procedures as used in the first experiment, we had participants read a boring passage and gave them low or high choice, by means of written instructions, to write a statement saying that the passage was interesting. Because choice was induced by means of written instructions, the experimenter was unaware of when dissonance was expected. Results from this experiment replicated those of the first experiment, with high-choice participants, as compared with low-choice participants, rating the boring passage as more interesting (E. Harmon-Jones et al., 1996, Experiment 2).

In another experiment (E. Harmon-Jones et al., 1996, Experiment 3), we measured nonspecific skin conductance responses (NS-SCRs) that occurred in the 3 minutes after the writing of the counterattitudinal statement but before the assessment of attitude. Previous research has indicated that increased NS-SCRs are associated with increased sympathetic nervous system activity, which is increased during emotional arousal. If our experimental procedure evoked dissonance, we would observe increased NS-SCRs. Results indicated that participants given high choice to write the counterattitudinal statement evidenced more NS-SCRs and reported that the passage was more interesting than did participants given low choice to write the statement.

Dissonance and a Hershey's Kiss. The previous results demonstrate that the production of aversive consequences is not necessary to arouse dissonance and dissonance-related attitude change. However, they may be subject to an alternative explanation: Perhaps the manipulation of choice to write the statement influenced individuals' reconstructive construal of the situation, so that high-choice participants felt as though they had high choice to engage with the unpleasant stimulus, whereas low-choice participants felt as though they had low choice to engage with the unpleasant stimulus. If this were so, then the aversive-consequences revision could explain these results as being due to feeling personally responsible for inflicting a negative event on oneself (choosing to drink the unpleasant Kool-Aid or read the boring passage). To eliminate this alternative explanation, another experiment was conducted (E. Harmon-Jones, 2000a, Experiment 1). In this experiment, instead of writing a counterattitudinal statement about a negative stimulus, participants wrote a counterattitudinal statement about a positive stimulus.

Under the same cover story as in the previous experiments, participants ate a pleasant-tasting Hershey's Kiss and then were given high or low choice to write that they did not enjoy it. Consistent with predictions, high-choice participants reported that they disliked the Hershey's Kiss more than did low-choice participants.

In addition, in this experiment, state self-reported affect was measured immediately after the writing of the counterattitudinal statement or after the attitude-change opportunity. Time between counterattitudinal action and attitude assessment was controlled by having participants complete an affect questionnaire or a filler questionnaire, comparable in length. From the state affect measure, four indexes of affect were derived. Discomfort was measured with the scale developed by Elliot and Devine (1994). State social self-esteem and appearance self-esteem were measured with the subscales of the State Self-Esteem Scale (Heatherton & Polivy, 1991). Positive affect was measured with the items happy, proud, and enthusiastic.

Results indicated that participants who were given high choice and who completed the affect questionnaire before the attitude measure reported significantly more discomfort than did participants in the other conditions. Positive affect, state social self-esteem, and state appearance self-esteem did not differ significantly among conditions. Another experiment reported in this article conceptually replicated these results (E. Harmon-Jones, 2000a, Experiment 2). These results suggest that the cognitive discrepancy evoked in this situation increased discomfort. The results also suggest that the cognitive discrepancy evoked in this situation was more likely to increase discomfort than to decrease state self-esteem or positive affect.[2]

Summary. The experiments presented thus far were all conducted using the induced-compliance paradigm. The results from these experiments support the original theory of dissonance and are inconsistent with the aversive-consequences revision. These experiments are important because they show that dissonance arousal, dissonance affect, and dissonance-produced attitude change can occur in situations in which a sufficient cognitive discrepancy is present but feeling personally responsible for the production of aversive consequences is not present. The present evidence convincingly demonstrates that dissonance effects can be generated by a cognitive discrepancy that does not produce aversive consequences. Indeed, these results suggest that the

---

[2] In the three induced-compliance experiments by E. Harmon-Jones et al. (1996) that are described in this chapter, compliance was approximately 85%. However, in the reported experiment by E. Harmon-Jones (2000a), in which participants ate a piece of chocolate and then wrote that they did not enjoy it, only 1 participant did not comply. In the experiments by E. Harmon-Jones et al. (1996), persons were asked to write that they believed a boring passage they had just read was interesting or that an unpleasant-tasting beverage was pleasant tasting. The attitudes toward these simple stimuli were quite negative, as evidenced by low-choice-condition and control-condition participants. In contrast, in the experiment by E. Harmon-Jones (2000a), persons' attitudes toward the chocolate were not extremely positive. Thus, although this latter experiment had compliance rates similar to the ones discussed above, it still produced dissonance. Thus, compliance rates are not an inviolable assessment of amount of justification within an experiment. Other factors, such as the size and importance of the discrepancy between attitude and behavior and number and importance of justifications for the behavior (promised rewards or punishments, which are probably largely social in nature), need to be taken into account. Attempts to measure size and importance of discrepancy and justifications would aid tremendously in specifying the magnitude of dissonance.

original version of the theory was abandoned prematurely (see Chapter 3, this volume).

Aversive Consequences and Attitude Change

Earlier we argued that producing aversive consequences might intensify dissonance. Why would this occur? The production of aversive consequences may intensify dissonance because aversive consequences are a cognition dissonant with one's preexisting attitude. If the attitude were the generative cognition, the cognition about the counterattitudinal behavior and the cognition of producing aversive consequences would be dissonant cognitions. Thus, the magnitude of dissonance aroused would be greater in psychological situations where counterattitudinal behavior and aversive consequences were produced than in situations where only counterattitudinal behavior was produced, because there are more dissonant cognitions in the former than in the latter situation. However, if the counterattitudinal behavior were the generative cognition (Beauvois & Joule, 1996), then the cognition of producing aversive consequences would be a consonant cognition (it follows from the behavior), and thus it would decrease the magnitude of dissonance aroused. Beauvois and Joule (1996) reported results consistent with this latter interpretation, but the past research on the aversive-consequences model is consistent with the former. This inconsistency between these two sets of results can be resolved by positing that in the induced-compliance paradigm, both the attitude and the behavior can serve as generative cognitions, and there may be a potential dissonance associated with each. That is, there is a potential dissonance associated with the attitude and a potential dissonance associated with the behavior. In general, the greater dissonance would be the one reduced. The generative cognition associated with that greater dissonance would not be altered, whereas the generative cognition associated with the lesser dissonance would be altered. However, the reduction of dissonance depends also on the availability of discrepancy-reduction routes. Hence, when the potential dissonances are not very different in magnitude, the discrepancy may be reduced by means of the most available route, which has been attitude change in most previous dissonance experiments.

An additional possibility is that the production of aversive consequences may increase the dissonance, because it increases the commitment to the behavior, making the behavior more resistant to change and attitude change more likely to result. In addition, when behavior produces important consequences, it will be regarded as a more important cognition and thus has the potential to create more dissonance. Although these explanations are more elegant in their simplicity, they do not fit with the large body evidence presented by Beauvois and Joule (1996), whereas the explanation offered in the previous paragraph does.

The Belief-Disconfirmation Paradigm

Research on the aversive-consequences revision has focused exclusively on the induced-compliance paradigm. However, other paradigms have been used to test predictions derived from dissonance theory, and evidence obtained in these paradigms is difficult to explain with the aversive-consequences revision (see also Berkowitz & Devine, 1989).

One such paradigm is the *belief-disconfirmation* paradigm. This paradigm is based on Festinger, Riecken, and Schachter's (1956) observations of belief intensification among members of a group whose belief that a flood would destroy the continent was disconfirmed. This evidence suggests that the cognitive discrepancy that occurs when an important and highly resistant to change belief is disconfirmed produces dissonance, leading to the use of dissonance-reducing strategies such as belief intensification. Results obtained in this paradigm are not subject to an aversive-consequences alternative explanation, because individuals involuntarily exposed to belief-discrepant information have not produced an aversive consequence and thus cannot feel responsible for having done so.

Past Evidence From the Belief-Disconfirmation Paradigm Inconsistent With the Aversion Consequences Revision

In an experiment by Brock and Balloun (1967), committed churchgoers were confronted with audiotaped information that did or did not support their religious values. When the information was inconsistent with their religious values, individuals were less likely to press a button to eliminate white noise from the communication and thus make it easier to comprehend. Other research has replicated these findings (e.g., Schwarz, Frey, & Kumpf, 1980), further suggesting that dissonance effects occur even when inconsistencies are produced by outside information, not from actions that produce aversive consequences.

In a quasi-experiment by Batson (1975), girls attending a church youth program were asked to declare publicly whether they believed in the divinity of Jesus. After completing a measure of Christian orthodoxy, the girls were then presented with belief-disconfirming information (i.e., information that indicated that Jesus was not the son of God). Orthodoxy was once again assessed. As expected, those who believed in the divinity of Jesus and accepted the truthfulness of the disconfirming information intensified their belief in Jesus' divinity, whereas those who were not believers or who believed but did not accept the truthfulness of the disconfirming information did not.

It is difficult to explain the results obtained in the belief-disconfirmation paradigm as resulting from the motivation to avoid feeling personally responsible for producing aversive consequences. That is, the person exposed to belief-inconsistent information has not acted in a manner to produce aversive consequences and thus cannot feel responsible for having done so. In this paradigm, persons are exposed to information from an external source; they have not done anything for which to feel responsible. Note that Cooper and Fazio (1989), two of the main proponents of the aversive-consequences revision, stated that according to the aversive-consequences revision, evidence obtained in the belief-disconfirmation paradigm is not the result of dissonance. Cooper and Fazio stated that exposure to belief-discrepant information "will not necessarily create an unwanted consequence and will not necessarily arouse dissonance" (p. 525). In our view, dissonance does occur in response to belief-discrepant information, and the aversive-consequences revision has unfortunately excessively narrowed the range of application of dissonance theory. One way to demonstrate that evidence obtained in the belief-disconfirmation paradigm is the result of dissonance processes is to show that the negative affect that motivates the cognitive effects occurs as a result of belief disconfirmation and is reduced after reconciliation of the cognitive discrepancy.

Recent Evidence From the Belief-Disconfirmation Paradigm Inconsistent With the Aversion Consequences Revision

Two belief-disconfirmation experiments have done exactly that: they assessed whether dissonance-related emotive pressures drove the cognitive effects (Burris, Harmon-Jones, & Tarpley, 1997). The design was based on Allport's (1950) idea that "the suffering of innocent persons is for most people the hardest of all facts to integrate into religious sentiment" (p. 81). In the experiments, Christian participants were exposed to a newspaper article that highlighted the discrepancy between belief in a loving, protecting, just, and omnipotent God and knowledge of the gratuitous suffering humans often experience. The newspaper article reported the drive-by shooting death of an infant boy in his grandmother's arms, as she and the child's father prayed for protection because a similar incident had occurred two nights earlier. The article concluded with a quote from the infant's grandfather that expressed his continued faith in God. The cognitive discrepancy between the participants' religious beliefs (God is a good God who protects the innocent and answers prayers) and this tragic outcome (the infant dies during a prayer for protection) was highlighted by having participants read, "Some people would think that the grandfather's continued belief and trust in a good God is naive and misguided."

Belief Disconfirmation and Transcendence Experiment. The first experiment tested the hypothesis, offered by Abelson (1959), that "the theosophical dilemma of God's presumed permissiveness toward evil is sometimes resolved by appeal to transcendent concepts" (p. 346). If participants exposed to this belief-discrepant story were allowed to engage in transcendence (i.e., allowed to reconcile dissonant cognitions under a superordinate principle), they would experience less negative affect. Moreover, the more they engaged in transcendence, the less their negative affect would be.

Participants were randomly assigned to one of two conditions. In the transcendence-opportunity condition, they read the newspaper article and then completed a questionnaire that allowed them to engage in transcendence. These participants were given the explicit opportunity to reconcile the cognitive discrepancy after the dissonance had been aroused, when they were most in need of reducing the dissonance brought about by exposure to the belief-inconsistent information. They then completed a measure of self-reported state negative affect. In the no-transcendent-opportunity condition, participants completed the transcendence measure, read the tragic newspaper article, and then completed the measure of negative affect. These participants were thus not given an explicit opportunity to engage in transcendence after the dissonance had been aroused, when they were most in need of reducing the dissonance. The transcendence measure included questions such as, "How much does God intervene in persons' lives?" and "How often do things happen to persons because of God's greater purpose?" The measure of negative affect included items to measure discomfort (uncomfortable, uneasy, bothered; Elliot & Devine, 1994) and agitation (angry, frustrated, distressed, and threatened).

Based on dissonance theory, the endorsement of higher levels of transcendence subsequent to reading the newspaper article should relate to lower levels of dissonance-related affect. In contrast, higher levels of transcendence before the reading should not relate to lower levels of dissonance-related affect. Consistent with predictions, results indicated that higher endorsement of transcendence predicted decreased agitation in the transcendence-opportunity condition, whereas it did not in the no-opportunity condition. A similar pattern emerged for discomfort. Moreover, individuals in the transcendence-opportunity condition engaged in more transcendence than did individuals in the no-transcendence-opportunity condition, who completed the transcendence measure prior to reading the belief disconfirming story.

As expected, more extreme endorsement of transcendent beliefs after exposure to a belief-discrepant article was associated with reduced dissonance-related affect. In contrast, belief transcendence before exposure to the belief-discrepant article did not relate to reduced dissonance-related affect. This evidence strongly suggests that exposure to belief-discrepant information arouses dissonance that motivates persons to engage in discrepancy reduction, which then reduces the dissonance. Because persons in the belief-disconfirmation paradigm do not produce aversive consequences for which to feel responsible, this evidence suggests that the production of aversive consequences is not necessary to create dissonance.

Belief Disconfirmation and Belief Affirmation Experiment. In the previous experiment, time and transcendence opportunity were confounded, making it difficult to infer what caused the observed effects. That is, those who completed the transcendence scale after reading the article and before responding to the affect measures may have been distracted by this intervening task compared with those who completed the transcendence scale before the article. This explanation does not seem plausible, given that there was no main effect of transcendence-opportunity condition on dissonance-related affect but only an interaction with level of transcendence endorsement. However, to eliminate this explanation, a second study was conducted to conceptually replicate the first. In addition, instead of assessing transcendence in response to belief disconfirmation, belief affirmation was manipulated, much like Batson (1975) and Festinger et al. (1956) did. This was done to test the hypothesis that religious individuals would "rigidly maintain or even intensify" (Batson, 1975, p. 178) their beliefs when faced with disconfirming evidence. Religiously interested participants completed religious belief measures either after (belief-affirmation condition) or before (no-affirmation condition) reading the belief-discrepant article or completed comparable-length nonreligious belief measures after the article (distraction condition). All then completed self-report affect measures. Results revealed that, as predicted, agitation was lower in the religious-affirmation condition than in either the no-affirmation or the distraction condition; agitation levels in the latter two conditions did not differ.

Past results from the belief-disconfirmation paradigm cannot be interpreted in terms of the aversive-consequences revision. This past research, however, suffers from an important limitation because no measures of dissonance-related affect were obtained either during the experience of dissonance or after discrepancy reduction, rendering it difficult to know whether the effects generated in this belief-disconfirmation paradigm were caused by the mechanisms proposed by dissonance theory. However, the research by Burris et al. (1997) demonstrates that the effects produced in the belief-disconfirmation paradigm are due to dissonance processes.

Other Experimental Results Inconsistent With the Aversive-Consequences Revision

Other experiments provide evidence of dissonance in situations void of the production of aversive consequences. For instance, Aronson and Carlsmith (1962) found that individuals with experimentally-created expectancies for failure reacted with dissonance to behaving successfully. In the experiment, after individuals had repeatedly failed at a task, they were given feedback indicating that they were succeeding at the task. Then the individuals were given an opportunity to change their responses. Results indicated that these individuals changed their responses from being correct to being incorrect. Because failure is regarded as negative and success as positive, the behavior of these individuals would be difficult to interpret in the aversive-consequences formulation. Other research has demonstrated that dissonance can occur even when participants engage in proattitudinal behavior that has positive consequences (see Chapter 6, this volume). Finally, additional experimental evidence indicates that dissonance can occur in the absence of the production of aversive consequences (e.g., Beauvois & Joule, 1996; see also Chapters 3 and 6, this volume).

Summary of Evidence Concerning Aversive-Consequences Revision

Results from experiments using several methodologies suggest that a cognitive discrepancy in the absence of feeling personally responsible for the production of aversive consequences can cause increased dissonance-related negative affect and discrepancy reduction. The results of these experiments suggest that a cognitive discrepancy is enough to generate dissonance and discrepancy reduction. Feeling personally responsible for producing aversive consequences is not necessary to generate dissonance and discrepancy reduction, but it may enhance the magnitude of dissonance effects because producing aversive consequences is an important cognition that is dissonant with one's pre-existing attitude or because the aversive consequences increase the commitment to behavior.

A cognitive discrepancy, however, will produce an aversive state, in keeping with Festinger's speculations and the results presented in this chapter. This aversive state is not equivalent to the aversive consequences that dissonance theory revisionists discussed. Two other prominent revisions of dissonance theory posited that dissonance responses were responses to self-threats (see Chapters 7 and 8, this volume). Other research and theoretical arguments have suggested that these revisions do not fully explain research generated by dissonance theory, and therefore, the original theory, with its focus on cognitive discrepancy, is still viable (E. Harmon-Jones, 2000b, 2000c, 2001, 2002; E. Harmon-Jones, Amodio, & Harmon-Jones, 2009; see also Chapters 3 and 5, this volume). However, the original theory never clearly specified why cognitive discrepancy creates a negative affective state and motivates discrepancy reduction. Below, we outline a conceptual model and some research that addresses these issues.

THE MOTIVATION UNDERLYING DISSONANCE EFFECTS—AN ACTION-BASED MODEL

The reviewed research cogently demonstrates that the motivation to avoid the production of aversive consequences is not the motivation underlying dissonance effects. The studies reviewed above affirmed Festinger's (1957) original version of the theory as being a more inclusive and elegant explanation for the evidence. However, the original version left several questions unanswered.

According to the original version of the theory, a sufficient cognitive discrepancy is the source of the motivation underlying dissonance and its effects. But why would a cognitive discrepancy evoke such a motivation? What function does the capacity to experience negative affect in response to a sufficient cognitive discrepancy and then be motivated to reduce it have for the organism? Is this set of psychological mechanisms adaptively beneficial? That is, is the dissonance mechanism functional or beneficial for the organism?

The action-based model was designed to address these questions. It extends dissonance theory by providing an explanation of why cognitive inconsistency arouses negative affect and how and why this negative affect motivates the cognitive and behavior adjustments. The model begins with the assumption that cognitions (broadly defined) can serve as action tendencies. The idea that cognition for action is seen not only in the 1890 writings of William James (1890/1950), but also in ecological approaches to perception (Gibson, 1979; McArthur & Baron, 1983) and in the study of attitudes (Bain, 1868; Spencer, 1865). In this sense, the cognitions that are of primary concern for this theoretical model are those that provide useful information, and usefulness of information is defined by its relevance to actions and goals. When information inconsistent with cognitions that guide action is encountered, negative emotion (dissonance) is aroused because the dissonant information has the potential to interfere with effective and unconflicted action. For the present model, effective behavior can occur in the absence of consciousness; in other words, effective behavior can be produced automatically. Thus, the present model does not propose that cognitive consistency is necessary for effective behavior. It only proposes that cognitive inconsistency interferes with effective behavior.

Thus, cognitive discrepancy may create negative affect because discrepancy among cognitions undermines the requirement for effective and unconflicted action (Beckmann & Irle, 1985; Jones & Gerard, 1967). Research on the theory of dissonance has identified commitment as an important, if not necessary, condition for the arousal of dissonance (Beauvois & Joule, 1996; Brehm & Cohen, 1962; Festinger, 1964). For most dissonance theorists, the notion of commitment implies that the person has engaged in a behavior for which he or she feels responsibility and that he or she has a definite understanding of the consequences of the behavior. However, persons can regard cognitions that may not involve an immediate behavioral commitment as true or certain (Mills, 1968) and would experience dissonance if information were presented that was inconsistent with these cognitions. A good example of this type of cognition is a person's belief in the law of gravity. Information that violates the law of gravity would probably arouse dissonance in most persons because it guides behavior in a general sense, regardless of whether the individual has made a specific, recent commitment to this knowledge. Therefore, we propose that a commitment occurs when a person regards a behavior, belief, attitude, or value as a meaningful truth. Defining commitment in this way allows for viewing commitment as a continuous variable. When commitment is defined as overt behavior, as with previous dissonance theorists, commitment is reduced to a categorical variable, which may not be an accurate representation of psychological states involving more and less commitment. The degree of psychological commitment to the cognition guides information processing, which serves the ultimate function of producing and guiding behavior.

If dissonant information is encountered, negative emotion may result and cause the person to engage in cognitive work to support the commitment. However, if dissonant information continues to mount, the negative emotion that results may motivate the person to disengage from the commitment and accept the dissonant information. Whether the person's cognitive work is aimed toward supporting the commitment or discontinuing the commitment is determined by the resistance to change of each cognition. If the commitment is more resistant to change than the dissonant information, then cognitive work would be aimed at supporting the commitment. If, however, the dissonant information is more resistant to change than the commitment, then the cognitive work would be aimed at discontinuing the commitment. Resistance to change of cognitions is determined by the responsiveness of the cognitions to reality (e.g., the grass is green), the extent to which the cognitions are in relations of consonance to other cognitions, the difficulty of changing the cognition, and so on. From the present view, resistance to change is ultimately determined by the degree to which individuals believe the information assists them in controlling and predicting outcomes and thus behaving effectively. When knowledge about the environment, about oneself, or about one's actions, beliefs, or attitudes is in a dissonant relation, the sense of being able to control and predict outcomes may be threatened, and ultimately, the need to act effectively would be undermined.

From the current perspective, the proximal motivation to reduce cognitive discrepancy stems from the need to reduce negative emotion, whereas the distal motivation to reduce discrepancy stems from the requirement for effective action. When the maintenance of true and certain knowledge, and thus the potential for effective action, is threatened by information that is sufficiently discrepant from the psychological commitment, negative emotion results, which prompts attempts at the restoration of cognitions supportive of the commitment (i.e., discrepancy reduction). Thus, negative emotion works much like pain in that it provides the information and motivation that prompts the person to engage in cognitive action aimed at resolving the discrepancy. These speculations about the adaptive function of dissonance processes suggest interesting avenues of research.

Many of the situations that evoke dissonance can be conceptualized as situations that involve a commitment to a specific action (e.g., after a difficult decision or chosen counterattitudinal behavior). The commitment to a specific action engages psychological processes that essentially prime one to act and thus motivate the organism to convert their commitment or intention into an effective action. This motivational state should be approach oriented and is revealed in changes in attitude that are consistent with and ultimately support the commitment.

Most dissonance research puts individuals in situations that involve a behavioral commitment. The action-based model proposes that making a commitment to a behavior primes the individual to translate that intention into action. Thus, a commitment should motivate individuals to engage in cognitive work to bring their cognitions into alignment, to engage in dissonance reduction. This should be an approach-motivated process that functions to facilitate effective action because it relieves the competing action tendencies of conflicting cognitions.

Imagine a person who makes the difficult decision of temporarily leaving the workforce to obtain an advanced degree. The potential benefits of the degree, such as greater potential for earnings and advancement, are consonant cognitions. The drawbacks, such as temporarily reduced income and the effort that will need to be expended, are dissonant cognitions. According to the action-based model, the more the individual can increase consonant cognitions and/or their importance, while decreasing dissonant cognitions and/or their importance, the greater the likelihood of success in seeking the degree. Conversely, if the individual continued to regret the temporary loss of income and increased workload, the action tendencies of these cognitions may interfere with taking the steps necessary to complete the degree. By increasing consonant cognitions and decreasing dissonant cognitions, the individual not only reduces the negative emotion of dissonance but also is better able to carry out a difficult decision.

Testing the Action-Based Model

This action-based model of dissonance has been tested in a variety of ways. We review these tests here.

Action Orientation and Spreading of Alternatives

The above example illustrates that, following a behavioral commitment, persons should be in a state of "getting things done" (Kuhl, 1984). This approach-motivated state is consistent with what other theorists have called an action-oriented or implemental mindset (Gollwitzer & Bayer, 1999). This state enhances goal accomplishment and the implementation of decisions (Gollwitzer & Sheeran, 2006).

The above reasoning suggests that an action-oriented state should make cognitive discrepancy reduction more efficient. To test this prediction, participants made a difficult decision (between performing two experiments they had rated as similar in attractiveness). They were also induced to experience an action-oriented state, by thinking of an important life goal and the steps they would need to take to accomplish it, compared with a positive, non-action-oriented state or neutral state. In support of the action-based model, participants in the action-oriented condition engaged in more spreading of alternatives than those in the other conditions (E. Harmon-Jones & Harmon-Jones, 2002).

Embodied Manipulation of Approach Motivation and Discrepancy Reduction

The action-based model proposes that dissonance reduction is an approach-motivated process. From this, it follows that reducing approach motivation should also inhibit discrepancy reduction. Approach motivation is an embodied process and may be influenced by changes in body posture. For example, the supine position (lying on one's back) leads to less approach motivation toward appetitive stimuli such as photographs of desirable individuals or delicious desserts (E. Harmon-Jones, Gable, & Price, 2011; Price, Dieckman, & Harmon-Jones, 2012). Thus, it would be expected that the supine position should reduce discrepancy reduction.

This hypothesis was supported by studies using both effort justification and the difficult decision paradigms. In one experiment, participants exerted unpleasant effort in order to obtain a goal. Those who did this while in a supine position rated the goal less positively compared to those who sat upright. That is, they engaged in less effort justification. In another experiment, participants made a difficult decision, and those who assumed a supine position engaged in less spreading of alternatives than those who sat upright (E. Harmon-Jones, Price, & Harmon-Jones, 2015). These studies suggest that dissonance reduction is an approach-motivated process.

Evidence That Dissonance Reduction Reduces Behavioral Conflict
Evidence that dissonance reduction assists in behavior comes from a study showing that meat-eaters are motivated to deny the mental capabilities of animals that are raised as food. Participants were assigned to taste either fruit or meat, and presented with a sample of that food. They were then instructed to write about the process of bringing meat from the farm to market, to include the slaughter of the animal. They rated the mental capacity of the animal they had written about. Participants in the meat-eating condition, who expected to eat that animal, rated the animal as having less mental capabilities. Additionally, greater denial of mind to the animal was related to less negative affect, suggesting that individuals who successfully reduced dissonance felt better about their intended behavior of eating meat (Bastian, Loughnan, Haslam, & Radke, 2012). In line with the action-based model, these results suggest that dissonance reduction lessens resistance toward behaviors for which individuals feel ambivalent.

Trait Approach Motivation and Discrepancy Reduction
The idea that dissonance reduction is approach motivated has also been supported at the trait level. In one study, trait approach motivation was positively correlated with spreading of alternatives in a difficult decision paradigm (C. Harmon-Jones, Schmeichel, Inzlicht, & Harmon-Jones, 2011). In a second study, individual differences in trait approach motivation were related to attitude change in an induced compliance paradigm in the high choice condition (where dissonance is expected to be high) but not in the low choice condition (where dissonance is expected to be low; C. Harmon-Jones et al., 2011). These results add support to the prediction that dissonance reduction is approach-motivated.

Neural Activity Involved in Dissonance Processes
The action-based model together with advances in cognitive and affective neuroscience suggested some patterns of neural activity that should be involved with various dissonance processes. Below, we review research that has revealed patterns of neural activity involved in dissonance processes.

Dissonance Arousal, Conflict Monitoring, and the Anterior Cingulate Cortex. The action-based model proposes that the reason for dissonance processes is that inconsistent cognitions lead to conflicted behaviors. Thus, it would be expected that discrepant cognitions would activate the brain regions that are activated by behavioral conflicts. The anterior cingulate cortex (ACC) is a brain region that is activated by cognitive tasks that involve behavioral conflicts, such as the incongruent Stroop task. The ACC may function to detect behavioral conflicts, to inhibit undesired behavior and allow other brain regions to substitute an appropriate response (Botvinick, Braver, Barch, Carter, & Cohen, 2001). Similar to dissonance, these simple cognitive conflicts also produce negative affect (Hajcak & Foti, 2008).

Activation of the ACC has been found for conflicts related to important values, as well as for low-level cognitive tasks. For example, when participants low in racial prejudice become aware that they have inadvertently behaved in a racist manner, they show ACC activation (Amodio et al., 2004). This activation is even greater for individuals who are strongly motivated to avoid being prejudiced (Amodio, Devine, & Harmon-Jones, 2008). When individuals behave contrary to their values, they experience dissonance, which is associated with activation in the ACC, a region that reflects conflicts.

More recently, ACC activation has also been found with paradigms typically used in dissonance research. One study used a within-subjects design difficult decision paradigm and measured functional magnetic resonance imaging (fMRI). Participants rated 160 foods on their desirability and then made choices between foods that were rated similarly (difficult decisions) and dissimilarly (easy decisions). They made these choices either before or after rating the foods for a second time. As the original theory of dissonance would predict, participants spread alternatives more when the decision was difficult and when they made their choices before rerating the foods. In addition, as the action-based model would predict, ACC activity was greater during the difficult decisions (Izuma et al., 2010; see also Chapter 11, this volume). Other studies have shown that individuals evidence increased ACC activity in induced compliance experiments (van Veen, Krug, Schooler, & Carter, 2009). Consistent with the action-based model, these results suggest both that dissonance is associated with cognitive conflict and that dissonance reduction affects motivation.

Dissonance Reduction and the Prefrontal Cortex. According to the action-based model, dissonance reduction should involve approach motivation so as to facilitate behaviorally following through with decisions and commitments. According to models of cognitive control, the prefrontal cortex functions to promote intended responses over unintended responses (Kerns et al., 2004). This suggests that whereas the unpleasant arousal due to a discrepancy should evoke ACC activation, dissonance reduction should involve the prefrontal cortex.

More specifically, as the left prefrontal cortex is activated during approach motivation (E. Harmon-Jones & Gable, 2018), the action-based model predicts that dissonance reduction should be associated with greater left frontal cortical activity. The results of three EEG experiments support this prediction. Individuals in the high choice conditions of induced compliance paradigms showed greater left frontal activation, as well as attitude change, compared to those in the low choice conditions (E. Harmon-Jones, Gerdjikov, & Harmon-Jones, 2008; E. Harmon-Jones, Harmon-Jones, Serra, & Gable, 2011).

Subsequently, experimental manipulation of left frontal cortical activity has been shown to influence the degree of dissonance reduction. Neurofeedback was used to increase or decrease left frontal cortical activation in one experiment

(E. Harmon-Jones, Harmon-Jones, Fearn, Sigelman, & Johnson, 2008), and transcranial direct current stimulation was used in another (Mengarelli, Spoglianti, Avenanti, & di Pellegrino, 2015). In both cases, greater induced left frontal cortical activity led to more dissonance reduction. Similarly, an fMRI study showed that activity in the left lateral prefrontal cortex after a difficult decision predicted greater spreading of alternatives (Qin et al., 2011). Furthermore, experimentally inducing an action-oriented state after a difficult decision increased both spreading of alternatives and left prefrontal cortical activity (E. Harmon-Jones, Harmon-Jones, et al., 2008).

The ventral striatum is another brain region associated with approach motivation, so the action-based model predicts that activity in this region should be associated with dissonance reduction. In support of this, fMRI studies have found that activity in the ventral striatum during difficult decisions predicts spreading of alternatives (Jarcho, Berkman, & Lieberman, 2011; Kitayama, Chua, Tompson, & Han, 2013). Conversely, stimuli that were rejected during in a difficult decision produce less activity in the ventral striatum, suggesting the dissonance reduction assists in motivationally disengaging from unchosen alternatives (Izuma et al., 2010).

Dissonance Reduction in Nonhuman Animals

Evidence that nonhuman animals engage in dissonance reduction is also consistent with the action-based model of dissonance. The dissonance revisions such as the aversive consequences model (Cooper & Fazio, 1984), as well as self-consistency (Aronson, 1969) and self-affirmation (Steele, 1988), propose that dissonance reduction is motivated by complex, high-level concepts about the self. It follows that organisms that lack a well-developed self, such as nonhuman animals and young children, would not experience dissonance affect or engage in dissonance reduction. In contrast, the action-based model proposes that dissonance affect and discrepancy reduction are basic, approach-motivated responses to inconsistency that need not be conscious nor related to the self-concept. Thus, the action-based model would presume that dissonance processes may occur in nonhuman animals.

Indeed, recent research has found evidence consistent with dissonance in pigeons, capuchin monkeys, and human preschoolers. Pigeons have been shown to prefer signals of reward that they have had to work harder to obtain (Zentall & Singer, 2007). Although Zentall (2016) interpreted this as a contrast effect, it is equally consistent with effort justification (C. Harmon-Jones, Haslam, & Bastian, 2017; E. Harmon-Jones, 2017). Similarly, both capuchin monkeys and preschool children have demonstrated spreading of alternatives (Egan, Santos, & Bloom, 2007). This effect occurs even in a blind-choice paradigm, when the subjects choose the rewards without knowing what they are until after making the choice (Egan, Bloom, & Santos, 2010). Consistent with the action-based model, these results suggest that dissonance does not rely on a well-developed self, but is a more basic motivational process.

CONCLUSION

Although the action-based model is consistent with the original theory of cognitive dissonance, it goes beyond in providing a functional explanation for why these effects occur. The model proposes that, in most situations, dissonance reduction promotes effective action. The discomfort that organisms experience when their cognitions are in opposition motivates changes that make action tendencies less conflicted.

Although most of the research on dissonance has employed situations in which participants are required to engage in behavior, dissonance may also result from conflicts between both high-level values and low-level perceptions (Proulx, Inzlicht, & Harmon-Jones, 2012). The action-based model presumes that these are important cognitions with strong implications for action, even when the individual may not be acting on them in the moment. For example, religious beliefs serve as an overarching guide to behavior in many situations, even if one is not sitting in church at that moment. Similarly, a perceptual illusion that causes one to misperceive the depth of a body of water could cause injury if one were to dive into it. According to the action-based model, important cognitions are those with strong action implications, whether or not they are being acted upon at a particular time. This perspective on dissonance has restored the breadth of the original theory, as well as integrated the theory with other research on motivation and emotion, cognitive conflict and control, and affective and cognitive neuroscience.

REFERENCES

Abelson, R. P. (1959). Modes of resolution of belief dilemmas. *The Journal of Conflict Resolution, 3,* 343–352. http://dx.doi.org/10.1177/002200275900300403

Allport, G. W. (1950). *The individual and his religion.* New York, NY: Macmillan.

Amodio, D. M., Devine, P. G., & Harmon-Jones, E. (2008). Individual differences in the regulation of intergroup bias: The role of conflict monitoring and neural signals for control. *Journal of Personality and Social Psychology, 94,* 60–74. http://dx.doi.org/10.1037/0022-3514.94.1.60

Amodio, D. M., Harmon-Jones, E., Devine, P. G., Curtin, J. J., Hartley, S. L., & Covert, A. E. (2004). Neural signals for the detection of unintentional race bias. *Psychological Science, 15,* 88–93. http://dx.doi.org/10.1111/j.0963-7214.2004.01502003.x

Aronson, E. (1969). The theory of cognitive dissonance: A current perspective. In L. Berkowitz (Ed.), *Advances in experimental social psychology* (Vol. 4, pp. 1–34). New York, NY: Academic Press.

Aronson, E., & Carlsmith, J. M. (1962). Performance expectancy as a determinant of actual performance. *Journal of Abnormal and Social Psychology, 65,* 178–182. http://dx.doi.org/10.1037/h0042291

Bain, A. (1868). *Mental science: A compendium of psychology, and the history of philosophy.* New York, NY: Appleton-Century-Crofts.

Bastian, B., Loughnan, S., Haslam, N., & Radke, H. R. (2012). Don't mind meat? The denial of mind to animals used for human consumption. *Personality and Social Psychology Bulletin, 38,* 247–256. http://dx.doi.org/10.1177/0146167211424291

Batson, C. D. (1975). Rational processing or rationalization?: The effect of disconfirming information on a stated religious belief. *Journal of Personality and Social Psychology, 32,* 176–184. http://dx.doi.org/10.1037/h0076771

Beauvois, J.-L., & Joule, R.-V. (1996). *A radical dissonance theory*. London, England: Taylor & Francis.

Beckmann, J., & Irle, M. (1985). Dissonance and action control. In J. Kuhl & J. Beckmann (Eds.), *Action control: From cognition to behavior* (pp. 129–150). Berlin, Germany: Springer-Verlag. http://dx.doi.org/10.1007/978-3-642-69746-3_7

Berkowitz, L., & Devine, P. G. (1989). Research traditions, analysis, and synthesis in social psychological theories: The case of dissonance theory. *Personality and Social Psychology Bulletin, 15*, 493–507. http://dx.doi.org/10.1177/0146167289154002

Botvinick, M. M., Braver, T. S., Barch, D. M., Carter, C. S., & Cohen, J. D. (2001). Conflict monitoring and cognitive control. *Psychological Review, 108*, 624–652. http://dx.doi.org/10.1037/0033-295X.108.3.624

Brehm, J. W., & Cohen, A. R. (1962). *Explorations in cognitive dissonance*. New York, NY: Wiley. http://dx.doi.org/10.1037/11622-000

Brock, T. C., & Balloun, J. L. (1967). Behavioral receptivity to dissonant information. *Journal of Personality and Social Psychology, 6*, 413–428. http://dx.doi.org/10.1037/h0021225

Burris, C. T., Harmon-Jones, E., & Tarpley, W. R. (1997). "By faith alone": Religious agitation and cognitive dissonance. *Basic and Applied Social Psychology, 19*, 17–31.

Calder, B. J., Ross, M., & Insko, C. A. (1973). Attitude change and attitude attribution: Effects of incentive, choice, and consequences. *Journal of Personality and Social Psychology, 25*, 84–99. http://dx.doi.org/10.1037/h0034264

Collins, B. E., & Hoyt, M. F. (1972). Personal responsibility-for-consequences: An integration and extension of the "forced compliance" literature. *Journal of Experimental Social Psychology, 8*, 558–593. http://dx.doi.org/10.1016/0022-1031(72)90080-7

Cooper, J., & Fazio, R. H. (1984). A new look at dissonance theory. In L. Berkowitz (Ed.), *Advances in experimental social psychology* (Vol. 17, pp. 229–264). Orlando, FL: Academic Press.

Cooper, J., & Fazio, R. H. (1989). Research traditions, analysis, and synthesis: Building a faulty case around misinterpreted theory. *Personality and Social Psychology Bulletin, 15*, 519–529. http://dx.doi.org/10.1177/0146167289154005

Cooper, J., & Worchel, S. (1970). Role of undesired consequences in arousing cognitive dissonance. *Journal of Personality and Social Psychology, 16*, 199–206. http://dx.doi.org/10.1037/h0029830

Cooper, J., Zanna, M. P., & Goethals, G. R. (1974). Mistreatment of an esteemed other as a consequence of affecting dissonance reduction. *Journal of Experimental Social Psychology, 10*, 224–233.

Egan, L. C., Bloom, P., & Santos, L. R. (2010). Choice-induced preferences in the absence of choice: Evidence from a blind two choice paradigm with young children and capuchin monkeys. *Journal of Experimental Social Psychology, 46*, 204–207. http://dx.doi.org/10.1016/j.jesp.2009.08.014

Egan, L. C., Santos, L. R., & Bloom, P. (2007). The origins of cognitive dissonance: Evidence from children and monkeys. *Psychological Science, 18*, 978–983. http://dx.doi.org/10.1111/j.1467-9280.2007.02012.x

Elliot, A. J., & Devine, P. G. (1994). On the motivational nature of cognitive dissonance: Dissonance as psychological discomfort. *Journal of Personality and Social Psychology, 67*, 382–394. http://dx.doi.org/10.1037/0022-3514.67.3.382

Faul, F., Erdfelder, E., Buchner, A., & Lang, A.-G. (2009). Statistical power analyses using G*Power 3.1: Tests for correlation and regression analyses. *Behavior Research Methods, 41*, 1149–1160. http://dx.doi.org/10.3758/BRM.41.4.1149

Festinger, L. (1957). *A theory of cognitive dissonance*. Evanston, IL: Row, Peterson.

Festinger, L. (1964). *Conflict, decision, and dissonance*. Palo Alto, CA: Stanford University Press.

Festinger, L., & Carlsmith, J. M. (1959). Cognitive consequences of forced compliance. *Journal of Abnormal and Social Psychology, 58*, 203–210. http://dx.doi.org/10.1037/h0041593

Festinger, L., Riecken, H. W., & Schachter, S. (1956). *When prophecy fails.* Minneapolis: University of Minnesota Press. http://dx.doi.org/10.1037/10030-000

Fraley, R. C., & Marks, M. J. (2007). The null hypothesis significance testing debate and its implications for personality research. In R. W. Robins, R. C. Fraley, & R. F. Krueger (Eds.), *Handbook of research methods in personality psychology* (pp. 149–169). New York, NY: Guilford Press.

Gibson, J. J. (1979). *The ecological approach to visual perception.* Boston, MA: Houghton Mifflin.

Goethals, G. R., & Cooper, J. (1972). Role of intention and postbehavioral consequence in the arousal of cognitive dissonance. *Journal of Personality and Social Psychology, 23,* 293–301. http://dx.doi.org/10.1037/h0033123

Goethals, G. R., & Cooper, J. (1975). When dissonance is reduced: The timing of self-justificatory attitude change. *Journal of Personality and Social Psychology, 32,* 361–367. http://dx.doi.org/10.1037/0022-3514.32.2.361

Gollwitzer, P. M., & Bayer, U. (1999). Deliberative versus implemental mindsets in the control of action. In S. Chaiken & Y. Trope (Eds.), *Dual-process theories in social psychology* (pp. 403–422). New York, NY: Guilford Press.

Gollwitzer, P. M., & Sheeran, P. (2006). Implementation intentions and goal achievement: A meta-analysis of effects and processes. In M. P. Zanna (Ed.), *Advances in experimental social psychology* (Vol. 38, pp. 69–119). San Diego, CA: Elsevier Academic Press. http://dx.doi.org/10.1016/S0065-2601(06)38002-1

Hajcak, G., & Foti, D. (2008). Errors are aversive: Defensive motivation and the error-related negativity. *Psychological Science, 19,* 103–108. http://dx.doi.org/10.1111/j.1467-9280.2008.02053.x

Harmon-Jones, C., Haslam, N., & Bastian, B. (2017). Dissonance reduction in non-human animals: Implications for cognitive dissonance theory. *Animal Sentience: An Interdisciplinary Journal on Animal Feeling, 1*(12), 4.

Harmon-Jones, C., Schmeichel, B. J., Inzlicht, M., & Harmon-Jones, E. (2011). Trait approach motivation relates to dissonance reduction. *Social Psychological & Personality Science, 2,* 21–28. http://dx.doi.org/10.1177/1948550610379425

Harmon-Jones, E. (2000a). Cognitive dissonance and experienced negative affect: Evidence that dissonance increases experienced negative affect even in the absence of aversive consequences. *Personality and Social Psychology Bulletin, 26,* 1490–1501. http://dx.doi.org/10.1177/01461672002612004

Harmon-Jones, E. (2000b). A cognitive dissonance theory perspective on the role of emotion in the maintenance and change of beliefs and attitudes. In N. H. Frijda, A. R. S. Manstead, & S. Bem (Eds.), *Emotions and beliefs* (pp. 185–211). Cambridge, England: Cambridge University Press. http://dx.doi.org/10.1017/CBO9780511659904.008

Harmon-Jones, E. (2000c). An update on cognitive dissonance theory, with a focus on the self. In A. Tesser, R. Felson, & J. Suls (Eds.), *Psychological perspectives on self and identity* (pp. 119–144). Washington, DC: American Psychological Association. http://dx.doi.org/10.1037/10357-005

Harmon-Jones, E. (2001). The role of affect in cognitive dissonance processes. In J. Forgas (Ed.), *Handbook of affect and social cognition* (pp. 237–255). Mahwah, NJ: Lawrence Erlbaum.

Harmon-Jones, E. (2002). A cognitive dissonance theory perspective on persuasion. In J. P. Dillard & M. Pfau (Eds.), *The persuasion handbook: Developments in theory and practice* (pp. 99–116). Mahwah, NJ: Lawrence Erlbaum.

Harmon-Jones, E. (2017). Clarifying concepts in cognitive dissonance theory: Commentary on Zentall on cognitive dissonance. *Animal Sentience, 12*(5).

Harmon-Jones, E., Amodio, D. M., & Harmon-Jones, C. (2009). Action-based model of dissonance: A review, integration, and expansion of conceptions of cognitive conflict. In M. P. Zanna (Ed.), *Advances in Experimental Social Psychology* (Vol. 41, pp. 119–166). San Diego, CA: Academic Press.

Harmon-Jones, E., Brehm, J. W., Greenberg, J., Simon, L., & Nelson, D. E. (1996). Evidence that the production of aversive consequences is not necessary to create cognitive dissonance. *Journal of Personality and Social Psychology, 70,* 5–16. http://dx.doi.org/10.1037/0022-3514.70.1.5

Harmon-Jones, E., & Gable, P. A. (2018). On the role of asymmetric frontal cortical activity in approach and withdrawal motivation: An updated review of the evidence. *Psychophysiology, 55,* e12879. http://dx.doi.org/10.1111/psyp.12879

Harmon-Jones, E., Gable, P. A., & Price, T. F. (2011). Leaning embodies desire: Evidence that leaning forward increases relative left frontal cortical activation to appetitive stimuli. *Biological Psychology, 87,* 311–313. http://dx.doi.org/10.1016/j.biopsycho.2011.03.009

Harmon-Jones, E., Gerdjikov, T., & Harmon-Jones, C. (2008). The effect of induced compliance on relative left frontal cortical activity: A test of the action-based model of dissonance. *European Journal of Social Psychology, 38,* 35–45. http://dx.doi.org/10.1002/ejsp.399

Harmon-Jones, E., & Harmon-Jones, C. (2002). Testing the action-based model of cognitive dissonance: The effect of action orientation on postdecisional attitudes. *Personality and Social Psychology Bulletin, 28,* 711–723. http://dx.doi.org/10.1177/0146167202289001

Harmon-Jones, E., Harmon-Jones, C., Fearn, M., Sigelman, J. D., & Johnson, P. (2008). Left frontal cortical activation and spreading of alternatives: Tests of the action-based model of dissonance. *Journal of Personality and Social Psychology, 94,* 1–15. http://dx.doi.org/10.1037/0022-3514.94.1.1

Harmon-Jones, E., Harmon-Jones, C., Serra, R., & Gable, P. A. (2011). The effect of commitment on relative left frontal cortical activity: Tests of the action-based model of dissonance. *Personality and Social Psychology Bulletin, 37,* 395–408. http://dx.doi.org/10.1177/0146167210397059

Harmon-Jones, E., Price, T. F., & Harmon-Jones, C. (2015). Supine body posture decreases rationalizations: Testing the action-based model of dissonance. *Journal of Experimental Social Psychology, 56,* 228–234. http://dx.doi.org/10.1016/j.jesp.2014.10.007

Heatherton, T. F., & Polivy, J. (1991). Development and validation of a scale for measuring state self-esteem. *Journal of Personality and Social Psychology, 60,* 895–910. http://dx.doi.org/10.1037/0022-3514.60.6.895

Hoyt, M. F., Henley, M. D., & Collins, B. E. (1972). Studies in forced compliance: Confluence of choice and consequence on attitude change. *Journal of Personality and Social Psychology, 23,* 205–210. http://dx.doi.org/10.1037/h0033034

Izuma, K., Matsumoto, M., Murayama, K., Samejima, K., Sadato, N., & Matsumoto, K. (2010). Neural correlates of cognitive dissonance and choice-induced preference change. *Proceedings of the National Academy of Sciences of the United States of America, 107,* 22014–22019. http://dx.doi.org/10.1073/pnas.1011879108

James, W. (1950). *The principles of psychology.* New York, NY: Dover. (Original work published 1890)

Jarcho, J. M., Berkman, E. T., & Lieberman, M. D. (2011). The neural basis of rationalization: Cognitive dissonance reduction during decision-making. *Social Cognitive and Affective Neuroscience, 6,* 460–467. http://dx.doi.org/10.1093/scan/nsq054

Johnson, R. W., Kelly, R. J., & LeBlanc, B. A. (1995). Motivational basis of dissonance: Aversive consequences or inconsistency. *Personality and Social Psychology Bulletin, 21,* 850–855. http://dx.doi.org/10.1177/0146167295218008

Jones, E. E., & Gerard, H. B. (1967). *Foundations of social psychology.* New York, NY: Wiley.

Kerns, J. G., Cohen, J. D., MacDonald, A. W., III, Cho, R. Y., Stenger, V. A., & Carter, C. S. (2004). Anterior cingulate conflict monitoring and adjustments in control. *Science, 303,* 1023–1026. http://dx.doi.org/10.1126/science.1089910

Kitayama, S., Chua, H. F., Tompson, S., & Han, S. (2013). Neural mechanisms of dissonance: An fMRI investigation of choice justification. *NeuroImage, 69*, 206–212. http://dx.doi.org/10.1016/j.neuroimage.2012.11.034

Kuhl, J. (1984). Volitional aspects of achievement motivation and learned helplessness: Toward a comprehensive theory of action-control. In B. A. Maher (Ed.), *Progress in experimental personality research* (Vol. 13, pp. 99–171). New York, NY: Academic Press.

McArthur, L. Z., & Baron, R. M. (1983). Toward an ecological theory of social perception. *Psychological Review, 90*, 215–238. http://dx.doi.org/10.1037/0033-295X.90.3.215

Mengarelli, F., Spoglianti, S., Avenanti, A., & di Pellegrino, G. (2015). Cathodal tDCS over the left prefrontal cortex diminishes choice-induced preference change. *Cerebral Cortex, 25*, 1219–1227. http://dx.doi.org/10.1093/cercor/bht314

Mills, J. (1968). Interest in supporting and discrepant information. In R. P. Abelson, E. Aronson, W. J. McGuire, T. M. Newcomb, M. J. Rosenberg, & P. H. Tannenbaum (Eds.), *Theories of cognitive consistency: A source book* (pp. 771–776). Skokie, IL: Rand McNally.

Nel, E., Helmreich, R., & Aronson, E. (1969). Opinion change in the advocate as a function of the persuasibility of his audience: A clarification of the meaning of dissonance. *Journal of Personality and Social Psychology, 12*, 117–124. http://dx.doi.org/10.1037/h0027566

Price, T. F., Dieckman, L. W., & Harmon-Jones, E. (2012). Embodying approach motivation: Body posture influences startle eyeblink and event-related potential responses to appetitive stimuli. *Biological Psychology, 90*, 211–217. http://dx.doi.org/10.1016/j.biopsycho.2012.04.001

Proulx, T., Inzlicht, M., & Harmon-Jones, E. (2012). Understanding all inconsistency compensation as a palliative response to violated expectations. *Trends in Cognitive Sciences, 16*, 285–291. http://dx.doi.org/10.1016/j.tics.2012.04.002

Qin, J., Kimel, S., Kitayama, S., Wang, X., Yang, X., & Han, S. (2011). How choice modifies preference: Neural correlates of choice justification. *NeuroImage, 55*, 240–246. http://dx.doi.org/10.1016/j.neuroimage.2010.11.076

Rabbie, J. M., Brehm, J. W., & Cohen, A. R. (1959). Verbalization and reactions to cognitive dissonance. *Journal of Personality, 27*, 407–417. http://dx.doi.org/10.1111/j.1467-6494.1959.tb02363.x

Richard, F. D., Bond, C. F., Jr., & Stokes-Zoota, J. J. (2003). One hundred years of social psychology quantitatively described. *Review of General Psychology, 7*, 331–363. http://dx.doi.org/10.1037/1089-2680.7.4.331

Scheier, M. F., & Carver, C. S. (1980). Private and public self-attention, resistance to change, and dissonance reduction. *Journal of Personality and Social Psychology, 39*, 390–405. http://dx.doi.org/10.1037/0022-3514.39.3.390

Scher, S. J., & Cooper, J. (1989). Motivational basis of dissonance: The singular role of behavioral consequences. *Journal of Personality and Social Psychology, 56*, 899–906. http://dx.doi.org/10.1037/0022-3514.56.6.899

Schwarz, N., Frey, D., & Kumpf, M. (1980). Interactive effects of writing and reading a persuasive essay on attitude change and selective exposure. *Journal of Experimental Social Psychology, 16*, 1–17. http://dx.doi.org/10.1016/0022-1031(80)90032-3

Simon, L., Greenberg, J., & Brehm, J. W. (1995). Trivialization: The forgotten mode of dissonance reduction. *Journal of Personality and Social Psychology, 68*, 247–260. http://dx.doi.org/10.1037/0022-3514.68.2.247

Spencer, H. (1865). *First principles*. New York, NY: Appleton.

Steele, C. M. (1988). The psychology of self-affirmation: Sustaining the integrity of the self. In L. Berkowitz (Ed.), *Advances in experimental social psychology* (Vol. 21, pp. 261–302). San Diego, CA: Academic Press. http://dx.doi.org/10.1016/S0065-2601(08)60229-4

van Veen, V., Krug, M. K., Schooler, J. W., & Carter, C. S. (2009). Neural activity predicts attitude change in cognitive dissonance. *Nature Neuroscience, 12,* 1469–1474. http://dx.doi.org/10.1038/nn.2413

Zentall, T. R. (2016). Cognitive dissonance or contrast? *Animal Sentience, 12*(1).

Zentall, T. R., & Singer, R. A. (2007). Within-trial contrast: Pigeons prefer conditioned reinforcers that follow a relatively more rather than a less aversive event. *Journal of the Experimental Analysis of Behavior, 88,* 131–149. http://dx.doi.org/10.1901/jeab.2007.27-06

5

What Is Cognitive Consistency, and Why Does It Matter?

Bertram Gawronski and Skylar M. Brannon

In spring 2015, the first author of this chapter attended a small group conference where he had the opportunity to chat with one of the most distinguished senior researchers in the area of cognitive dissonance. Puzzled by the increasingly narrow focus of dissonance research since the publication of Festinger's (1957) seminal book, the said author asked this eminent scholar about his views on exposure to belief-conflicting information as a source of dissonance. Causing even more puzzlement, the scholar replied that such mental conflicts do not involve any dissonance. He further stated that dissonance is exclusively caused by discrepancies between attitudes and behavior and occurs only for behaviors with aversive consequences for which the actor takes personal responsibility (Cooper & Fazio, 1984). After a short back-and-forth, the two researchers ended the conversation by agreeing to disagree. Yet, one of them was left with an unpleasant feeling caused by the conflict between his belief that dissonance is a much broader phenomenon and the views of the eminent scholar he had just been exposed to.

One potential interpretation of the two conflicting views is that they reflect different empirical assumptions that could be tested in a carefully designed study. For example, one could design an experiment in which participants are presented with information that conflicts with their personal beliefs and measure whether exposure to this information elicits unpleasant feelings. Yet, another potential interpretation is that the two conflicting views are rooted in different definitions of theoretical concepts. In the latter case, it would be very difficult (if not impossible) to resolve the disagreement on the basis of empirical data (Gawronski & Bodenhausen, 2015). For example, even if participants experienced unpleasant feelings in response to information that conflicts with their beliefs, a skeptic might argue that these feelings are distinct from dissonance, because dissonance is (by definition) limited to discrepancies between attitudes and behavior.[1]

Expanding on the second interpretation, the current chapter aims to make a theoretical case for broader conceptualizations of cognitive consistency and dissonance that go beyond the relation between attitudes and behavior. In line with earlier concerns (e.g., Gawronski, 2012a; Greenwald & Ronis, 1978; Proulx, Inzlicht, & Harmon-Jones, 2012), we argue that the increasingly narrow focus on attitude-behavior discrepancies has led researchers to neglect the potential of Festinger's (1957) original theory in providing valuable insights into a much broader set of psychological phenomena (see Gawronski & Strack, 2012). Our main arguments are that (a) cognitive consistency plays a much more fundamental role for information processing than is commonly assumed in the dissonance literature and (b) embracing the ubiquitous role of cognitive consistency provides valuable insights into a wide range of phenomena that are rarely discussed in terms of Festinger's theory. In support of these arguments, we highlight various lines of consistency research beyond attitude-behavior discrepancies and suggest theoretical clarifications aimed at uniting these phenomena under the umbrella of dissonance theory.

WHAT IS COGNITIVE CONSISTENCY?

Although Festinger (1957) preferred the term *dissonance* over *inconsistency* (treating the two terms as interchangeable synonyms), we deem it important to distinguish between *(in)consistency* as a property of the relation between cognitive elements and *dissonance* as the aversive feeling that is assumed to arise from inconsistent cognitive elements. According to Festinger's (1957) original definition, two cognitive elements are inconsistent if one element follows from the opposite of the other. More formally, this definition can be restated as: "x and y are [inconsistent] if not-x follows from y" (p. 13), with x and y subsuming "any knowledge, opinion, or belief about the environment, about oneself, or about one's behavior" (p. 3).

What Are the Elements of Cognitive Consistency?

An important, yet frequently overlooked, aspect of Festinger's (1957) specification of x and y is that it refers to cognitive elements with propositional content (Gawronski & Strack, 2004). Conceptually, propositional thoughts

---

[1] As we explain in this chapter, even this example could be interpreted in terms of dissonance, such that scientists may experience aversive feelings when they are exposed to evidence that contradicts their theoretical views. From this perspective, the resolution of inconsistency via reinterpretation of theoretical concepts could be regarded as a strategy to reduce dissonance (cf. Quine & Ullian, 1978).

involve mentally represented statements about states of affairs that are regarded as true or false by the individual. This specification is important, because it distinguishes cognitive consistency from other types of relations between cognitive elements.

First, a conceptualization in terms of propositional thoughts distinguishes cognitive consistency from purely semantic relations between mental concepts (Gawronski, 2012a). To illustrate this argument, consider the antonyms *agreeable* and *disagreeable*. Although the two concepts have semantically opposite meanings, simultaneous activation of the two concepts would lead to cognitive inconsistency only if they are part of two propositional thoughts that relate them to the same object (e.g., *Hillary is agreeable* and *Hillary is disagreeable*). Yet, simultaneous activation of the two concepts would not lead to cognitive inconsistency if they are part of two propositional thoughts that refer to different objects (e.g., *Hillary is agreeable* and *Donald is disagreeable*). Moreover, even if the two antonyms are part of propositional thoughts that refer to the same object, there would be no cognitive inconsistency if one of the involved propositions is regarded as true (e.g., *It is true that Hillary is agreeable*) and the other one as false (e.g., *It is false that Hillary is disagreeable*).

From this perspective, the elements of cognitive (in)consistency can be understood as propositional beliefs about states of affairs that (a) describe a particular relation between concepts (e.g., *Peter is extraverted; Smoking causes cancer; Jennifer likes dogs*) and (b) the assignment of a positive or negative truth value to the described relation (i.e., the subjective belief that the proposition is true or false). Propositional beliefs can be either general if they refer to categories of objects (e.g., *Canadians are friendly*) or specific if they refer to individual objects (e.g., *Uli is unfriendly*). Thus, different from Festinger's (1957) concern with the relation between two cognitive elements, inconsistency is most often the result of more than two propositional beliefs (e.g., *Canadians are friendly; Uli is unfriendly; Uli is Canadian*).

Second, a conceptualization in terms of propositional beliefs helps to distinguish cognitive (in)consistency from processing (dis)fluency (see Winkielman, Huber, Kavanagh, & Schwarz, 2012). Although the two constructs may seem rather similar, they are conceptually distinct in that cognitive *(in)consistency* refers to the content of mentally represented information (*what?*), whereas *(dis)fluency* refers to the ease of processing information (*how?*). For example, exposure to a news article reporting that a particular political candidate is leading in the polls may be inconsistent with the belief that a different candidate will win the election, and this inconsistency is driven by the contents of one's belief and the new information. Irrespective of the inconsistency in terms of contents, the new information may be more or less difficult to process as a result of content-unrelated features, such as the font in which the article is printed (e.g., Song & Schwarz, 2008) or the perceptual contrast between the text and the background (e.g., Reber, Winkielman, & Schwarz, 1998). Nevertheless, cognitive (in)consistency may sometimes influence processing fluency, in that new information that conflicts with one's beliefs may be more difficult to process compared to new information that is consistent with one's beliefs (see Sherman, Lee, Bessenoff, & Frost, 1998). Conversely, high levels of processing fluency may contribute to cognitive inconsistency when fluent processing of belief-conflicting information increases the perceived validity of that information (see Reber & Schwarz, 1999).

What Determines the Relation Between Cognitive Elements?

Although Festinger's (1957) original definition puts a strong emphasis on logical relations between cognitive elements (i.e., x and y are inconsistent if not-x follows from y), he explicitly acknowledged the role of cultural mores, opinions, and personal experiences as important determinants of perceived (in)consistency. In this sense, cognitive (in)consistency can be said to describe psycho-logical (rather than strictly logical) relations between cognitive elements. Although psycho-logic and formal logic have considerable overlap, they are not equivalent. First, perceptions of (in)consistency have been shown to deviate from the laws of formal logic in a systematic fashion. Second, psycho-logical (in)consistency subsumes a broader range of relations between cognitive elements that go beyond the laws of formal logic.

Consistent with the notion of systematic deviations from the laws of formal logic, research by Johnson-Laird, Girotto, and Legrenzi (2004) showed that (a) people sometimes perceive consistency when there is logical inconsistency, and (b) people sometimes perceive inconsistency when there is logical consistency (for a review, see Johnson-Laird et al., 2004). According to Johnson-Laird et al., people assess the (in)consistency of a given set of propositions by creating a mental model in which all assumptions are true. To the extent that they can create such a mental model, the set of propositions is judged as being consistent. To the extent that they cannot find a mental model in which all assumptions are true, the set of propositions is judged as being inconsistent. Although this strategy leads to logically accurate judgments of consistency in most cases, it can lead to (a) systematic illusions of consistency in cases of logical inconsistency and (b) systematic illusions of inconsistency in cases of logical consistency.

An illustrative example of psycho-logical relations that go beyond the laws of formal logic is Heider's (1958) hypothesis that people strive for patterns of interpersonal relations that constitute balanced triads. According to Heider, a triad of interpersonal relations is balanced when it has either no or an even number of disliking relations, but it is imbalanced when it has an odd number of disliking relations. Consistent with Heider's hypothesis, several studies found that people tend to like individuals who are liked by people they like, but they tend to dislike individuals who are disliked by people they like. Conversely, people tend to dislike individuals who are liked by people they dislike, but they tend to like individuals who are disliked by people they dislike (e.g., Aronson & Cope, 1968; Gawronski, Walther, & Blank, 2005). In theoretical terms, these patterns can be interpreted as reflections of people's desire to achieve psycho-logical consistency between three cognitive elements: (a) their personal attitude toward another

Person A, (b) their knowledge of Person A's attitude toward another Person B, and (c) their personal attitude toward Person B. Formal logic does not have any implications for the (in)consistency between these three elements. Their perceived (in)consistency is determined by psycho-logic, not formal logic.

WHY IS COGNITIVE CONSISTENCY IMPORTANT?

Festinger (1957) described the desire for cognitive consistency as a psychological need that is as basic as hunger and thirst. Although some researchers argued that cognitive consistency might be better described as a means to an end rather than an end in itself (e.g., Kruglanski & Shteynberg, 2012), an important question is why cognitive consistency is so important (either as a means to an end or an ends in itself). According to Gawronski (2012a), an important aspect of cognitive inconsistency is that it serves as a cue for potential errors in one's system of beliefs (see Quine & Ullian, 1978). Although consistency is insufficient to establish accuracy, inconsistency is an unambiguous cue for errors that require belief updating. For example, if a person believes that (a) *Good friends always support each other when they need help*, (b) *Jill and Janet are good friends*, and (c) *Jill did not support Janet when Janet needed help*, the inconsistency between the three propositional beliefs requires a reassessment of their validity, which may lead to the revision of either one of them. It may lead to a revision of the belief that good friends always support each other by allowing for exceptions (e.g., *Good friends may sometimes fail to support each other when they have their own problems*); it may lead to a revision of the belief that Jill is actually a good friend of Janet (e.g., *Jill always claimed that she is a good friend of Janet, but that's not true*); or it may lead to a revision of the belief that Jill did not support Janet when Janet needed help (e.g., *Jill offered to help Janet, but Janet did not want Jill's help*).

From a pragmatic view, the identification of errors in one's system of beliefs is important, because erroneous beliefs can undermine context-appropriate behavior by suggesting inadequate courses of action (Quine & Ullian, 1978). Moreover, cognitive inconsistency itself can sometimes undermine context-appropriate behavior, because inconsistent beliefs may suggest mutually exclusive courses of action (Harmon-Jones, Amodio, & Harmon-Jones, 2009). In both cases, the aversive feeling that is assumed to be elicited by inconsistent beliefs serves as a signal that the current system of beliefs has to be revised for the sake of context-appropriate action. From this perspective, the need for cognitive consistency can be said to arise from its function as a means to an end rather than an end in itself (see Kruglanski & Shteynberg, 2012), in that (a) cognitive inconsistency signals a potential error in one's system of beliefs (*epistemic function*; see Gawronski, 2012a), and (b) errors in one's system of beliefs undermine context-appropriate action (*pragmatic function*; see Harmon-Jones et al., 2009).

The notion that cognitive consistency has basic epistemic and pragmatic functions is remarkably different from its presumed role in various revisions of Festinger's (1957) original theory. Several theorists have argued that phenomena of dissonance-related attitude change are driven by mechanisms of ego-defense rather than cognitive inconsistency per se (e.g., Aronson, 1968; Cooper & Fazio, 1984; Steele & Liu, 1983; Stone & Cooper, 2001). The general idea underlying this hypothesis is that discrepancies between one's attitude and one's behavior pose a threat to the self, which triggers mental and behavioral reactions aimed at restoring a positive self-view. However, as noted by Greenwald and Ronis (1978), the exclusive focus on ego-defense in response to attitude-behavior discrepancies ignores the fundamental role of cognitive (in)consistency in various phenomena that do not involve any attitude-behavior discrepancies. For example, a large body of research has demonstrated pervasive effects of expectancy-violations on various stages of information processing, including attention, encoding, attribution, memory, and judgment (Roese & Sherman, 2007). One of the most common examples in these studies is the disconfirmation of social stereotypes via exposure to counterstereotypical exemplars (for a review, see Sherman, Allen, & Sacchi, 2012). None of these studies involve discrepancies between attitudes and behavior. Yet, they fit well to our argument that cognitive inconsistency can arise from conflicts between personal beliefs and exposure to belief-conflicting information, with downstream effects on various stages of information processing.

To be sure, self-relevance might be an important moderator of these downstream effects, in that self-relevance may determine the subjective significance of cognitive inconsistency. According to Festinger (1957), the degree of dissonance that is aroused by inconsistent cognitions depends on the subjective importance of the involved elements, which should increase as a function of their self-relevance. From this perspective, self-relevance may moderate the level of negative affect that is elicited by cognitive inconsistency. Yet, this moderating role pertains to the effect of cognitive inconsistency on the elicitation of aversive feelings, and therefore does not eliminate the fundamental role of cognitive (in)consistency as an antecedent of downstream effects on information processing.

A THREE-STAGE MODEL OF INCONSISTENCY PROCESSES

In our view, a major source of theoretical confusion is the conflation of three distinct stages in the processing of inconsistency (see Figure 5.1): (a) the identification of inconsistency, (b) the elicitation of aversive feelings of dissonance, and (c) the resolution of inconsistency (see Gawronski, Peters, & Strack, 2008). This conflation is particularly common in research on attitude-behavior discrepancies, where it has led to premature conclusions about the psychological properties of inconsistency and dissonance.

Inconsistency Identification

The first step in the sequence of inconsistency processes is the identification of inconsistency. People often hold inconsistent beliefs, but they may not

FIGURE 5.1. Three-Stage Model of Inconsistency Processes

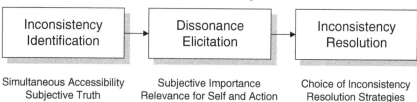

Identification of inconsistency within one's system of beliefs is assumed to elicit aversive feelings of dissonance, which in turn motivate agents to resolve the inconsistency that gave rise to these feelings. General variables influencing the three steps are depicted below the respective boxes. From "Cross-Cultural Differences vs. Universality in Cognitive Dissonance: A Conceptual Reanalysis," by B. Gawronski, K. R. Peters, and F. Strack, in R. M. Sorrentino & S. Yamaguchi (Eds.), *Handbook of motivation and cognition across cultures* (p. 301), 2008, New York, NY: Elsevier. Copyright 2008 by Elsevier. Adapted with permission.

realize their inconsistency when these beliefs are not activated simultaneously (McGregor, Newby-Clark, & Zanna, 1999; see also Chapter 6, this volume). For example, many of our attitudes may be inconsistent with our behavior, but we may not experience any dissonance if we fail to think about one of the two elements. There will be no inconsistency identified if we fail to think about our behavior whenever we reflect on our attitudes; and there will be no inconsistency identified if we fail to think about our attitudes whenever we reflect on our behavior. For inconsistency to arise, both types of thoughts need to be simultaneously accessible.

Even though simultaneous accessibility is necessary for the identification of cognitive inconsistency, it is not sufficient. As noted previously, the contents of the relevant cognitions have to be regarded as true or false in order to acquire the potential of being (in)consistent with each other. For example, negative stereotypic associations pertaining to a disadvantaged minority group may not result in inconsistency with explicitly endorsed egalitarian goals when accessible stereotypic associations are rejected as inaccurate or false (Gawronski, Peters, Brochu, & Strack, 2008). Hence, the two major determinants of inconsistency identification are (a) the simultaneous accessibility of potentially inconsistent cognitions (McGregor et al., 1999) and (b) the assignment of truth values that makes these cognitions factually inconsistent (Gawronski & Strack, 2004).

The relevance of these arguments for the effects of attitude-behavior discrepancies can be illustrated with the experimental situation in the hypocrisy paradigm (e.g., Fried & Aronson, 1995; Stone, Aronson, Crain, Winslow, & Fried, 1994; Stone, Wiegand, Cooper, & Aronson, 1997). In this paradigm, participants are first asked to indicate their general opinion about a specific issue in a pro-attitudinal manner (e.g., advocating the importance of safe sex), and are then made aware of past failures to behave in line with their attitudes (e.g., past failures to use condoms). The common finding in this paradigm is that the inconsistency between personal attitudes and past behavior influences subsequent behavior in a manner consistent with the endorsed attitude (e.g., buying condoms). In other words, the inconsistency between participants' attitudes and their cognitions about past behavior leads them to change the cognitions about their behavior, in this case by actually changing their behavior.[2] However, for this behavioral change to occur, it is necessary that (a) the attitude and the cognitions about past behavior are made simultaneously accessible by the experimental procedure, and (b) both of them are explicitly endorsed as valid. If one of the two conditions is not met, there will be no inconsistency identified in the first place, and thus no dissonance-related changes in behavior.

Dissonance Elicitation

If inconsistency in one's system of beliefs has been identified, this inconsistency may arouse aversive feelings of dissonance and the relative magnitude of dissonance should depend on the subjective importance of the involved elements (Festinger, 1957). As we noted earlier, one important determinant of subjective importance is the self-relevance of the involved elements. Another important determinant of subjective importance is the relevance of the involved cognitions for a current task (Harmon-Jones et al., 2009). If inconsistency is identified and the involved elements are either self-relevant or task-relevant, it should arouse aversive feelings of dissonance, and thereby set the stage for downstream effects of cognitive inconsistency. Yet, if inconsistency is identified, but the involved elements are neither self-relevant nor task-relevant, the degree of dissonance that is aroused by the inconsistency should be relatively low (e.g., Nohlen, van Harreveld, Rotteveel, Barends, & Larsen, 2016), which should reduce the likelihood of downstream reactions aimed at resolving the inconsistency.

An important aspect of our distinction between inconsistency identification and dissonance elicitation is that strategies to reduce aversive feelings of dissonance may target either (a) the aversive feelings themselves or (b) the inconsistency underlying these feelings (see Harmon-Jones et al., 2009). In fact, some strategies may effectively reduce the aversive feelings arising from inconsistency without resolving the underlying inconsistency. For example, trivialization of inconsistency, one of the strategies proposed by Festinger (1957), may help to reduce the aversive feeling arising from inconsistency, but it does little to resolve underlying inconsistency (Simon, Greenberg, & Brehm, 1995). Similarly, self-affirmation may be an effective strategy to reduce aversive feelings arising from inconsistency (Steele & Liu, 1983), but it seems ineffective in resolving the inconsistency that gave rise to these feelings. Although effects of self-affirmation on dissonance-related attitude change are typically interpreted as evidence for the role of ego-defense mechanisms (Steele & Liu, 1983), they do not question Festinger's (1957) original ideas about the

---

[2] An alternative means of changing cognitions about behavior that does not imply actual changes in behavior would be a reinterpretation of the meaning of past behavior to make it consistent with one's attitude. To our knowledge, this possibility has not yet been investigated empirically.

fundamental nature of cognitive (in)consistency when self-affirmation is interpreted as a strategy to cope with the negative feelings arising from inconsistency. To the extent that aversive feelings of dissonance can be reduced without resolving the underlying inconsistency, any downstream reactions aimed at restoring consistency may become unnecessary from an emotion-regulation point of view.

Another important aspect of the distinction between inconsistency identification and dissonance elicitation is that people may be aware of the aversive feelings arising from cognitive inconsistency, but they may not be aware that these feelings were caused by cognitive inconsistency. Whereas the former refers to people's awareness of their affective state, the latter refers to people's awareness of the cause of their affective state (see Gawronski & Bodenhausen, 2012). Lack of knowledge about the cause of one's affective state opens the door for causal misattribution, such that people may attribute aversive feelings of dissonance to salient factors other than cognitive inconsistency. The most well-known demonstration of this phenomenon is Zanna and Cooper's (1974) "dissonance and the pill" study, in which participants were led to believe that their aversive feelings were caused by a (placebo) pill. As result, downstream reactions aimed at restoring consistency became unnecessary, thereby eliminating the effect of counterattitudinal behavior on attitude change.

Inconsistency Resolution

Harmon-Jones et al. (2009) used the term *proximal motivation* to describe the desire to reduce the aversive feelings arising from cognitive inconsistency and the term *distal motivation* to describe the desire to resolve the inconsistency that gave rise to these feelings (see also Jonas et al., 2014). As we noted in the preceding section, distal motivation to restore consistency may often be low when people are able to reduce the aversive feeling arising from inconsistency in a direct manner (e.g., trivialization, self-affirmation). Yet, even if they aim to resolve the inconsistency underlying their aversive feelings of dissonance, they can rely on a broad range of potential strategies. According to Festinger (1957), inconsistency can be resolved either by adding a new cognitive element or by changing one of the inconsistent elements. In terms of the current framework, the former strategy can be described as the search for a new proposition that resolves the inconsistency, whereas the latter strategy involves a change of the (subjective) truth value of one of the inconsistent propositions (Gawronski & Strack, 2004). Applied to the case of attitude-behavior discrepancies, an example of "addition" is the search for consonant information (e.g., search for a situational factor that explains the counterattitudinal behavior); examples involving "change" are attitude change and behavior change.[3]

---

[3] In a strict sense, inconsistency is resolved by changing the cognition about one's behavior. Although actual behavior change is an effective strategy to change cognitions about one's behavior, the latter may be changed without actual changes in behavior (e.g., reinterpretation of one's behavior).

The fact that inconsistency can always be resolved in multiple ways has important implications for the interpretation of moderator effects on dissonance-related attitude change. A widespread assumption in dissonance research is that the degree of attitude change in dissonance paradigms can be interpreted as a direct indicator of the degree of dissonance. For example, in Festinger and Carlsmith's (1959) induced compliance paradigm, the observed degree of attitude change is typically interpreted as an indicator of the degree of dissonance that is aroused by counterattitudinal behavior. Similarly, in Brehm's (1956) free-choice paradigm, the observed size of the spreading-of-alternatives effect is typically interpreted as an indicator of the degree of postdecisional dissonance. Thus, to the extent that a given factor influences either one of these effects, it is often inferred that this factor influenced the degree of dissonance that was aroused by participants' behavior.

A clear distinction between dissonance elicitation and inconsistency resolution suggests that any such interpretations may be premature. After all, it is possible that the observed difference in attitude change reflects a change in the strategy to restore consistency, and such changes may occur without any differences in the degree of dissonance that motivated the resolution of inconsistency. Similarly, observed differences in attitude change across conditions may be driven by differences in the employed strategies to reduce dissonance, such that participants in one condition may adopt a strategy to reduce their aversive feelings without resolving the underlying inconsistency (i.e., proximal motivation) whereas participants in another condition may aim to reduce their aversive feelings by restoring consistency (i.e., distal motivation). In either of these cases, it would be ill-founded to treat the observed differences in attitude change as direct indicators of differences in the degree of dissonance aroused by inconsistent cognitions.

In our view, this inferential problem has been the driving force behind the increasingly narrow focus of dissonance research. A puzzling finding in the early days of Festinger's (1957) theory was that attitude change in dissonance paradigms depends on numerous factors that have not been anticipated on the basis of the theory. For example, some studies found attitude change as a result of counterattitudinal behavior only when the counterattitudinal behavior had aversive consequences (for a review, see Cooper & Fazio, 1984; but see also Harmon-Jones, Brehm, Greenberg, Simon, & Nelson, 1996). Instead of interpreting these factors as determinants of different strategies to cope with the aversive feelings arising from inconsistency, many researchers treated the obtained effects as direct reflections of the aversive feelings themselves. These interpretations led to major revisions of Festinger's (1957) original theory (e.g., Aronson, 1968; Cooper & Fazio, 1984; Steele & Liu, 1983; Stone & Cooper, 2001). Yet, as we noted earlier in this chapter, most of these revisions are unable to capture the wide range of phenomena used by Festinger (1957) to illustrate the explanatory power of his theory (Greenwald & Ronis, 1978). Examples of these phenomena include responses to new information that conflicts with one's personal beliefs and various other instances in which people hold conflicting propositional beliefs.

IMPLICATIONS

Our conceptual reanalysis of cognitive consistency has a number of interesting implications that go far beyond the dominant focus on attitude-behavior discrepancies. The shared assumptions underlying these implications is that (a) people have a desire to maintain consistency among their propositional beliefs, (b) inconsistency between propositional beliefs arouses aversive feelings of dissonance, and (c) aversive feelings of dissonance trigger mental and behavioral reactions aimed at reducing these feelings (e.g., by resolving the inconsistency that gave rise to these feelings).

Cognitive Consistency and Belief Updating

By expanding the focus from attitude-behavior relations to relations between propositional beliefs, our analysis highlights not only the role of inconsistency processes in the retention and change of personal beliefs; it also explains how people can hold on to their beliefs when they are confronted with belief-conflicting information. After infiltrating a doomsday cult, Festinger, Riecken, and Schachter (1956) argued that human beings are motivated to vehemently defend their beliefs in the face of even overwhelming disconfirming information. Following the observations in their famous *When prophecy fails* study, Festinger (1957) proposed different ways in which dissonance can be abated without updating any beliefs. One such strategy is to simply ignore the new information. For example, people who are convinced that *Trump would make a good president* may willfully ignore any information that would question this belief (e.g., *Economists say that Trump's policy proposals would increase unemployment rates*). Further, to the extent that it is not possible to ignore such information, they may actively discount it (e.g., *The economists who say such things about Trump's policy proposals are Democrats, and their analysis is biased by their political views*) or generate alternative explanations if it is impossible to discount the available evidence (e.g., *The reason why the unemployment rate may increase under Trump's presidency is that his opponents will actively sabotage the economy*). Expanding on these ideas, Proulx et al. (2012) identified various other ways in which people may respond to inconsistency without updating their beliefs, including the perception of new patterns in the environment or affirmation of unrelated beliefs. For example, those who believe that *Trump would make a good president* may deal with new information that *economists say that Trump's policy proposals would increase unemployment rates* by perceiving patterns in the environment that do not exist or by enhancing their endorsement of unrelated beliefs (e.g., *iPhones are superior to Androids*). Neither of these strategies involves a resolution of the underlying inconsistency, but they are aimed at reducing the aversive feelings arising from the inconsistency.

Research on subtyping further suggests that people may respond to belief-conflicting information by treating it as an "exception to the rule" (Weber & Crocker, 1983). For example, upon meeting a gay man who is masculine, people who endorse the stereotype that *gay men are feminine* may protect their stereotypic belief by creating a subtype for gay men who are masculine. Research has identified various moderators of subtyping, which provides valuable insights for research on cognitive consistency and belief updating. Examples of these moderators are the extremity of counterstereotypical exemplars (i.e., extreme exemplars promote subtyping; see Kunda & Oleson, 1997), ambiguous information about counterstereotypical exemplars (e.g., ambiguous information promotes subtyping; see Kunda & Oleson, 1995), and the availability of cognitive resources (e.g., subtyping requires cognitive resources; see Moreno & Bodenhausen, 1999; Yzerbyt, Coull, & Rocher, 1999).

Our emphasis on psycho-logic in the identification of inconsistency also provides valuable insights into how people can maintain their beliefs in response to disconfirming information. Specifically, people may not update their beliefs in the face of new information when they do not perceive that information as inconsistent with their beliefs. Indeed, recent research suggests that people prefer unfalsifiable beliefs over falsifiable ones and add elements of unfalsifiability to their beliefs in order to protect them (Friesen, Campbell, & Kay, 2015). For example, parents who are against vaccinating their children may argue that their choice is based on moral beliefs (unfalsifiable) rather than making appeals to testable facts (falsifiable). Thus, when presented with information that challenges their decision (e.g., *studies linking vaccinations and autism have been debunked*), they can continue holding their stance against vaccination because no evidence can falsify a moral belief. Similarly, mental models allow adherence to personal beliefs in response to conflicting information by providing additional support for one's beliefs and discounting any information that may conflict with these beliefs (cf. Johnson-Laird et al., 2004). For example, as long as one can come up with a mental model supporting the link between vaccination and autism (e.g., *Jenny McCarthy's child has autism as a result of vaccinations*), scientific studies disconfirming the proposed link will not change the belief that vaccines cause autism. Thus, people may protect their beliefs against contradictory information by (a) avoiding exposure to such information, (b) reducing negative feelings arising from inconsistency, (c) actively discounting the inconsistent information, (d) generating alternative explanations for the contradictory information, (e) deeming it as an exception to the rule, or (f) reinterpreting the status of one's beliefs in a manner that makes them unfalsifiable.

An important question for future research concerns the conditions under which each of these strategies is used to protect one's beliefs. Neither Festinger's (1957) original theory nor recently developed frameworks (e.g., Proulx et al., 2012) are precise enough to stipulate when each strategy is utilized. Similarly, neither of these theories includes specific assumptions about the conditions under which people will change their beliefs or try to protect them (see Gawronski, 2012b). Preliminary insights regarding the latter question can be gained by research on the moderators of subtyping, but more research is needed to demonstrate the generality of the identified principles. By adopting a broader interpretation of cognitive consistency in terms of propositional beliefs, we can move towards more refined frameworks that are broad in scope, yet precise in their assumptions about the conditions under which people respond to conflicting information in a specific manner.

Contextualized Representation of Expectancy-Violating Information

Because inconsistency between personal beliefs and newly acquired information signals the presence of an erroneous component in one's system of beliefs (Gawronski, 2012a), a by-product of exposure to belief-incongruent information is enhanced attention. This idea has become a central component in developmental research with preverbal infants, which heavily relies on visual attention as an indicator of expectancy-violation (for a similar approach in animal research, see Tinklepaugh, 1928). In terms of the current framework, expectancy-violation indexed by enhanced attention can be interpreted as an instance of identified cognitive inconsistency, in which prior beliefs about states of affairs conflict with new information.

The notion that exposure to expectancy-violating information enhances attention was adopted by Gawronski, Ye, Rydell, and De Houwer (2014) to investigate the integration of incidental context cues into the mental representation of newly acquired information. The basic idea underlying this work is that exposure to expectancy-violating information enhances attention to the momentary context, which leads to an integration of the context into the mental representation of the expectancy-violating information. To test this hypothesis, Gawronski et al. (2014) asked participants to form an impression of a target individual and presented them with 30 behavioral statements about the individual one-by-one against different background colors. The initial 20 statements suggested either a positive or a negative trait. The 21st statement was used as a target statement and described a behavior that was either congruent or incongruent with the valence of the initial 20 statements. The target statement was followed by nine distracter statements that matched the valence of the initial 20 statements. After the impression formation task, participants completed a surprise recognition test, in which they had to identify the background color against which the target statement was presented during the impression formation task. Supporting the idea that expectancy-violation enhances attention to incidental context cues, participants showed better recognition memory for the background color of the target statement when it was incongruent than when it was congruent with the valence of the initial statements (see also Cacioppo, Crites, Berntson, & Coles, 1993).

An interesting implication of Gawronski et al.'s (2014) findings is that mental representations of expectancy-violating information often become linked to the context in which this information was acquired. That is, incidental context cues are more likely to become integrated into the representation of expectancy-incongruent information compared to expectancy-congruent information. As a result, subsequent activation of expectancy-incongruent information depends on the presence of contextual cues that had been present during the acquisition of the expectancy-incongruent information. Consistent with these hypotheses, a series of studies by Gawronski and Rydell found that expectancy-violating information about another person influenced spontaneous evaluative responses only in the context in which this information had been acquired, whereas spontaneous evaluative responses in any other context continued to reflect the previously acquired information that gave rise to the initial expectancy (e.g., Gawronski, Rydell, Vervliet, & De Houwer, 2010; Rydell & Gawronski, 2009). In line with the above arguments, Gawronski et al. (2010) hypothesized that exposure to expectancy-violating information enhances attention to incidental context cues. Thus, new information that contradicts a first impression tends to be stored in contextualized representations, which leaves initially formed context-free representations intact. Interestingly, the mental contextualization of expectancy-violating information also prevents cognitive inconsistency from the simultaneous activation of conflicting representations (and thus the elicitation of dissonance), because context cues modulate which representation will be activated in a given situation: (a) the previously formed context-free representation that gave rise to the initial expectancy or (b) the subsequently formed contextualized representation of the expectancy-violating information (for reviews, see Gawronski & Cesario, 2013; Gawronski et al., 2018).

Cognitive Consistency and the Relation Between Implicit and Explicit Evaluations

Another interesting implication of our conceptualization of cognitive consistency in terms of propositional beliefs concerns the relation between explicit and implicit evaluations. Dissociations between explicit and implicit evaluations are commonly framed in terms of conscious versus unconscious attitudes (e.g., Greenwald & Banaji, 1995) or self-presentational effects on explicit evaluations (e.g., Fazio, Jackson, Dunton, & Williams, 1995). Different from these conceptualizations, Gawronski and Bodenhausen (2006) argued that (a) implicit evaluations reflect spontaneous affective reactions resulting from activated associations and (b) explicit evaluations reflect deliberate evaluative judgments that have passed a propositional assessment of subjective validity. Moreover, although spontaneous affective reactions often provide the basis for deliberate evaluative judgments, the two kinds of evaluative responses can differ when inconsistency leads to a rejection of one's affective reaction as a valid basis for an evaluative judgment.

To illustrate the role of consistency in this process, consider a case in which the activation of negative associations related to the stereotype of African Americans elicits a negative affective reaction in response to Black people. According to Gawronski, Peters, Brochu, et al. (2008), this affective reaction may be translated into a corresponding propositional evaluation (e.g., *I dislike Black people*), which may be assessed for its validity on the basis of its consistency with other propositional beliefs that are considered relevant for an evaluative judgment. In general, propositional evaluations of a given object may be assessed for their consistency with (a) nonevaluative beliefs about states of affairs and (b) propositional evaluations of other attitude objects (Jones & Gerard, 1967). In the current example, these two kinds of propositions may include propositional beliefs about the prevalence of racial discrimination and propositional evaluations of discriminatory behavior. More specifically, the set of judgment-relevant elements may include the following three propositions:

1. *I dislike Black people.*
2. *Black people represent a disadvantaged group.*
3. *Negative evaluations of disadvantaged groups are wrong.*

Together, these three propositions are inconsistent with each other in that they cannot be endorsed at the same time without violating the basic notion of cognitive consistency (see Figure 5.2, Panel A). Proposition 1 is inconsistent with the joint implication of Propositions 2 and 3; Proposition 2 is inconsistent with the joint implication of Propositions 1 and 3; and Proposition 3 is inconsistent with the joint implication of Propositions 1 and 2. To the extent that consistency is achieved through a rejection of either Proposition 2 (see Figure 5.2, Panel B) or Proposition 3 (see Figure 5.2, Panel C), the negative evaluation of Proposition 1 may be endorsed in a verbally reported evaluative judgment. In these cases, implicit and explicit evaluations should show corresponding responses, such that both reflect the negativity of the affective reaction resulting from activated associations. If, however, consistency is achieved through a rejection of Proposition 1 (see Figure 5.2, Panel D), people may endorse a neutral or positive evaluation in their verbally reported judgments. Importantly, merely reversing the subjective truth value of Proposition 1 does not necessarily deactivate the associations that gave rise to the affective reaction that served as the basis for this proposition (see Deutsch, Gawronski, & Strack, 2006). As a result, a rejection of Proposition 1 should lead to a dissociation between implicit and explicit evaluations, such that implicit evaluations should reflect the negativity of the affective reaction, whereas explicit evaluations should reflect the neutral or positive evaluation that is inferred in the propositional validation process. These predictions have been empirically confirmed for several target groups (e.g., African Americans, people who are overweight) using various measure of implicit evaluations (for a review, see Gawronski, Brochu, Sritharan, & Strack, 2012).

Cognitive Consistency and Changes in Implicit and Explicit Evaluations

Related to the notion that cognitive (in)consistency determines the relation between implicit and explicit evaluations, our conceptualization in terms of propositional beliefs implies that a reassessment of validity triggered by dissonance should lead to changes on explicit, but not implicit evaluations (Gawronski & Strack, 2004). The basic idea underlying this hypothesis is that a change of the (subjective) truth value of one of the inconsistent propositions does not necessarily deactivate the mental associations that provided the basis

FIGURE 5.2. Interplay Between Affective Reactions (Circles) and Propositional Beliefs (Squares) in Racial Prejudice Against Black People

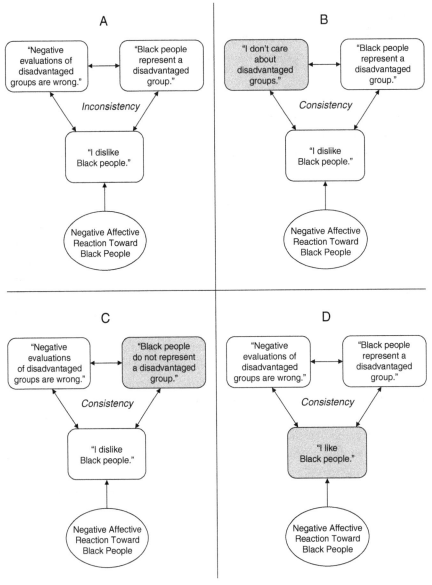

Panel A depicts the case of an inconsistent belief system; Panels B, C, and D depict consistent belief systems, involving either a reliance on affective reactions for evaluative judgments (Panels B and C) or a rejection of affective reactions for evaluative judgments (Panel D). From "Understanding the Relations Between Different Forms of Racial Prejudice: A Cognitive Consistency Perspective," by B. Gawronski, K. R. Peters, P. M. Brochu, and F. Strack, 2008, *Personality and Social Psychology Bulletin, 34*, p. 651. Copyright 2008 by SAGE. Adapted with permission.

for this proposition (see Deutsch et al., 2006). For example, in Festinger and Carlsmith's (1959) induced compliance paradigm, counterattitudinal behavior may give rise to a mental proposition about the participant engaging in that behavior, which may conflict with the participant's propositional evaluation of the relevant target object. To the extent that the behavior was not freely chosen, this conflict may be resolved by an additional proposition that provides a situational explanation for the counterattitudinal behavior. Yet, if there is no situational explanation for the counterattitudinal behavior, the conflict may be resolved by reversing the (subjective) truth value of the propositional evaluation of the target object, leading to a change in deliberate evaluative judgments (i.e., change in explicit evaluation). Importantly, because reversing the truth value of a propositional evaluation does not deactivate its underlying associations, the spontaneous affective reaction resulting from these associations should remain unaffected (i.e., no change in implicit evaluations). Consistent with these hypotheses, Gawronski and Strack (2004) found that counterattitudinal behavior in the induced compliance paradigm changes explicit, but not implicit, evaluations (for similar findings, see Wilson, Lindsey, & Schooler, 2000). Moreover, whereas explicit and implicit evaluations were highly correlated when inconsistency could be resolved by means of a situational explanation for the counterattitudinal behavior, explicit and implicit evaluations were uncorrelated when there was no situational explanation for the counterattitudinal behavior.

Does this mean that implicit evaluations should never change in traditional dissonance paradigms? The short answer is no, because change in implicit evaluations in these paradigms can be the result of other mechanisms that do not involve any dissonance. To illustrate this argument, consider Brehm's (1956) free-choice paradigm in which participants tend to show more favorable evaluations of chosen compared to rejected objects. The most common interpretation of this spreading-of-alternatives effect is that choosing between two equally valued alternatives elicits postdecisional dissonance. To reduce this aversive feeling, participants are assumed to selectively search for positive features of the chosen object and negative features of the rejected object, leading to more favorable evaluations of the chosen object and less favorable evaluations of the rejected object (i.e., spreading-of-alternatives effect).

Although there is no doubt that postdecisional dissonance can cause the spreading-of-alternatives effect, there is at least one alternative mechanism that can lead to similar outcomes. Importantly, this mechanism (a) does not involve any dissonance and (b) influences implicit evaluations via the formation of new associations. In line with the notion of mere-ownership effects, Gawronski, Bodenhausen, and Becker (2007) argued that the act of choosing an object creates an association between the chosen object and the self (cf. Ye & Gawronski, 2016). By virtue of this association, implicit evaluations of the self transfer to the chosen object, such that implicit evaluations of the chosen object depend on implicit evaluations of the self. To the extent that people show positive implicit evaluations of the self (e.g., Greenwald & Farnham,

2000; Koole, Dijksterhuis, & van Knippenberg, 2001), this mechanism can lead to ownership-related changes in implicit evaluations, and these changes may occur even in the absence of postdecisional dissonance (e.g., when people receive an object as a gift).[4] Moreover, mere-ownership effects on implicit evaluations may lead to downstream effects on explicit evaluations to the extent that people rely on their spontaneous affective reactions resulting from activated associations. Yet, if people reject their spontaneous affective reactions as a basis for evaluative judgments, mere-ownership effects should be limited to implicit evaluations without generalizing to explicit evaluations (see Gawronski & LeBel, 2008, Experiment 3).

EMERGING THEMES

In addition to the insights reviewed in the preceding section, our analysis raises a number of important questions for future research. One such question concerns the determinants of people's lay perceptions of (in)consistency at the identification stage (see Figure 5.1). As we noted earlier in this chapter, lay perceptions of (in)consistency go beyond the laws of formal logic, such that psycho-logical (in)consistency subsumes a much broader range of relations between cognitive elements. One example is the relation between warmth and competence in person perception (see Cuddy, Fiske, & Glick, 2008; Judd, James-Hawkins, Yzerbyt, & Kashima, 2005). Using participants' memory for incidental context cues as an indicator of expectancy-violation during the encoding of novel information about a target individual (see Gawronski et al., 2014), Brannon, Sacchi, and Gawronski (2017) found an expectancy-violation effect for information that was incongruent with the valence of prior impressions. Interestingly, this expectancy-violation effect occurred regardless of whether the new information matched the dimension of the initial impression. That is, when participants formed an initial impression of the target as being warm (cold), they showed a surprise reaction when they were presented with new information suggesting that the target is incompetent (competent). Conversely, when participants formed an initial impression of the target as being competent (incompetent), they showed a surprise reaction when they were presented with new information suggesting that the target is cold (warm). Together, these results suggest that expectancy-violation effects in impression formation are

---

[4] Another important implication of these findings is that they prohibit interpretations of the spreading-of-alternatives effect as a direct indicator of postdecisional dissonance. For example, it has been argued that the mere emergence of a spreading-of-alternatives effect demonstrates postdecisional dissonance in amnesic patients who do not remember their choice (Lieberman, Ochsner, Gilbert, & Schacter, 2001). From the perspective of our analysis, such a conclusion seems rather implausible, given that lack of memory for the choice implies low accessibility of one of the involved cognitions (see Figure 5.1). A more plausible conclusion is that spreading-of-alternatives effects in amnesic patients result from a mechanism that does not involve any dissonance, such as the formation of a new association between the chosen object and the self (Gawronski et al., 2007).

driven by the valence of prior expectations and novel information, and these effects occur regardless of whether prior expectations and novel information match in terms of their trait dimension.

Another interesting implication of Brannon et al.'s (2017) findings is that they echo the significance of distinguishing between the principles that guide inconsistency identification and those that guide inconsistency resolution. Given that negative behavior is often assumed to be more informative about the presence of a corresponding trait than positive behavior (for a review, see Skowronski & Carlston, 1989), new information about negative behavior may be perceived as more inconsistent with an initial positive impression than the reverse. Counter to this hypothesis, Brannon et al. (2017) found no evidence for valence asymmetries in lay perceptions of inconsistency (see also Brannon & Gawronski, 2018). That is, expectancy-incongruent negative information showed the same expectancy-violation effect as expectancy-incongruent positive information. Further, there were no valence asymmetries regardless of whether the impression dimension involved warmth or competence. These results suggest that the negativity bias in impression formation is most likely driven by the differential weighting of positive and negative information during the resolution of inconsistency. Yet, there seems to be no negativity bias in the identification of inconsistency (see Figure 5.1).

Another emerging question is whether the affective feelings elicited by cognitive inconsistency are generally aversive, or whether there are conditions under which inconsistency can elicit positive affect. An interesting example is the case of negative expectations that are violated by a positive outcome (e.g., a student expects a low grade on an exam, and this expectation is violated by a high grade). From a cognitive consistency view, expectancy-violations of this kind should elicit negative affect despite the positive outcome. Yet, from a purely hedonic view, it seems more likely that affective reactions to the unexpected outcome reflect the positive valence of the outcome. Reconciling the conflicting evidence on the two hypotheses, Noordewier, Topolinski, and Van Dijk (2016) argued that the nature of the affective response depends on the particular stage of information processing. According to their theory, the identification of inconsistency between expected and actual outcomes elicits a negative affective reaction regardless of whether the unexpected outcome is positive or negative. Yet, once the inconsistency is resolved and the belief system is updated in favor of the actual outcome, the initial negative reaction is overridden by the positive affect resulting from the valence of the outcome (e.g., Noordewier & Breugelmans, 2013; Topolinski & Strack, 2015).

IS THE NEED FOR COGNITIVE CONSISTENCY UNIVERSAL?

A final question that needs to be addressed in any chapter on the fundamental nature of cognitive consistency concerns its universal significance. Festinger (1957) famously argued that the need for consistency is as basic as hunger and thirst. In line with this claim, researchers in developmental and comparative psychology have claimed that dissonance-related attitude change can be observed in infants and various animals (e.g., Egan, Santos, & Bloom, 2007; Lawrence & Festinger, 1962; Lydall, Gilmour, & Dwyer, 2010). Yet, counter to the presumed universality, many cross-cultural researchers have argued that dissonance is a culture-specific phenomenon that is limited to Western, individualist countries and less likely in Eastern, collectivist countries (e.g., Heine & Lehman, 1997; Markus & Kitayama, 1991). Although we agree with the view that consistency and dissonance phenomena can be found across age, species, and cultures, it seems important to carefully scrutinize the evidence that has been cited in support of the conflicting views.

With regard to claims about cultural differences, we want to reiterate our concerns about treating the absence of attitude change in traditional dissonance paradigms as evidence for a lack of dissonance (or even a lack of a need for consistency). As we explained earlier in this chapter, any factor that moderates the emergence of attitude change in these paradigms may do so by influencing (a) lay perceptions of what is deemed consistent versus inconsistent, (b) the relative importance of the involved elements, and thus the degree of dissonance that is elicited by inconsistent propositional beliefs, (c) the proximal focus on the aversive feelings versus the distal focus on the inconsistency that gave rise to these feelings, and (d), if the focus is on the underlying inconsistency, the particular strategy that is used to restore consistency (see Figure 5.1). Because cultural differences may influence any one of these processes (for a review, see Gawronski et al., 2008), claims that a lack of attitude change in dissonance paradigms among Eastern participants indicates the absence of a basic need for cognitive consistency seem premature.

Similar caveats seem appropriate for claims about dissonance in infants and various animals. Many studies cited in support of these claims relied on the free-choice paradigm (Brehm, 1956) to demonstrate the emergence of a spreading-of-alternatives effect (e.g., Egan et al., 2007; but see Lawrence & Festinger, 1962). However, as we explained earlier in this chapter, the mere demonstration of a spreading-of-alternatives effect is insufficient to establish the operation of dissonance processes, because this effect can be due to other mechanisms (Gawronski et al., 2007) and sometimes reflects artifacts of the experimental design (Chen & Risen, 2010). These issues make it impossible to draw inferences about the involvement of inconsistency or dissonance from the mere observation of a spreading-of-alternatives effect without additional measures or appropriate control conditions.

Despite these ambiguities, it is important to note that they do not undermine the ubiquitous effect of cognitive inconsistency on attention (Vachon, Hughes, & Jones, 2012), which is widely used as an indicator of expectancy-violation in infants (for a similar approach in animal research, see Tinklepaugh, 1928). To be sure, animals and infants may have lower working memory capacity than human adults, which may constrain the complexity of mental models to identify inconsistency (see Johnson-Laird et al., 2004). However, this constraint does not imply the absence of a universal need for cognitive consistency. After all, any organism requires an accurate representation of the world for context-appropriate action, and inconsistency serves as an important signal of inaccurate representations.

CONCLUSION

The main goal of the current chapter was to make a theoretical case for broader interpretations of cognitive consistency and dissonance that go beyond the relation between attitudes and behavior. A central aspect of our analysis is the conceptualization of cognitive (in)consistency as a relation between propositional beliefs. In addition to shedding new light on the effects of attitude-behavior discrepancies, this conceptualization provides novel insights into a wide range of other phenomena, including belief updating, the formation of contextualized representations, the relation between implicit and explicit evaluations, and changes in implicit and explicit evaluations. Our analysis also raises interesting questions for future research regarding lay perceptions of (in)consistency, the affective feelings elicited by inconsistency, and the particular processing stages that are responsible for consistency phenomena. On the basis of these insights, we deem a broader conceptualization of consistency and dissonance as superior compared to narrow interpretations in terms of attitude-behavior discrepancies. We apologize for any dissonance this conclusion may elicit in people who endorse such narrow interpretations.

REFERENCES

Aronson, E. (1968). Dissonance theory: Progress and problems. In R. P. Abelson, E. Aronson, W. J. McGuire, T. M. Newcombe, M. J. Rosenberg, & P. H. Tannenbaum (Eds.), *Theories of cognitive consistency: A sourcebook* (pp. 5–27). Skokie, IL: Rand-McNally.

Aronson, E., & Cope, V. (1968). My enemy's enemy is my friend. *Journal of Personality and Social Psychology, 8*, 8–12. http://dx.doi.org/10.1037/h0021234

Brannon, S. M., & Gawronski, B. (2018). In search of a negativity bias in expectancy violation. *Social Cognition, 36*, 199–220. http://dx.doi.org/10.1521/soco.2018.36.2.199

Brannon, S. M., Sacchi, D. L. M., & Gawronski, B. (2017). (In)consistency in the eye of the beholder: The roles of warmth, competence, and valence in lay perceptions of inconsistency. *Journal of Experimental Social Psychology, 70*, 80–94. http://dx.doi.org/10.1016/j.jesp.2016.12.011

Brehm, J. W. (1956). Postdecision changes in the desirability of alternatives. *Journal of Abnormal and Social Psychology, 52*, 384–389. http://dx.doi.org/10.1037/h0041006

Cacioppo, J. T., Crites, S. L., Jr., Berntson, G. G., & Coles, M. G. H. (1993). If attitudes affect how stimuli are processed, should they not affect the event-related brain potential? *Psychological Science, 4*, 108–112. http://dx.doi.org/10.1111/j.1467-9280.1993.tb00470.x

Chen, M. K., & Risen, J. L. (2010). How choice affects and reflects preferences: Revisiting the free-choice paradigm. *Journal of Personality and Social Psychology, 99*, 573–594. http://dx.doi.org/10.1037/a0020217

Cooper, J., & Fazio, R. H. (1984). A new look at dissonance theory. *Advances in Experimental Social Psychology, 17*, 229–266. http://dx.doi.org/10.1016/S0065-2601(08)60121-5

Cuddy, A. J. C., Fiske, S. T., & Glick, P. (2008). Warmth and competence as universal dimensions of social perception: The stereotype content model and the BIAS map. *Advances in Experimental Social Psychology, 40,* 61–149. http://dx.doi.org/10.1016/S0065-2601(07)00002-0

Deutsch, R., Gawronski, B., & Strack, F. (2006). At the boundaries of automaticity: Negation as reflective operation. *Journal of Personality and Social Psychology, 91,* 385–405. http://dx.doi.org/10.1037/0022-3514.91.3.385

Egan, L. C., Santos, L. R., & Bloom, P. (2007). The origins of cognitive dissonance: Evidence from children and monkeys. *Psychological Science, 18,* 978–983. http://dx.doi.org/10.1111/j.1467-9280.2007.02012.x

Fazio, R. H., Jackson, J. R., Dunton, B. C., & Williams, C. J. (1995). Variability in automatic activation as an unobtrusive measure of racial attitudes: A bona fide pipeline? *Journal of Personality and Social Psychology, 69,* 1013–1027. http://dx.doi.org/10.1037/0022-3514.69.6.1013

Festinger, L. (1957). *A theory of cognitive dissonance.* Evanston, IL: Row Peterson.

Festinger, L., & Carlsmith, J. M. (1959). Cognitive consequences of forced compliance. *Journal of Abnormal and Social Psychology, 58,* 203–210. http://dx.doi.org/10.1037/h0041593

Festinger, L., Riecken, H. W., & Schachter, S. (1956). *When prophecy fails.* Minneapolis, MN: University of Minnesota Press. http://dx.doi.org/10.1037/10030-000

Fried, C. B., & Aronson, E. (1995). Hypocrisy, misattribution, and dissonance reduction. *Personality and Social Psychology Bulletin, 21,* 925–933. http://dx.doi.org/10.1177/0146167295219007

Friesen, J. P., Campbell, T. H., & Kay, A. C. (2015). The psychological advantage of unfalsifiability: The appeal of untestable religious and political ideologies. *Journal of Personality and Social Psychology, 108,* 515–529. http://dx.doi.org/10.1037/pspp0000018

Gawronski, B. (2012a). Back to the future of dissonance theory: Cognitive consistency as a core motive. *Social Cognition, 30,* 652–668. http://dx.doi.org/10.1521/soco.2012.30.6.652

Gawronski, B. (2012b). Meaning, violation of meaning, and meaninglessness in meaning maintenance. *Psychological Inquiry, 23,* 346–349. http://dx.doi.org/10.1080/1047840X.2012.706507

Gawronski, B., & Bodenhausen, G. V. (2006). Associative and propositional processes in evaluation: An integrative review of implicit and explicit attitude change. *Psychological Bulletin, 132,* 692–731. http://dx.doi.org/10.1037/0033-2909.132.5.692

Gawronski, B., & Bodenhausen, G. V. (2012). Self-insight from a dual-process perspective. In S. Vazire & T. D. Wilson (Eds.), *Handbook of self-knowledge* (pp. 22–38). New York, NY: Guilford Press.

Gawronski, B., & Bodenhausen, G. V. (2015). Theory evaluation. In B. Gawronski & G. V. Bodenhausen (Eds.), *Theory and explanation in social psychology* (pp. 3–23). New York, NY: Guilford Press.

Gawronski, B., Bodenhausen, G. V., & Becker, A. P. (2007). I like it, because I like myself: Associative self-anchoring and post-decisional change of implicit evaluations. *Journal of Experimental Social Psychology, 43,* 221–232. http://dx.doi.org/10.1016/j.jesp.2006.04.001

Gawronski, B., Brochu, P. M., Sritharan, R., & Strack, F. (2012). Cognitive consistency in prejudice-related belief systems: Integrating old-fashioned, modern, aversive and implicit forms of prejudice. In B. Gawronski & F. Strack (Eds.), *Cognitive consistency: A fundamental principle in social cognition* (pp. 369–389). New York, NY: Guilford Press.

Gawronski, B., & Cesario, J. (2013). Of mice and men: What animal research can tell us about context effects on automatic responses in humans. *Personality and Social Psychology Review, 17,* 187–215. http://dx.doi.org/10.1177/1088868313480096

Gawronski, B., & LeBel, E. P. (2008). Understanding patterns of attitude change: When implicit measures show change, but explicit measures do not. *Journal of Experimental Social Psychology, 44,* 1355–1361. http://dx.doi.org/10.1016/j.jesp.2008.04.005

Gawronski, B., Peters, K. R., Brochu, P. M., & Strack, F. (2008). Understanding the relations between different forms of racial prejudice: A cognitive consistency perspective. *Personality and Social Psychology Bulletin, 34,* 648–665. http://dx.doi.org/10.1177/0146167207313729

Gawronski, B., Peters, K. R., & Strack, F. (2008). Cross-cultural differences versus universality in cognitive dissonance: A conceptual reanalysis. In R. M. Sorrentino & S. Yamaguchi (Eds.), *Handbook of motivation and cognition across cultures* (pp. 297–314). New York, NY: Elsevier. http://dx.doi.org/10.1016/B978-0-12-373694-9.00013-1

Gawronski, B., Rydell, R. J., De Houwer, J., Brannon, S. M., Ye, Y., Vervliet, B., & Hu, X. (2018). Contextualized attitude change. *Advances in Experimental Social Psychology, 57,* 1–52. http://dx.doi.org/10.1016/bs.aesp.2017.06.001

Gawronski, B., Rydell, R. J., Vervliet, B., & De Houwer, J. (2010). Generalization versus contextualization in automatic evaluation. *Journal of Experimental Psychology: General, 139,* 683–701. http://dx.doi.org/10.1037/a0020315

Gawronski, B., & Strack, F. (2004). On the propositional nature of cognitive consistency: Dissonance changes explicit, but not implicit attitudes. *Journal of Experimental Social Psychology, 40,* 535–542. http://dx.doi.org/10.1016/j.jesp.2003.10.005

Gawronski, B., & Strack, F. (Eds.). (2012). *Cognitive consistency: A fundamental principle in social cognition.* New York, NY: Guilford Press.

Gawronski, B., Walther, E., & Blank, H. (2005). Cognitive consistency and the formation of interpersonal attitudes: Cognitive balance affects the encoding of social information. *Journal of Experimental Social Psychology, 41,* 618–626. http://dx.doi.org/10.1016/j.jesp.2004.10.005

Gawronski, B., Ye, Y., Rydell, R. J., & De Houwer, J. (2014). Formation, representation, and activation of contextualized attitudes. *Journal of Experimental Social Psychology, 54,* 188–203. http://dx.doi.org/10.1016/j.jesp.2014.05.010

Greenwald, A. G., & Banaji, M. R. (1995). Implicit social cognition: Attitudes, self-esteem, and stereotypes. *Psychological Review, 102,* 4–27. http://dx.doi.org/10.1037/0033-295X.102.1.4

Greenwald, A. G., & Farnham, S. D. (2000). Using the implicit association test to measure self-esteem and self-concept. *Journal of Personality and Social Psychology, 79,* 1022–1038. http://dx.doi.org/10.1037/0022-3514.79.6.1022

Greenwald, A. G., & Ronis, D. L. (1978). Twenty years of cognitive dissonance: Case study of the evolution of a theory. *Psychological Review, 85,* 53–57. http://dx.doi.org/10.1037/0033-295X.85.1.53

Harmon-Jones, E., Amodio, D. M., & Harmon-Jones, C. (2009). Action-based model of dissonance. *Advances in Experimental Social Psychology, 41,* 119–166. http://dx.doi.org/10.1016/S0065-2601(08)00403-6

Harmon-Jones, E., Brehm, J. W., Greenberg, J., Simon, L., & Nelson, D. E. (1996). Evidence that the production of aversive consequences is not necessary to create cognitive dissonance. *Journal of Personality and Social Psychology, 70,* 5–16. http://dx.doi.org/10.1037/0022-3514.70.1.5

Heider, F. (1958). *The psychology of interpersonal relations.* New York, NY: Wiley. http://dx.doi.org/10.1037/10628-000

Heine, S. J., & Lehman, D. R. (1997). Culture, dissonance, and self-affirmation. *Personality and Social Psychology Bulletin, 23,* 389–400. http://dx.doi.org/10.1177/0146167297234005

Johnson-Laird, P. N., Girotto, V., & Legrenzi, P. (2004). Reasoning from inconsistency to consistency. *Psychological Review, 111,* 640–661. http://dx.doi.org/10.1037/0033-295X.111.3.640

Jonas, E., McGregor, I., Klackl, J., Agroskin, D., Fritsche, I., Holbrook, C., . . . Quirin, M. (2014). Threat and defense: From anxiety to approach. *Advances in Experimental Social Psychology, 49*, 219–286. http://dx.doi.org/10.1016/B978-0-12-800052-6.00004-4

Jones, E. E., & Gerard, H. B. (1967). *Foundations of social psychology*. New York, NY: Wiley.

Judd, C. M., James-Hawkins, L., Yzerbyt, V., & Kashima, Y. (2005). Fundamental dimensions of social judgment: Understanding the relations between judgments of competence and warmth. *Journal of Personality and Social Psychology, 89*, 899–913. http://dx.doi.org/10.1037/0022-3514.89.6.899

Koole, S. L., Dijksterhuis, A., & van Knippenberg, A. (2001). What's in a name: Implicit self-esteem and the automatic self. *Journal of Personality and Social Psychology, 80*, 669–685. http://dx.doi.org/10.1037/0022-3514.80.4.669

Kruglanski, A. W., & Shteynberg, G. (2012). Cognitive consistency as means to an end: How subjective logic affords knowledge. In B. Gawronski & F. Strack (Eds.), *Cognitive consistency: A unifying concept in social psychology* (pp. 245–264). New York, NY: Guilford Press.

Kunda, Z., & Oleson, K. C. (1995). Maintaining stereotypes in the face of disconfirmation: Constructing grounds for subtyping deviants. *Journal of Personality and Social Psychology, 68*, 565–579. http://dx.doi.org/10.1037/0022-3514.68.4.565

Kunda, Z., & Oleson, K. C. (1997). When exceptions prove the rule: How extremity of deviance determines the impact of deviant examples on stereotypes. *Journal of Personality and Social Psychology, 72*, 965–979. http://dx.doi.org/10.1037/0022-3514.72.5.965

Lawrence, D. H., & Festinger, L. (1962). *Deterrents and reinforcement: The psychology of insufficient reward*. Palo Alto, CA: Stanford University Press.

Lieberman, M. D., Ochsner, K. N., Gilbert, D. T., & Schacter, D. L. (2001). Do amnesics exhibit cognitive dissonance reduction? The role of explicit memory and attention in attitude change. *Psychological Science, 12*, 135–140. http://dx.doi.org/10.1111/1467-9280.00323

Lydall, E. S., Gilmour, G., & Dwyer, D. M. (2010). Rats place greater value on rewards produced by high effort: An animal analogue of the "effort justification" effect. *Journal of Experimental Social Psychology, 46*, 1134–1137. http://dx.doi.org/10.1016/j.jesp.2010.05.011

Markus, H., & Kitayama, S. (1991). Culture and the self: Implications for cognition, emotion, and motivation. *Psychological Review, 98*, 224–253. http://dx.doi.org/10.1037/0033-295X.98.2.224

McGregor, I., Newby-Clark, I. R., & Zanna, M. P. (1999). "Remembering" dissonance: Simultaneous accessibility of inconsistent cognitive elements moderates epistemic discomfort. In E. Harmon-Jones & J. Mills (Eds.), *Cognitive dissonance: Progress on a pivotal theory in social psychology* (pp. 325–353). Washington, DC: American Psychological Association. http://dx.doi.org/10.1037/10318-013

Moreno, K. N., & Bodenhausen, G. V. (1999). Resisting stereotype change: The role of motivation and attentional capacity in defending social beliefs. *Group Processes & Intergroup Relations, 2*, 5–16. http://dx.doi.org/10.1177/1368430299021001

Nohlen, H. U., van Harreveld, F., Rotteveel, M., Barends, A. J., & Larsen, J. T. (2016). Affective responses to ambivalence are context-dependent: A facial EMG study on the role of inconsistency and evaluative context in shaping affective responses to ambivalence. *Journal of Experimental Social Psychology, 65*, 42–51. http://dx.doi.org/10.1016/j.jesp.2016.02.001

Noordewier, M. K., & Breugelmans, S. M. (2013). On the valence of surprise. *Cognition and Emotion, 27*, 1326–1334. http://dx.doi.org/10.1080/02699931.2013.777660

Noordewier, M. K., Topolinski, S., & Van Dijk, E. (2016). The temporal dynamics of surprise. *Social and Personality Psychology Compass, 10*, 136–149. http://dx.doi.org/10.1111/spc3.12242

Proulx, T., Inzlicht, M., & Harmon-Jones, E. (2012). Understanding all inconsistency compensation as a palliative response to violated expectations. *Trends in Cognitive Sciences, 16,* 285–291. http://dx.doi.org/10.1016/j.tics.2012.04.002

Quine, W. V. O., & Ullian, J. S. (1978). *The web of belief* (2nd ed.). New York, NY: McGraw-Hill.

Reber, R., & Schwarz, N. (1999). Effects of perceptual fluency on judgments of truth. *Consciousness and Cognition, 8,* 338–342. http://dx.doi.org/10.1006/ccog.1999.0386

Reber, R., Winkielman, P., & Schwarz, N. (1998). Effects of perceptual fluency on affective judgments. *Psychological Science, 9,* 45–48. http://dx.doi.org/10.1111/1467-9280.00008

Roese, N. J., & Sherman, J. W. (2007). Expectancies. In E. T. Higgins & A. W. Kruglanski (Eds.), *Social psychology: Handbook of basic principles* (2nd ed., pp. 91–115). New York, NY: Guilford Press.

Rydell, R. J., & Gawronski, B. (2009). I like you, I like you not: Understanding the formation of context-dependent automatic attitudes. *Cognition and Emotion, 23,* 1118–1152. http://dx.doi.org/10.1080/02699930802355255

Sherman, J. W., Allen, T. J., & Sacchi, D. L. M. (2012). Stereotype confirmation and disconfirmation. In B. Gawronski & F. Strack (Eds.), *Cognitive consistency: A unifying concept in social psychology* (pp. 390–423). New York, NY: Guilford Press.

Sherman, J. W., Lee, A. Y., Bessenoff, G. R., & Frost, L. A. (1998). Stereotype efficiency reconsidered: Encoding flexibility under cognitive load. *Journal of Personality and Social Psychology, 75,* 589–606. http://dx.doi.org/10.1037/0022-3514.75.3.589

Simon, L., Greenberg, J., & Brehm, J. (1995). Trivialization: The forgotten mode of dissonance reduction. *Journal of Personality and Social Psychology, 68,* 247–260. http://dx.doi.org/10.1037/0022-3514.68.2.247

Skowronski, J. J., & Carlston, D. E. (1989). Negativity and extremity biases in impression formation: A review of explanations. *Psychological Bulletin, 105,* 131–142. http://dx.doi.org/10.1037/0033-2909.105.1.131

Song, H., & Schwarz, N. (2008). If it's hard to read, it's hard to do: Processing fluency affects effort prediction and motivation. *Psychological Science, 19,* 986–988. http://dx.doi.org/10.1111/j.1467-9280.2008.02189.x

Steele, C. M., & Liu, T. J. (1983). Dissonance processes as self-affirmation. *Journal of Personality and Social Psychology, 45,* 5–19. http://dx.doi.org/10.1037/0022-3514.45.1.5

Stone, J., Aronson, E., Crain, A. L., Winslow, M. P., & Fried, C. B. (1994). Inducing hypocrisy as a means of encouraging young adults to use condoms. *Personality and Social Psychology Bulletin, 20,* 116–128. http://dx.doi.org/10.1177/0146167294201012

Stone, J., & Cooper, J. (2001). A self-standards model of cognitive dissonance. *Journal of Experimental Social Psychology, 37,* 228–243. http://dx.doi.org/10.1006/jesp.2000.1446

Stone, J., Wiegand, A. W., Cooper, J., & Aronson, E. (1997). When exemplification fails: Hypocrisy and the motive for self-integrity. *Journal of Personality and Social Psychology, 72,* 54–65. http://dx.doi.org/10.1037/0022-3514.72.1.54

Tinklepaugh, O. L. (1928). An experimental study of representative factors in monkeys. *Journal of Comparative Psychology, 8,* 197–236. http://dx.doi.org/10.1037/h0075798

Topolinski, S., & Strack, F. (2015). Corrugator activity confirms immediate negative affect in surprise. *Frontiers in Psychology, 6,* 134. http://dx.doi.org/10.3389/fpsyg.2015.00134

Vachon, F., Hughes, R. W., & Jones, D. M. (2012). Broken expectations: Violation of expectancies, not novelty, captures auditory attention. *Journal of Experimental Psychology: Learning, Memory, and Cognition, 38,* 164–177. http://dx.doi.org/10.1037/a0025054

Weber, R., & Crocker, J. (1983). Cognitive processes in the revision of stereotypic beliefs. *Journal of Personality and Social Psychology, 45,* 961–977. http://dx.doi.org/10.1037/0022-3514.45.5.961

Wilson, T. D., Lindsey, S., & Schooler, T. Y. (2000). A model of dual attitudes. *Psychological Review, 107,* 101–126. http://dx.doi.org/10.1037/0033-295X.107.1.101

Winkielman, P., Huber, D. E., Kavanagh, L., & Schwarz, N. (2012). Fluency of consistency: When thoughts fit nicely and flow smoothly. In B. Gawronski & F. Strack (Eds.), *Cognitive consistency: A fundamental principle in social cognition* (pp. 89–111). New York, NY: Guilford Press.

Ye, Y., & Gawronski, B. (2016). When possessions become part of the self: Ownership and implicit self-object linking. *Journal of Experimental Social Psychology, 64,* 72–87. http://dx.doi.org/10.1016/j.jesp.2016.01.012

Yzerbyt, V. Y., Coull, A., & Rocher, S. J. (1999). Fencing off the deviant: The role of cognitive resources in the maintenance of stereotypes. *Journal of Personality and Social Psychology, 77,* 449–462. http://dx.doi.org/10.1037/0022-3514.77.3.449

Zanna, M. P., & Cooper, J. (1974). Dissonance and the pill: An attribution approach to studying the arousal properties of dissonance. *Journal of Personality and Social Psychology, 29,* 703–709. http://dx.doi.org/10.1037/h0036651

6

Dissonance Now

How Accessible Discrepancies Moderate Distress and Diverse Defenses

Ian McGregor, Ian R. Newby-Clark, and Mark P. Zanna

The evolution of Festinger's (1957) cognitive dissonance theory was shaped by its research methods. In its early years, behaviorally based inductions indirectly demonstrated that experimentally implanted "non-fitting cognitions" (p. 3) could cause surprisingly irrational reactions. These indirect methods involved elaborate social interactions, however, that invited revisions that moved the theory away from its core proposition that cognitive inconsistency, per se, is aversive enough to cause such reactions. Here we describe research on two phenomena related to Festinger's dissonance construct—ambivalence (Jamieson, 1993; Luttrell, Stillman, Hasinski, & Cunningham, 2016) and discrepancy detection (Hirsh, Mar, & Peterson, 2012; Proulx, Inzlicht, & Harmon-Jones, 2012; Randles, Inzlicht, Proulx, Tullett, & Heine, 2015). Research on both of these kindred topics supports the original claim of dissonance theory—that mere cognitive inconsistency is psychologically uncomfortable. Moreover, when dissonance and these kindred phenomena are considered in light of research on the simultaneous accessibility of cognitive elements (Bassili, 1994), a more complete perspective comes into view of dissonance theory's historical development and contemporary relevance. What becomes clear is that discomfort arising from inconsistent cognitive elements is moderated by their simultaneous accessibility/salience.

In what follows, after reviewing the evolution of classic dissonance and related literatures from the perspective of simultaneous accessibility, we describe how the same perspective can illuminate recent advances in research

---

http://dx.doi.org/10.1037/0000135-006
Cognitive Dissonance, Second Edition: Reexamining a Pivotal Theory in Psychology,
E. Harmon-Jones (Editor)
Copyright © 2019 by the American Psychological Association. All rights reserved.

on psychological threat and defense. We then outline how accessible conflict may be modulated by two basic motivational systems related to accessible conflict and approach motivation, and review research on how people use personal and social phenomena to leverage approach motivation for relief from the distress arising from accessible conflict.

Across paradigms and perspectives, accessible cognitive conflict is revealed as the essential, active ingredient in various psychological threats. Moreover, it is what motivates diverse, defensively extreme reactions, including religious extremism (Hirsh et al., 2012; Jonas et al., 2014; McGregor, 2006a; Proulx et al., 2012). This relevance of dissonance-related processes to important real-world outcomes brings the theory back full circle to one of its original intents. It reconnects dissonance with the important question of why people so regularly hold the dubious beliefs that sustain enigmatic social phenomena (Festinger, Riecken, & Schachter, 1956).

COGNITIVE DISSONANCE THEORY AND REVISIONS

The arrival of cognitive dissonance theory excited social psychologists for at least two reasons. First, it challenged the relatively bland version of reinforcement theory that was popular at the time (Aronson, 1992, p. 303). Second, it lent scientific support to the notion of motivated thinking, which had been percolating in other disciplines for many years. In philosophy, Schopenhauer (1818/1883) claimed that desire "is the strong blind man who carries on his shoulders the lame man (reason) who can see" (p. 421). In psychoanalytic psychology, rationalization was presented as a prevalent defense mechanism. The outcomes of the first high-impact dissonance studies demonstrated that people's opinions sometimes just reflect what they want to believe, for self-defensive reasons.

Early high-impact studies cleverly demonstrated participants' tendency to justify the counterattitudinal behaviors they had been subtly tricked into performing. In most experiments, however, inconsistent cognitions were only assumed to follow from behaviors that implied an inconsistent position, and psychological discomfort was inferred from attitude change. Festinger's core proposition, that inconsistent cognitions cause psychological discomfort, was not directly tested. Reliance on behavioral induction and indirect assessment of dissonance via attitude change opened the door for challenges to the epistemic basis of the theory.

The first major challenge came from Bem's (1967) self-perception theory. Bem argued that attributional processes could explain attitude change in conventional dissonance paradigms and that no aversive motivational state need exist. Participants noticed themselves behaving in a particular way, and because no external reason for their behavior was apparent, they inferred that their behavior must have arisen from internal factors (i.e., attitudes consistent with the behavior). The cognitive dissonance interpretation prevailed over the self-perception challenge after it became clear that if participants have an opportunity to misattribute dissonance arousal to another source, such as a pill

(Zanna & Cooper, 1974) or an unpleasant environment (Fazio, Zanna, & Cooper, 1977), attitude change does not occur. Eventually both theories found their appropriate domain of applicability. Dissonance processes are operative when counterattitudinal behaviors are outside the range of what participants can imagine endorsing; self-perception processes are operative when counterattitudinal behaviors are within that latitude of acceptance (Fazio et al., 1977).

Self-perception theory challenged dissonance theory at the back end of the counterattitudinal behavior paradigm, that is, it questioned Festinger's (1957) contention that psychological discomfort mediates the attitude change following counterattitudinal behavior. A second set of challenges to the original conception of cognitive dissonance theory came at the front end of the paradigm. Most notably, self-consistency (E. Aronson, 1968; see also Chapter 7, this volume), self-affirmation (Steele, 1988; see also Chapter 8, this volume), and the new look (Cooper & Fazio, 1984; see also Chapter 9, this volume) perspectives questioned whether inconsistent cognitions were sufficient or even necessary to produce discomfort and attitude change.

E. Aronson proposed that inconsistent cognitions are uncomfortable only when they impugn the self-concept. For example, most people believe that they are competent and good. Thus, when they are tricked by a dissonance researcher into doing something stupid or bad, they experience discomfort. According to E. Aronson, discomfort arises, not because, for example, a counterattitudinal essay is inconsistent with a prior attitude. Rather, it arises because the behavior of writing in support of the wrong cause is inconsistent with a positive self-concept. Two subsequent revisions took E. Aronson's focus on stupid or bad actions even further and contended that inconsistency is not even a necessary condition for dissonance to be experienced. Cooper and Fazio (1984) proposed a new look for dissonance theory, arguing that psychological discomfort in dissonance experiments occurs because people feel personally responsible for the production of aversive consequences. Similarly, Steele's (1988) self-affirmation revision posited that it is threat to global self-integrity, not inconsistency that causes the discomfort in dissonance experiments. New look and self-affirmation perspectives proposed that people simply rationalize behaviors that imply their guilt, incompetence, or immorality, and Abelson (1983) concluded that dissonance reduction is primarily a social strategy for saving face following experimentally engineered embarrassment. These perspectives viewed *cognitive dissonance* as a misnomer and saw the discomfort in "dissonance" paradigms as arising from social, not epistemic, factors.

AMBIVALENCE RESEARCH: RETURNING TO THE EPISTEMIC ROOTS OF DISSONANCE THEORY

Conventional dissonance experiments made an important contribution to the field's understanding of social behavior and motivated cognition, but invited revisions that deemphasized the theory's initial focus on epistemic motivation.

Ambivalence research complements conventional dissonance work by investigating implications of native inconsistencies (i.e., naturally occurring inconsistencies that are not behaviorally induced by a researcher). A direct technology for assessing inconsistency, developed by Scott (1966) and later by Kaplan (1972), separately measures both the positive and negative aspects of a given attitude (holding aspects of the opposite valence constant) and provides the means for direct assessment of native discrepancies within attitudes.

Using this technique, Thompson, Zanna, and Griffin (1995) found that intra-attitudinal discrepancies were associated ($r = .40$) with the experience of felt ambivalence—or feeling "torn and conflicted," as measured by Jamieson's (1993) scale. Jamieson's felt ambivalence questions refer to experienced conflict between issue-related elements. The conflicts could be cognitive (e.g., confusion about thoughts while making up mind), affective (e.g., feeling torn by the directions of feelings), or mixed (e.g., head and heart disagree). Felt ambivalence is accordingly a measure of targeted dissonance, specific to an issue under consideration. Although devoid of the provocative outcomes and high-impact appeal associated with the original dissonance tradition, ambivalence research (and later, discrepancy-detection research) reaffirmed the epistemic core of Festinger's proposition that had been deemphasized by the new look and self-affirmation revisions. Inconsistent cognitions, whether native or implanted via dissonance experiments, are experienced as uncomfortable and can activate areas of the brain that process discrepancy-related distress (Luttrell et al., 2016; Proulx et al., 2012; Randles et al., 2015; van Veen, Krug, Schooler, & Carter, 2009).

At around the same time as this research on the link between potential and felt ambivalence was being conducted, conventional dissonance research was further bolstering Festinger's original epistemic conception. E. Harmon-Jones, Brehm, Greenberg, Simon, and Nelson (1996) found that dissonance (directly measured by skin conductance) was aroused and attitude change occurred after "freely" chosen counterattitudinal expression, even if participants discarded their counterattitudinal statements before anyone else could see them. This finding contradicted the new look revision's requirement that negative consequences be present. In another experiment, Elliot and Devine (1994) found that counterattitudinal expression increased self-reported psychological discomfort (bothered, uneasy, uncomfortable) and that the discomfort was alleviated by attitude change.[1]

How can the reassertion of the original conception of dissonance theory be reconciled with the various revisions? The revisions may have capitalized on factors that influence the simultaneous accessibility (Bassili, 1994) of inconsistent cognitions. If inconsistent cognitions are not accessible at the same time, dissonance discomfort will be minimized. On the other hand, if inconsistent cognitions are simultaneously accessible, dissonance discomfort will be maximized.

---

[1] Elliot and Devine's (1994) "dissonance thermometer" is specific to agitation-related affect, which may be why it succeeded where past dissonance research typically failed to find self-reported changes in generalized negative affect.

Indeed, according to Festinger, Riecken, and Schachter (1956), one way to reduce dissonance is to "forget or reduce the importance of those cognitions that are in dissonant relationship" (p. 26).

A SIMULTANEOUS-ACCESSIBILITY ACCOUNT OF THE REVISIONS

E. Aronson's (1968) original claim that dissonance will occur only when the dissonant cognitions are self-relevant can be understood in terms of accessibility. According to the self-reference effect, information related to the self is recalled more easily than non-self-related information (Rogers, Kuiper, & Kirker, 1977). Dissonance may be heightened when self-related cognitions are involved because the two cognitions may be more likely to remain simultaneously accessible and less likely to drift out of awareness.

Cooper and Fazio's (1984) new look revision can similarly be explained in terms of accessibility. The perception that one has just done harm to an audience that does not deserve it is likely a relatively novel and unexpected realization for most participants. The increase in attributional activity (Pyszczynski & Greenberg, 1981; Wong & Weiner, 1981) that accompanies such an experientially striking realization may very well render the behavior, and the inconsistent cognition the behavior implies, hyper-accessible. In addition, guilt associated with a bad behavior might motivate an attempt to suppress awareness of it, which could cause rebound hyper-accessibility (Wegner, 1994), and anxiety arising from the guilt might motivate further self-focus and accessibility (Todd, Forstmann, Burgmer, Brooks, & Galinsky, 2015). Note also that in the E. Harmon-Jones et al. (1996) research in which dissonance ensued without the presence of aversive consequences, the "recall-task" cover story may have inadvertently ensured that the original attitude and the counterattitudinal expression remained simultaneously accessible (participants were told at the outset that they were to remember what they wrote).

The self-affirmation revision of dissonance theory is also amenable to an accessibility interpretation. "Stupid" or "bad" behaviors are more likely to remain accessible because of self-reference and heightened attributional activity. Moreover, Steele and Liu (1983) demonstrated that affirmation can alleviate dissonance but did not demonstrate that dissonance discomfort necessarily arises from threatened self-worth. We propose that affirmation ameliorates dissonance because it activates powerful cognitive processes related to approach motivation (E. Harmon-Jones & Harmon-Jones, 2008; Jonas et al., 2014) that mute accessibility of the inconsistent cognitions (E. Harmon-Jones, Amodio, & Harmon-Jones, 2009). This muting or shielding function may be why participants prefer to affirm themselves in domains unrelated to the dissonant elements (J. Aronson, Blanton, & Cooper, 1995; Blanton, Cooper, Skurnik, & Aronson, 1997).

Steele and Liu (1983) attempted to rule out muting and distraction accounts of their results by demonstrating in a counterattitudinal essay study that affirmation still reduces attitude change (and therefore dissonance) even when participants are reminded of their dissonant essay after the affirmation and before the attitude measure. The reminder procedure simply required participants to write down three key words from their earlier essay, however, and so may not have been enough to return the inconsistent elements to simultaneous accessibility. It is unlikely that they would have mentioned with those three words, anything about their original attitude.

SIMULTANEOUS ACCESSIBILITY AND EARLY DISSONANCE RESEARCH

The importance of accessibility as a moderator of cognitive dissonance was supported by experimental results from the early days of cognitive dissonance research. Several studies demonstrated that dissonance reduction through attitude change depends on whether participants are distracted from or confronted by the dissonant cognitions. In one of these first salience experiments, Brock (1962) found that after being induced to "freely" write an essay about why they would like to become Catholic, non-Catholics' attitudes became more favorable toward Catholicism if they focused on essay convincingness as opposed to grammatical structure in the interval between the essay writing and attitude assessment. Thus, extra attention to inconsistent elements apparently increased dissonance. In contrast, one of the first distraction experiments (Allen, 1965) found that when participants engaged in an absorbing technical task between a free-choice behavior and the assessment of attitudes, the dissonance-reducing spread of alternatives was eliminated (see also Zanna & Aziza, 1976).

In these early experiments, all avenues of dissonance reduction were closed off except attitude change, and the inconsistent cognitions were highly salient (unless a distraction was introduced). This state of affairs maximized the likelihood of finding self-justificatory attitude change but obscured investigation of distraction as a natural route of dissonance reduction. According to Rosenberg and Abelson (1960), people follow a principle of least effort when attempting to restore cognitive consistency. Because changing one's attitude presumably takes some cognitive work, Hardyck and Kardush (1968) proposed that stopping thinking, a form of self-distraction, might be the preferred strategy for coping with dissonance. A research technique was needed that would incorporate the spontaneous distraction that presumably occurs in real life.

The forbidden-toy paradigm (E. Aronson & Carlsmith, 1963) is unique in that during the "temptation period," in which children are forbidden to play with a well-liked toy, they can easily take their minds off their cognitive dilemma by playing with toys that are not forbidden. Thus, in contrast to other kinds of dissonance procedures in which participants are left to simmer in their counterattitudinal behavior, participants are free to immerse themselves in other engaging activities. This provides a relatively naturalistic setting for the dissonance-reduction strategy that Pallak, Brock, and Kiesler (1967) referred to as throwing oneself into one's work. Carlsmith et al. (1969) augmented the built-in distraction feature of the forbidden-toy paradigm with two manipulations of forced attention. In one experiment, a "janitor" made the forbidden toy salient by walking into the room during the temptation period and incidentally asking the children why they were not playing with it. In the other experiment, the forbidden toy was made salient by a "defective" lamp, which flashed on and off above it. The general procedure and results were as follows.

Each child was brought into a room, shown how to use six attractive toys, and asked to rank the attractiveness of the toys. The experimenter then explained that he had to run an errand and that while he was gone, the child was forbidden to play with the second-ranked toy (which was placed on a different table). In the mild-threat condition, the experimenter said, "If you play with the [second-ranked toy], I will be a little bit annoyed with you." In the severe-threat condition, he said instead, "If you play with the [second-ranked toy], I will be very upset and very angry with you, and I'll have to do something about it." The experimenter then left the room for a 6-minute temptation period, during which the forced-attention manipulations occurred for those in the experimental conditions. After the temptation period, the experimenter asked the children to rerank the toys. Thus, both experiments had a simple 2 (mild threat vs. severe threat) × 2 (forced attention vs. control) format.

In both experiments, two main effects resulted. There was more derogation of the second-ranked toy in the mild-threat conditions than in the severe-threat conditions, and there was more derogation in the forced-attention conditions than the control conditions. Carlsmith et al. (1969) had expected that attention would increase derogation, but only when dissonance existed in the first place, that is, in the mild-threat condition. Zanna, Lepper, and Abelson (1973) conducted a follow-up experiment, to see whether the expected interaction (forced attention increasing derogation only under mild threat) might result if forced attention was directed simultaneously toward both of the inconsistent cognitions ("I'm not playing with the desirable toy" and "there's no strong reason not to") instead of just the one ("I'm not playing with the desirable toy"). They reasoned that the absence of an interaction in the first two experiments might be due to the fact that, although the blinking light or janitor's comment focused the children's attention on the fact that they were not playing with a valued toy, it did not simultaneously remind them of the initial justification for that compliant behavior. For dissonance to occur, both cognitions would have to be simultaneously accessible.

To accomplish forced attention to both cognitions, the janitor experiment was modified in two ways. First, after the threat manipulation, the experimenter placed a sticker marked with an X on the side of the forbidden toy. Children were told that this sticker was being put on the toy as a reminder that the experimenter would either "be a little annoyed" or "very angry and upset" (depending on the threat condition) if they played with the forbidden toy. Second, in the high-accessibility condition, when the janitor entered the room in the middle of the temptation period, instead of simply calling attention to the forbidden toy, he said, "What's this toy doing over here on the table?" and "How come this toy has a sticker on it?" These two modifications apparently succeeded in simultaneously focusing children's attention on both of the dissonant cognitions. The expected interaction between potential dissonance (severe vs. mild threat) and simultaneous accessibility (control vs. reminder) resulted, with the greatest amount of dissonance reduction (toy derogation) in the high-reminder-mild-threat condition, suggesting that the experience of dissonance does seem to be moderated by the simultaneous accessibility of the potentially dissonant cognitions. These studies underscore how easily inconsistent elements can become inaccessible when distraction opportunities are present.

SIMULTANEOUS ACCESSIBILITY AND AMBIVALENCE

The early experiments suggest that simultaneous accessibility can play an important role in dissonance processes, but like most dissonance research in the counterattitudinal behavior paradigm, interpretation is vulnerable to the revisionist critiques mentioned above. Further, the early experiments manipulated salience. Although it is likely that salient elements will also be highly accessible, it would still be desirable to measure accessibility directly. The rise of social cognition in the 1980s brought new techniques for manipulating and measuring accessibility of knowledge structures (e.g., Bassili & Fletcher, 1991; Fazio, Sanbonmatsu, Powell, & Kardes, 1986). In three studies, we used Bassili's (1996) technique for measuring whether psychological discomfort may be influenced not just by the existence of ambivalent cognitions but also by the simultaneous accessibility of those cognitions (Newby-Clark, McGregor, & Zanna, 2002). These studies are described below.

Recall that Thompson et al. (1995) found that intra-attitudinal inconsistency was correlated at 0.40 with Jamieson's (1993) measure of felt ambivalence (i.e., how torn people felt about that attitude issue). This finding is consistent with the core of Festinger's (1957) original thesis that the existence of non-fitting cognitions leads to psychological discomfort. In the following two studies, we were interested in whether simultaneous accessibility of inconsistent cognitions would moderate the relation between the existence of inconsistent cognitions (what we call *potential* ambivalence), as measured by the Kaplan (1972) technique,[2] and *felt* ambivalence, as measured by Jamieson's (1993) scale. We hypothesized that felt ambivalence would be highest when inconsistent cognitions not only existed, but were available to awareness at the same time. We recorded how long it took participants to answer the Kaplan questions about

---

[2] To assess potential ambivalence, we asked participants to separately rate the favorable and unfavorable aspects of each attitude issue (Kaplan, 1972). The lower of the two ratings was squared and divided by the higher rating. Thus, as the favorable and unfavorable components became increasingly and equally extreme, potential ambivalence scores increased (for more detail, see Newby-Clark et al., 2002).

the favorable and unfavorable aspects of each issue and used these latencies to calculate an index of simultaneous accessibility.[3] Our contention is that potential ambivalence is experienced as felt ambivalence when contradictory cognitions are highly and equally accessible.

In the first study, we telephoned 187 undergraduates and asked them questions about two issues: abortion and capital punishment. As expected, there was a significant positive relation between felt ambivalence and potential ambivalence for both attitude issues. Further, the interaction between potential ambivalence and simultaneous accessibility was significantly associated with felt ambivalence for abortion and marginally associated with felt ambivalence for capital punishment. These results supported our hypothesis that the relation between potential and felt ambivalence would be moderated by the simultaneous accessibility of the relevant cognitions.

In a computerized replication, 69 undergraduates responded to the same questions as in Study 1, but the questions were presented on a computer screen, and response latencies were more automatically recorded. Results were similar. Again, potential ambivalence and felt ambivalence were significantly correlated, and again, the interaction between simultaneous accessibility and potential ambivalence was significantly associated with felt ambivalence for abortion and marginally for capital punishment. Meta-analyses across the two studies yielded significant interactions for both attitude issues. For descriptive purposes, we also combined participants from the upper and lower quartiles of simultaneous accessibility from both studies, and (a) calculated the correlation between potential and felt ambivalence and (b) regressed felt ambivalence on potential ambivalence. For participants high in simultaneous accessibility, the correlation between potential and felt ambivalence about abortion was 0.73; for those low in simultaneous accessibility, the correlation was only 0.32. Viewed another way, the slope of felt ambivalence (standardized) about abortion regressed on potential ambivalence (low = −2 SD, high = 2 SD) was steeper for those in the upper (as compared with the lower) quartile of simultaneous accessibility.

In the third study, to move past the correlational findings in these first two studies, we experimentally manipulated simultaneous accessibility by randomly assigning participants to either repeatedly express (or not) their potential ambivalence with a procedure that significantly increased simultaneous accessibility (on the manipulation check). To further underscore the epistemic nature of the expected effect we had also assessed participants' aversion to discrepancies with a trait scale—preference for consistency (PFC) that was created to moderate cognitive dissonance phenomena (Cialdini, Trost, & Newsom, 1995). For high PFC participants, the results mirrored those found in the first two studies: potential ambivalence interacted with manipulated simultaneous

---

[3] We performed a reciprocal transformation on the latency data, to normalize the positive skew and translate latency scores to speed scores. Speed scores were then used to calculate simultaneous accessibility, by squaring the slower response time and dividing it by the faster (following Bassili, 1996). Thus, as the two response speeds become increasingly and equally extreme, simultaneous-accessibility scores increase.

accessibility to predict felt ambivalence about abortion. In contrast, there was no interaction for low PFC participants. Overall, the highest felt ambivalence was experience by high PFC participants with substantial and simultaneously accessible cognitive conflict.

The results from these three ambivalence studies demonstrate that felt ambivalence arising from the existence of inconsistent cognitions is moderated by the extent to which both cognitions are readily and equally accessible. Consistent with distraction-salience findings from conventional dissonance paradigms, the results support the more general conclusion that simultaneous accessibility of inconsistent cognitive elements is an important factor in determining how much epistemic discomfort will be experienced. We see simultaneous accessibility as an essential and underemphasized aspect of dissonance theory that can not only help explain and integrate the revisions described earlier, but that can also help make sense of how dissonance-related processes operate in the real world to affect outcomes other than behavioral justification. We now turn to some of these extensions.

A SIMULTANEOUS-ACCESSIBILITY ACCOUNT OF SOME EXTENSIONS OF DISSONANCE RESEARCH

Understanding the role of simultaneous accessibility helps make sense of other phenomena with important social implications. It helps explain how people manage to maintain desired but irrational opinions by appealing to other unrelated beliefs of transcendent importance (trivialization); it helps explain the prevalence of hypocrisy; and it also helps explain the appeal of alcohol. Trivialization, hypocrisy, and (at least some of) the pleasures of alcohol all revolve around dynamics of simultaneous accessibility.

Trivialization

Simon, Greenberg, and Brehm (1995) demonstrated that participants often resolve dissonance by trivializing counter-attitudinal behavior. Imagine that you are a participant in a trivialization experiment. You have just freely completed a counterattitudinal essay and are experiencing dissonance discomfort as a result. Four questions are now provided by the researcher that essentially ask whether it is really so important in the grand scheme of things that you wrote a counter-attitudinal essay. Might you not gladly agree with this suggestion and use it as a way to become less preoccupied with the counter-attitudinal behavior? In essence, the four questions suggest not to worry about it, it doesn't really matter all that much. It seems plausible that trivialization works because it gives participants permission to forget about their inconsistent behavior. Trivialization may relieve dissonance by decreasing the simultaneous accessibility of the inconsistent cognitions. The loss of importance may allow the conflicting cognitions to wander from awareness more easily (see Krosnick, 1989, for the link between importance and accessibility).

Hypocrisy

Hypocrisy researchers demonstrated that after being made mindful of their hypocrisy, individuals reduce dissonance by changing their future behaviors and intentions (e.g., Stone, Wiegand, Cooper, & Aronson, 1997). In the typical hypocrisy experiment, after participants publicly advocate a prosocial attitude (e.g., condom use, water conservation, recycling), they are reminded of their past failures to practice what they have just preached. Participants caught in this dilemma, of high simultaneous accessibility of an advocated attitude and awareness of past behavioral shortcomings, resolve the predicament by acting and intending to act in a manner consistent with the advocated attitude. But it is only when participants are reminded of their past behavior that they experience dissonance. Remarkably, even when asked to think about behaviors of friends or roommates that are inconsistent with the advocated attitude, intentions and behaviors do not change, indicating that participants' own contradictory past behavior somehow eludes awareness. The hypocrisy paradigm highlights an impressive capacity to limit accessibility of personal inconsistencies under normal circumstances.

Alcohol

According to Steele and Josephs's (1990) alcohol myopia theory, alcohol intoxication makes people able to focus only on the most salient cue in the environment. If so, this should make alcohol an ideal solution for dissolving simultaneous accessibility. Indeed, Steele, Southwick, and Critchlow (1981) found evidence that alcohol relieves discomfort from internal inconsistencies, presumably because alcohol myopia reduces attentional breadth and permits awareness of only one element of the inconsistency.

Based on this alcohol myopia theory and research, and animal research specifically linking alcohol to relief from conflict-related distress (reviewed in Gray & McNaughton, 2000), two experiments tested whether people would spontaneously drink more when confronted with simultaneously accessible cognitive conflicts (reported in McGregor, 2007). In the first study, 199 undergraduates first completed the PFC scale (described above in the ambivalence studies) to assess trait aversion to cognitive conflict. They were then randomly assigned to either ruminate and write about both sides of a difficult personal dilemma, or to write about a decision they had already made. They were then given the chance to taste-test sample as much of various kinds of beer and sports drink (in the afternoon during the work day) as necessary to be able to rate how much they liked the drinks. Results revealed that for experienced drinkers (self-reported in a pretest) the cognitive conflict manipulation caused high PFC participants to drink more beer (residualized on sports drink consumption).

In the second experiment, 100 undergraduates completed a measure of implicit self-esteem (low scores on which have been associated with self-focus and reactivity to cognitive conflict; McGregor & Jordan, 2007). They were then all reminded of uncertainties and conflicts about close personal relationships, and then randomly assigned to conduct the same taste test described in the previous study while either sitting in front of a large mirror (to increase self-focus and presumably rumination about the conflicts) or not. Results revealed a significant interaction with highest alcohol consumption (residualized on sports drink) among participants with low implicit self-esteem in the mirror condition. These studies suggest that people spontaneously turn to alcohol as a way to dodge the simultaneous accessibility of conflicting cognitions. The capacity of alcohol to myopically limit focus to only a single cognition may be what makes it such a potent and attractive means of escape from simultaneously accessible conflict.

ACCESSIBLE CONFLICT IN THREAT AND DEFENSE RESEARCH

Contemporary theory and research on various forms of psychological threat and defense can also be integrated from the perspective of this chapter. It is now clear that, as in dissonance and ambivalence research, various threats cause distress and defensiveness to the extent that they highlight cognitive conflicts. Conflict is the active ingredient that motivates the defenses, and the defenses serve to mute accessibility of the conflicts.

One of the basic motivational systems governing goal regulation is dedicated to managing salient conflicts. When conflicts or uncertainties are detected, the behavioral inhibition system (BIS) initiates three responses designed to help the organism reorient toward less conflicted courses of action: anxious arousal, loss of interest in current goals, and diffuse vigilance (Gray & McNaughton, 2000). Together, these responses can encourage switching to more viable goals in the face of conflict. BIS activation makes people agitated and volatile as a way to disrupt conflicted goals and facilitate change. Importantly, the BIS responds to either behavioral or cognitive conflicts (Hirsh et al., 2012).

When the BIS is experimentally activated by deliberative mind-set instructions that require participants to ruminate about both sides of an intractable personal dilemma, mood, self-esteem, and optimism become depressed (Taylor & Gollwitzer, 1995). Deliberative mind-set clearly highlights simultaneous accessibility of important conflicts. Importantly, the epistemic discomfort it arouses mediates a decrease in self-control. In a large preregistered experiment, deliberative mind-set (vs. a value-affirmation comparison condition) increased participants' self-reported feelings of BIS-related agitation that in turn mediated loss of persistence on an anagram task. Participants in the deliberation condition were significantly more likely than participants in the affirmation condition to drop out of the experiment, and for those who stayed in the experiment the BIS-related agitation predicted poor performance on the anagram task (Alquist et al., 2018). It is important to note that the measure of BIS-related agitation was derived from dissonance and self-discrepancy research findings (by McGregor, Zanna, Holmes, & Spencer, 2001, Study 1) and included the dissonance thermometer items: bothered, uneasy, uncomfortable (from Elliot & Devine, 1994).

In contrast to the BIS-related agitation and volatility arising from salient conflict, singular focus on implementing goals one has already committed to elevates mood, self-esteem, and optimism (Taylor & Gollwitzer, 1995). Implemental goal commitment activates a companion motivational system to the BIS—the behavioral approach system (BAS), which bolsters tenacity and determination by providing a kind of motivational tunnel vision that mutes the salience of inconsistencies and discrepancies (C. Harmon-Jones, Schmeichel, Mennitt, & Harmon-Jones, 2011; E. Harmon-Jones et al., 2009). The BAS operates reciprocally with the BIS (Corr, 2004; Nash, Inzlicht, & McGregor, 2012), which means it could be expected to shield people from distractions directly, but also indirectly by muting the diffuse vigilance of the BIS. Importantly for our argument here, commitments that activate the BAS could thus be turned to for merely palliative and defensive purposes, for relief from the distress and demotivation arising from simultaneously accessible conflicts (Jonas et al., 2014; McGregor, Nash, Mann, & Phills, 2010). This tendency for people to seize on BAS-activating commitments for relief from conflict/dissonance-related BIS-arousal is referred to as reactive approach motivation (RAM).

From Conflict to RAM

RAM in the face of conflict-related threats can be accomplished via compensatory conviction about opinions, values, goals, self-worth, and groups (McGregor, 2003). The first demonstration of this tendency came from research showing that experimentally manipulated deliberative mind-set (vs. thinking about someone else's dilemma) caused participants to react with exaggerated conviction about their social-issue opinions, identity-commitments, and in-group biases. Importantly, the exaggerated conviction relieved the epistemic discomfort that had been aroused by the deliberative mind-set manipulation (McGregor et al., 2001, Study 1). Subsequent research demonstrated that conviction and other of the various defenses people spontaneously turn to after conflict-related threats effectively reduce the subjective salience of the distress-arousing conflicts (McGregor, 2006b; McGregor & Marigold, 2003; McGregor, Nail, Marigold, & Kang, 2005).

How do the conviction reactions mute subjective salience? The same threats that cause compensatory conviction reactions also cause RAM on self-report, implicit, behavioral, and neural measures of approach motivation (McGregor, Nash, & Inzlicht, 2009; McGregor, Nash, Mann, et al., 2010), and do so only in response to threats that highlight simultaneously accessible conflicts (Nash, McGregor, & Prentice, 2011). Specifically, in the Nash et al. (2011) research, experimentally manipulated failure or rejection threats only caused dissonance/agitation-related distress and then reactive idealism and RAM when participants had first been experimentally primed with failure or rejection-related goals (respectively). This finding, that threats are consequential only when they are applied in the context of a simultaneously accessible conflict (the relevant goal) links research on threats (e.g., failure or rejection) to basic motivational processes related to salient conflict.

Threats, Conflict-Related Distress, and Worldview Defense

Findings like those just described have now accumulated in research with other threats as well (e.g., mortality salience or loss of control). Various threats interchangeably cause various RAM-related defenses (Jonas et al., 2014). It is becoming clear that, in general, threats are threatening to the extent that they arouse conflict-BIS-related neural processes by highlighting simultaneously accessible discrepancies (e.g., want to succeed but may be failing; want inclusion but may be rejected; want to live but will die; want control but lack it).

The anterior cingulate cortex of the brain plays a vital role in conflict and discrepancy detection (Bush, Luu, & Posner, 2000) and in initiating the cascade of reactions that culminate in BIS-activation and dissonance-like distress (Hirsh et al., 2012; Jonas et al., 2014). Many of the various threats that cause RAM-related defenses cause increased activation of the anterior cingulate cortex (Proulx et al., 2012). Importantly, the classic counter-attitudinal-advocacy technique for experimentally implanting dissonant cognitions also heightens anterior cingulate cortex activity, which mediates the defensive attitude change (van Veen et al., 2009). Thus, it now seems likely that classic dissonance manipulations activate this same generic threat response as other threats, and that defensive attitude change may be only one of many RAM responses participants could mount to activate BAS for relief from BIS-related discomfort (cf. E. Harmon-Jones & Harmon-Jones, 2008; Jonas et al., 2014). Indeed, if given the chance, participants will respond to classic dissonance manipulations with heightened moral conviction, belief in God, and worldview defense reactions that involve punishment of moral transgressors (Randles et al., 2015).

A prominent line of research that can be interpreted from this perspective focuses on worldview defense reactions to mortality salience (Pyszczynski, Solomon, & Greenberg, 2015). Mortality salience (thinking about one's own death) has recently been linked to the same kind of discrepancy-related distress as is caused by ambivalence and dissonance (Jonas et al., 2014; Klackl, Jonas, & Fritsche, 2018; Luttrell et al., 2016; Proulx et al., 2012; Quirin & Klackl, 2016; van Veen et al., 2009). Worldview defense reactions often take the form of amalgam defenses that wrap together compensatory convictions about opinions, values, goals, self-worth, and groups (McGregor, 2003, 2006a). They involve heightened zeal for culturally-mediated value systems that one identifies with and strives to morally exemplify. Hundreds of experiments have now demonstrated that personal mortality reminders cause various instantiations of worldview defense, from defense of consensual moral propriety (e.g., recommending stiffer punishments for prostitutes) to religious extremism, political partisanship, and exaggerated outgroup derogation (reviewed in Pyszczynski et al., 2015).

The claim of mortality salience researchers was initially that there was something special about mortality that made it a uniquely potent cause of such reactions (Greenberg, Solomon, & Pyszczynski, 1997). Early compensatory conviction work, however, revealed that conflict-related threats unrelated to mortality salience could cause the same outcomes (McGregor et al., 2001; van den Bos,

Poortvliet, Maas, Miedema, & van den Ham, 2005), including reactive approach-motivation (McGregor, Gailliot, Vasquez, & Nash, 2007; McGregor, Prentice, & Nash, 2013). Subsequent work further revealed that exposure to simultaneously accessible cognitive inconsistencies (absurd stories or nonsense word pairs), and also to original cognitive dissonance manipulations, could cause the same kinds of worldview defense reactions as mortality salience, and that these reactions were eliminated if participants had some other way to relieve the conflict-related distress (McGregor et al., 2001; Randles et al., 2015; Randles, Heine, & Santos, 2013; Randles, Proulx, & Heine, 2011).

Religious Zeal

A powerful form of worldview defense is religious zeal. Various conflict-related threats, including mortality salience, cause people to amplify their religious zeal, for better or for worse (e.g., Kay, Gaucher, McGregor, & Nash, 2010; McGregor et al., 2013; McGregor, Haji, Nash, & Teper, 2008; Rothschild, Abdollahi, & Pyszczynski, 2009; Schumann, McGregor, Nash, & Ross, 2014). Importantly, there is also evidence that religious zeal can function as a form of RAM. Participants react to the same threats (e.g., academic confusion and rejection) that cause reactive approach of personal goals and left frontal asymmetry associated with approach motivation (McGregor et al., 2009; McGregor, Nash, Mann, et al., 2010) by becoming more extremely certain and devoted to their identified religious belief system (McGregor et al., 2008; McGregor, Nash, & Prentice, 2010). Importantly, this occurs only under conditions of simultaneously accessible conflict. Academic achievement threats after achievement-goal primes or relationship uncertainty threats after relationship-goal primes caused religious zeal, but there was no increase in religious zeal after threats that followed the unrelated goal prime (McGregor et al., 2013). The view of reactive-religious zeal as generalized means for relieving salient conflict-related distress is supported by evidence that religious zeal does effectively relieve conflict-related distress as assessed by event-related potentials associated with psychological distress that have been source localized to the area of the anterior cingulate cortex (Bush et al., 2000; Inzlicht, McGregor, Hirsh, & Nash, 2009; Inzlicht & Tullett, 2010).

Early cognitive dissonance research on religious zeal focused on the way that people use dubious religious convictions to relieve the discomfort arising from awareness of conflict between their dubious religious commitments and reality, as in the case of how doomsday cult members coped with the revelation that the world did not end when their cult predicted it would (Festinger et al., 1956). From the present perspective, religious zeal has a more versatile anxiolytic function for relieving conflict-related distress by way of generalized reduction of anterior cingulate cortex activation. Religious zeal and other idealistic forms of moral enthusiasm may be a convenient and socially sanctioned way for people to self-sooth in the face of conflict-related distress by approaching relief via idealistic certainties and commitments that can spur approach-motivated states (McGregor, Prentice, & Nash, 2012).

Importantly, in contrast to the bizarre religious beliefs of Festinger's cult members, the religious beliefs of the undergraduates in our experiments tend to revolve around compassionate ideals. In a series of experiments (Schumann et al., 2014), either mortality salience or academic confusion threats caused similar amounts of distress and hostile worldview defense reactions when religion had not been primed. If religion had been primed at the beginning of the study, however, both threats had opposite effects—they caused participants to become reactively forgiving of fictitious moral offenders and of ostensibly real groups in their community who had used up more than their share of resources. Anger and forgiveness have both been linked to approach-motivation (Carver & Harmon-Jones, 2009; Molden & Finkel, 2010; Struthers et al., 2014). Evidence that both the hostile and forgiving reactions may be forms of RAM comes from a further Schumann et al. (2014, Study 7) finding, that the hostile and forgiving reactions alike emerged only among participants with approach-oriented personality traits. This finding is consistent with other research showing that RAM for relief from conflict-related distress is most prevalent among people who are dispositionally inclined toward approach motivation in the first place (reviewed in Jonas et al., 2014; McGregor & Jordan, 2007; McGregor et al., 2009). In sum, threat and defense research has coalesced around the view that basic processes related to accessible conflict and BIS activation are what spur various defenses. Threats highlight cognitive conflicts, and defenses activate approach-motivated states that mute simultaneous accessibility of the conflicting cognitions (Jonas et al., 2014; cf. E. Harmon-Jones & Harmon-Jones, 2008).

CONCLUSION

The basic premise of dissonance theory has travelled a long way. Its claim that "nonfitting cognitions" are aversive and cause defensive reactions survived multiple revision attempts, and is thriving in contemporary research on ambivalence, discrepancy-detection, and threat and defense. Along the way, it has become clear that for dissonance (or ambivalence, or discrepancy, or threat) to be distressing and consequential, the inconsistent cognitions must be simultaneously accessible. The notion of simultaneously accessible conflict can help integrate disparate findings across dissonance and related research areas. It also allows for the integration of classic dissonance research with contemporary research on ambivalence and discrepancy detection. Moreover, processes related to simultaneous accessibility have been guiding recent advances in threat and defense research. Diverse threats activate discrepancy-related distress mediated by the BIS, to the extent that they highlight simultaneously accessible conflicts (Hirsh et al., 2012; Luttrell et al., 2016; Proulx et al., 2012). Defensive reactions serve as levers for heightening the BAS, which can shield people from simultaneous accessibility of conflicts, thereby providing relief from BIS-related (dissonance) distress (Jonas et al., 2014).

REFERENCES

Abelson, R. P. (1983). Whatever became of consistency theory? *Personality and Social Psychology Bulletin, 9*, 37–54. http://dx.doi.org/10.1177/0146167283091006

Allen, V. L. (1965). Effect of extraneous cognitive activity on dissonance reduction. *Psychological Reports, 16*, 1145–1151. http://dx.doi.org/10.2466/pr0.1965.16.3c.1145

Alquist, J. L., Baumeister, R. F., McGregor, I., Core, T. J., Benjamin, I., & Tice, D. M. (2018). Personal conflict impairs performance on an unrelated self-control task: Lingering costs of uncertainty and conflict. *Journal of Experimental Social Psychology, 74*, 157–160. http://dx.doi.org/10.1016/j.jesp.2017.09.010

Aronson, E. (1968). Dissonance theory: Progress and problems. In R. P. Abelson, E. Aronson, W. J. McGuire, T. M. Newcomb, M. J. Rosenberg, & P. H. Tannenbaum (Eds.), *Theories of cognitive consistency: A sourcebook* (pp. 5–27). Chicago, IL: Rand McNally.

Aronson, E. (1992). The return of the repressed: Dissonance theory makes a comeback. *Psychological Inquiry, 3*, 303–311. http://dx.doi.org/10.1207/s15327965pli0304_1

Aronson, E., & Carlsmith, J. M. (1963). Effect of the severity of threat on the devaluation of forbidden behavior. *Journal of Abnormal and Social Psychology, 66*, 584–588. http://dx.doi.org/10.1037/h0039901

Aronson, J., Blanton, H., & Cooper, J. (1995). From dissonance to disidentification: Selectivity in the self-affirmation process. *Journal of Personality and Social Psychology, 68*, 986–996. http://dx.doi.org/10.1037/0022-3514.68.6.986

Bassili, J. N. (1994, November). *On the relationship between attitude ambivalence and attitude accessibility.* Paper presented at the University of Waterloo, Waterloo, Ontario, Canada.

Bassili, J. (1996). The "how" and "why" of response latency measurement in telephone surveys. In N. Schwarz & S. Sudman (Eds.), *Answering questions: Methodology for determining cognitive and communicative processes in survey research* (pp. 319–346). San Francisco, CA: Jossey-Bass.

Bassili, J. N., & Fletcher, J. F. (1991). Response-time measurement in survey research: A method for CATI and a new look at nonattitudes. *Public Opinion Quarterly, 55*, 331–346. http://dx.doi.org/10.1086/269265

Bem, D. J. (1967). Self-perception: An alternative interpretation of cognitive dissonance phenomena. *Psychological Review, 74*, 183–200. http://dx.doi.org/10.1037/h0024835

Blanton, H., Cooper, J., Skurnik, I., & Aronson, J. (1997). When bad things happen to good feedback: Exacerbating the need for self-justification with self-affirmations. *Personality and Social Psychology Bulletin, 23*, 684–692. http://dx.doi.org/10.1177/0146167297237002

Brock, T. C. (1962). Cognitive restructuring and attitude change. *Journal of Abnormal and Social Psychology, 64*, 264–271. http://dx.doi.org/10.1037/h0043376

Bush, G., Luu, P., & Posner, M. I. (2000). Cognitive and emotional influences in anterior cingulate cortex. *Trends in Cognitive Sciences, 4*, 215–222. http://dx.doi.org/10.1016/S1364-6613(00)01483-2

Carlsmith, J. M., Ebbesen, E. B., Lepper, M. R., Zanna, M. P., Joncas, A. J., & Abelson, R. P. (1969). Dissonance reduction following forced attention to the dissonance. *Proceedings of the 77th Annual Convention of the American Psychological Association, 4* (Pt. 1), 321–322.

Carver, C. S., & Harmon-Jones, E. (2009). Anger is an approach-related affect: Evidence and implications. *Psychological Bulletin, 135*, 183–204. http://dx.doi.org/10.1037/a0013965

Cialdini, R. B., Trost, M. R., & Newsom, J. T. (1995). Preference for consistency: The development of a valid measure and the discovery of surprising behavioral implications. *Journal of Personality and Social Psychology, 69*, 318–328. http://dx.doi.org/10.1037/0022-3514.69.2.318

Cooper, J., & Fazio, R. H. (1984). A new look at dissonance theory. In L. Berkowitz (Ed.), *Advances in experimental social psychology*, (Vol. 17, pp. 229–266). Orlando, FL: Academic Press.

Corr, P. J. (2004). Reinforcement sensitivity theory and personality. *Neuroscience and Biobehavioral Reviews, 28*, 317–332. http://dx.doi.org/10.1016/j.neubiorev.2004.01.005

Elliot, A. J., & Devine, P. (1994). On the motivational nature of cognitive dissonance: Dissonance as psychological discomfort. *Journal of Personality and Social Psychology, 67*, 382–394. http://dx.doi.org/10.1037/0022-3514.67.3.382

Fazio, R. H., Sanbonmatsu, D. M., Powell, M. C., & Kardes, F. R. (1986). On the automatic activation of attitudes. *Journal of Personality and Social Psychology, 50*, 229–238. http://dx.doi.org/10.1037/0022-3514.50.2.229

Fazio, R. H., Zanna, M. P., & Cooper, J. (1977). Dissonance and self-perception: An integrative view of each theory's proper domain of application. *Journal of Experimental Social Psychology, 13*, 464–479. http://dx.doi.org/10.1016/0022-1031(77)90031-2

Festinger, L. (1957). *A theory of cognitive dissonance*. Evanston, IL: Row, Peterson.

Festinger, L., Riecken, H. W., & Schachter, S. (1956). *When prophecy fails*. Minneapolis: University of Minnesota Press. http://dx.doi.org/10.1037/10030-000

Gray, J. A., & McNaughton, N. (2000). *The neuropsychology of anxiety: An enquiry into the functions of the septo-hippocampal system*. New York, NY: Oxford University Press.

Greenberg, J., Solomon, S., & Pyszczynski, T. (1997). Terror management theory of self-esteem and cultural worldviews: Empirical assessments and conceptual refinements. In M. P. Zanna (Ed.), *Advances in experimental social psychology*, (Vol. 29, pp. 61–139). San Diego, CA: Academic Press. http://dx.doi.org/10.1016/S0065-2601(08)60016-7

Hardyck, J. A., & Kardush, M. (1968). A modest modish model for dissonance reduction. In R. P. Abelson, E. Aronson, W. J. McGuire, T. M. Newcomb, M. J. Rosenberg, & P. H. Tannenbaum (Eds.), *Theories of cognitive consistency: A sourcebook* (pp. 684–692). Chicago, IL: Rand McNally.

Harmon-Jones, C., Schmeichel, B. J., Mennitt, E., & Harmon-Jones, E. (2011). The expression of determination: Similarities between anger and approach-related positive affect. *Journal of Personality and Social Psychology, 100*, 172–181. http://dx.doi.org/10.1037/a0020966

Harmon-Jones, E., Amodio, D. M., & Harmon-Jones, C. (2009). Action-based model of dissonance: A review, integration, and expansion of conceptions of cognitive conflict. *Advances in Experimental Social Psychology, 41*, 119–166.

Harmon-Jones, E., Brehm, J. W., Greenberg, J., Simon, L., & Nelson, D. E. (1996). Evidence that the production of aversive consequences is not necessary to create cognitive dissonance. *Journal of Personality and Social Psychology, 70*, 5–16. http://dx.doi.org/10.1037/0022-3514.70.1.5

Harmon-Jones, E., & Harmon-Jones, C. (2008). Action-based model of dissonance: A review of behavioral, anterior cingulate, and prefrontal cortical mechanisms. *Social and Personality Psychology Compass, 2*, 1518–1538. http://dx.doi.org/10.1111/j.1751-9004.2008.00110.x

Hirsh, J. B., Mar, R. A., & Peterson, J. B. (2012). Psychological entropy: A framework for understanding uncertainty-related anxiety. *Psychological Review, 119*, 304–320. http://dx.doi.org/10.1037/a0026767

Inzlicht, M., McGregor, I., Hirsh, J. B., & Nash, K. (2009). Neural markers of religious conviction. *Psychological Science, 20*, 385–392. http://dx.doi.org/10.1111/j.1467-9280.2009.02305.x

Inzlicht, M., & Tullett, A. M. (2010). Reflecting on God: Religious primes can reduce neurophysiological response to errors. *Psychological Science, 21*, 1184–1190. http://dx.doi.org/10.1177/0956797610375451

Jamieson, D. W. (1993, August). *The attitude ambivalence construct: Validity, utility, and measurement*. Paper presented at the 101st Annual Convention of the American Psychological Association, Toronto, Ontario, Canada.

Jonas, E., McGregor, I., Klackl, J., Agroskin, D., Fritsche, I., Holbrook, C., . . . Quirin, M. (2014). Threat and defense: From anxiety to approach. *Advances in Experimental Social Psychology, 49*, 219–286. http://dx.doi.org/10.1016/B978-0-12-800052-6.00004-4

Kaplan, K. J. (1972). On the ambivalence-indifference problem in attitude theory and measurement: A suggested modification of the semantic differential technique. *Psychological Bulletin, 77*, 361–372. http://dx.doi.org/10.1037/h0032590

Kay, A. C., Gaucher, D., McGregor, I., & Nash, K. (2010). Religious belief as compensatory control. *Personality and Social Psychology Review, 14*, 37–48. http://dx.doi.org/10.1177/1088868309353750

Klackl, J., Jonas, E., & Fritsche, I. (2018). Neural evidence that the behavioral inhibition system is involved in existential threat processing. *Social Neuroscience, 13*, 355–371. http://dx.doi.org/10.1080/17470919.2017.1308880

Krosnick, J. A. (1989). Attitude importance and attitude accessibility. *Personality and Social Psychology Bulletin, 15*, 297–308. http://dx.doi.org/10.1177/0146167289153002

Luttrell, A., Stillman, P. E., Hasinski, A. E., & Cunningham, W. A. (2016). Neural dissociations in attitude strength: Distinct regions of cingulate cortex track ambivalence and certainty. *Journal of Experimental Psychology: General, 145*, 419–433. http://dx.doi.org/10.1037/xge0000141

McGregor, I. (2003). Defensive zeal: Compensatory conviction about attitudes, values, goals, groups, and self-definition in the face of personal uncertainty. In S. J. Spencer, S. Fein, M. P. Zanna, & J. M. Olson (Eds.), *Motivated social perception: The Ontario symposium* (Vol. 9, pp. 73–92). Mahwah, NJ: Erlbaum.

McGregor, I. (2006a). Offensive defensiveness: Toward an integrative neuroscience of compensatory zeal after mortality salience, personal uncertainty, and other poignant self-threats. *Psychological Inquiry, 17*, 299–308. http://dx.doi.org/10.1080/10478400701366977

McGregor, I. (2006b). Zeal appeal: The allure of moral extremes. *Basic and Applied Social Psychology, 28*, 343–348. http://dx.doi.org/10.1207/s15324834basp2804_7

McGregor, I. (2007). Personal projects as compensatory convictions: Passionate pursuit and the fugitive self. In B. R. Little, K. Salmela-Aro, & S. D. Phillips (Eds.), *Personal project pursuit: Goals, action and human flourishing* (pp. 171–195). Mahwah, NJ: Erlbaum.

McGregor, I., Gailliot, M. T., Vasquez, N. A., & Nash, K. A. (2007). Ideological and personal zeal reactions to threat among people with high self-esteem: Motivated promotion focus. *Personality and Social Psychology Bulletin, 33*, 1587–1599. http://dx.doi.org/10.1177/0146167207306280

McGregor, I., Haji, R., Nash, K. A., & Teper, R. (2008). Religious zeal and the uncertain self. *Basic and Applied Social Psychology, 30*, 183–188. http://dx.doi.org/10.1080/01973530802209251

McGregor, I., & Jordan, C. H. (2007). The mask of zeal: Low implicit self-esteem, threat, and defensive extremism. *Self and Identity, 6*, 223–237. http://dx.doi.org/10.1080/15298860601115351

McGregor, I., & Marigold, D. C. (2003). Defensive zeal and the uncertain self: What makes you so sure? *Journal of Personality and Social Psychology, 85*, 838–852. http://dx.doi.org/10.1037/0022-3514.85.5.838

McGregor, I., Nail, P. R., Marigold, D. C., & Kang, S.-J. (2005). Defensive pride and consensus: Strength in imaginary numbers. *Journal of Personality and Social Psychology, 89*, 978–996. http://dx.doi.org/10.1037/0022-3514.89.6.978

McGregor, I., Nash, K. A., & Inzlicht, M. (2009). Threat, high self-esteem, and reactive approach-motivation: Electroencephalographic evidence. *Journal of Experimental Social Psychology, 45*, 1003–1007. http://dx.doi.org/10.1016/j.jesp.2009.04.011

McGregor, I., Nash, K., Mann, N., & Phills, C. E. (2010). Anxious uncertainty and reactive approach motivation (RAM). *Journal of Personality and Social Psychology, 99*, 133–147. http://dx.doi.org/10.1037/a0019701

McGregor, I., Nash, K., & Prentice, M. (2010). Reactive approach motivation (RAM) for religion. *Journal of Personality and Social Psychology, 99*, 148–161. http://dx.doi.org/10.1037/a0019702

McGregor, I., Prentice, M., & Nash, K. (2012). Approaching relief: Compensatory ideals relieve threat-induced anxiety by promoting approach-motivated states. *Social Cognition, 30*, 689–714. http://dx.doi.org/10.1521/soco.2012.30.6.689

McGregor, I., Prentice, M., & Nash, K. (2013). Anxious uncertainty and reactive approach motivation (RAM) for religious, idealistic, and lifestyle extremes. *Journal of Social Issues, 69*, 537–563. http://dx.doi.org/10.1111/josi.12028

McGregor, I., Zanna, M. P., Holmes, J. G., & Spencer, S. J. (2001). Compensatory conviction in the face of personal uncertainty: Going to extremes and being oneself. *Journal of Personality and Social Psychology, 80*, 472–488. http://dx.doi.org/10.1037/0022-3514.80.3.472

Molden, D. C., & Finkel, E. J. (2010). Motivations for promotion and prevention and the role of trust and commitment in interpersonal forgiveness. *Journal of Experimental Social Psychology, 46*, 255–268. http://dx.doi.org/10.1016/j.jesp.2009.10.014

Nash, K., Inzlicht, M., & McGregor, I. (2012). Approach-related left prefrontal EEG asymmetry predicts muted error-related negativity. *Biological Psychology, 91*, 96–102. http://dx.doi.org/10.1016/j.biopsycho.2012.05.005

Nash, K., McGregor, I., & Prentice, M. (2011). Threat and defense as goal regulation: From implicit goal conflict to anxious uncertainty, reactive approach motivation, and ideological extremism. *Journal of Personality and Social Psychology, 101*, 1291–1301. http://dx.doi.org/10.1037/a0025944

Newby-Clark, I. R., McGregor, I., & Zanna, M. P. (2002). Thinking and caring about cognitive inconsistency: When and for whom does attitudinal ambivalence feel uncomfortable? *Journal of Personality and Social Psychology, 82*, 157–166. http://dx.doi.org/10.1037/0022-3514.82.2.157

Pallak, M. S., Brock, T. C., & Kiesler, C. A. (1967). Dissonance arousal and task performance in an incidental verbal learning paradigm. *Journal of Personality and Social Psychology, 7*, 11–20. http://dx.doi.org/10.1037/h0024894

Proulx, T., Inzlicht, M., & Harmon-Jones, E. (2012). Understanding all inconsistency compensation as a palliative response to violated expectations. *Trends in Cognitive Sciences, 16*, 285–291. http://dx.doi.org/10.1016/j.tics.2012.04.002

Pyszczynski, T. A., & Greenberg, J. (1981). Role of disconfirmed expectancies in the instigation of attributional processing. *Journal of Personality and Social Psychology, 40*, 31–38. http://dx.doi.org/10.1037/0022-3514.40.1.31

Pyszczynski, T. A., Solomon, S., & Greenberg, J. (2015). Thirty years of terror management theory: From genesis to revelation. *Advances in Experimental Social Psychology, 52*, 1–70. http://dx.doi.org/10.1016/bs.aesp.2015.03.001

Quirin, M., & Klackl, J. (2016). Existential neuroscience. In E. Harmon-Jones, & M. Inzlicht (Eds.), *Social neuroscience: Biological approaches to social psychology* (pp. 134–152). New York, NY: Routledge.

Randles, D., Heine, S. J., & Santos, N. (2013). The common pain of surrealism and death: Acetaminophen reduces compensatory affirmation following meaning threats. *Psychological Science, 24*, 966–973. http://dx.doi.org/10.1177/0956797612464786

Randles, D., Inzlicht, M., Proulx, T., Tullett, A. M., & Heine, S. J. (2015). Is dissonance reduction a special case of fluid compensation? Evidence that dissonant cognitions cause compensatory affirmation and abstraction. *Journal of Personality and Social Psychology, 108*, 697–710. http://dx.doi.org/10.1037/a0038933

Randles, D., Proulx, T., & Heine, S. J. (2011). Turn-frogs and careful-sweaters: Non-conscious perception of incongruous word pairings provokes fluid compensation. *Journal of Experimental Social Psychology, 47*, 246–249. http://dx.doi.org/10.1016/j.jesp.2010.07.020

Rogers, T. B., Kuiper, N. A., & Kirker, W. S. (1977). Self-reference and the encoding of personal information. *Journal of Personality and Social Psychology, 35*, 677–688. http://dx.doi.org/10.1037/0022-3514.35.9.677

Rosenberg, M. J., & Abelson, R. R. (1960). An analysis of cognitive balancing. In M. J. Rosenberg, C. I. Hovland, W. J. McGuire, R. R. Abelson, & J. W. Brehm (Eds.), *Attitude organization and change* (pp. 112–163). New Haven, CT: Yale University Press.

Rothschild, Z. K., Abdollahi, A., & Pyszczynski, T. (2009). Does peace have a prayer? The effect of mortality salience, compassionate values, and religious fundamentalism on hostility toward out-groups. *Journal of Experimental Social Psychology, 45*, 816–827. http://dx.doi.org/10.1016/j.jesp.2009.05.016

Schopenhauer, A. (1883). *The world as will and idea* (R. B. Haldane & J. Kemps, Trans.). London, England: Routledge & Kegan Paul. (Original work published 1818)

Schumann, K., McGregor, I., Nash, K. A., & Ross, M. (2014). Religious magnanimity: Reminding people of their religious belief system reduces hostility after threat. *Journal of Personality and Social Psychology, 107*, 432–453. http://dx.doi.org/10.1037/a0036739

Scott, W. A. (1966). Brief Report: Measures of cognitive structure. *Multivariate Behavioral Research, 1*, 391–395.

Simon, L., Greenberg, J., & Brehm, J. (1995). Trivialization: The forgotten mode of dissonance reduction. *Journal of Personality and Social Psychology, 68*, 247–260. http://dx.doi.org/10.1037/0022-3514.68.2.247

Steele, C. M. (1988). The psychology of self-affirmation: Sustaining the integrity of the self. In L. Berkowitz (Ed.), *Advances in experimental social psychology* (pp. 261–302). San Diego, CA: Academic Press. http://dx.doi.org/10.1016/S0065-2601(08)60229-4

Steele, C. M., & Josephs, R. A. (1990). Alcohol myopia. Its prized and dangerous effects. *American Psychologist, 45*, 921–933. http://dx.doi.org/10.1037/0003-066X.45.8.921

Steele, C. M., & Liu, T. J. (1983). Dissonance processes as self-affirmation. *Journal of Personality and Social Psychology, 45*, 5–19. http://dx.doi.org/10.1037/0022-3514.45.1.5

Steele, C. M., Southwick, L. L., & Critchlow, B. (1981). Dissonance and alcohol: Drinking your troubles away. *Journal of Personality and Social Psychology, 41*, 831–846. http://dx.doi.org/10.1037/0022-3514.41.5.831

Stone, J., Wiegand, A. W., Cooper, J., & Aronson, E. (1997). When exemplification fails: Hypocrisy and the motive for self-integrity. *Journal of Personality and Social Psychology, 72*, 54–65. http://dx.doi.org/10.1037/0022-3514.72.1.54

Struthers, C. W., Santelli, A. G., Khoury, C., Pang, M., Young, R. E., Kashefi, Y., . . . Vasquez, N. A. (2014). The role of victim embarrassment in explaining why apologies affect reported (but not actual) forgiveness. *Journal of Language and Social Psychology, 33*, 517–525. http://dx.doi.org/10.1177/0261927X14520983

Taylor, S. E., & Gollwitzer, P. M. (1995). Effects of mindset on positive illusions. *Journal of Personality and Social Psychology, 69*, 213–226. http://dx.doi.org/10.1037/0022-3514.69.2.213

Thompson, M. M., Zanna, M. P., & Griffin, D. W. (1995). Let's not be indifferent about (attitudinal) ambivalence. In R. E. Petty & J. A. Krosnick (Eds.), *Attitude strength: Antecedents and consequences* (pp. 361–386). Hillsdale, NJ: Erlbaum.

Todd, A. R., Forstmann, M., Burgmer, P., Brooks, A. W., & Galinsky, A. D. (2015). Anxious and egocentric: How specific emotions influence perspective taking. *Journal of Experimental Psychology: General, 144*, 374–391. http://dx.doi.org/10.1037/xge0000048

van den Bos, K., Poortvliet, P. M., Maas, M., Miedema, J., & van den Ham, E.-J. (2005). An enquiry concerning the principles of cultural norms and values: The impact of uncertainty and mortality salience on reactions to violations and bolstering of cultural worldviews. *Journal of Experimental Social Psychology, 41*, 91–113. http://dx.doi.org/10.1016/j.jesp.2004.06.001

van Veen, V., Krug, M. K., Schooler, J. W., & Carter, C. S. (2009). Neural activity predicts attitude change in cognitive dissonance. *Nature neuroscience, 12,* 1469–1474.

Wegner, D. M. (1994). Ironic processes of mental control. *Psychological Review, 101,* 34–52.

Wong, P. T., & Weiner, B. (1981). When people ask "why" questions, and the heuristics of attributional search. *Journal of Personality and Social Psychology, 40,* 650–663. http://dx.doi.org/10.1037/0022-3514.40.4.650

Zanna, M. P., & Aziza, C. (1976). On the interaction of repression-sensitization and attention in resolving cognitive dissonance. *Journal of Personality, 44,* 577–593. http://dx.doi.org/10.1111/j.1467-6494.1976.tb00139.x

Zanna, M. P., & Cooper, J. (1974). Dissonance and the pill: An attribution approach to studying the arousal properties of dissonance. *Journal of Personality and Social Psychology, 29,* 703–709. http://dx.doi.org/10.1037/h0036651

Zanna, M. P., Lepper, M. R., & Abelson, R. P. (1973). Attentional mechanisms in children's devaluation of a forbidden activity in a forced-compliance situation. *Journal of Personality and Social Psychology, 28,* 355–359. http://dx.doi.org/10.1037/h0035119

II

THE ROLE OF THE SELF IN DISSONANCE

7

Dissonance, Hypocrisy, and the Self-Concept

Elliot Aronson

This chapter focuses primarily on the relationship between cognitive dissonance and the self-concept. At the outset, however, note that when Leon Festinger invented the theory of cognitive dissonance, he conceived of dissonance arousal and reduction as a much more universal phenomenon—not as tied to a person's self-concept. Accordingly, before getting to the heart of this chapter, I trace the evolution of the theory from its exciting universalistic beginnings, in 1957, when it revolutionized the way social psychologists think about human behavior, through its "doldrums" period (roughly, 1975–1990), when it was largely ignored by most researchers, to its reemergence in the 1990s as a powerful means of predicting and changing human behavior in a variety of areas, including those that have abiding societal importance (such as condom use and water conservation).

Because dissonance theory arrived on the social psychological scene at virtually the same moment I started graduate school, my involvement with the theory is a personal one as well as an intellectual one. Accordingly, it might be useful to tell the story of the dissonance "revolution" through my own rather fortuitous experience with the theory—almost from its inception.

As a 1st-year graduate student at Stanford, in 1956, I had very little interest in social psychology, and what little I knew about that discipline seemed both boring and pedestrian. Central to social psychology was the issue of social influence, which is certainly an important topic, but in the mid-1950s, the existing

http://dx.doi.org/10.1037/0000135-007
Cognitive Dissonance, Second Edition: Reexamining a Pivotal Theory in Psychology,
E. Harmon-Jones (Editor)
Copyright © 2019 by the American Psychological Association. All rights reserved.

knowledge of social influence seemed fairly cut and dried and rather obvious. What did social psychologists know for sure about social influence at that time?

1. If you want people to go along with your position, offer tangible rewards for compliance and clear punishments for noncompliance.

2. Present an audience with a reasonable communication, attributing it to a highly credible communicator.

3. Present the individual with the illusion that everyone else in sight agrees with one another.

4. If a member of your discussion group disagrees with you, you will send him more messages (in attempt to get him to see the light) than if he agrees with you. If he persists in being stubborn, you will try to eject him from the group.

In those days, the overwhelming trend in all of American empirical psychology was "Let's find the reinforcer." If a person (or a rat) does something, there must be a reason, and that reason has to be the gaining of an identifiable reward, such as food, money, or praise, or the removing of a noxious state of affairs, such as pain, fear, or anxiety. If food will induce a hungry rat to press the lever of a Skinner box or turn left in a Y maze, surely conceptually similar rewards can induce a person to adopt a given opinion. The classic experiment that seemed to epitomize experimental social psychology in the mid-1950s was the still-classic Asch (1951) experiment, in which a unanimous majority apparently disagreed with an individual on a simple, unambiguous perceptual judgment. Why do most people conform to this kind of group pressure? Perhaps it makes them anxious to be alone against a unanimous majority; they fear being considered crazy, being held in low esteem, and so on. It's comforting to be in agreement with others. That's the reward for conformity.

Or take the equally classic experiment done by Hovland and Weiss (1951). Why do people tend to believe a statement attributed to a credible source (such as Oppenheimer) rather than a noncredible one (such as Pravda)? Perhaps it increases the probability of being right, and being right reduces anxiety and makes one feel good, smart, and esteemed. That is the reward for changing one's belief.

These data are true enough, but hardly worth getting excited about. My old bobbeh (grandmother), a fountainhead of folk wisdom, could have told me those things without having done an elaborate experiment to demonstrate the obvious. Then, in 1957, Leon Festinger invented the theory of cognitive dissonance, deftly combining cognition and motivation, and produced a revolution that revitalized social psychology and changed it forever. I first read Festinger's book in the form of a prepublication carbon copy that he thrust into my hands (rather disdainfully!) after I told him I was trying to decide whether to enroll in his graduate seminar. Reading that manuscript was something of an epiphany for me. It was (and still is) the single most exciting book I have ever read in all of psychology.

The core proposition of the theory is a very simple one: If a person were to hold two cognitions that were psychologically inconsistent, she or he would experience dissonance. Because dissonance is an unpleasant drive state (like hunger, thirst, or pain), the person will attempt to reduce it—much like she or he would try to reduce hunger, thirst, or pain. Viewed more broadly, cognitive dissonance theory is essentially a theory about sense making: how people try to make sense out of their environment and their behavior and, thus, try to lead lives that are (at least in their own mind) sensible and meaningful.

As I implied above, one of the theory's most important aspects was in the challenge it presented to the long-standing dominance of reinforcement theory as an all-purpose explanation for social psychological phenomena. To illustrate this challenge (as well as its importance), I put forth the following scenario: A young man performs a monotonous, tedious task as part of an industrial relations experiment. After completing it, he is informed that his participation as a participant is over. The experimenter then appeals to him for help. He states that his research assistant was unable to be there and asks the participant if he would help run the experiment. The experimenter explains that he is investigating the effect of people's preconceptions about their performance of a task; specifically, he wants to see if a person's performance is influenced by whether he or she is told either positive things about the task (in advance), negative things about the task (in advance), or nothing at all about the task. The next participant, who is about to arrive, is assigned to be in the favorable-information condition. The experimenter asks the participant if he would tell the incoming participant that he had just completed the task (which is true) and that he found it to be an exceedingly enjoyable one (which is not true, according to the participant's own experience). The participant is offered either $1 or $20 for telling this lie and for remaining on call in case the regular assistant cannot show up in the future.

The astute reader will recognize this as the scenario of the classic experiment by Festinger and Carlsmith (1959). I regard this experiment, because of the enormous impact it had on the field, as the single most important study ever done in social psychology. The results were striking. The participants who said that they found the task enjoyable to earn the paltry payment of $1 came to believe that it actually was enjoyable to a far greater extent than those who said it to earn the princely payment of $20. The experiment was a direct derivation from the theory of cognitive dissonance. Needless to say, reinforcement theory would suggest that, if you reward individuals for saying something, they might become infatuated with that statement (through secondary reinforcement). But dissonance theory makes precisely the opposite prediction. If I were a participant in the Festinger–Carlsmith (1959) experiment, my cognition that the task I performed was boring would be dissonant with the fact that I informed another person that it was enjoyable. If I were paid $20 for making that statement, this cognition would provide ample external justification for my action, thus reducing the dissonance. However, if I were paid only $1, I would lack sufficient external justification for having made the statement (I would be experiencing the discomfort of dissonance) and would be motivated to reduce it. In this situation, the most convenient way to reduce dissonance would be for me to try to convince myself that the task was somewhat more interesting than it seemed at first. In effect, in the process of persuading myself that the task was actually interesting, I would convince myself that my statement to the other student was not a great lie.

Similarly, in another early experiment aimed at testing dissonance theory, Aronson and Mills (1959) demonstrated that people who go through a severe initiation, to gain admission to a group, come to like that group better than people who go through a mild initiation to get into the same group. Reinforcement theory would suggest that we like people and groups that are associated with reward; dissonance theory led Aronson and Mills to the prediction that we come to like things for which we suffer. All cognitions having to do with the negative aspects of the group are dissonant with the cognition that we suffered to be admitted to the group; therefore, they get distorted in a positive direction, effectively reducing the dissonance.

Even in the early years, it was crystal clear that dissonance-generated attitude change was not limited to such trivial judgments as the dullness of a boring task or the attractiveness of a discussion group. The early researchers extended the theory to much more important opinions and attitudes, such as a striking reassessment of the dangers of smoking marijuana among students at the University of Texas (Nel, Helmreich, & Aronson, 1969), and the softening of Yale students' negative attitudes toward the alleged antistudent brutality of the New Haven police (Cohen, 1962).

IMPACT ON THE FIELD

It is hard to convey the impact these early experiments had on the social psychological community at the time of their publication. The findings startled a great many social psychologists largely because they challenged the general orientation accepted either tacitly or explicitly by the field. These results also generated enthusiasm among most social psychologists because, at the time, they represented a striking and convincing act of liberation from the dominance of a general reward-reinforcement theory. The findings of these early experiments demonstrated dramatically that at least under certain conditions, reward theory was inadequate. In doing so, dissonance research sounded a clarion call to cognitively oriented social psychologists, proclaiming in the most striking manner that human beings think, they do not always behave in a mechanistic manner. It demonstrated that human beings engage in all kinds of cognitive gymnastics aimed at justifying their own behavior.

Perhaps most important, dissonance theory inspired an enormous number and variety of hypotheses that were specific to the theory and could be tested in the laboratory. The wide array of research that dissonance theory has produced is truly astonishing. Dissonance research runs the gamut from decision making to color preferences, from the socialization of children to curing people's snake phobias, from interpersonal attraction to antecedents of hunger and thirst, from the proselytizing behavior of religious zealots to the behavior of gamblers at racetracks, from inducing people to conserve water by taking showers to selective informational exposure, from helping people curb their temptation to cheat at a game of cards to inducing people to practice safer sex.

The impact of dissonance theory went even beyond the generation of new and exciting knowledge. Given the nature of the hypotheses we were testing, dissonance researchers were forced to develop a new experimental methodology—a powerful, high-impact set of procedures that allowed us to ask truly important questions in a very precise manner. As we all know, the laboratory tends to be an artificial environment. But dissonance research made it necessary to overcome that artificiality by developing a methodology that would enmesh participants in a set of events—a drama, if you will—which made it impossible for them to avoid taking these events seriously.

In my writing on research methods (Aronson & Carlsmith, 1968; Aronson, Ellsworth, Carlsmith, & Gonzales, 1990) I have referred to this strategy as establishing *experimental reality* where, within the admittedly phony confines of the lab, the experimenter makes certain that real things are happening to real people. Because of the nature of our hypotheses, we could not afford the luxury, so common in contemporary research, of having participants passively look at a videotape of events happening to someone else and then make judgments about them. Rather, our research questions required the construction of an elaborate scenario in which participants became immersed. Thus, what dissonance research brought into focus more clearly than any other body of work is the fact that the social psychological laboratory, with all of its contrivances and complex scenarios, can produce clear, powerful effects that are conceptually replicable in both the laboratory and the real world.

DISSONANCE AND THE SELF: THE POWER OF SELF-PERSUASION

Research has shown that the persuasive effects in the experiments discussed previously are more powerful and more persistent than those resulting from persuasion techniques based on rewards, punishments, or source credibility (e.g., Freedman, 1965). The major reason is that the arousal of dissonance always entails relatively high levels of personal involvement and, therefore, the reduction of dissonance requires some form of self-justification. From the very outset, some of us who were working closely with the theory felt that at its core it led to clear and unambiguous predictions, but around the edges it was a little too vague. Several situations arose in which it was not entirely clear what dissonance theory would predict or, indeed, whether dissonance theory even made a prediction. Around 1958, the standing joke among Festinger's research assistants was, "If you really want to be sure whether A is dissonant with B, ask Leon!" Although this was said with our tongues firmly planted in our cheeks, it reflected the fact that we argued a lot about whether dissonance theory applied in a wide variety of situations.

What comes to mind most specifically are two strenuous running arguments that Festinger and I had about two of his classic examples. The first involved a person stepping outside in a rainstorm and not getting wet. Festinger was convinced that this would arouse a great deal of dissonance, whereas I had considerable difficulty seeing it. My disagreement went something like this: "What's that got to do with him? It's a strange phenomenon, all right, but unless he feared he was losing his mind, I don't see the dissonance."

The second was Festinger's classic example of a situation in which dissonance theory did not apply. This was the case of a man driving, late at night, on a lonely country road and getting a flat tire (Festinger, 1957, pp. 277–278). Lo and behold, when he opened the trunk of his car, he discovered he did not have a jack. Leon maintained that, although the person would experience frustration, disappointment, and perhaps even fear, there were no dissonant cognitions in that situation. My argument was succinct: "Of course there is dissonance! What kind of idiot would go driving late at night on a lonely country road without a jack in his car?" "But," Leon countered, "where are the dissonant cognitions?"

It took me a couple of years, but it gradually dawned on me that what was at the heart of my argument in both of those situations was the self-concept. That is, when I said above that dissonance theory made clear predictions at its core, what I implicitly meant by *at its core* were situations in which the person's self-concept was at issue. Thus, in the raindrop situation, as far as I could judge, the self was not involved. In the flat tire situation, the self-concept was involved; what was dissonant was (a) the driver's cognition about his idiotic behavior with (b) his self-concept of being a reasonably smart guy. Accordingly, I wrote a monograph (Aronson, 1960), in which I argued that dissonance theory makes its strongest predictions when an important element of the self-concept is threatened, typically when a person performs a behavior that is inconsistent with his or her sense of self. Initially, I intended this not to be a major modification of the theory, but only an attempt to tighten the predictions a bit. That is, in my opinion, this tightening retained the core notion of inconsistency but shifted the emphasis to the self-concept—thus, clarifying more precisely when the theory did or did not apply. I believe that this apparently minor modification of dissonance theory turned out to have important ramifications inasmuch as it increased the predictive power of the theory without seriously limiting its scope.

In addition, this modification uncovered a hidden assumption contained in the original theory. Festinger's original statement and all of the early experiments rested on the implicit assumption that people have a reasonably positive self-concept. But if a person considered himself or herself to be a "schnook," he or she might expect to do schnooky things—like go through a severe initiation to get into a group or say things that he or she didn't quite believe. For such people, dissonance would not be aroused under the same conditions as for people with a favorable view of themselves. Rather, dissonance would occur when negative self-expectancies were violated, that is, when the person with a poor self-concept engaged in a behavior that reflected positively on the self.

To test this assumption, Merrill Carlsmith and I conducted a simple little experiment that demonstrated that under certain conditions, college students would be made uncomfortable with success; that they would prefer to be accurate in predicting their own behavior, even if it meant setting themselves up for failure. Specifically, we found that students who had developed negative self-expectancies regarding their performance on a task showed evidence of dissonance arousal when faced with success on that task. That is, after repeated failure at the task, participants who later achieved a successful performance actually changed their responses from accurate to inaccurate ones, to preserve a consistent, though negative, self-concept (Aronson & Carlsmith, 1962). (In recent years, Swann and his students have confirmed this basic finding in a number of experiments and quasi-experiments; Swann, 1984, 1990, 1996; Swann & Pelham, 1988; Swann & Read, 1981).

A few years later, I carried this reasoning a step further (Aronson, 1968; Aronson, Chase, Helmreich, & Ruhnke, 1974), elaborating on the centrality of the self-concept in dissonance processes and suggesting that in this regard, people generally strive to maintain a sense of self that is both consistent and positive. That is, because most people have relatively favorable views of themselves, they want to see themselves as (a) competent, (b) moral, and (c) able to predict their own behavior.

In summary, efforts to reduce dissonance involve a process of self-justification because, in most instances, people experience dissonance after engaging in an action that leaves them feeling stupid, immoral, or confused (see Aronson et al., 1974). Moreover, the greater the personal commitment or self-involvement implied by the action and the smaller the external justification for that action, the greater the dissonance and, therefore, the more powerful the need for self-justification. Thus, in the Festinger–Carlsmith experiment, the act of deceiving another person would make one feel immoral or guilty. To reduce that dissonance, one must convince oneself that little or no deception was involved, in other words, that the task was, in fact, a rather interesting activity. By justifying one's actions in this fashion, one is able to restore a sense of self as morally good. In the Aronson and Mills' (1959) experiment, going through hell and high water to gain admission to a boring discussion group was dissonant with one's self-concept as a smart and reasonable person, who makes smart and reasonable decisions.

SCOPE VERSUS TIGHTNESS IN THEORY BUILDING

All theories are lies. That is, all theories are only approximations of the empirical domain they are trying to describe. Accordingly, it is inevitable that theories will evolve and change to accommodate new data that are being generated. Indeed, it is the duty of theorists to modify their theory in the face of new data and new ideas. Festinger understood this better than most theorists. At the same time, understandably, he was deeply enamored of both the elegant simplicity and the breadth of his original theoretical statement. When I first came out with the self-concept notion of dissonance, Festinger was not pleased. He felt that although my revision had led to some interesting research, conceptually, I was limiting the scope of the theory far too much. I agreed that the scope was a bit smaller, but I believed that the increased accuracy of prediction (the added tightness) was worth the slightly more limited scope. In 1987, while serving as a discussant at the American Psychological Association symposium on cognitive dissonance, Festinger acknowledged the dilemma of the theorist who has a hard time seeing his theory change yet knows that change it must. (One might say that this is a situation bound to produce considerable dissonance in the theorist!). In typical fashion, Leon poked fun at himself for trying to cling to the original conceptualization even though he knew better (see Appendix B, this volume, for the complete transcript of this talk):

> No theory is going to be inviolate. Let me put it clearly. The only kind of theory that can be proposed and ever will be proposed that absolutely will remain inviolate for decades, certainly centuries, is a theory that is not testable. If a theory is at all testable, it will not remain unchanged. It has to change. All theories are wrong. One doesn't ask about theories, can I show that they are wrong or can I show that they are right, but rather one asks, how much of the empirical realm can it handle and how must it be modified and changed as it matures?
>
> As a lot of people know, I ended up leaving social psychology, meaning dissonance theory, and I want to clarify that. Lack of activity is not the same as lack of interest. Lack of activity is not desertion. I left and stopped doing research on the theory of dissonance because I was in a total rut. The only thing I could think about was how correct the original statement had been . . . how every word in that book was perfect. So to me, I did a good thing for cognitive dissonance by leaving it. I think if I had stayed in it, I might have retarded progress for cognitive dissonance for at least a decade. (pp. 382–383)

In theory building, there is always a tension between scope and precision; generally speaking, one usually gains precision at the price of scope. The self-concept notion strikes a pretty good balance between scope and precision. My guess is that sooner or later, someone will come along with a richer conceptualization that will strike a better balance. When that happens, I hope I will have the good grace to applaud.

THE SELF-CONCEPT AND THE INDUCTION OF HYPOCRISY

In recent years, the self-concept notion of dissonance has led us into areas of investigation that would not have been feasible under the rubric of Festinger's initial formulation. One of these involves the induction of feelings of hypocrisy. This discovery came about quite by accident. At the time, I was not even thinking about theory development but was struggling to find an effective way to convince sexually active college students to use condoms in this, the era of AIDS. The problem is not an easy one to solve, because it transcends the simple conveying of information to rational people. College students already have the requisite information, that is, virtually all sexually active college students know that condoms are an effective way to prevent AIDS. The problem is that the vast majority are not using condoms, because they consider them to be a nuisance, unromantic, and unspontaneous. In my research, I had run into a stone wall; I had tried several of the traditional, direct persuasive techniques (powerful videos, aimed at arousing fear or at eroticizing the condom) with very limited success. Whatever impact my videos did have was of very short duration; our participants would try condoms once or twice and then stop using them.

Eventually, I thought about using the counterattitudinal-attitude paradigm. That is, why not try to get people to argue against their own attitudes, as in the Festinger–Carlsmith (1959) experiment? On the surface, it seemed like a great idea. After all, we had found that this strategy was powerful and, when judiciously applied, had long-term effects on attitudes and behavior—precisely what was needed in this societal situation. But wait a minute: In the condom use situation, there were no counterattitudinal attitudes to address. That is, our surveys and interviews had demonstrated that sexually active young adults already were in favor of people using condoms to prevent AIDS. They simply weren't using them. They seemed to be in a state of denial: denying that the dangers of unprotected sex applied to them in the same way they applied to everyone else. How could we invoke the counterattitudinal-attitude paradigm if there was no counterattitude to invoke?

It occurred to me that the solution had to come from the self-concept, because being in denial is not an attractive thing to be doing. The challenge was to find a way to place the person in a situation where the act of denial would be infeasible, because it would conflict, in some way, with his or her positive image of their selves. And then it struck me. Suppose you are a sexually active college student and, like most, (a) you do not use condoms regularly, and (b) being in denial, you have managed to ignore the dangers inherent in having unprotected sex. Suppose, upon going home for Christmas vacation, you find that Charlie, your 16-year-old brother has just discovered sex and is in the process of boasting to you about his many and varied sexual encounters. What do you say to him? Chances are, as a caring, responsible older sibling, you will dampen his enthusiasm a bit by warning him about the dangers of AIDS and other sexually transmitted diseases and urge him to, at least, take proper precautions by using condoms.

Suppose that I am a friend of the family who was invited to dinner and who happened to overhear this exchange between you and your brother. What if I were to pull you aside and say, "That was very good advice you gave Charlie. I am very proud of you for being so responsible. By the way, how frequently do you use condoms?" In other words, by getting you to think about that, I am confronting you with your own hypocrisy. According to the self-concept version of the theory, this would produce dissonance because you are not practicing what you are preaching. That is, for most people, their self-concept does not include behaving like a hypocrite.

My students and I then proceeded to design and conduct a simple little experiment following the scenario outlined above (Aronson, Fried, & Stone, 1991). In a 2 × 2 factorial design, in one condition, college students were induced to make a videotape in which they urged their audience to use condoms; they were told that the video would be shown to high school students. In the other major condition, the college students simply rehearsed the arguments without making the video. Cutting across these conditions was the "mindfulness" manipulation: In one set of conditions, our participants were made mindful of the fact that they themselves were not practicing what they were preaching. To accomplish this, we asked them to think about all those situations where they found it particularly difficult or impossible to use condoms in the recent past. In the other set of conditions, we did nothing to make the students mindful of their past failures to use condoms.

The one cell we expected to produce dissonance was the one high in hypocrisy, that is, where participants made the video and were given the opportunity to dredge up memories of situations where they failed to use condoms. Again, how did we expect them to reduce dissonance? By increasing the strength of their intention to use condoms in the future. And that is precisely what we got. Those participants who were in the high-dissonance (hypocrisy) condition showed the greatest intention to increase their use of condoms. Moreover, 2 months later, there was a tendency for the participants in the high-dissonance cell to report using condoms a higher percentage of the time than in any of the other three cells.

In a follow-up experiment (Stone, Aronson, Crain, Winslow, & Fried, 1994), we strengthened the manipulations of the initial experiment and used a "behavioroid" measure of the dependent variable. Specifically, in each of the conditions described above, participants were subsequently provided with an opportunity to purchase condoms at a very substantial discount (10¢ each). The results were unequivocally as predicted. Fully 83% of the participants in the hypocrisy condition purchased condoms; this was a significantly greater percentage than in each of the other three conditions, none of which were reliably different from each other. The effect was a powerful and long-lasting one: Three months after the induction of hypocrisy, a telephone survey indicated that 92% of the participants in the hypocrisy condition were still using condoms regularly, a figure that was significantly different from the control conditions.

Subsequently, we increased our confidence in the efficacy of the induction-of-hypocrisy paradigm by testing the paradigm in a different situation, one in which we could get a direct behavioral measure of the dependent variable. We found one in the shower room of our campus field house. As you may know, central California has a chronic water shortage. On our campus, the administration is constantly trying to find ways to induce students to conserve water. So we decided to test our hypothesis by using dissonance theory and the induction of hypocrisy to convince students to take shorter showers. What we discovered was that although it is impossible, within the bounds of propriety, to follow people into their bedrooms and observe their condom-using behavior, it was easily possible to follow people into the shower rooms and observe their shower-taking behavior.

In this experiment (Dickerson, Thibodeau, Aronson, & Miller, 1992), we went to the university field house and intercepted college women who had just finished swimming in a highly chlorinated pool and were on their way to take a shower. Just like in the condom experiment, it was a 2 × 2 design, in which we varied commitment and mindfulness. In the commitment conditions, each student was asked if she would be willing to sign a flyer encouraging people to conserve water at the field house. The students were told that the flyers would be displayed on posters, and each was shown a sample poster: a large, colorful, very public display. The flyer read: "Take shorter showers. Turn off water while soaping up. If I can do it, so can you!" After the student signed the flyer, we thanked her for her time, and she proceeded to the shower room, where our undergraduate research assistant (unaware of condition) was unobtrusively waiting (with hidden waterproof stopwatch) to time the student's shower. In the mindful conditions, we also asked the students to respond to a water conservation survey, which consisted of items designed to make them aware of their proconservation attitudes and the fact that their typical showering behavior was sometimes wasteful.

The results are consistent with those in the condom experiment: We found dissonance effects only in the cell where the participants were preaching what they were not always practicing. That is, in the condition where the students were induced to advocate short showers and were made mindful of their own past behavior, they took very short showers. To be specific, in the high-dissonance cell, the length of the average shower (which, because of the chlorine in the swimming pool, included a shampoo and cream rinse) averaged just over 3 min 30 sec (that's short!) and was significantly shorter than in the control condition.

How can we be certain that dissonance is involved in these experiments? Although the data are consistent with the self-concept formulation of dissonance theory, there is another plausible interpretation. It is conceivable that the effects of the hypocrisy manipulation may have been due to the effects of priming. The combination of proattitudinal advocacy and the salience of past behavior may have served, in an additive fashion, to make participants' positive attitudes toward condom use or water conservation highly accessible, thus fostering a stronger correspondence between their attitudes and behavior (e.g., Fazio, 1989). What is needed to pin it down is evidence that the hypocrisy effect involves physiological arousal, thereby indicating the presence of dissonance rather than the mere influence of attitude salience.

An experiment by Fried and Aronson (1995) provides exactly this sort of evidence. Within the context of the hypocrisy paradigm, this experiment used a misattribution-of-arousal manipulation, a strategy brilliantly developed in earlier research to document the existence of dissonance as an uncomfortable state of arousal by Zanna and Cooper (1974). Zanna and Cooper found that when participants were given an opportunity to misattribute their arousal to a source other than their dissonance-arousing behavior—for example, to an overheated room, a placebo, or glaring florescent lights—the attitude change typically associated with dissonance reduction no longer occurs.

Using a modified version of the earlier condom experiments, Fried and Aronson's (1995) study required participants to compose and deliver proattitudinal, videotaped speeches advocating the importance of recycling. These speeches were ostensibly to be shown to various groups as part of a campaign to increase participation in recycling programs on campus and in the larger community. Hypocrisy was induced in half the participants by asking them to list recent examples of times when they had failed to recycle; the other half simply wrote and delivered the speech, without being reminded of their wasteful behavior. In addition, half the participants in each condition were given an opportunity to misattribute arousal to various environmental factors within the laboratory setting. Specifically, participants were asked to answer questions regarding the room's fighting, temperature, and noise level, including how these ambient factors might have affected them. (This was accomplished under the guise of asking participants to rate the room's suitability for use as laboratory space—a request that was made to appear unrelated to the activities in which participants were participating.) To summarize, proattitudinal advocacy was held constant, and the salience of past behavior and the opportunity for misattribution were manipulated, yielding a 2 × 2 factorial design with the following conditions: (a) hypocrisy (high salience), (b) hypocrisy with misattribution, (c) no hypocrisy (low salience), and (d) no hypocrisy with misattribution. Dissonance reduction was measured by asking participants to volunteer to help a local recycling organization by making phone calls soliciting support for recycling.

The results of this experiment revealed that arousal was indeed present within the hypocrisy conditions. Hypocrisy participants who were not afforded the opportunity to misattribute the source of their arousal volunteered significantly more often, and for longer blocks of time, than participants in the other experimental conditions. Moreover, volunteer behavior for hypocrisy participants who were allowed to misattribute their arousal was no greater than for participants who were not exposed to the hypocrisy manipulation.

More recently, the hypocrisy paradigm has been tested and extended to a great many areas, including health, the environment, and politics by Jeff Stone and his students (e.g., Focella & Stone, 2013; Focella, Stone, Fernandez, Cooper, & Hogg, 2016; Stone & Fernandez, 2011; Stone & Focella, 2011).

HYPOCRISY: DISSONANCE IN THE ABSENCE OF AVERSIVE CONSEQUENCES

As I stated above, the initial reason for the development of the hypocrisy paradigm was couched in my attempt to apply dissonance theory to the solution of a societal problem. The hidden bonus was that it also shed some light on an interesting theoretical controversy among dissonance theorists. I should say at the outset that dissonance research tends to be a family business; thus, the controversies are invariably friendly arguments, around the dinner table as it were. One such controversy involves the new look theory, developed several years ago by Cooper and Fazio (1984). In examining the early forced-compliance experiments, such as the Festinger–Carlsmith (1959) experiment and the Nel et al. (1969) experiment, Cooper and Fazio made an interesting discovery: In these experiments, participants not only experienced cognitive dissonance but also inflicted aversive consequences on the recipient of their communication; that is, lying to another person is presumed to have aversive consequences to that person. Their next step was a bold one: Cooper and Fazio asserted that dissonance was not due to inconsistent cognitions at all, but, rather, was aroused only when a person felt personally responsible for bringing about an aversive or unwanted event. Or, to put it in my terms, dissonance was caused solely by the person's doing harm to another person, which was a threat to the person's self-concept as a morally good human being.

Although I always appreciated the boldness implicit in Cooper and Fazio's (1984) theorizing, I could never bring myself to buy into the notion that aversive consequences are essential for the existence of dissonance. Moreover, in terms of my earlier discussion of scope versus tightness, it seems to me that Cooper and Fazio's conception is limiting the scope of the theory enormously while gaining nothing in tightness that wasn't already present in the self-concept notion.

How would one test this difference empirically? Several years ago, I was at a loss as to how to produce inconsistency in the Festinger and Carlsmith (1959) type of experiment without also producing aversive consequences for the recipient of one's message. That is, if you are misleading another person, by telling her or him something you believe is false, then you are always bringing about aversive consequences. But without quite realizing it, my students and I seem to have stumbled onto the solution with the hypocrisy experiments. In this procedure, the participants are preaching what they are not practicing (and are, therefore, experiencing dissonance), but where are the aversive consequences for the audience in the condom experiment? There are none. Indeed, to the extent that the "hypocrites" succeed in being persuasive, far from producing aversive consequences for the recipients, they may well be saving their lives. And still, it is clear from the data that our participants were experiencing dissonance. For a fuller discussion of this theoretical controversy, see Thibodeau and Aronson (1992).

SELF-JUSTIFICATION AND SELF-ESTEEM— SOME UNSUBSTANTIATED SPECULATIONS

From the very beginning, I found dissonance theory to be a powerful explanation for a wide swath of human behavior. The scientist in me was always delighted by the exciting, nonobvious predictions generated by the theory, as well as the creative experimentation used to test these predictions. But at the same time, the humanist in me was always a bit troubled by the rather bleak, rather unappetizing picture the theory painted of the human condition—forever striving to justify our actions after the fact. Over the past few years, my reasoning about dissonance and the self-concept has led me to speculate about how a person's self-esteem might interact with the experiencing and reduction of dissonance. These speculations might suggest a more complete picture of human nature. Note two intriguing experiments in the dissonance literature. First, consider an experiment I did a great many years ago with David Mettee (Aronson & Mettee, 1968), in which we demonstrated that if we temporarily raised a person's self-esteem, it would serve to insulate him or her from performing an immoral act such as cheating. We found that the higher self-esteem served to make the anticipation of doing something immoral more dissonant than it would have been otherwise. Thus, when our participants were put in a situation in which they had an opportunity to win money by unobtrusively cheating at a game of cards, they were able to say to themselves, in effect, "Wonderful people like me don't cheat!" And they succeeded in resisting the temptation to cheat to a greater extent than those in the control condition.

Now consider an experiment performed by Glass (1964). In this study, people were put in a situation where they were induced to deliver a series of electric shocks to other people. They then had an opportunity to evaluate their victims. Dissonance theory predicts that if individuals are feeling awful about having hurt someone, one way to reduce the dissonance is to convince themselves that their victim is a dreadful person who deserved to suffer the pain of electric shock. What Glass found was that it was precisely those individuals who had the highest self-esteem who derogated their victims the most. Consider the irony: It is precisely because I think I am such a nice person that if I do something that causes you pain, I must convince myself that you are a rat. In other words, because nice guys like me don't go around hurting innocent people, you must have deserved every nasty thing I did to you. On the other hand, if I already consider myself to be something of a scoundrel, then causing others to suffer does not introduce as much dissonance; therefore, I have less of a need to convince myself that you deserved your fate. The ultimate tragedy, of course, is that once I succeed in convincing myself that you are a dreadful person, it lowers my inhibitions against doing you further damage.

Aronson and Mettee (1968) showed that high self-esteem can serve as a buffer against immoral behavior, whereas Glass (1964) showed that once a person commits an immoral action, high self-esteem leads him or her into a situation where he or she might commit further mischief. In pondering these two experiments, I have come to the conclusion that it is far too simplistic to think of self-esteem as a one-dimensional phenomenon—either high or low. My reasoning here is similar to that of Baumeister (1998); Kernis, Cornell, Sun, Berry, and Harlow (1993); Rohan (1996); and Waschull and Kernis (1996). My notion is that self-esteem can be high or low and either fragile or well-grounded. *Well-grounded* in this context means that a positive self-image has been developed and held during a great deal of past behavior, whereas *fragile* suggests that a positive self-image has never been securely developed. People with high and well-grounded self-esteem need not be concerned with developing or verifying their self-image and can enter situations with the confident knowledge that they are competent, moral people. On the other hand, people with high and fragile self-esteem, because of their lack of a secure self-image, are overly concerned with trying to preserve images of themselves as being competent and moral at all costs.

Typically, people with high and fragile self-esteem, in their zeal to maintain a belief in their own competence and virtue, often boast about their achievements—trying desperately to convince themselves and others that they are terrific. But their boasting behavior, their misjudgments, their errors, and the wrong turns they make because they are thinking more about themselves than the situation they are in all tend to shatter the fragile image they are trying to defend. As a result, they frequently feel like impostors and are forever trying to prove that they are not. Thus, they are trying to win every possible argument, pushing themselves to believe they are always right, justifying their behavior to themselves at every turn, and explaining away failures and mistakes instead of attending to them long enough to learn from them.

In contrast, people with high and well-grounded self-esteem are not invested in winning arguments for winning's sake, do not need to believe they are always right, do not need to explain away failures and mistakes, and do not need to engage in the almost frantic self-justification in which high and fragile self-esteem people constantly engage. Instead, when they fail or make mistakes, people with high and well-grounded self-esteem can look at their failures and mistakes and learn from them. For example, a person with high, well-grounded self-esteem can look at his or her errors and say, in effect, "I screwed up. I did a stupid (or hurtful or immoral) thing. But just because I did a stupid (or hurtful or immoral) thing this time, this doesn't make me a stupid (or hurtful or immoral) person. Let me look at it. How did it come about? How can I make it better? What can I learn from this situation, so that I might decrease the possibility that I'll screw up in a similar way again?"

At this point, I have no idea whether the fragile and well-grounded dimension of self-esteem is normally distributed. If I were to hazard a guess, I would speculate that high, well-grounded self-esteem is not a common thing; accordingly, my guess is that the majority of people who score high on general measures of self-esteem would cluster near the fragile end of the continuum. If this were true, it would certainly account for the behavior of Glass's (1964) high-self-esteem participants who did not hesitate to derogate their victim. In contrast, people with high, well-grounded self-esteem would not use derogation of the victim as a way to reduce their dissonance; rather, they would be more likely to take responsibility for their actions and try, in some way, to make amends for their cruel behavior.

This strikes me as an important area of inquiry. Again, these are mere speculations; I have no data to confirm them. Somehow, it seems reasonable to end this chapter with unsubstantiated speculation because, for me, it has always been the interesting loose ends that make science such an exciting enterprise.

REFERENCES

Aronson, E. (1960). *The cognitive and behavioral consequences of the confirmation and disconfirmation of expectancies* [Grant proposal]. Harvard University.

Aronson, E. (1968). Dissonance theory: Progress and problems. In R. P. Abelson, E. Aronson, W. J. McGuire, T. M. Newcomb, M. J. Rosenberg, & P. H. Tannenbaum (Eds.), *Theories of cognitive consistency: A sourcebook*. Chicago, IL: Rand McNally.

Aronson, E., & Carlsmith, J. M. (1962). Performance expectancy as a determinant of actual performance. *Journal of Abnormal and Social Psychology, 65*, 178–182. http://dx.doi.org/10.1037/h0042291

Aronson, E., & Carlsmith, J. M. (1968). Experimentation in social psychology. In G. Lindzey & E. Aronson (Eds.), *The handbook of social psychology* (2nd ed., Vol. 2, pp. 1–79). Reading, MA: Addison-Wesley.

Aronson, E., Chase, T., Helmreich, R., & Ruhnke, R. (1974). A two-factor theory of dissonance reduction: The effect of feeling stupid or feeling awful on opinion change. *International Journal for Research and Communication, 3*, 59–74.

Aronson, E., Ellsworth, P., Carlsmith, J. M., & Gonzales, M. H. (1990). *Methods of research in social psychology*. New York, NY: McGraw Hill.

Aronson, E., Fried, C., & Stone, J. (1991). Overcoming denial and increasing the intention to use condoms through the induction of hypocrisy. *American Journal of Public Health, 81*, 1636–1638. http://dx.doi.org/10.2105/AJPH.81.12.1636

Aronson, E., & Mettee, D. R. (1968). Dishonest behavior as a function of differential levels of induced self-esteem. *Journal of Personality and Social Psychology, 9*, 121–127. http://dx.doi.org/10.1037/h0025853

Aronson, E., & Mills, J. (1959). The effect of severity of initiation on liking for a group. *Journal of Abnormal and Social Psychology, 59*, 177–181. http://dx.doi.org/10.1037/h0047195

Asch, S. E. (1951). Effects of group pressure upon the modification and distortion of judgments. In H. Guetzkow (Ed.), *Groups, leadership and men* (pp. 177–190). Pittsburgh, PA: Carnegie Press.

Baumeister, R. E. (1998). The self. In D. Gilbert, S. Fiske, & G. Lindzey (Eds.), *The handbook of social psychology* (4th ed., pp. 680–740). Boston, MA: McGraw-Hill.

Cohen, A. R. (1962). An experiment on small rewards for discrepant compliance and attitude change. In J. W. Brehm & A. R. Cohen (Eds.), *Explorations in cognitive dissonance* (pp. 73–78). New York, NY: Wiley.

Cooper, J., & Fazio, R. H. (1984). A new look at dissonance theory. In L. Berkowitz (Ed.), *Advances in experimental social psychology* (Vol. 17, pp. 229–266). Orlando, FL: Academic Press.

Dickerson, C., Thibodeau, R., Aronson, E., & Miller, D. (1992). Using cognitive dissonance to encourage water conservation. *Journal of Applied Social Psychology, 22*, 841–854. http://dx.doi.org/10.1111/j.1559-1816.1992.tb00928.x

Fazio, R. H. (1989). On the power and functionality of attitudes: The role of attitude accessibility. In A. R. Pratkanis, S. J. Breckler, & A. G. Greenwald (Eds.), *Attitude structure and function* (pp. 153–179). Hillsdale, NJ: Erlbaum.

Festinger, L. (1957). *A theory of cognitive dissonance*. Evanston, IL: Row, Peterson.

Festinger, L., & Carlsmith, J. M. (1959). Cognitive consequences of forced compliance. *Journal of Abnormal and Social Psychology, 58*, 203–210. http://dx.doi.org/10.1037/h0041593

Focella, E., & Stone, J. (2013). The use of hypocrisy for promoting environmentally sustainable behaviors. In H. van Tripp (Ed.), *Encouraging Sustainable Behavior* (pp. 203–218). New York, NY: Psychology Press.

Focella, E., Stone, J., Fernandez, N. C., Cooper, J., & Hogg, M. (2016). Vicarious hypocrisy: Bolstering attitudes and taking action after exposure to a hypocritical ingroup member. *Journal of Experimental Social Psychology, 62*, 89–102. http://dx.doi.org/10.1016/j.jesp.2015.09.014

Freedman, J. (1965). Long-term behavioral effects of cognitive dissonance. *Journal of Experimental Social Psychology, 1*, 145–155. http://dx.doi.org/10.1016/0022-1031(65)90042-9

Fried, C. B., & Aronson, E. (1995). Hypocrisy, misattribution, and dissonance reduction. *Personality and Social Psychology Bulletin, 21,* 925–933. http://dx.doi.org/10.1177/0146167295219007

Glass, D. C. (1964). Changes in liking as a means of reducing cognitive discrepancies between self-esteem and aggression. *Journal of Personality, 32,* 531–549. http://dx.doi.org/10.1111/j.1467-6494.1964.tb01357.x

Hovland, C. I., & Weiss, W. (1951). The influence of source credibility on communication effectiveness. *Public Opinion Quarterly, 15,* 635–650. http://dx.doi.org/10.1086/266350

Kernis, M. H., Cornell, D. P., Sun, C.-R., Berry, A., & Harlow, T. (1993). There's more to self-esteem than whether it is high or low: The importance of stability of self-esteem. *Journal of Personality and Social Psychology, 65,* 1190–1204. http://dx.doi.org/10.1037/0022-3514.65.6.1190

Nel, E., Helmreich, R., & Aronson, E. (1969). Opinion change in the advocate as a function of the persuasibility of his audience: A clarification of the meaning of dissonance. *Journal of Personality and Social Psychology, 12,* 117–124. http://dx.doi.org/10.1037/h0027566

Rohan, M. J. (1996). *The performance-integrity framework: A new solution to an old problem* (Unpublished doctoral dissertation). University of Waterloo, Waterloo, Ontario, Canada.

Stone, J., Aronson, E., Crain, A. L., Winslow, M. P., & Fried, C. B. (1994). Inducing hypocrisy as a means of encouraging young adults to use condoms. *Personality and Social Psychology Bulletin, 20,* 116–128. http://dx.doi.org/10.1177/0146167294201012

Stone, J., & Fernandez, N. C. (2011). When thinking about less failure causes more dissonance: The effect of elaboration and recall on behavior change following hypocrisy. *Social Influence, 6,* 199–211. http://dx.doi.org/10.1080/15534510.2011.618368

Stone, J., & Focella, E. (2011). Hypocrisy, dissonance and the self-regulation processes that improve health. *Self and Identity, 10,* 295–303. http://dx.doi.org/10.1080/15298868.2010.538550

Swann, W. B., Jr. (1984). Quest for accuracy in person perception: A matter of pragmatics. *Psychological Review, 91,* 457–477. http://dx.doi.org/10.1037/0033-295X.91.4.457

Swann, W. B., Jr. (1990). To be adored or to be known? The interplay of self-enhancement and self-verification. In R. M. Sorrentino & E. T. Higgins (Eds.), *Handbook of motivation and cognition* (pp. 408–448). New York, NY: Guilford Press.

Swann, W. B., Jr. (1996). *Self-traps: The elusive quest for higher self-esteem.* New York, NY: Freeman.

Swann, W. B., Jr., & Pelham, B. W. (1988). *The social construction of identity: Self-verification through friend and intimate selection* (Unpublished manuscript). University of Texas at Austin.

Swann, W. B., Jr., & Read, S. J. (1981). Acquiring self-knowledge: The search for feedback that fits. *Journal of Personality and Social Psychology, 41,* 1119–1128. http://dx.doi.org/10.1037/0022-3514.41.6.1119

Thibodeau, R., & Aronson, E. (1992). Taking a closer look: Reasserting the role of the self-concept in dissonance theory. *Personality and Social Psychology Bulletin, 18,* 591–602. http://dx.doi.org/10.1177/0146167292185010

Waschull, S., & Kernis, M. (1996). Level and stability of self-esteem as predictors of children's intrinsic motivation and reasons for anger. *Personality and Social Psychology Bulletin, 22,* 4–13. http://dx.doi.org/10.1177/0146167296221001

Zanna, M. P., & Cooper, J. (1974). Dissonance and the pill: An attribution approach to studying the arousal properties of dissonance. *Journal of Personality and Social Psychology, 29,* 703–709. http://dx.doi.org/10.1037/h0036651

Self-Affirmation Theory
An Update and Appraisal

Joshua Aronson, Geoffrey Cohen, and Paul R. Nail

Because the main propositions of dissonance theory have been confirmed with sufficient regularity, there is not a great deal to be gained from further research in this area.
—E. E. JONES, THE HANDBOOK OF
SOCIAL PSYCHOLOGY (1985, P. 57)

Uncharacteristically, time has proven Ned Jones (E.E. Jones, 1985) wrong. Dissonance theory is now more than 60 years old, and as the content of this volume demonstrates, there is much to be gained from researching dissonance phenomena. Moreover, it is clear that the reports by Jones and others of waning interest in the theory were premature. This volume attests to the considerable research activity that has repopulated the journals with dissonance studies. In a computer search on *PsycINFO*, we found 68 journal articles published between 1991 and 1996 explicitly focusing on dissonance theory, a healthy increase from the 38 articles published between 1985 and 1990.

In this chapter, we discuss *self-affirmation theory* (Steele, 1988),[1] a theoretical development that we see as a major force in sparking the resurgent interest and progress in the study of dissonance processes. Although it is a broad theory, addressing self-esteem maintenance processes underlying an array of phenomena, a good deal of the published research on self-affirmation theory has sought to provide alternative explanations for dissonance effects.

---

[1] The writing of this chapter benefited greatly from many delightful conversations with Claude Steele.

http://dx.doi.org/10.1037/0000135-008
Cognitive Dissonance, Second Edition: Reexamining a Pivotal Theory in Psychology,
E. Harmon-Jones (Editor)
Copyright © 2019 by the American Psychological Association. All rights reserved.

We do not argue that self-affirmation theory is a more correct statement about human thought and action than Festinger's original theory (see Steele, 1988, Steele & Spencer, 1992; Steele, Spencer, & Lynch, 1993) or than other revisions of the theory (e.g., Cooper & Fazio, 1984; Thibodeau & Aronson, 1992). Instead, we hope to show that the self-affirmation perspective is particularly valuable in the way that Festinger s original formulation was valuable—in its simplicity, scope, and richness as a source of new, interesting, and testable hypotheses. In addition to celebrating its progress, we discuss a few of the challenges posed to the theory by recent data on the role of the self-concept in dissonance phenomena.

THE THEORY IN A NUTSHELL

According to self-affirmation theory, thought and action are guided by a strong motivation to maintain an overall self-image of moral and adaptive adequacy. We want to see ourselves as good, capable, and able to predict and control outcomes in areas that matter. Awareness of information that threatens this image motivates us to restore it to a state of integrity. Like dissonance motivation, the self-affirmation drive can be strong or weak, depending on the size of the threat to the self-image. But because the objective is global self-worth and not cognitive consistency, we have tremendous flexibility in satisfying the need to restore a sense of general goodness. Self-worth derives from many resources, the myriad self-conceptions that are hypothesized to constitute a larger self-system. Thus, the larger self can be reaffirmed by thought or action addressed to one or more of these self-resources. So long as the affirming self-conception is important enough, this manner of restoring feelings of self-integrity can obviate the need to resolve the provoking inconsistency or threat, because "it is the war, not the battle, that orients this [self] system" (Steele, 1988, p. 289). For instance, a person does not have to rationalize a regrettable decision at work if his or her global sense of self-worth is secured by being a good parent or community member. Nor do cigarette smokers need to deny the risks of their self-incriminating habit if they can find other ways to bolster the global self, say, by affirming their capacities and worth in the workplace.

On the basis of this logic, Steele and Liu (1983) predicted that people would have no problem tolerating cognitive inconsistency in a forced-compliance paradigm, provided that the experimental procedure gave them the opportunity to affirm some important feature of the self—in this case, a cherished value. Students wrote essays in favor of a large tuition increase at their university. Immediately after writing the essay but before a measure of their attitudes, some participants were reminded of an important aspect of their self-concept by completing an aesthetic-values scale (value-oriented participants). Other participants went through the same procedure, but they were chosen for the study because aesthetic values were unimportant to them (non-value-oriented participants). As predicted, filling out the values scale eliminated dissonance—there was no attitude change in the direction of the essay—but only among value-oriented participants. According to Steele and Liu, these findings support self-affirmation theory over Festinger's (1957) consistency-based explanation because completing the values scale did nothing to reduce attitude–behavior inconsistency, yet the values-oriented participants showed no need to rationalize their behavior. In subsequent studies, "value affirmation" also has been shown to reduce rationalizing in the free-choice paradigm (Steele, Hopp, & Gonzales, [cited in Steele, 1988]).

In more recent work, Steele and his colleagues (Steele, Spencer, & Lynch, 1993) carried the self-affirmation logic a step further, to make an additional prediction about the role of dispositional self-esteem in dissonance processes. People with high self-esteem, they argued, should be less inclined to rationalize in dissonance-inducing situations than people with low self-esteem. Why? Because people with high self-esteem presumably have more internal resources, that is, more favorable self-concepts, with which to affirm away the self-esteem threat inherent in the dissonance-arousing episode. The simple version of this hypothesis was not supported in Steele et al.'s research. That is, people with high self-esteem were no less likely to rationalize in a standard dissonance procedure than people with low self-esteem. But the hypothesis was confirmed if just before the dissonance manipulation, participants' self-concepts were made salient by having them complete a self-esteem measure. In this scenario, only low-self-esteem individuals rationalized, whereas their high-self-esteem counterparts showed no evidence of rationalization. This last finding provides strong support for the resource model of dissonance reduction.

The student of dissonance theory may note that the results of the Steele et al. (1993) study fly in the face of the *self-consistency* reformulation of dissonance (see Chapter 7, this volume). Like self-affirmation theory, the self-consistency model sees dissonance as mediated by the ego and not in a freestanding need for cognitive consistency (see Greenwald & Ronis, 1978, p. 55). However, unlike the self-affirmation model, the self-consistency model still puts the need for consistency at the heart of dissonance. In this view, a given cognition arouses dissonance because it is inconsistent with a self-concept—people experience dissonance because they perceive an inconsistency between a behavior (e.g., writing a counterattitudinal essay) and a valued self-concept (being an honest person; see Chapter 7, this volume, for a complete discussion). Thus, self-affirmation and self-consistency theories make opposite predictions with regard to whether low- or high-self-esteem individuals will be more likely to rationalize a dissonant action. Self-affirmation theory predicts that low-self-esteem individuals will rationalize more, because they have fewer esteem-saving resources with which to counter a threatening inconsistency. By contrast, self-consistency theory predicts that high self-esteem individuals will rationalize more, because their positive self-concept will be more inconsistent with the dissonant act. Thus, the Steele et al. (1993) finding that people with low self-esteem rationalize more than those with high self-esteem is an important theoretical advance—both for dissonance theory and for the study of the role of the self-concept in social cognition.

ANALYSIS: SOME EMERGENT THEORETICAL ISSUES

Do We Need a New Theory?

Notwithstanding the impressive support for self-affirmation theory provided by Steele and his colleagues (e.g., Steele & Liu, 1983; Steele et al., 1993) and others (e.g., Tesser & Cornell, 1991), some dissonance theorists have questioned the need for a new and separate theory to explain the results of self-affirmation studies (e.g., Beauvois & Joule, 1996; Simon, Greenberg, & Brehm, 1995; Thibodeau & Aronson, 1992; Chapter 7, this volume). For example, Thibodeau and Aronson (1992) remind us that one of Festinger's (1957) hypothesized modes of dissonance reduction is adding new, consonant cognitions to the dissonant elements. Presumably these cognitions are postulated to reduce dissonance because the magnitude of dissonance is defined by the ratio of dissonant elements to dissonant plus consonant elements $[D/(D + C)]$. Thibodeau and Aronson asserted that once participants' central values have been affirmed, they have little need for attitude change because affirmation reminds them of valued, self-relevant cognitive elements that are consonant with a positive self-concept. Once these consonant elements are added to the dissonance equation, the magnitude of dissonance is reduced. Thus, the self-affirmation findings, one could argue, can be readily accommodated by the original dissonance formulation.

However, the strong version of this argument is challenged by the results of Steele et al. (1993), which suggest that reminding people of their self-concepts not only alleviates rationalization among high-self-esteem individuals but also tends to exacerbate it among low-self-esteem individuals. Thibodeau and Aronson (1992) have predicted the opposite with regard to low-self-esteem participants. Among these participants, completing the self-esteem scale decreased the magnitude of dissonance by reducing the number of cognitions consonant with a positive self-image. In any event, one strategy to illuminate this theoretical tension is to examine whether an irrelevant esteem threat increases or decreases rationalization in a dissonance paradigm. An increase would support the resources model; a decrease would support the original consistency formulation. To our knowledge, no direct test of this question exists.

In a slightly different vein, Simon et al., (1995) have proposed that self-affirmation interventions may eliminate the need for dissonance reduction not because they restore one's self-image, but because they establish a trivializing frame of reference whereby the relative importance of dissonant elements is reduced. One of Festinger's (1957) proposed methods of dissonance reduction was to decrease the importance of dissonant cognitions. Simon et al. found that reminding participants of a generally important issue (e.g., world hunger) after counterattitudinal behavior eliminated the need for dissonance reduction. This occurred regardless of the issue's personal importance to the participants. This finding contradicts self-affirmation theory because, by definition, an issue cannot be self-affirming unless it is of high personal importance.

Effects of Dispositional Self-Esteem

Another theoretical problem concerns the data discussed regarding the *resources* model and the role of self-esteem. As noted, the self-esteem differences predicted by self-affirmation theory emerge only when steps are taken to remind participants of their resources. When people are made mindful of their resources, the model works. But some evidence by Stone and his colleagues (see Stone, 1999) suggests a new twist. This research showed that people with high self-esteem actually rationalize more than people with low self-esteem if the self is brought on-line *after* dissonance has been aroused—in direct opposition to the resources model. When self-focus precedes the dissonance-arousing act, the self-affirmation resources model is supported; when self-focus follows the dissonance manipulation, the self-consistency model holds.

Moreover, some studies have shown that self-affirmation, under certain circumstances, can backfire—that positive feedback can increase rationalization if it focuses attention onto the domain threatened by dissonant behavior (J. Aronson, Blanton, & Cooper, 1995; Blanton, Cooper, Skurnik, & Aronson, 1997). For example, Blanton et al. had college students write dissonant essays arguing against increased university funding to help students with disabilities, a topic designed to impugn the essay writer's self-image as compassionate. After writing the essay, participants received feedback from a bogus personality test they had taken earlier. In one condition of the experiment, the feedback extolled the essay writer's compassion (thus, it was relevant to the uncompassionate essay the participant had written); in the other condition, the feedback praised the participant's creativity (irrelevant feedback). After reading the feedback, participants' attitudes toward the funding issue were assessed. The results showed that relevant affirmations—affirming the writers' compassion after the noncompassionate act—exacerbated dissonance, causing them to change their attitude in the direction of the essay more than participants who received no affirmation. In the irrelevant-feedback condition, there was no such rationalizing attitude change. Clearly, then, there are some constraints on the self-affirmation process; it appears that to reduce dissonance, the affirmation may need to be irrelevant rather than relevant to the dissonance-arousing act.

It is unclear what this research implies for dissonance reduction in the real world, where no one else may be around to focus a person on his or her resources—relevant or irrelevant, before or after the fact. Outside of the laboratory, does high self-esteem lead to less rationalizing? A recent study by Gibbons, Eggleston, and Benthin (1997) suggests not. Gibbons et al. looked at the rationalizations of nonsmokers who fell off the wagon and started smoking again. Contrary to self-affirmation predictions, it was the high-self-esteem relapsers who were most likely to rationalize their renewed habit by denying the risks of smoking. The relapsers with low self-esteem behaved as self-consistency theory would predict: They seemed to accept their failure as befitting their low self-image.

What can be made of the difficulty in making clear predictions about the role of dispositional self-esteem and dissonance or, more specifically, of results suggesting that affirmations sometimes reduce but at other times exacerbate dissonance? What can dissonance theorists conclude about the relative merits of self-affirmation theory and more conventional self-consistency theories? The self-image may at times serve as a standard of conduct, evoking dissonance when behavior fails to meet this standard. And at other times, the self-concept may serve as a resource, replenishing self-worth in the wake of a threat. Various factors (such as the relevance and timing of the affirmation) will influence whether the self functions as a standard or resource.

In support of this argument, one study examined whether people avoid affirmations that are relevant to a dissonance-arousing act (J. Aronson et al., 1995). J. Aronson et al. reasoned that relevant affirmations provide a threatening reminder of one's failure to live up to a valued standard of conduct. Accordingly, after behaving in an uncompassionate manner, people were found to eschew personality-test feedback that extolled their compassion. Although such feedback was flattering, it nonetheless was threatening, because it reminded participants that they had violated their usual standards of compassionate behavior, and it thus intensified the dissonance induced by their earlier unsympathetic actions.

Thus, positive self-conceptions can function both as resources (as in Steele et al., 1993) and as standards of conduct (as in J. Aronson et al., 1995), depending on the particulars of the situation. As the Stone, Cooper, Galinsky, and Kelly (1997) research demonstrates, the timing of an affirmation, like its relevance, may also be an important determinant of when a self-concept will *function* as an affirmational resource. There are undoubtedly other factors—such as the severity of the threat presented in the experiment—that must matter a great deal. The effect of self-image motivations on thought and behavior depends on several factors, and neither self-affirmation nor self-consistency offers a complete picture of the complex and manifold ways in which people regulate to their self-concepts. A straightforward calculus of the amount of dissonance from the number of positive self-conceptions may be impossible given the importance of the situation in determining whether a particular self-conception will be a source of pride or shame.

This last point raises a broader critique of dissonance research. Many investigators presume, either explicitly or implicitly, a general, universal, invariant process underlying all cognitive dissonance phenomena. This is a delusion; the form of the process, we believe, will depend on the specifics of the situation. Accordingly, the preconditions for dissonance will vary across contexts; sometimes freely chosen decisions whose outcomes are aversive will be necessary (Cooper & Fazio, 1984), and sometimes they will not be necessary (Thibodeau & E. Aronson, 1992; Harmon-Jones, 1999). There may be situational regularities common to dissonance phenomena, such as the perception of self-threat. But the process that creates this threat, and the strategies people deploy for reducing it, will vary a great deal depending on the nature of the situation. The delusion of a single pristine and precise mental process fuels much research both in the dissonance tradition and in other areas of psychological inquiry. It derives from an implicit assumption in general psychology that there is an abstract central processing unit (CPU) called *mind*, and that it is the task of researchers to discern its properties and algorithms with more and more precise laboratory methods (Shweder, 1991). Because the goal is understanding the nature of this disembedded, context-free CPU, researchers assume that they can stick to one paradigm and through systematic variations on this paradigm, they will eventually divine the exact nature of the universal psychological processes—the fundamental laws—underlying psychological phenomena, in this case, cognitive dissonance phenomena. It is assumed that these processes will apply to all situations everywhere. But a great deal of evidence has accumulated suggesting that the nature of the psychological process depends on the content of the situation—a critique made time and again by researchers in cultural psychology (e.g., Shweder, 1991).

SYNTHESIS AND SOME NEW DIRECTIONS

Cognitive dissonance theory was inspiring in part because it encompassed so many different phenomena. It gave a way of understanding and talking about a vast array of human behavior with a relatively simple construct. For example, it could explain patterns of rumor transmission after catastrophes (Festinger, 1957) or the behavior of cultists (Festinger, Riecken, & Schachter, 1956). It helped us understand why people come to love the things they suffer for (E. Aronson & Mills, 1959) and hate the people they inflict suffering on (Glass, 1964). It offered useful techniques for parenting, for example, how to get children to learn to like their vegetables (Brehm, 1959), or how to get them to dislike a forbidden toy (E. Aronson & Carlsmith, 1962). Other topics within dissonance's explanatory purview included defensive projection (Bramel, 1962), consumer behavior (Doob, Carlsmith, Freedman, Landauer, & Tom, 1969), and the treatment of phobias (Cooper, 1980) and obesity (Axsom & Cooper, 1985). In short, it was synthetic rather than analytic. That is, it opened doors to new and unthought-of manifestations of a process rather than cautiously describing the boundary conditions of a theoretical process. Perhaps spurred by theoretical critiques (e.g., Bem, 1967) and the rise of the cognitive approach, dissonance research became more and more analytic and less and less synthetic (Berkowitz & Devine, 1989).

One downside of the analytic approach has been that theory testing tends to limit itself to one or two paradigms, leading to the mistaken idea that a theory largely applies to processes occurring in those paradigms. In the case of dissonance theory, most of the studies conducted after the early 1970s used the *induced-compliance* paradigm, a state of affairs that created the false impression that dissonance theory was mostly about what happened to people's attitudes after being induced to contradict those attitudes by writing an essay that argued against one's true beliefs. For example, Cooper and Fazio's (1984) reformulation of dissonance theory refers exclusively to the studies using the induced-compliance paradigm, focusing on the necessary preconditions for creating sufficient dissonance to induce attitude change (e.g., foreseeable, aversive consequences). Gone was dissonance theory's enormous scope.

Self-affirmation theory has had tremendous value in moving the study of dissonance—or at least dissonance-like—phenomena in the direction of synthesis and in uncovering new areas in which self-image maintenance affects beliefs and behavior. Self-affirmation theory provides a theoretical framework that like Festinger's original theory, captures many disparate phenomena with a single, compelling formulation. Unfettered by the excess baggage that the definition of *dissonance* has picked up in the last six decades and equipped with new methodological techniques derived from the dissonance-as-self-threat perspective, self-affirmation theory is reexamining some old terrain with a fresh perspective. Below, we offer a few examples of recent research derived from the logic of self-affirmation theory. Note that very little if any of the hypotheses could have been derived from the version of dissonance that was predominant when Jones (1985) declared that dissonance had ceased to bear fruit. Note also the return of motivation to phenomena, like prejudice and inferential biases, that for the past few decades have been understood from a primarily cognitive perspective. Self-affirmation theory offers both a conceptual framework and a methodological technique for demonstrating the influence of motivation on cognition and behavior.

Self-Affirmation and Prejudice

Reasoning that people make themselves feel better about themselves by putting down members of socially devalued groups, Fein and Spencer (1997) asked whether affirming people's self-concepts might reduce their tendency to evaluate members of stereotyped groups negatively. Participants in their study evaluated a job candidate who, by manipulating her last name and showing her with or without a Star of David or a Crucifix, was either presented as a member of a negatively stereotyped group (a "Jewish-American princess") or was not (an Italian-American woman). Despite having identical credentials, the Jewish woman received significantly lower ratings than the Italian-American woman when evaluated by participants asked to rate her personality. However, half of Fein and Spencer's participants were given the opportunity to affirm their self-concepts by writing about an important value (e.g., art, music, or theater). These affirmed participants were not influenced by the stereotype, that is, they did not give negative ratings to the Jewish woman; they saw her as just as nice, honest, and intelligent, as when she was portrayed as Italian American.

In a subsequent study, Fein and Spencer (1997) showed that threatening people's self-esteem by giving them negative feedback on a bogus test of intelligence increased their prejudiced reactions to a stereotype target, in this case, a presumably gay man. The negative feedback had no effect on their evaluations of the same person when he was not presented as gay. This work is the first empirical demonstration of the motivational forces underlying prejudice: It suggests that negative stereotypes provide a "cognitively justifiable" means to bolster self-regard.

Self-Affirmation and Health

Drawing from the increased awareness of the link between stress and physical illness, Keough and colleagues (Keough, 1997; Garcia & Steele, 1997) reasoned that the net effect of one's daily self-esteem threats could be reduced health. Drawing from the work on self-affirmation theory, they tested this notion by affirming a group of undergraduate students over a period of time and then comparing their health (as measured by a number of self-report instruments) to a control group of unaffirmed students. Specifically, during an academic vacation, affirmed students wrote about their daily experiences and about their feelings about those experiences with regard to a centrally important personal value. The results showed that compared with two other writing control conditions, those who completed the affirmation assignments were physically healthier at the end of the vacation than those who wrote about things that made them feel good or about their friends' activities. This research ruled out other, more conventional explanations (such as mood effects or the importance of positive thoughts) and suggested that it was the unique exercise of integrating daily experiences into a personally important value, rather than simply reflecting on happy events, that improved health.

Biases in Persuasion and Negotiation

People with strong beliefs on a topic tend to cling to their attitudes in the face of ambiguous and even well-reasoned disconfirming information. They tend also to see people who espouse opposing views as misguided. This tendency has typically compelled nonmotivational explanations (e.g., Lord, Ross, & Lepper, 1979). Cohen, Aronson, and Steele (1997) wondered if part of the reason that people dig in their heels and refuse to change their minds is because it is self-threatening—or dissonant—to do so, because these opinions are self-defining. The hypothesis was straightforward. Partisans of a particular belief (e.g., advocates of the abortion issue or opponents and proponents of capital punishment) would be more open to arguments against their position if they were given an affirmation of an alternative source of identity or self-worth. In a series of studies, this hypothesis was supported. In one study, opponents and proponents of capital punishment were more persuaded by an article impugning their views when, before reading the article, they were given a self-affirmation in the form of positive feedback on their social perceptiveness skills. Self-affirmed partisans also were less likely to dismiss advocates of opposing views as political extremists, and they even became more critical in their evaluation of evidence that confirmed their own pre-existing beliefs. In another study, a self-affirmation procedure reduced people's tendency to engage in "reactive devaluation"—the problematic impulse of negotiators to derogate a concession that has been offered relative to one that has been withheld (Atkins, Ward, & Lepper, 1997). Other research has revealed that self-affirmation reduces biased processing of potentially threatening information in a variety of domains including potentially threatening health information (Sherman & Cohen, 2006). Moreover, self-affirmation has been found to increase healthy intentions and behaviors, presumably because of the reduction in biased processing of potentially threatening information (Sweeney & Moyer, 2015). Although an extension of self-affirmation theory, this research also begins to resolve classic issues in social psychology regarding the effect of motivational forces on cognitive biases (see also Dunning, Leuenberger, & Sherman, 1995; Kunda, 1987).

Self-Affirmation and the Academic Underperformance of Black Students

The underperformance of Blacks on standardized tests and in school has been explained in terms ranging from the *sociological disadvantage* (Bereiter & Engelmann, 1966) to *genetic differences* in intelligence (e.g., Benbow & Stanley, 1980; Herrnstein & Murray, 1994; Jensen, 1969). Noting the insufficiency of these explanations, Steele and his colleagues (J. Aronson, Quinn, & Spencer, 1997; Spencer, Steele, & Quinn, 1997; Steele, 1997; Steele & Aronson, 1995) drew on self-affirmation logic to offer a new explanation. They hypothesized that being the target of a negative stereotype (e.g., "Black people are unintelligent") in a situation where that stereotype is relevant (e.g., taking a test of intelligence) functioned as a self-threat, with some of the same arousal properties. They further reasoned that the underperformance of Blacks (and of women in mathematics) might be due in part to the extra test anxiety brought on by this sense of "stereotype threat." In one series of studies testing this reasoning (Steele & Aronson, 1995), Black and White college students were given a difficult standardized test (the Verbal Ability subscale of the Graduate Record Examinations) under conditions designed to either eliminate or exacerbate this stereotype threat. When stereotype threat was increased by underscoring the evaluative nature of the test, the Black students performed much worse than the White students. But when stereotype threat was minimized by introducing the same test as nonevaluative, the Black students performed just as well as the White students.

Despite the fact that the stereotype-threat situation bears no resemblance to a traditional dissonance–self-affirmation paradigm, thinking about the test-taking situation in those terms has been extremely useful. In a recent study (J. Aronson & Damiani, 1997), we tested whether self-affirmations could mitigate the underperformance engendered by the stereotype threat. In essence, we asked if being reminded of one's general sense of goodness could protect one from the threatening and performance-disruptive implications of a negative stereotype about one's intellectual abilities. Could we help a Black test taker to perform better by affirming him or her in some valued domain of the self-concept? To find out, we replicated the Steele and Aronson (1995) procedure described above. But in this experiment, half of the test takers received a self-affirmation just before starting the test. For one group, the affirmation was relevant: We affirmed their verbal skills. The other two groups received an irrelevant affirmation (of either their social skills or their ethnic identity). The results were very clear. The only affirmation that benefited the test takers was the affirmation of their verbal skills. Relevance, in this instance, buffered participants against a self-threat.

Self-Affirmation and the Effect of Positive Role Models

Reading through the literature on academic underperformance, one frequently confronts the role model argument: Why do Black and Latino students fail to do as well as White students in school? One explanation is that they lack adequate Black and Latino role models, who demonstrate, by example, that people of their race can succeed in academics. This argument also surfaces frequently during discussions of affirmative action. But despite the intuitive appeal of this argument, evidence that the presence of minority role models improves the outcomes of minority students is hard to come by. It is not at all clear, for example, that on integrated college campuses, there is a correlation between the number of Black professors and the academic performance of the Black student body (J. Aronson & Disko, 1997).

In a recent study, we (J. Aronson & Disko, 1997) examined the hypothesis, derived from self-affirmation theory, that role models can actually be threatening if they excel in domains where a person feels threatened. As a result, we may denigrate rather than identify with such role models. To test this reasoning, we gave students a test of either their verbal skills or their hand-eye coordination skills. Regardless of experimental condition, the students were made to feel that they had performed poorly on the test. Later, in the context of a supposedly unrelated survey, we told students that we needed their help in putting together some interventions aimed at motivating high school students to excel in academics. Specifically, we asked them to rate the suitability of various role models who could be used as spokespeople for this cause. The list of role models they rated came from various walks of life: famous scientists, athletes, politicians, writers, and so on. Our key hypothesis centered on the ratings of the writers on our list (e.g., Stephen King and Anne Rice) because they represented the category of people with excellent verbal skills, the same skills that half of our participants were presumably doubting because of their failure in the first part of the study. As predicted, the participants in the verbal-skills-failure condition gave much more negative ratings to the writers than they did to the other role model candidates. This pattern of role model bashing did not occur for participants in the hand-eye-coordination condition. This study, we believe, helps to explain why the mere presence of positive role models may not be enough. Students may feel threatened, rather than inspired, by excellent role models, especially in domains where they feel under suspicion.

Self-Concept Change Through Disidentification

One additional advantage of the self-affirmation approach is that it considers the self as an element in the dissonance process. Because the self is an element, changing one's self-concept may be an effective means to reduce dissonance. According to this reasoning, when one's behavior or performance in a domain casts a negative light on oneself, one can maintain global self-esteem by disidentifying with the domain in question. For example, we (J. Aronson & Fried, 1997) have found that Blacks with relatively low academic performance in school cope by making academics less important to their self-concepts, that is, they rationalize their lower achievement by reorganizing their priorities (see also Steele, 1997). We have studied the *disidentification* hypothesis in the domain of moral goodness as well. For example, J. Aronson et al. (1995) found that after behaving uncompassionately, participants attempted to affirm themselves by denying the importance of compassion to their self-concepts. Although such effects were certainly conceivable under the older formulations of dissonance theory, the effect of dissonance on the self was never a focal point. In a conceptually related study, it was found that in the face of a self-threat, people recruited lost self-esteem by heightening their identification with a valued reference group, a defensive reaction that was attenuated when people were able to affirm another unrelated aspect of their self-concept. This research demonstrates how identification and disidentification processes may produce changes in self-concept—a finding that poses serious challenges for conventional theories that view social identity as fixed rather than malleable (Garcia & Steele, 1997).

CONCLUSION

Self-affirmation theory contributed a great deal to bringing dissonance and motivational processes back to the analysis of significant social psychological phenomena (see Sherman & Cohen, 2006, for a review). Like the early version of dissonance theory, self-affirmation theory lacks precision with regard to some of its postulates and with regard to the mediating process (but see Critcher & Dunning, 2015, for some mediating evidence). But, like dissonance theory, this imprecision comes with the benefit of an expansive range of application. It is a useful tool for examining a broad range of phenomena where self-protective motivations play a role, and it pushes dissonance theory beyond the consideration of simple consistency drives to a broader and richer territory. That is, self-affirmation theory directs our attention to the many manifestations and implications of the motivation to manage and protect self or identity. How this motivation plays out depends on the opportunities and threats presented by a particular situation, whether it be a dissonance paradigm (Steele & Liu, 1983), the more common daily stressors people face in their lives (Keough et al., 1997), the context of debate or negotiation (Atkins et al., 1997; Cohen et al., 1997), or the schooling environment (Steele & Aronson, 1995).

This synthetic approach of applying self-affirmation theory to new phenomena is likely to shed light on the processes underlying these phenomena (including stress and illness, stereotyping and inferential biases, and academic identification). But it is also likely to provide insights into the nature of dissonance processes, especially when such synthesis is tempered by a consideration of the constraints and limiting conditions uncovered by more analytically inclined experimenters. For example, one message of self-affirmation research is that self-image motivations permeate a wide range of phenomena, even very basic and everyday tasks like causal attribution (e.g., Liu & Steele, 1986). Thus, it may be premature to assert that the precondition for all dissonance phenomena is the commission of a freely chosen act with aversive, foreseeable consequences (Cooper & Fazio, 1984). Although in some situations, this may hold, in other situations, different factors may create self-threat and arouse dissonance.

At present, using self-affirmation theory as opposed to a more analytic theory is a bit like trading in a fine-tuned sports sedan for an all-terrain vehicle with huge tires and a bulky suspension system. One sacrifices the ability to sense slight variations in the texture of the road for the ability to venture into uncharted, unpaved territory. As research continues and the theory becomes more precise, the trade-off will become less and less significant.

REFERENCES

Aronson, E., & Carlsmith, J. M. (1962). Performance expectancy as a determinant of actual performance. *Journal of Abnormal and Social Psychology, 65,* 178–182. http://dx.doi.org/10.1037/h0042291

Aronson, E., & Mills, J. (1959). The effect of severity of initiation on liking for a group. *Journal of Abnormal and Social Psychology, 59,* 177–181. http://dx.doi.org/10.1037/h0047195

Aronson, J., Blanton, H., & Cooper, J. (1995). From dissonance to disidentification: Selectivity in the self-affirmation process. *Journal of Personality and Social Psychology, 68,* 986–996. http://dx.doi.org/10.1037/0022-3514.68.6.986

Aronson, J., & Damiani, M. (1997). *Stereotype threat, attributional ambiguity and fragile self-competence.* Unpublished manuscript, University of Texas at Austin.

Aronson, J., & Disko, D. (1997). *Why role models aren't enough: The influence of self-affirmation processes on positive social influence.* Paper presented at the 77th annual meeting of the Western Psychological Association, Seattle.

Aronson, J., & Fried, C. (1997). *Reducing disidentification and boosting the academic achievement of stereotype vulnerable students: The role of theories of intelligence.* Unpublished manuscript, University of Texas at Austin.

Aronson, J., Quinn, D., & Spencer, S. (1997). Stereotype threat and the academic performance of minorities and women. In J. Swim & C. Stangor (Eds.), *Prejudice: The target's perspective* (pp. 83–103). San Diego, CA: Academic Press.

Atkins, D., Ward, A., & Lepper, M. (1997). *Reducing reactive devaluation with a self-affirmation.* Unpublished manuscript, Stanford University, Palo Alto, CA.

Axsom, D., & Cooper, J. (1985). Cognitive dissonance and psychotherapy: The role of effort justification in inducing weight loss. *Journal of Experimental Social Psychology, 21,* 149–160. http://dx.doi.org/10.1016/0022-1031(85)90012-5

Beauvois, J.-L., & Joule, R.-V. (1996). *A radical dissonance theory.* London, England: Taylor & Francis.

Bem, D. J. (1967). Self-perception: An alternative interpretation of cognitive dissonance phenomena. *Psychological Review, 74*, 183–200. http://dx.doi.org/10.1037/h0024835

Benbow, C. P., & Stanley, J. C. (1980). Sex differences in mathematical ability: Fact or artifact? *Science, 210*, 1262–1264. http://dx.doi.org/10.1126/science.7434028

Bereiter, C., & Engelmann, S. (1966). *Teaching disadvantaged children in the preschool.* Englewood Cliffs, NJ: Prentice-Hall.

Berkowitz, L., & Devine, P. G. (1989). Research traditions, analysis, and synthesis in social psychological theories: The case of dissonance theory. *Personality and Social Psychology Bulletin, 15*, 493–507. http://dx.doi.org/10.1177/0146167289154002

Blanton, H., Cooper, J., Skurnik, I., & Aronson, J. (1997). When bad things happen to good feedback: Exacerbating the need for self-justification with self-affirmations. *Personality and Social Psychology Bulletin, 23*, 684–692. http://dx.doi.org/10.1177/0146167297237002

Bramel, D. (1962). A dissonance theory approach to defensive projection. *Journal of Abnormal and Social Psychology, 64*, 121–129. http://dx.doi.org/10.1037/h0043741

Brehm, J. W. (1959). Increasing cognitive dissonance by a fait accompli. *Journal of Abnormal and Social Psychology, 58*, 379–382. http://dx.doi.org/10.1037/h0047791

Cohen, G. L., Aronson, J., & Steele, C. M. (1997). *When beliefs yield to evidence: Reducing biased evaluation by affirming the self.* Manuscript submitted for publication.

Cooper, I. (1980). Reducing fears and increasing assertiveness: The role of dissonance reduction. *Journal of Experimental Social Psychology, 16*, 199–213. http://dx.doi.org/10.1016/0022-1031(80)90064-5

Cooper, J., & Fazio, R. H. (1984). A new look at dissonance theory. In L. Berkowitz (Ed.), *Advances in experimental social psychology* (Vol. 17, pp. 229–262). Hillsdale, NJ: Erlbaum.

Critcher, C. R., & Dunning, D. (2015). Self-affirmations provide a broader perspective on self-threat. *Personality and Social Psychology Bulletin, 41*, 3–18. http://dx.doi.org/10.1177/0146167214554956

Doob, A., Carlsmith, J., Freedman, J., Landauer, T., & Tom, S. (1969). Effect of initial selling price on subsequent sales. *Journal of Personality and Social Psychology, 11*, 345–350. http://dx.doi.org/10.1037/h0027415

Dunning, D., Leuenberger, A., & Sherman, D. A. (1995). A new look at motivated inference: Are self-serving theories of success a product of motivational forces? *Journal of Personality and Social Psychology, 69*, 58–68. http://dx.doi.org/10.1037/0022-3514.69.1.58

Fein, S., & Spencer, S. J. (1997). Prejudice as self-image maintenance: Affirming the self through derogating others. *Journal of Personality and Social Psychology, 73*, 31–44.

Festinger, L. (1957). *A theory of cognitive dissonance.* Palo Alto, CA: Stanford University Press.

Festinger, L., Riecken, H. W., & Schachter, S. (1956). *When prophecy fails.* New York, NY: Harper & Row. http://dx.doi.org/10.1037/10030-000

Garcia, J., & Steele, C. M. (1997). *Social identity and self-affirmation.* Manuscript submitted for publication.

Gibbons, F. X., Eggleston, T. J., & Benthin, A. C. (1997). Cognitive reactions to smoking relapse: The reciprocal relation between dissonance and self-esteem. *Journal of Personality and Social Psychology, 72*, 184–195. http://dx.doi.org/10.1037/0022-3514.72.1.184

Glass, D. C. (1964). Changes in liking as a means of reducing cognitive discrepancies between self-esteem and aggression. *Journal of Personality, 32*, 531–549. http://dx.doi.org/10.1111/j.1467-6494.1964.tb01357.x

Greenwald, A. G., & Ronis, D. L. (1978). Twenty years of cognitive dissonance: Case study of the evolution of a theory. *Psychological Review, 85,* 53–57. http://dx.doi.org/10.1037/0033-295X.85.1.53

Harmon-Jones, E. (1999). Toward an understanding of the motivation underlying dissonance effects: Is the production of aversive consequences necessary? In E. Harmon-Jones & J. Mills (Eds.), *Cognitive dissonance: Perspectives on a pivotal theory in social psychology* (pp. 71–99). Washington, DC: American Psychological Association. http://dx.doi.org/10.1037/10318-004

Herrnstein, R. J., & Murray, C. (1994). *The bell curve: Intelligence and class structure in American life.* New York, NY: Free Press.

Jensen, A. R. (1969). How much can we boost IQ and scholastic achievement? *Harvard Educational Review, 39,* 1–123. http://dx.doi.org/10.17763/haer.39.1.l3u15956627424k7

Jones, E. E. (1985). Major developments in social psychology during the past five decades. In G. Lindzey & E. Aronson (Eds.), *The handbook of social psychology* (3rd ed., Vol. 1, pp. 47–108). New York, NY: Random House.

Keough, K. A. (1997). *When the self is at stake: Integrating the self into stress and physical health research.* Unpublished manuscript, University of Texas at Austin.

Keough, K. A., Garcia, J., & Steele, C. M. (1997). *Reducing stress and illness by affirming the self.* Unpublished manuscript, University of Texas at Austin.

Kunda, Z. (1987). Motivated inference: Self-serving generation and evaluation of causal theories. *Journal of Personality and Social Psychology, 53,* 636–647. http://dx.doi.org/10.1037/0022-3514.53.4.636

Liu, T. J., & Steele, C. M. (1986). Attributional analysis as self-affirmation. *Journal of Personality and Social Psychology, 51,* 531–540. http://dx.doi.org/10.1037/0022-3514.51.3.531

Lord, C. G., Ross, L., & Lepper, M. R. (1979). Biased assimilation and attitude polarization: The effects of prior theories on subsequently considered evidence. *Journal of Personality and Social Psychology, 37,* 2098–2109. http://dx.doi.org/10.1037/0022-3514.37.11.2098

Sherman, D. K., & Cohen, G. L. (2006). The psychology of self-defense: Self-affirmation theory. *Advances in Experimental Social Psychology, 38,* 183–242. http://dx.doi.org/10.1016/S0065-2601(06)38004-5

Shweder, R. A. (1991). *Thinking through cultures: Expeditions in cultural psychology.* Cambridge, MA: Harvard University Press.

Simon, L., Greenberg, J., & Brehm, J. (1995). Trivialization: The forgotten mode of dissonance reduction. *Journal of Personality and Social Psychology, 68,* 247–260. http://dx.doi.org/10.1037/0022-3514.68.2.247

Spencer, S. J., Steele, C. M., & Quinn, D. M. (1997). *Stereotype threat and women's math performance.* Unpublished manuscript, University of Waterloo, Waterloo, Ontario, Canada.

Steele, C. M. (1988). The psychology of self-affirmation: Sustaining the integrity of the self. In L. Berkowitz (Ed.), *Advances in experimental social psychology* (Vol. 21, pp. 261–302). Hillsdale, NJ: Erlbaum. http://dx.doi.org/10.1016/S0065-2601(08)60229-4

Steele, C. M. (1997). A threat in the air: How stereotypes shape intellectual identity and performance. *American Psychologist, 52,* 613–629. http://dx.doi.org/10.1037/0003-066X.52.6.613

Steele, C. M., & Aronson, J. (1995). Stereotype threat and the intellectual test performance of African Americans. *Journal of Personality and Social Psychology, 69,* 797–811. http://dx.doi.org/10.1037/0022-3514.69.5.797

Steele, C. M., & Liu, T. J. (1983). Dissonance processes as self-affirmation. *Journal of Personality and Social Psychology, 45,* 5–19. http://dx.doi.org/10.1037/0022-3514.45.1.5

Steele, C. M., & Spencer, S. J. (1992). The primacy of self-integrity. *Psychological Inquiry, 3*, 345–346. http://dx.doi.org/10.1207/s15327965pli0304_14

Steele, C. M., Spencer, S. J., & Lynch, M. (1993). Self-Image resilience and dissonance: The role of affirmational resources. *Journal of Personality and Social Psychology, 64*, 885–896. http://dx.doi.org/10.1037/0022-3514.64.6.885

Stone, J. (1999). What exactly have I done? The role of self-attribute accessibility in dissonance. In E. Harmon-Jones & J. Mills (Eds.), *Cognitive dissonance: Progress on a pivotal theory in social psychology* (pp. 175–200). Washington, DC: American Psychological Association.

Stone, J., Cooper, J., Galinsky, A., & Kelly, K. (1997). *Self-attribute accessibility in dissonance: The mirror has many faces.* Manuscript submitted for publication.

Sweeney, A. M., & Moyer, A. (2015). Self-affirmation and responses to health messages: A meta-analysis on intentions and behavior. *Health Psychology, 34*, 149–159. http://dx.doi.org/10.1037/hea0000110

Tesser, A., & Cornell, D. R. (1991). On the confluence of self processes. *Journal of Experimental Social Psychology, 27*, 501–526. http://dx.doi.org/10.1016/0022-1031(91)90023-Y

Thibodeau, R., & Aronson, E. (1992). Taking a closer look: Reasserting the role of the self-concept in dissonance theory. *Personality and Social Psychology Bulletin, 18*, 591–602. http://dx.doi.org/10.1177/0146167292185010

In Search of the Motivation for Dissonance Reduction
The Drive to Lessen Aversive Consequences

Joel Cooper

More than 60 years ago, Leon Festinger (1957) made the marvelously elegant suggestion that inconsistency between pairs of cognitive elements causes the psychological discomfort known as *cognitive dissonance*. That statement, and a modest number of supporting postulates, spawned more than 2,000 empirical investigations examining the nonobvious predictions of the theory and expanding its reach into new areas of applicability.

The longevity of dissonance at or near the center stage of social psychology is impressive. The early days of dissonance research were characterized by novel, high-impact experimentation conducted by clever and intuitive experimenters. But this alone could not have been sufficient to carry the dissonance tradition through six decades. More impressive than the impact of the original experiments was Festinger's foresight to recognize the careful interplay between motivation and cognition. Festinger recognized, before it was fashionable, that knowledge of the environment and knowledge of one's own behaviors, attitudes, and emotions were represented cognitively and that it was the relationship among the cognitive representations that prompted motivation. Thus, when social psychology strayed toward the purely motivational, dissonance theory was present to remind the field of the importance of cognitive representations of the person and the environment. Similarly, and perhaps more important, when social psychology strayed toward the purely

---

I gratefully acknowledge the help of Adam Galinsky in the preparation of an earlier draft of this chapter.

http://dx.doi.org/10.1037/0000135-009
Cognitive Dissonance, Second Edition: Reexamining a Pivotal Theory in Psychology,
E. Harmon-Jones (Editor)
Copyright © 2019 by the American Psychological Association. All rights reserved.

cognitive, dissonance theory reminded us that cognitive representations lead to motivation and that motivation affects the representations themselves (cf. Kunda, 1990, 1999). Thus, in addition to being a provocative theory in its own right, dissonance's reliance on the cognitive and the motivational provided an important middle ground to which social psychology could consistently return.

In this chapter, I examine the motivational basis of dissonance reduction. Why does inconsistency motivate people to go about the difficult task of cognitive change? What makes people experience arousal and negative affect? For Festinger, the answer lay in the mere presence of inconsistency. But more recent work has suggested alternative mechanisms for change, including the elimination of aversive consequences and the bolstering of the self-concept. In the current chapter, I consider the difference between motivational views that focus on the self and those that focus on behavioral consequences. Although there is considerable wisdom drawn from the representation of the self, I argue that the motivation for dissonance reduction arises from the perception of aversive consequences and that changes of attitudes that generally follow from dissonance arousal are at the service of rendering those consequences nonaversive.

CURING THE "BUT ONLYS": FROM INCONSISTENCY TO AVERSIVE OUTCOMES

When dissonance theory was merely 25 years old, Russell Fazio and I set out to put together much of the research that had accumulated over dissonance's first quarter century. We wanted to see if comprehensive sense could be made of a theory that had an impressive history but that was saddled with a bad case of the "but onlys." Dissonance arose from inconsistent cognitions, *but only* if there was free choice to act counterattitudinally; *but only* if there was commitment to the counterattitudinal act; *but only* if an unwanted consequence had occurred; *but only* if the consequence was foreseeable, and so forth.

Fazio and I wanted to see if we could plot the best fitting theoretical curve that passed through the numerous replications of dissonance and the impressive list of "but only" exceptions. In the end, we concluded that the best fitting curve did not pass through cognitive inconsistency at all (Cooper & Fazio, 1984). Rather, we concluded that dissonance was a state of arousal caused by behaving in such a way as to feel personally responsible for bringing about an aversive event. If that arousal was not misattributed to another source or reduced in some other way, dissonance arousal became *dissonance motivation*, an instigation to engage in cognitive changes for the fundamental purpose of rendering the consequence nonaversive. That is why the consequence, the unwanted result of a person's behavior, is so critical in driving the dissonance engine. It is the essential ingredient, the primary reason for people engaging in the effort of dissonance reduction.

The new look model was intended not as a new theory, but rather as a change in emphasis of a venerable theory. We suggested that the emphasis on inconsistency in causing dissonance arousal had been misplaced. Because acting inconsistently usually has the potential to result in an aversive or unwanted consequence, inconsistency is a reasonable stand-in variable for aversive consequences in producing dissonance. However, it is not the inconsistency per se that causes the arousal, but rather the result of that inconsistency, the unwanted consequence. When viewed this way, the "but onlys" fall into place, not as exceptions to the theory, but as explicable and important components of dissonance.

Nonetheless, the difference in the two approaches is not trivial. On those occasions in which inconsistency can be separated from aversive consequences, it is the latter and not the former that holds up to empirical test (Cooper, 2007). Empirically, Cooper and Worchel (1970) found that inconsistency was not a sufficient condition for dissonance arousal if aversive consequences were lacking. Scher and Cooper (1989) showed that inconsistency was neither sufficient nor necessary for dissonance arousal if the production of aversive consequences had been carefully disentangled from the cognitive inconsistency.

WHAT IS AN AVERSIVE CONSEQUENCE?

Meeting the Positivistic Test

In our new look paper (1984), Fazio and I defined aversive consequences *positivistically* rather than a priori. According to the positivistic view, the ultimate authority for theoretical terms is how they are experienced by the perceiver. Similarly, in our view, *aversive* consequences are best defined by the way they are experienced by the actor rather than by an abstract definition in advance of an act that fails to consider the actor's experience. We defined an *aversive* consequence as the real or potential result of behavior that a person would rather have not brought about. The emphasis in this definition is on the actor who determines, by his or her experience of an event, whether it is wanted or unwanted. What makes a consequence aversive is the way an outcome of an act is perceived by the actor. If the actor perceives the consequence as unwanted, then it successfully meets the test of being an aversive consequence.

The experiment by Cooper and Worchel (1970) established a procedure that perhaps became the paradigmatic example of an aversive consequence. Worchel and I had student volunteers participate in a procedure substantially similar to the original well-known induced-compliance experiment of Festinger and Carlsmith (1959). In the original study, participants engaged in a truly boring task and then were induced, for either a low or high monetary inducement, to tell a waiting participant (actually, a confederate of the experimenter) that the task was truly exciting and interesting. Festinger and Carlsmith had reasoned that the inconsistency between saying the task was interesting while privately believing that the task was deadly dull was sufficient to cause dissonance. As is well known, they also established and confirmed the nonobvious prediction that acting inconsistently for a small monetary inducement would create more dissonance and thus lead to more attitude change than acting inconsistently for a large inducement. People came to believe that the task was more interesting if they had lied to the waiting participant for only a meager amount of financial inducement.

Worchel and I argued that it was not the inconsistency between saying the task was interesting and believing it was dull that led to dissonance, but rather the unwanted event of having duped a fellow student to look forward to an exciting experience. The participant knew full well that the waiting participant was in for an immense letdown. Indeed, we found that if the student who was waiting explicitly stated that he believed the participant and was looking forward to performing the task, there was dissonance-produced attitude change. But if that consequence was removed by the waiting confederate, indicating that he did not believe the participant, then, despite the participant's having behaved inconsistently, his actions produced no dissonance.

From that study, and several others that confirmed its basic tenet (e.g., Blackman, Keller, & Cooper, 2016; Cooper, Zanna, & Goethals, 1974; Hoyt, Henley, & Collins, 1972; Norton, Monin, Cooper, & Hogg, 2003), it might appear that an aversive consequence is necessarily characterized as doing something bad to someone else, like duping a fellow student, or bringing about an unwanted policy which could harm hundreds of students. Undoubtedly, these are unwanted consequences for most people and serve to initiate the arousal of dissonance. However, causing negative consequences to others and bringing about unwanted political ends are but two of the myriad behavioral outcomes that a person may find aversive. Rejecting a particular consumer item in the research procedure made famous by Brehm (1956) and his colleagues causes the potentially aversive consequence to oneself of giving up the positive benefits associated with that choice and accepting all of the negative features associated with the chosen alternative. Indeed, people may differ in their opinions of the kinds of consequences they find aversive. My list may bear significant similarities to yours, although differences would almost certainly exist. I may think it is particularly aversive to dupe a fellow student, but someone else may find it pleasant to have successfully completed a task requested by the experimenter.

Normative and Ideographic Standards

The fact that people may differ in what they find aversive does not plunge us toward definitional chaos. Regularities exist. Some behavioral outcomes violate generally shared expectations of what is appropriate in a particular situation. That is, they violate normative standards of behavior. Most people in a culture know that it is unacceptable to bring harm to others or knowingly and freely create harmful policies that affect one's university, society, or social group. As Stone and Cooper (2001, 2003) have argued, the discrepancy between one's behavioral outcome and the normative standard gives that behavior its psychological meaning. For most people, violating normative standards designates the consequence as aversive and unwanted and drives the arousal of dissonance.

On the other hand, behavior can also be discrepant from *ideographic*, or personal standards, and the violation of personal standards also can create dissonance. Years ago, Cooper and Scalise (1974) showed that introverts, as measured by the Myers-Briggs Type Indicator, experience dissonance from different behavioral outcomes than do extraverts. To the extent that personal, ideographic standards are made salient, behavioral outcomes that violate those standards serve as unwanted consequences. The standard that is made accessible in the situation gives meaning to a particular behavioral outcome. If normative standards are most easily accessible—and they usually are—then behavioral outcomes that violate those standards will cause dissonance. If personal standards become accessible, then behaviors that violate such standards will be considered aversive and lead to the arousal of dissonance. Stone and Cooper (2003) showed that making personal standards salient by having participants engage in a scrambled sentence task facilitated their use of personal standards in considering whether a consequence was aversive.

In essence, then, a behavioral consequence is aversive only when it is psychologically measured against a standard. Typically, that standard is defined by cultural and societal norms, meaning that it is consistent with what most people find aversive about a particular outcome. Occasionally, through chronic accessibility of a personal standard or through an environmental prime, a personal standard becomes highly accessible and then that standard functions as the measuring stick for determining aversiveness (Stone & Cooper, 2001).

THE ROLE OF THE SELF IN DISSONANCE

What systematic role does the self play in the dissonance process? There have been several fascinating and provocative theoretical accounts that have implicated self-esteem in the dissonance process. For E. Aronson (1968, 1992), a person's perception of him- or herself as a competent and moral person necessarily forms one of the cognitions that lead to dissonance arousal. The inconsistent cognition arises from the representation of behavior that compromises or threatens the person's preferred assessment of being a highly moral and competent individual. For Steele and his colleagues (e.g., Steele, 1988; Steele & Liu, 1983), *dissonance reduction* is a strategy designed to protect a person's global feeling of self-worth and self-esteem.

Counterattitudinal behavior threatens the self and thus needs to be dealt with, often through attitude change. Ironically, these two versions of the role of self-esteem have made dramatically different predictions. E. Aronson's *self-consistency* view argues that the typical dissonance situation is arousing only for people with high self-esteem, whereas *self-affirmation* theory argues that people with low self-esteem are primarily upset or threatened by attitude-inconsistent behavior (Steele, Spencer, & Lynch, 1993). These predictions stem from fundamentally different views of the self. Self-consistency views the self as an expectancy, with high self-esteem serving as a more exacting and stringent expectation for one's behavior. For self-affirmation, high self-esteem is a resource that can be brought to bear to buffer the actor against the experience of discomfort.

In our self-standards model of dissonance, Jeff Stone and I took the position that there is no consistent or systematic role for the self in the dissonance process (Stone & Cooper, 2001). Dissonance is not limited to people of high self-esteem, as suggested by self-consistency, nor is it limited to people with low self-esteem, as indicated by self-affirmation. It is not a process that occurs only for introverts, high achievers, or people high in nurturance needs, and so forth. To the contrary, dissonance is a process that is aroused in all people whenever they are responsible for bringing about an aversive consequence. As I suggested previously, the self may become involved in helping to determine when a behavioral consequence is considered aversive. If a personal, self-relevant standard is promoted to a position of high accessibility in a person's cognitive field, then behavioral outcomes that are at variance with the self-standard will create dissonance. But this is a very different view from the totalitarian sense of self in which one aspect of self (e.g., self-esteem) dominates and determines the existence of dissonance.

A CASE IN POINT: IS DISSONANCE SELF-AFFIRMATION?

The general proposition of self-affirmation is that people are concerned with the integrity of their self-worth and will take great pains to protect it. There is nothing in dissonance theory that contradicts this important message. The question at issue is whether dissonance reduction may be conceived solely as a strategic maneuver to accomplish self-affirmation. What Steele and his colleagues have contended is that participants' changes of the representations of their attitudes in dissonance experiments are merely strategic maneuvers to satisfy the self-affirmation motive. The theory holds that people who commit counterattitudinal acts see that they have compromised their integrity. There is nothing special about a dissonant act; it is simply one more way that people can have their self-integrity threatened.

In self-affirmation's view, people with shaky self-concepts (i.e., people with low self-esteem) are the ones most threatened. They will be most in need of finding a way to restore their self-integrity. However, in dissonance experiments, there is only one way provided for them: They can change their attitudes, so that their behavior no longer seems like a compromise to their integrity. Coming to believe what they said is a way for participants in a dissonance experiment to restore their self-integrity and to accomplish the task of self-affirmation. There are other ways that the self can be affirmed if people are given the opportunity. If, after performing some dastardly, consequential, counterattitudinal act, one can think of positive features that support her or his self-integrity, then, according to the self-affirmation approach, consequential, counterattitudinal behavior will not lead to attitude change.

Thus, Steele and Liu (1983) found that if people are reminded of their basic and important values by, for example, filling out an Allport–Vernon–Lindzey Study of Values (AVL; Allport, Vernon, & Lindzey, 1960) then counterattitudinal behavior does not lead to dissonance-produced attitude change.

If it were true that merely thinking about one's good attributes eliminates cognitive dissonance, it would be a major challenge to the new look model. This is not just because it was unpredicted, but because it is at variance with the presumed motivational underpinning of dissonance. Why do people change their attitudes after counterattitudinal advocacy or after making difficult decisions among choice alternatives? As mentioned previously, it is to render the consequence of the behavior nonaversive. If you convince fellow voters to elect a disliked candidate to your city council, for example, thinking about how good a tennis player you are hardly solves the dilemma in which you placed yourself—assuming the dilemma is that the wrong councilperson has been elected. Only changing your attitude to favor the newly elected councilperson will render the outcome nonaversive. Of course, that is the crux of the theoretical difference: Is dissonance reduction a way to deal with the arousal created by the behavioral outcome, or is it merely a strategy of self-affirmation?

Consider the following thought-experiment: You are a person who thinks it is important to provide services for the handicapped. Nonetheless, an experimenter convinces you to write an essay advocating a cut in handicapped services at your university. You feel upset and negatively aroused at what you have done. If the motivation posited by self-affirmation is correct, you have all the wherewithal at your disposal to reduce your discomfort and reaffirm yourself any time you wish to do it. All of the ingredients you need are currently in your head. There are values you possess, abilities you have, accomplishments you have produced—all of these and more are waiting for you in memory if you only choose to use them. Any of those mnemonic cognitions can be used for self-affirmation and should be every bit as good as, for example, the filling out of an AVL, which forms the self-affirmation manipulation in Steele and Liu's (1983) experiment. The question is, will you use these memory traces? Will you end your discomfort by conjuring up the recollection of some of your positive values or achievements?

Most probably, this would not happen. The results of so many experiments in which people advocated attitude-discrepant positions argue that people will not make use of the potentially self-affirming cognitions they already possess in memory. If they did—and surely such cognitions were available for use—then counterattitudinal advocacy would never lead to attitude change. It would seem so much more efficient and require so little effort to think quickly of your prowess at tennis or of the great meal you cooked the other night. Even these thoughts are only indirect ways of restoring the self-concept that was threatened by your heartless, noncompassionate essay. It would seem so much more effective to take a frontal attack on your seeming lack of concern for the handicapped by remembering how compassionate you typically have been toward people in need. There must have been some occasion in which your compassion and concern come to mind. However, we know that people do not conjure up such cognitions because cognitions that could provide such direct self-affirming information are always available in memory but are not used by people in any of the research in counterattitudinal advocacy.

It could be argued that, although they are potentially available, such cognitions are largely inaccessible in the context of a psychology experiment. You chose to make a speech, you wove an argument in support of your disliked position, you risked bringing about an unwanted consequence, and you were then given an attitude scale. Perhaps there was no opportunity for your compassionate memories to become accessible in memory.

Avoidance of Relevant Affirmations

Joshua Aronson, Hart Blanton, and I decided to assess this possibility (J. Aronson, Blanton, & Cooper, 1995). It was our plan to place people in a dissonant situation, make self-affirming cognitions readily accessible, and examine their impact on the dissonance process. It was not at all clear to us that making cognitions accessible that were directly related to the self-concept dimension threatened by the counterattitudinal advocacy would make people more comfortable. Although directly self-affirming on the threatened dimension, such cognitions might make the behavioral outcome seem worse and increase, rather than decrease, the uncomfortable arousal state of dissonance. Thus, such cognitions might be avoided rather than sought and not lower the need for dissonance-reducing attitude change.

In our study, we had volunteers participate in an experiment described as a study in personality structure. Participants were seated by a computer and were asked to respond on-line to the items generated on the screen. When they had completed the inventory, they were told that it would take approximately 15 min for the computer to analyze their responses and present a personality profile.

The study used a two-experimenter procedure, with participants being ushered into the office of a second experimenter while waiting for the computer to analyze the personality results. The second experimenter explained that he was working with the university on research about handicapped facilities on campus. He explained that the university was considering curtailing some of its services for the handicapped, and that the policymakers wanted to study students' opinions. In keeping with procedures that have often been used in counterattitudinal advocacy research, the experimenter explained that one of the best ways to obtain people's thoughts on both sides of an issue was to have people write strong and forceful essays favoring one of the two sides. He explained that he had plenty of essays opposing any curtailing of services for the handicapped, and that what he needed now were essays taking the strong and forceful position that services should be reduced. The first independent variable was the magnitude of the choice that participants were given to write the essay. In the high-choice conditions, participants were told that the choice to write this essay was completely their own, whereas in the low-choice conditions, they were merely told to write the antihandicapped services essay.

When the essay was completed and before any assessment of the participant's attitudes, the participant was sent back to the office of the first experimenter to complete the personality structure research. The timing of the attitude assessment, relative to the participant's opportunity to learn how compassionate he or she was, served as the second independent variable in the study. In the attitude-first condition, the second experimenter immediately knocked on the first experimenter's door. Embarrassed and somewhat out of breath, he explained that he had forgotten to give the participant a questionnaire that the university needed. This questionnaire contained the crucial measurement of the participant's opinion about reducing handicapped funding. In the attitude-second condition, the embarrassed first experimenter knocked on the door after the participant's opportunity to receive information on how highly compassionate he or she was.

The first experimenter explained to all participants that the feedback from the personality profile was ready and there was both good news and bad news. The good news was that the computer had identified a large number of factors on which the participant scored greater than the median. The computer printed a paragraph describing the participant's personality profile on all items in which he or she scored above the median. The bad news was that so many items had been identified, there was not time to read all of them. Thus, the participant was told he or she would have to choose which of 10 personality dimensions to read. Would the participants seek or avoid the directly affirming paragraphs that identified him or her as high in compassion? The participants' choice of which paragraphs to read served as a second important dependent measure.

First, let us look at the attitude measure. Recall that in the attitude-first condition, participants had their attitudes assessed before receiving any feedback that could have served as self-affirmation. Both self-affirmation theory and dissonance theory would predict greater opinion change for high-choice than for low-choice participants (i.e., the typical induced-compliance effect found in many studies). However, in the attitude-second condition, participants had already had an opportunity to read about their good qualities, including—if they so desired—direct confirmation of their goodness in the area of compassion. This manipulation made positive self-information both available and accessible and should have provided ample opportunity for self-affirmation. Nonetheless, Figure 9.1 shows that reading about one's good personality traits had absolutely no effect on attitudes. In the attitude-second condition, just like the attitude-first condition, high-choice participants expressed attitudes that were significantly more in favor of reducing handicapped funding than did participants in an attitude-only control condition in which attitudes were assessed without any experimental manipulations. Low-choice participants, however, did not differ from the control. The analysis of the data revealed a main effect for choice and significant simple effects for choice within the attitude-first and attitude-second conditions. Simply put, the opportunity to self-affirm had no impact on reducing the need to change attitudes following freely chosen, counterattitudinal advocacy.

We now address a related question: Did participants even want to see how compassionate they were? It follows from the basic assumptions of self-affirmation that people who have had their compassionate selves compromised by their counterattitudinal advocacy should jump at the opportunity to reinstate

FIGURE 9.1. Attitudes Toward Handicapped Funding After Counterattitudinal Behavior

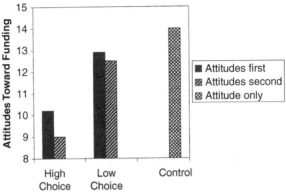

Low numbers indicate greater attitude change. Adapted from "From Dissonance to Disidentification: Selectivity in the Self-Affirmation Process," by J. Aronson, H. Blanton, and J. Cooper, 1995, *Journal of Personality and Social Psychology, 68*, p. 989. Copyright 1995 by the American Psychological Association.

their compassion. The results, presented in Figure 9.2, showed that this did not happen. To the contrary, a main effect for choice showed that the more dissonance the participants had, the less they wanted to read about their compassion. And within the attitude-second condition, high-choice participants particularly wanted no part of learning about their compassion, showing the greatest avoidance of the compassion paragraphs of all the participants in the study.

FIGURE 9.2. Interest in Reading Affirming Information About Compassion as a Function of Choice and Affirmation Opportunity

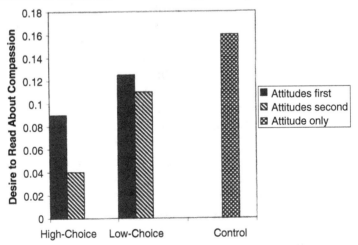

Dependent measure is the proportion of paragraphs chosen about compassion relative to the total number of paragraphs chosen. Adapted from "From Dissonance to Disidentification: Selectivity in the Self-Affirmation Process," by J. Aronson, H. Blanton, and J. Cooper, 1995, *Journal of Personality and Social Psychology, 68*, p. 990. Copyright 1995 by the American Psychological Association.

From this study, conducted at Princeton University, and a nearly identical replication run at Stanford University, we have learned a number of important facts: First, when in the throes of cognitive dissonance, people do not want to know about affirming, positive information relevant to the attribute that has been challenged by the potential consequences of their counterattitudinal behavior. Second, not only do participants not want such information, but its increased accessibility does not alter their need to reduce dissonance. Instead, participants continue to deal with the unwanted consequences of their behavior by changing their attitudes, presumably to render those consequences less aversive than they otherwise would have been.

Confronting People With Affirmation

The next question that my colleagues and I tried to answer was the effect of confronting people directly with self-affirming information (Blanton, Cooper, Skurnik, & Aronson, 1997). The previous study had shown that people who are experiencing dissonance avoid information that could directly affirm the valued personality trait that had been compromised by their counterattitudinal behavior. What would happen if people were presented with the information that showed that they were indeed compassionate, helpful people? Would making such praiseworthy information immediately salient help to reduce people's discomfort, that is, would it reduce the need for attitude change?

Our prediction was that although a directly relevant affirmation might bolster a person's self-esteem, it also could make salient a personal standard to which the behavioral outcome of an action could be compared. If people were forced to consider that they are helpful, compassionate people, that might cause the ideographic, personal standard to be brought to bear on the dissonant act.

Now, writing an essay against funding for the handicapped is aversive when considered against the normative standard and when considered against the personal standard of compassion. If compassionate people bring about effects that are antithetical to compassion, then the counterattitudinal behavior would be especially aversive. In summary, supplying a person with relevant, self-affirming information can lead to greater dissonance because the accessible personal standard makes the behavioral outcome seem even more noxious and aversive than when considered against the normative standard alone.

As in the previous study, Blanton et al. (1997) had participants volunteer for a study on personality structure. Participants were then asked by a second experimenter to write an essay arguing against funding for handicapped services at their university, under conditions of high or low choice. Participants returned to the first experimenter and read a paragraph that described an aspect of their personality that was identified by the computerized personality inventory. Some participants received positive, relevant feedback: They were told that they had scored highly in the trait of compassion. Other participants received positive, irrelevant feedback: They were

FIGURE 9.3. Attitudes Toward Proposing Relevant and Irrelevant Affirming Information

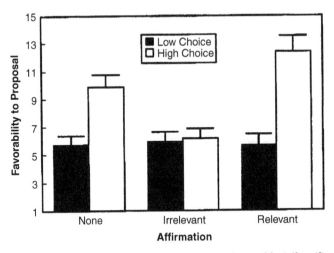

From "When Bad Things Happen to Good Feedback: Exacerbating the Need for Self-Justification With Self-Affirmations," by H. Blanton, J. Cooper, I. Skurnik, and J. Aronson, 1997, *Personality and Social Psychology Bulletin, 23*, p. 689. Copyright 1997 by Sage. Reprinted with permission.

told that they scored highly in the trait of creativity. A control group received no feedback at all.

A knock on the door brought the return of the out-of-breath, embarrassed second experimenter. As in the J. Aronson et al. (1995) procedure, he explained that he had forgotten to administer the questionnaire that the university wanted all participants to complete. This questionnaire included the major dependent measure: the assessment of attitudes toward handicapped funding.

The results showed strong evidence for our predictions. As can be seen in Figure 9.3, we found a main effect for choice and an interaction between choice and affirmation. In keeping with dissonance theory predictions, the results for the control (no-feedback) conditions showed a significant simple effect for choice: High-choice participants expressed attitudes that were more in line with the position of their essay than did low-choice participants. When participants read information that showed how positively compassionate they were (relevant-affirmation conditions), dissonance was increased. The same simple effect between high and low choice that had been found in the control condition was also found in the relevant-affirmation condition, but the effect was larger. Finally, the 2 × 3 factorial resulted in a significant interaction between choice and affirmation, aided by the lack of any difference between choice conditions when the affirming information was irrelevant to the topic of the essay. Thus, facing directly affirming information drives people further toward the need for dissonance reduction and increases, rather than decreases, dissonance-produced attitude change.

The Fuzzy (but Temporary) Good Feeling of Self-Affirmation

There is evidence in the Blanton et al. (1997) study that suggests that positive information people receive about themselves does seem to reduce the need for attitude change, provided that the information is not relevant to the self-attribute threatened by the counterattitudinal behavior. Note the lack of attitude change in the high-choice, irrelevant-feedback condition depicted in Figure 9.3. If direct self-affirmations result in increased dissonance, why does the indirect affirmation lead to less dissonance?

We think that the reason people show less dissonance motivation when receiving positive, but irrelevant, information is that they are literally distracted from the task at hand. They are distracted from the behavioral consequence by the fuzzy, good feeling of learning about a good attribute they possess. As we have argued, responsibly creating an aversive consequence creates arousal that is experienced as negative affect. When people add to that hedonic equation some positive news about themselves, their discomfort is reduced, and the exigent need to change their attitude is diminished.

However, such positive affect is fragile. We already know, from the results of the research presented here, that positive information will not lead to distracting, positive affect if it serves to make accessible a personal standard that has been directly violated by the attitude-discrepant behavior. We suspect that even irrelevant information (i.e., information that does not make the violated personal standard salient) will reduce negative affect only temporarily. It can fail: People can cease paying attention to it, or the information might be shown to be wrong. In such cases, we predict that the dissonance will return with a magnitude at least as great as that which existed before the positive, irrelevant information was introduced.

Galinsky, Stone, and Cooper (2000) conducted a study to examine the latter hypothesis. We allowed participants in a dissonance experiment to think of some of their positive self-values. Similar to previous affirmation experiments, we facilitated participants' basking in this information and feeling good about its implications by giving them the AVL. Then, for some participants, we negated the information by providing information that questioned whether they indeed possessed these positive values. We predicted that the participants would no longer have their fuzzy, good feeling. Instead, they would need to reconfront their psychological discomfort, and the need to change their attitude would reemerge.

During the 1990s, there was a tradition at Princeton University that was enthusiastically supported by undergraduate students and opposed by the town police and university officials. It occurred on the day of the first snowfall of the season and was euphemistically known as the Nude Olympics. This now-defunct tradition provided a particularly good context to conduct our induced-compliance procedure. We asked (or told) students to make speeches arguing for an end to their treasured Nude Olympics. Then, in keeping with the procedure of Steele and Liu (1983), participants filled out the AVL, which gave them the opportunity to express themselves on valued dimensions of their personality.

Some participants immediately filled out an attitude survey that asked their positions on a number of campus issues, including the degree to which they supported the Nude Olympics. Other participants were given the opportunity to affirm the self by expressing their values on the AVL. Two other conditions, one that performed the dissonant behavior under conditions of high choice and the other under conditions of low choice, were randomly assigned to the disconfirmed condition. These participants received alleged feedback based on their responses to the AVL. They were shown graphs that placed their scores in the context of other university students. The graphs showed them that the positive values they thought characterized their personalities were, in fact, not characteristic of them at all. Essentially, their affirmations were negated and disconfirmed. Following the viewing of the graphs, participants in the affirmation and disconfirmed conditions filled out attitude scales and other measures.

The results of the attitude measure are depicted in Figure 9.4. We found that participants who were distracted by the positive information about their values did not manifest attitude change toward the Nude Olympics and differed significantly from the high-choice-no-feedback participants. However, when the participants learned that they had scored low on those treasured values that they thought characterized their personalities, their attitudes

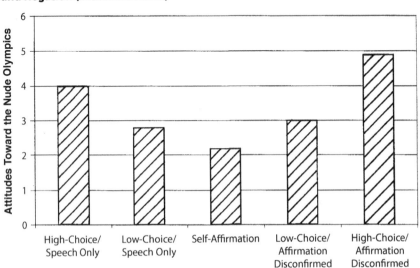

FIGURE 9.4. Attitudes Toward the Nude Olympics After Affirmation and Negation (Disconfirmation)

From "The Reinstatement of Dissonance and Psychological Discomfort Following Failed Affirmations," by A. D. Galinsky, J. Stone, and J. Cooper, 2000, *European Journal of Social Psychology, 30*, p. 140. Copyright 2000 by John Wiley & Sons. Reprinted with permission.

reverted to those expressed by the high-choice, no-feedback participants. In other words, the relief from needing to deal with the aversive consequences of their behavior was short-lived. As soon as the positive information was disconfirmed, the need to deal with the reality of the aversive event returned and so did dissonance-produced attitude change.

Low-choice disconfirmed participants did not show justification of their dissonant behavior. This result indicates that it was not negative feedback per se that caused attitude change. Rather, discrediting participants' values produced attitude change only for those participants who initially experienced dissonance and who had attempted to deal with the situation by focusing on their positive values.

In a separate experiment, using a very similar procedure, we examined the effect of affirming or negating positive, self-relevant information on the participants' emotional experience. Using a measure developed by Elliot and Devine (1994), participants were asked to rate their affect after producing a counterattitudinal speech, after self-affirming on the AVL, or after receiving information that negated their affirmation, depending on the experimental condition to which they had been assigned. They were asked to rate their psychological discomfort by indicating the degree to which they felt uncomfortable, uneasy, and bothered.

In keeping with the attitude data presented in Figure 9.4, participants in the high-choice, no-feedback condition who did not have the opportunity to think about their favorite values showed a high degree of psychological discomfort, as dissonance theory predicts. On the other hand, participants who contemplated their positive values expressed a very low level of psychological discomfort, as predicted by self-affirmation. However, when the positive thoughts were negated by information showing that participants did not possess a high degree of those values, the psychological discomfort reemerged at a level similar to that of the high-choice, no-feedback participants. As in the previous experiment, low-choice, negative-feedback participants did not experience discomfort. This demonstrates that the negation information per se did not have a negative impact on the participants' discomfort level. Rather, writing a counterattitudinal essay under high-choice conditions appears to be necessary to invoke the feeling of discomfort, a feeling state akin to Festinger's (1957) original conceptualization of dissonance. Writing under low choice produced no psychological discomfort, even when it was accompanied by information showing people that the degree to which they held certain treasured values was not very high. Allowing people to bask in the belief that they did have treasured values reduced psychological discomfort, but the relief was fragile and fleeting. Discomfort reemerged in full force when the participants' belief in their values was negated by the computerized feedback.

Putting the Pieces Together

In summary, the current portion of my argument is that dissonance reduction is not a strategy to make the self feel better or affirmed. Rather, it is the result of an unpleasant arousal state and is designed to render the consequence of a behavior nonaversive. Our data have shown that (a) people do not wish to find out about positive features of the self that have been threatened by attitude-discrepant behaviors, even though such information could directly repair the integrity of the compromised self; (b) people who are induced to confront affirming information directly manifest an increased need to reduce dissonance through attitude change; and (c) people who receive positive information that is not related to the compromised part of the self may show less of a need for attitude change after counterattitudinal behavior, but such reduction is temporary and fragile, with attitude change re-emerging if the affirmations fail. I am not arguing that people do not have an independent motive to feel good about themselves or to direct their actions toward restoring self-integrity. However, I am arguing that in situations in which people responsibly produce unwanted consequences, they must deal directly with the cognitive representation of those consequences—usually by changing their attitudes. Attempts to deal with their compromised self-integrity must wait until they have dealt with the unwanted consequences of their behavior.

SPECULATIONS ON A NEW ROLE FOR THE SELF IN DISSONANCE

Earlier, I indicated that there was no necessary role played by the self in dissonance reduction. That statement is now qualified to mean that dissonance is not confined to people with a particular self-view or to people with a particular level of self-esteem or to people with a particular personality trait. Much of the data presented in this chapter has focused on whether dissonance is merely one of many possible strategies to make a shattered self feel better and concluded that that was not a proper role for the self in dissonance theory.

However, the self is very much involved in dissonance if one takes a somewhat broader perspective (Stone & Cooper, 2001). First, the self plays a role as a standard against which a consequence can be considered wanted or unwanted. When self-standards are made highly accessible by environmental events or, in what I suspect are rare circumstances, by chronic accessibility, then they supersede normative standards in determining the aversiveness of a behavioral outcome (Stone & Cooper, 2003). Second, and somewhat more speculatively, the self may be intimately connected to the ontogeny of dissonance.

In the original new look paper (Cooper & Fazio, 1984) and a subsequent empirical study (Cooper, 1998), Fazio and I suggested that dissonance developed as a learned drive. Think about how children may learn to anticipate negative events in their lives. They learn that certain behaviors are followed by punishments and threats. Soon, children learn to anticipate the connection between behaviors and negative outcomes, and they avoid behaving in ways that bring such outcomes. Sullivan (1953), in his social psychiatric theory of personality development, discussed the creation of the self-system as a way of bringing about security while avoiding anxiety. The key to the system is that the self develops as a complex system of cognitions and behaviors, all designed to anticipate and cope with anxiety-producing reactions from people in the environment. It seems reasonable that one such negative, painful reaction from the environment occurs when a child brings about a consensually agreed, negative outcome. Hurting one's mother, or a baby sister, or even knocking over a lamp may qualify as normatively defined negative events. Children thus learn to anticipate that such events lead to profound negative responses and are to be avoided. So an uncomfortable emotional reaction may develop at any hint or anticipation of responsibly bringing about an aversive event. If children do bring about an aversive event, then they need to develop ways to cope. One way might be to deny responsibility; if that fails, they may need to change what was once aversive into something nonaversive. What may develop as a response to the anxiety reactions and sanctions of significant people in the environment may eventually develop its own autonomy and become the tension state known as dissonance.

The gist of the analysis is to speculate that the development of ways to cope with producing aversive behavioral outcomes may be intimately related to the development of the entire self-system. Avoiding dissonance situations is learned as part of the self-system, as are coping mechanisms, should unwanted, aversive events occur. Dealing with significant others in the environment helps us form our self-systems, and, part and parcel of that development, is the development of cognitive dissonance.

Dissonance theory, throughout its long history, has been marked by extensions and applications into new and uncharted territory. Examining the role of the self in dissonance theory may provide another new opportunity. Although I have taken issue with the precise way that theories of self-consistency and self-affirmation view the involvement of self in dissonance, examining dissonance within the context of the self-system may prove a fertile area for future theory and research.

REFERENCES

Allport, G. W., Vernon, P. E., & Lindzey, G. (1960). *Allport–Vernon–Lindzey Study of Values.* Chicago, IL: Riverside.

Aronson, E. (1968). Dissonance theory: Progress and problems. In R. Abelson, E. Aronson, W. McGuire, T. Newcomb, M. Rosenberg, & P. Tannenbaum (Eds.), *Theories of cognitive consistency: A sourcebook* (pp. 5–27). Chicago, IL: Rand McNally.

Aronson, E. (1992). The return of the repressed: Dissonance theory makes a comeback. *Psychological Inquiry, 3*, 303–311. http://dx.doi.org/10.1207/s15327965pli0304_1

Aronson, J., Blanton, H., & Cooper, J. (1995). From dissonance to disidentification: Selectivity in the self-affirmation process. *Journal of Personality and Social Psychology, 68*, 986–996. http://dx.doi.org/10.1037/0022-3514.68.6.986

Blackman, S. F., Keller, K. T., & Cooper, J. (2016). Egocentrism and vicarious dissonance. *Journal of Experimental Social Psychology, 62*, 1–6. http://dx.doi.org/10.1016/j.jesp.2015.09.001

Blanton, H., Cooper, J., Skurnik, I., & Aronson, J. (1997). When bad things happen to good feedback: Exacerbating the need for self-justification with self-affirmations. *Personality and Social Psychology Bulletin, 23*, 684–692. http://dx.doi.org/10.1177/0146167297237002

Brehm, J. W. (1956). Postdecision changes in the desirability of alternatives. *Journal of Abnormal and Social Psychology, 52*, 384–389. http://dx.doi.org/10.1037/h0041006

Cooper, J. (1998). Unlearning cognitive dissonance: Toward an understanding of the development of dissonance. *Journal of Experimental Social Psychology, 34*, 562–575. http://dx.doi.org/10.1006/jesp.1998.1365

Cooper, J. (2007). *Cognitive dissonance: Fifty years of a classic theory*. Thousand Oaks, CA: Sage.

Cooper, J., & Fazio, R. H. (1984). A new look at dissonance theory. In L. Berkowitz (Ed.), *Advances in experimental social psychology* (Vol. 17, pp. 229–266). New York, NY: Academic Press.

Cooper, J., & Scalise, C. J. (1974). Dissonance produced by deviations from life styles: The interaction of Jungian typology and conformity. *Journal of Personality and Social Psychology, 29*, 566–571. http://dx.doi.org/10.1037/h0036217

Cooper, J., & Worchel, S. (1970). Role of undesired consequences in arousing cognitive dissonance. *Journal of Personality and Social Psychology, 16*, 199–206. http://dx.doi.org/10.1037/h0029830

Cooper, J., Zanna, M. P., & Goethals, G. R. (1974). Mistreatment of an esteemed other as a consequence affecting dissonance reduction. *Journal of Experimental Social Psychology, 10*, 224–233. http://dx.doi.org/10.1016/0022-1031(74)90069-9

Elliot, A., & Devine, P. (1994). On the motivational nature of cognitive dissonance: Dissonance as psychological discomfort. *Journal of Personality and Social Psychology, 67*, 382–394. http://dx.doi.org/10.1037/0022-3514.67.3.382

Festinger, L. (1957). *A theory of cognitive dissonance*. Palo Alto, CA: Stanford University Press.

Festinger, L., & Carlsmith, J. M. (1959). Cognitive consequences of forced compliance. *Journal of Abnormal and Social Psychology, 58*, 203–210. http://dx.doi.org/10.1037/h0041593

Galinsky, A. D., Stone, J., & Cooper, J. (2000). The reinstatement of dissonance and psychological discomfort following failed affirmations. *European Journal of Social Psychology, 30*, 123–147. http://dx.doi.org/10.1002/(SICI)1099-0992(200001/02)30:1<123::AID-EJSP981>3.0.CO;2-T

Hoyt, M. F., Henley, M. D., & Collins, B. E. (1972). Studies in forced compliance: Confluence of choice and consequence on attitude change. *Journal of Personality and Social Psychology, 23*, 205–210. http://dx.doi.org/10.1037/h0033034

Kunda, Z. (1990). The case for motivated reasoning. *Psychological Bulletin, 108*, 480–498. http://dx.doi.org/10.1037/0033-2909.108.3.480

Kunda, Z. (1999). *Social cognition: Making sense of people*. Boston, MA: MIT press.

Norton, M. I., Monin, B., Cooper, J., & Hogg, M. A. (2003). Vicarious dissonance: Attitude change from the inconsistency of others. *Journal of Personality and Social Psychology, 85*, 47–62. http://dx.doi.org/10.1037/0022-3514.85.1.47

Scher, S. J., & Cooper, J. (1989). Motivational basis of dissonance: The singular role of behavioral consequences. *Journal of Personality and Social Psychology, 56*, 899–906. http://dx.doi.org/10.1037/0022-3514.56.6.899

Steele, C. M. (1988). The psychology of self-affirmation: Sustaining the integrity of the self. In L. Berkowitz (Ed.), *Advances in experimental social psychology* (pp. 261–302). Hillsdale, NJ: Erlbaum. http://dx.doi.org/10.1016/S0065-2601(08)60229-4

Steele, C. M., & Liu, T. J. (1983). Dissonance processes as self-affirmation. *Journal of Personality and Social Psychology, 45*, 5–19. http://dx.doi.org/10.1037/0022-3514.45.1.5

Steele, C. M., Spencer, S. J., & Lynch, M. (1993). Self-image resilience and dissonance: The role of affirmational resources. *Journal of Personality and Social Psychology, 64,* 885–896. http://dx.doi.org/10.1037/0022-3514.64.6.885

Stone, J., & Cooper, J. (2001). A self-standards model of cognitive dissonance. *Journal of Experimental Social Psychology, 37,* 228–243. http://dx.doi.org/10.1006/jesp.2000.1446

Stone, J., & Cooper, J. (2003). The effect of self-attribute relevance on how self-esteem moderates attitude change in dissonance processes. *Journal of Experimental Social Psychology, 39,* 508–515. http://dx.doi.org/10.1016/S0022-1031(03)00018-0

Sullivan, H. S. (1953). *Interpersonal theory of psychiatry.* New York, NY: Norton.

MATHEMATICAL MODELS, NEURAL ACTIVATIONS, AND AFFECTIVE RESPONSES

10

Modeling Cognitive Dissonance as a Parallel Constraint Satisfaction Network With Learning

Stephen J. Read and Brian M. Monroe

One of the most famous and productive theories in social psychology has been Festinger's (1957) theory of cognitive dissonance. The term *cognitive dissonance* has entered everyday language and is often used to describe inconsistencies among cognitions. According to cognitive dissonance theory, when two cognitions are dissonant with each other, an individual is motivated to reduce that dissonance. Researchers have used dissonance theory to generate a number of counterintuitive findings, such as finding that people like groups better the more painful the initiation is to join that group (Gerard & Mathewson, 1966), and that people like a boring task better, if they agree to tell someone that the task is actually interesting in exchange for a small amount of money compared to receiving a large amount (Festinger & Carlsmith, 1959).

Several authors (e.g., Read & Miller, 1994; Read & Simon, 2012; Read, Vanman, & Miller, 1997; Shultz & Lepper, 1996, 1998; Simon & Holyoak, 2002; Spellman, Ullman, & Holyoak, 1993) have argued that cognitive dissonance (Festinger, 1957) and related consistency phenomena (Abelson et al., 1968) can be modeled as a parallel constraint-satisfaction process in a neural network, where the relevant cognitions are treated as nodes that have activation levels representing the initial strength of the corresponding cognitions, and the consistent and inconsistent relations between cognitions are treated as excitatory and inhibitory relationships among nodes, respectively. After the nodes in the network are initially activated, activation spreads, over time, across the excitatory and inhibitory links until the activation of the nodes in the network settles into a stable state that best represents the parallel satisfaction of the constraints

http://dx.doi.org/10.1037/0000135-010
Cognitive Dissonance, Second Edition: Reexamining a Pivotal Theory in Psychology,
E. Harmon-Jones (Editor)
Copyright © 2019 by the American Psychological Association. All rights reserved.

imposed by the excitatory and inhibitory links and the level of activation of the nodes.

Read et al. (1997) noted that parallel constraint-satisfaction processes provide a computational implementation of the Gestalt processes that are the theoretical underpinnings of dissonance theory. These authors, and particularly Shultz and Lepper (1996, 1998), have shown that a number of different cognitive dissonance findings can be successfully modeled in a parallel constraint-satisfaction network that is implemented as a feedback or recurrently connected network. Many of Shultz and Lepper's (1999) simulations were reviewed in their modeling chapter in the previous edition of this book.

Van Overwalle and Jordens (2002) noted that these approaches to modeling cognitive dissonance can only model immediate attitude and belief change; because they lack a learning mechanism, they are incapable of modeling long-term change that might result from resolving dissonance. Although learning could be implemented in these models, none did so.

Van Overwalle and Jordens's (2002) proposed solution was a feedforward neural network, consisting of one input layer (representing the key features of the experimental situation), feeding into one output layer (representing a feeling and a behavior). Because it is a feedforward network, activation only flows from input to output. And because there are no connections among the nodes in the output layer, the feeling and the behavior have no influence on each other. Delta-rule (or error-correcting) learning is used to change the weights.

A learning mechanism is critical for any model of cognitive dissonance that wishes to address long-term attitude change resulting from dissonance reduction. However, a major shortcoming of a two-layer, feedforward network is that it cannot capture the short-term attitude change, represented by changes in activation, that is easily represented in a feedback model. In the current chapter, we present a connectionist model of cognitive dissonance that integrates the strengths of the two types of connectionist models that have been previously proposed and that avoids many of their weaknesses. It is a recurrent or feedback network with learning. Here we successfully model four classic cognitive dissonance experiments: Free Choice, Forbidden Toy, Forced Compliance, and Severity of Initiation.

ISSUES WITH FEEDFORWARD MODELS, SUCH AS THE ONE USED BY VAN OVERWALLE AND JORDENS (2002)

One major issue with a feedforward model is that the characterization of cognitive dissonance is a radical departure from the consensual understanding of cognitive dissonance processes. Rather than treating dissonance reduction processes as a Gestalt-like seeking for good form and coherence (the historical view) or as a constraint-satisfaction process (the modern rendition of Gestalt ideas of coherence; see Read & Simon, 2012; Read et al., 1997; Simon & Holyoak, 2002), van Overwalle and Jordens's (2002) model treats dissonance reduction *purely* as an error correcting learning process in which the individual receives *explicit* feedback as to their behavior toward an object or situation *and* their evaluative response to that object or situation, and then uses error correcting learning to update its predictions. They model the dissonance process as follows: the network predicts its attitude (measured as the average of the activation of a behavior and a feeling node) and then the *researcher* tells the network what its actual behavior and feelings were; the network then adjusts its weights to reduce the discrepancy between the predicted attitude and the actual attitude provided by the researcher. The suggestion is that we think about dissonance reduction, not as driven by consistency maintenance processes, but instead as learning to correct errors about our predicted behaviors given explicit feedback.

In contrast, a recurrent model provides an account of consistency seeking or dissonance reduction in terms of parallel constraint-satisfaction processes that are a computational implementation of the Gestalt-like seeking for good form that underlies cognitive dissonance theory and its variants (Read & Simon, 2012; Read et al., 1997). These parallel constraint-satisfaction processes are an inherent part of a recurrent model.

In addition to presenting a different conceptualization of the dissonance process, another major issue is that van Overwalle and Jordens's (2002) model does not actually infer a new attitude. Instead it is explicitly given the attitude by the researcher. Their network predicts its behavior and feeling and then receives explicit feedback about what its measured behavior and feeling should be. In the simulations we present, the recurrent network receives direct feedback about its behavior, but it does *not* receive any direct feedback about evaluation or attitude. It uses feedback about the behavior to determine the new activation of the evaluation node. This is consistent with most dissonance studies where participants are encouraged to perform *behaviors* that are inconsistent with their *attitudes*. The activation of the evaluation (the new attitude) in our model is a result of a process of parallel constraint-satisfaction, in which the network of nodes pass activation around, until the network settles into a new stable state.

For instance, our network for the Forbidden Toy paradigm can be seen in Figure 10.1. Here, two evaluation nodes (one positive, one negative) are in the path (mediate the relationship) between the attitude object (the toy) and the behavior nodes. These evaluation nodes represent the attitude. We provide feedback only about how the child behaved. In response, the behavior nodes first send activation back to the evaluation nodes, resulting in changes to the momentary attitude, as represented by changes in the activation of the evaluation nodes. The network then subsequently changes its long-term attitude by changing the relevant weights from the toy to the evaluation nodes. That is, we simply tell the network that it performed a behavior counter to what would be expected, given its previous experience. This results in a change in the patterns of activations, including activations of the evaluation nodes, which the learning process then transforms into long-term attitude change by appropriate weight changes. The model changes the evaluations of the object and the relevant weights so that the previously unexpected behavior becomes consistent with the network's new evaluation and relations.

FIGURE 10.1. Network for Simulation 2: Freedman's (1965) Forbidden Toy

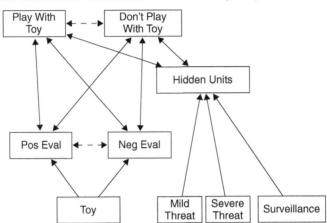

Further, van Overwalle and Jordens's (2002) attitude measurement confounds feelings and behavior. Attitude is measured as the average of the activation of the behavior and feeling nodes, so it is impossible to get a measure of behavior that is not confounded with the measure of attitude. By contrast, we rely on the idea that an attitude is the *evaluation* of the attitude object (Fazio, 2007) and that this evaluation influences behavior toward the attitude object. Thus, we have separate evaluation and behavior nodes and can measure attitude and behavior separately.

Finally, because their model lacks connections between feeling and behavior in the output layer, the behavior node and the feeling node cannot influence each other. In our network the evaluation and behavior nodes are bidirectionally connected, so that activation from the evaluation and the behavior nodes can reciprocally influence each other. An example of why this is important can be seen if we simulated someone's attitude and behavior toward a social group using van Overwalle and Jordens's model. Someone could have an extremely negative feeling about a particular social group, yet that feeling could not affect their behavior toward the group because there would be no pathway between the feeling and the behavior.

Summary

We present a model that is consistent with the theoretical underpinnings of Dissonance Theory and that we believe appropriately captures the psychological mechanisms involved in dissonance. It is a recurrent (feedback) network with Contrastive Hebbian Learning (CHL), which can capture learning in a multi-layer network. Because it is recurrent, it can capture the constraint-satisfaction processes that are central to dissonance processes. Further, because it is recurrent, changes in the behavior nodes can be propagated back to the evaluation nodes and lead to momentary changes in their activation, representing momentary attitude change. Thus, if the network is given information only about its behavior, it uses that information to change its attitudes, without needing direct feedback about its new attitudes. And the network then uses this new pattern of activation of the attitude nodes to modify its weights to capture long-term attitude change represented by changes in the weights in a multilayer network.

In the remainder of the chapter, we first outline a recurrent neural network model with learning that integrates the strengths of previous neural network models of dissonance, while avoiding some of their limitations. Second, we show how this network can simulate four classic dissonance studies.

DESCRIPTION OF THE DISSONANCE MODELING PROCEDURE AND RESULTS

We first provide an overview of the network that we used in our simulations, then describe the general simulation procedure we used in all our simulations, and finally describe the results for the simulations of several classic cognitive dissonance phenomena.

Network Overview

The simulations were done using the constraint-satisfaction module (cs++) in the PDP++ neural network package (Dawson, O'Reilly, & McClelland, 2003).[1] This is a freely available, powerful, well-known, and well-supported package. A major advantage of using a package such as *emergent* is that any simulations can easily be run and investigated by anyone with access to the software. In addition, *emergent* has been used to build a variety of large-scale cognitive systems, which means that cognitive dissonance ideas could be integrated into large scale cognitive models.

The model used a Contrastive Hebbian Learning (CHL) algorithm developed for the Boltzmann machine and then generalized by O'Reilly (1996). This algorithm compares the activation of the network in a plus phase (when both inputs and desired outputs are presented to the network) to its activation in a minus phase (when only the inputs are presented). CHL then adjusts weights to reduce the difference in activation between the two phases. What CHL is doing is that in the minus phase, the network uses its inputs to predict what its outputs should be whereas the plus phase represents what the inputs actually lead to. This is compatible with the typical dissonance study, where the minus phase can be thought of as what the individual expects to do and the plus phase can be thought of as what the individual actually did. CHL allows for learning in multilayer networks (e.g., networks with hidden units) and adjusts weights in a more biologically plausible way than does back propagation, which requires the use of

---

[1] They could also be done in cs++ in *emergent* (Aisa, Mingus, & O'Reilly, 2008; see https://grey.colorado.edu/emergent/index.php/Main_Page), the newly rewritten version of PDP++.

a nonlocal error term and assumes that the error can be propagated back through multiple layers. CHL uses a local error term and thus does not require the propagation of an error signal. However, we are not making any strong claims about the superiority of CHL over back propagation. The central issue is being able to address learning in a multilayer network, where attitudes can intervene between attitude objects and behavior.

We used the default sigmoidal (S-shaped) activation function for the units in the networks, with activations limited to the range −1 to +1. Bias weights were set at zero. During the predissonance learning phase of the simulations, the learning rate was set to 0.1. Because in some of the experiments, more complicated conjunctive relationships were required to be learned, learning in these simulations proceeded for more epochs (that is, more passes through the learning instances). The number of learning epochs ranged from 20 for Simulation 1: Free Choice to 100 epochs for Simulations 2–4. The specific details of the learning procedure in the predissonance phase are not critical to the model, as this learning was done simply to ensure that each network represented an appropriate pattern of cognitions.

General Overview of the Simulation Procedure

The general logic of the simulations is as follows. First, the network is exposed to a set of learning examples so that it develops a set of weights that correspond to the initial pattern of cognitions in the relevant experiment. For example, in the Forbidden Toy simulation (Freedman, 1965; see Figure 10.1), the model learns such things as that the toy is attractive (that is, the presence of the toy leads to positive activation of a positive evaluation node and negative activation of a negative evaluation node). And the positive evaluation node is positively associated with the "play with the toy" node. Thus, when the toy is presented to the network, it should highly activate the positive evaluation node, which should then highly activate the "play with the toy" node.

In the current simulations, we are using the training simply to make sure that the network represents the appropriate cognitions. Thus, when there are different patterns of relevant cognitions in different conditions, we will capture that by giving the networks different learning histories. In other work it would be interesting to use learning to investigate the impact of different evaluations and beliefs, as a result of different experiences, on dissonance processes.

Once the networks have learned the relevant pattern of cognitions, we expose the network to a set of cues that correspond to a condition in a dissonance experiment. Essentially, we first expose the network to the relevant cues and let it generate a prediction for how it will behave. We then give the network feedback as to how it did behave in the environment. For example, consider the different conditions in the Linder, Cooper, and Jones (1967) Forced Compliance study, where participants are asked to write a counter-attitudinal essay under either "Free Choice" or coercion, with high or low payment (see Figure 10.2 for the network). In the coercion condition, with high payment,

FIGURE 10.2. Network for Simulation 3: Linder, Cooper, and Jones's (1967) Forced Compliance

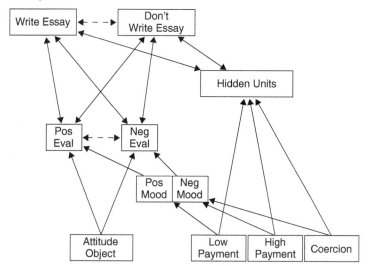

features for the attitude object, the coercion, and the high payment would be strongly activated, and we would then let the network generate a prediction. In this case, the node for writing a counterattitudinal essay would be highly activated. The network would then be given feedback indicating that the network did write a counterattitudinal essay. Because there is no discrepancy between the predicted behavior and the actual behavior, and because there would be very little change in the activations of the other nodes in the network, particularly the evaluation nodes, there will be little weight change and therefore little attitude change.

However, the behavior of the network in the dissonance condition: the Free Choice, low-payment condition would be different. Here, the nodes corresponding to the attitude object, the Free Choice, and low payment would be activated and the network would generate a prediction, which is that the individual would not write the counterattitudinal essay. However, the teaching feedback is that the individual did write the counterattitudinal essay. Thus, the predicted behavior and the actual behavior are dissonant. This is represented in the network by positive activation of both nodes, which have an inhibitory or negative link between them. Thus, they seek to inhibit each other, with the "writing the counterattitudinal essay" node, because it receives external input, successfully inhibiting the original prediction. Activation is then propagated from the behavior nodes back to the evaluation nodes, resulting in changes of the activation of the evaluation nodes to become more consistent with the activation of the behavior nodes. This change in activation of the evaluation nodes represents short-term attitude change.

The weights in the network are then adjusted, capturing long-term attitude change, so that in the future, the predicted activation of the behavior nodes is closer to the teaching activation and the predicted activation of the evaluation nodes is closer to their actual activation. We then test for the new attitude by activating the attitude object and seeing how strongly activated are the positive and negative evaluation nodes.

Simulation 1: Shultz, Léveillé, and Lepper (1999) Free Choice

This experiment was a refinement of the classic study by Brehm (1956), where participants were asked to rate a set of appliances, then to choose one they wanted from among those items (they were then allowed to keep the item), and finally asked to rate the objects again. The manipulation was whether the choice was easy to make (if the difference in the attractiveness of the items was large, the choice of which item they wanted would be clear) or if the choice was a difficult one (where the attractiveness of the items was very similar).

In the Shultz, Léveillé, and Lepper (1999) version, there were three conditions, as opposed to the two in Brehm's (1956) experiment. The "easy" condition from Brehm's study was preserved, but instead of one difficult condition there were two. In Brehm, the difficult condition had two highly rated items. This condition was translated into the difficult-high condition. The new condition was one in which the items were rated similarly but were both poorly rated (difficult-low). The rationale for adding this condition was that Shultz and Lepper's (1996) consonance model predicted that dissonance would manifest itself differently depending upon whether the difficult choice was between two highly rated objects or between two poorly rated choices. In Brehm's difficult condition (difficult-high rating), the nonchosen item was derogated to preserve consonance of thought, while Shultz and Lepper's (1996) model predicted that if the items were both rated poorly to begin with (difficult-low), derogation of the nonchosen item would not be a feasible option, so the chosen item would be bolstered instead.

So, Shultz, Léveillé, and Lepper's (1999) experiment was set up as follows: In the easy condition, one item was a highly rated poster and the other was a poorly rated poster. In the difficult-low condition, both posters were rated poorly, and in the difficult-high condition, both posters were rated highly. Shultz and Lepper's (1996) consonance model predicted that in the difficult-high condition, the nonchosen item would be derogated more severely than in the easy condition. In the difficult-low condition, the prediction was that the chosen item would be bolstered more than in the easy condition, because the rejected item was already poorly rated and so the only reasonable way to rearrange cognitions would be to raise the evaluation of the chosen item. These predictions were borne out in the experiment (see Figure 10.3a).

Structure of the Network

To model this simulation, we used a setup whose basic features are used in all subsequent models in this report. The model had three layers (see Figure 10.4). The first of these layers corresponded to the object(s) in question and served as the primary input layer. The second layer incorporated the evaluation of the

FIGURE 10.3. Results for (a) Shultz, Léveillé, and Lepper's (1999) Free Choice; and (b) Simulation 1

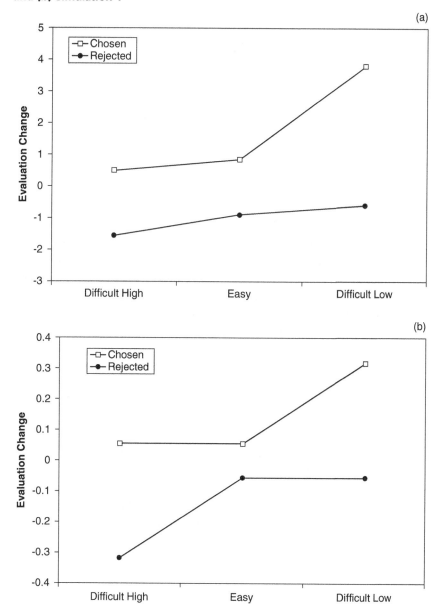

FIGURE 10.4. Network for Simulation 1: Shultz, Léveillé, and Lepper's (1999) Free Choice

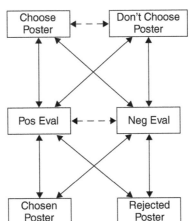

object (positive or negative, one node for each). The third layer corresponded to the relevant behaviors in the experiment. The connections between the input layer and the evaluation were feedforward only. This makes sense because the objects/issues under evaluation in dissonance experiments depend purely on external activation, that is, the evaluation comes to mind as a result of activation coming from the object, rather than the object being present as a result of activation from the evaluation. The connections between the evaluation and the behavior were recurrent (bidirectional). Here it is important that the evaluation be allowed to influence the behavior, and vice versa, so activation is allowed to flow in both directions. Thus, in our model information about the behavior and the underlying evaluation can mutually influence each other. This contrasts with van Overwalle and Jordens's (2002) model in which there is no way for information about the behavior to affect the affective response (or vice versa). This limits the kinds of processing it can do.

The evaluation units were connected to each other with a permanent negative weight (−0.5), and the behavior units were also connected to each other with permanent negative weights (−1), because for all practical purposes these units are mutually exclusive. The behavior nodes had such strong negative weights in order to model the idea that the behaviors were completely mutually exclusive (i.e., you either choose the poster or you don't). The evaluation nodes had weaker negative weights to allow for the possibility of ambivalence. That is, although these negative weights tend to make the units mutually exclusive, both evaluation nodes can be positively activated at the same time, if they each receive strong enough activation.

In the specific model for this simulation, there were two units in the object layer: one for each of the two posters between which the participant was choosing. The evaluation layer had one unit each for positive and negative evaluations, and the behavior layer had two units, one for each of the behaviors: choose and reject. See Figure 10.4 for a depiction of this model.

Learning Initial Cognitions

To set up the cognitions that were relevant in this simulation, we put the model through a learning process (see Appendix 10.1 at the end of this chapter for details). The associations we had the model learn were the following: (a) a positive evaluation is positively associated with choosing an item; and (b) a negative evaluation is positively associated with rejecting an item. In the difficult-high condition both posters had high evaluations (high activation on the positive evaluation node); in the difficult-low condition, both posters had low evaluations (low activation on the positive evaluation node); and in the easy condition, one poster had a high evaluation and the other poster a low evaluation. Across all conditions, the more attractive item was ensured to be at least very slightly more positively evaluated (activated) than the less attractive item. After initial learning, the model was tested to ensure that these associations were learned correctly.

To insure the generalizability of our results, in this and all subsequent simulations we generated 20 different "individuals." We did this by generating 20 different networks with different random initial weights and then exposed each network to the learning environment. Each of the 20 individuals or networks was then put through the dissonance phase and attitude change procedure. Thus, the results presented for this and all the subsequent simulations are the average across 20 runs with different random initializations.

Dissonance Phase and Attitude Change

For the dissonance phase of the simulation, the three conditions were implemented identically. In this simulation, the key differences were in terms of the different evaluations for the different items, which were implemented by the different learning histories, resulting in different networks for the different conditions. That is, in the difficult-high condition, the corresponding network had learned high evaluations for both posters; in the difficult-low condition, the corresponding network had learned low evaluations for both posters; and in the easy condition, the corresponding network had learned a high evaluation for one poster and a low evaluation for the other poster.

The following procedure was implemented in each of the three conditions. First, the more attractive item was paired with the behavior of being chosen (i.e., the corresponding nodes were activated), the network was allowed to settle, and the weights were updated. Second, the less attractive item was paired with the behavior of being rejected, the network was allowed to settle, and the weights were updated. This was done once for each pairing. In all the simulations reported in this paper, a learning rate of 0.5 was used in the dissonance conditions.

In the difficult-high condition, the slightly less attractive alternative was still highly evaluated, which would lead the network to predict that it would be chosen. However, the feedback was that it was *not* chosen, which creates dissonance. Thus, to resolve this dissonance, we expected that the attractiveness of the nonchosen alternative would decrease.

In the easy condition, because the network had learned a high evaluation for the chosen poster and a low evaluation for the nonchosen poster, there shouldn't be an expectation that the low evaluation poster would be chosen. Thus, there would be no dissonance and we would expect minimal weight change.

Finally, in the difficult-low condition, choosing the slightly more attractive, unattractive alternative was dissonant with the fact that it was unattractive and with the network's prediction that it would not be chosen. To resolve that dissonance, the weights should change so that the chosen alternative would be more attractive. However, for the nonchosen alternative, because it was unattractive, the network would also predict that it would not be chosen. Thus, there would be no dissonance here and we would predict little weight change for this choice.

After the dissonance process, we assessed the "new" evaluations of the two items by separately activating the respective object units and reading off the activation of the positive evaluation unit (for these simulations, the negative evaluation unit had virtually the exact opposite activation, so only the positive unit activation is reported.) Further, we reasoned that when the person was asked for their evaluation only and did not actually perform a behavior, it did not make sense to allow activation to flow through the behavior units, so those units were deactivated during this assessment by lesioning this portion of the network (that is, setting the weights from the behavior nodes to 0). Results are presented in Figure 10.3b and are the average across the 20 runs. In the difficult-high condition, the rejected item was derogated, while the evaluation of the chosen item increased only very slightly. In the easy choice condition, the chosen item's evaluation increased very slightly, and the rejected item's evaluation decreased very slightly. In the difficult-low condition, the rejected item's evaluation decreased very slightly, yet the chosen item's evaluation increased much more significantly.

Our simulation is more successful in capturing the results from Shultz et al.'s (1999) experiment than is van Overwalle and Jordens's (2002) model. Shultz et al. found greater spreading apart of alternatives in both difficult choice conditions (high- and low-attractiveness of the posters), compared to the easy choice condition, whereas van Overwalle and Jordens's simulation only shows spreading apart of the highly attractive, but not the low-attractiveness alternatives. In contrast, our model demonstrates spreading of alternatives in both high- and low-attractiveness, difficult-choice conditions.

Simulation 2: Freedman (1965) Forbidden Toy

In this paradigm, a young child is brought into the experimental room and shown an attractive toy: an interesting robot. The experimenter than administers either a mild or a severe threat to the child to not play with the robot. The experimenter then either leaves the room or stays in the room. So, the child is in one of four conditions: (a) mild threat, no surveillance; (b) mild threat, surveillance; (c) severe threat, no surveillance; or (d) severe threat, surveillance. The child is then observed through a one-way mirror. In this initial observation, none of the children play with the robot.

Forty days later the child is brought back to the experiment room and again left alone in the room with the toy. The experimenters observed the child through a one-way mirror and recorded whether the child played with the toy. The researchers predicted that all of the children should play with the toy except for those who were initially in the mild threat, no surveillance condition. The rationale is that, in all the other conditions, the child believes that they did not play with the toy because of the threat of punishment (or because of the combination of mild threat and surveillance). Thus, they didn't need to rationalize why they didn't play with the attractive toy. There shouldn't have been any change in the child's liking for the toy, and when they are later given an opportunity to play with the toy without any possibility of punishment, they will happily play with the toy. In contrast, the argument is that for the children in the mild threat, no surveillance condition, their failure to play with the robot earlier was perceived as inconsistent with the fact that they had only received a mild threat. To justify this inconsistency, they would decrease their liking for the toy. As predicted, the only children who do not play with the toy were those who were given the mild threat and thought they were not watched.

Structure of the Network

The network for this simulation is presented in Figure 10.1. As with Simulation 1, this model has a layer for the object in question (the toy), a second layer for the evaluations of that object, and a third layer for the behaviors relevant to the experiment (playing with the toy, not playing with the toy). However, this experiment was more complicated in that there were additional inputs that were relevant. Specifically, there was an additional input layer that contained additional important features of the situation: one node for the presence of the mild threat given to the child, one for severe threat, and one for the presence of surveillance during the critical phase of the experiment. Finally, in addition to these inputs, a hidden layer with eight nodes was implemented, in order to capture the conjunctive relationship between the threat and surveillance. The connections from the input layers were feedforward and all other connections were recurrent. Again, there were permanent negative connections between the positive and negative evaluations (−0.5), and between the two mutually exclusive behaviors (−1).

Learning Initial Cognitions

The initial learning history for this model was as follows (see Appendix 10.1 for details), across all four conditions: (a) the toy was associated with a positive evaluation, (b) the positive evaluation was associated with playing, and (c) the negative evaluation was associated with not playing. Additionally, the following conjunctive relationships were learned: (a) when the toy was present under surveillance only (and no threat), the toy was still played with; (b) when the toy was present with a mild threat, the toy was still played with; (c) when the toy was present with a severe threat, the toy was not played with; and (d) when the toy was present with surveillance and either a mild or severe threat, the toy was not played with. Testing confirmed these associations were learned properly. As noted above, this and all simulations in this paper are based on averages across 20 randomly initialized networks.

A key aspect of training the network in this way is that when the threat was mild, with no surveillance, the network predicted the child would play with the toy. This behavior is central to the dissonance effect in this network. According to the classic interpretation, the child, under mild threat and no surveillance, was expected to play with the toy, yet did not. Thus, there was dissonance between what the child expected to do and what s/he actually did. It was argued that the child resolved this dissonance by deciding that the toy was less attractive. However, with all other combinations of inputs (i.e., mild threat, surveillance; severe threat, surveillance; or severe threat, no surveillance) the network predicted that the child would not play with the toy.

Dissonance Phase and Attitude Change

The dissonance phase of the simulation presented one event to the network that varied across conditions. In the mild threat, no surveillance condition, the toy and the mild threat were activated and the initial prediction of the network was that the child would play with the toy. However, the feedback was that when the toy and mild threat were present, the output was not playing with the toy (represented by a positive activation on the don't play unit, and negative activation on the play unit). Thus, there was a discrepancy between what was predicted and what actually happened. The behavior nodes sent activation back to the evaluation nodes, the network then settled and the weights were changed to try to better fit this new pattern of activations.

However, in the other three conditions, the predictions of the network and the actual behavior were consistent. In all three conditions, the network predicted that it would not play with the toy, and the feedback was that it did not play with the toy. In the severe threat, no surveillance condition, the toy and the severe threat node were activated, along with the don't play node. In the mild threat, surveillance condition, the toy, mild threat, and surveillance were activated, along with the don't play output. In the severe threat, surveillance condition, the toy, severe threat, and surveillance were activated along with the don't play node. Because there was no inconsistency or dissonance in these three conditions, we did not expect to see any changes in weights.

Subsequent assessment of the attitude, after the dissonance phase, was done by activating the toy unit by itself, and reading out the activation on the play unit. (The hidden layer was deactivated by lesioning, since the purpose of this layer was to represent conjunctions of the other inputs, which were not present in this phase.) In this simulation, in contrast to the others, we focused on the activation of the behavior units, rather than the evaluation units. We did this because the primary dependent variable in the original study was the child's behavior, whereas in the other studies simulated here, the dependent variable was the participants' attitudes.

Results are presented in Figure 10.5a (original study results) and Figure 10.5b (simulation results). Consistent with previous simulations and the experiment

FIGURE 10.5. Results for (a) Freedman's (1965) Forbidden Toy; and (b) Simulation 2

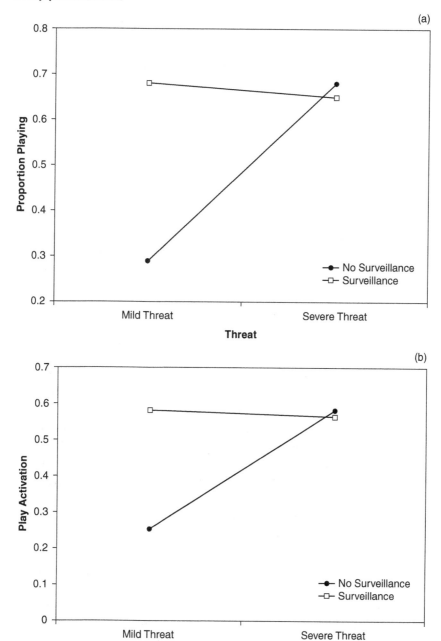

itself, only in the mild threat, no surveillance condition did the activation on the play unit decrease after the dissonance phase. This makes sense as only in that condition would there be a discrepancy between how the child was expected to behave and how they actually behaved. To ensure that our results weren't biased by looking at the activations on the behavior units in this simulation, we also examined the results by deactivating the behavior units and looking at activation of the evaluation units. The pattern of results was virtually the same.

Simulation 3: Linder et al. (1967): Forced Compliance

This experiment was designed to conceptually extend an experiment by Festinger and Carlsmith (1959) where participants were paid to tell someone that a boring task was in fact interesting, and participants who were paid less actually changed their attitude about the task more in a positive direction. The Linder et al. (1967) experiment examined whether the existence of dissonance in studies such as Festinger and Carlsmith (1959) depended on whether participants perceived that their behavior was freely chosen. Thus, they introduced an additional factor besides how much the participant was paid: whether they had a perceived choice in performing the counterattitudinal act. Students were asked, either under conditions of choice or Forced Compliance, to write an essay supporting a policy that they were not personally in favor of. The low payment was $0.50 and the high payment was $2.50.

Structure of the Network

The critical features for simulating this experiment were the attitude object (e.g., legalization of marijuana, abortion), their evaluation of it (either for or against the policy; promarijuana vs. antimarijuana), the behaviors (either writing a counterattitudinal essay or not writing it), and the situational features of coercion and small and large payments (see Figure 10.2). The form of this model is almost the same as the model in Simulation 2 (the Forbidden Toy experiment), except for changes in the definitions of the input and behavior units. In this model though, we have added a mechanism to account for the mood effects as a result of the payment and coercion that are apparent in the experimental results. In short, the input units representing payment lead directly to a positive mood, which then has an effect on the evaluation. This relationship was structured with fixed weights. The weight between the high payment and positive mood was set at +1, the weight between the low payment and positive mood was set at +0.2, and the weight between the coercion and positive mood was set at +0.7. It is reasoned that some of the negative mood resulting from writing the counterattitudinal essay was relieved by knowing it was done under coercion, thus leading to a more positive mood in these conditions. Weights between positive mood and a favorable evaluation and between positive mood and unfavorable evaluation were set at +0.5 and −0.5, respectively.

The rationale for introducing the mood nodes and their connections arises from the need to capture reward and punishment effects in this and the subsequent simulation. In this study, in the Forced Compliance conditions (the nondissonance conditions), participants in the high-payment condition changed their attitude more than did participants in the low-payment condition. And in the next simulation on Severity of Initiation, participants in the no-initiation condition were more negative toward the discussion group when they received higher levels of shock. One plausible way to capture this is to assume that people who received a higher payment are in a better mood, whereas people who receive a higher level of shock are in a worse mood. There is considerable evidence that such moods can strongly affect people's evaluations and judgments (Isen, 2000; Schwarz & Clore, 2007).

Learning Initial Cognitions

Here the prior learning history was as follows (see Appendix 10.1 for details): the attitude object was associated with an evaluation against the policy; an evaluation against the policy was associated with not writing the essay supporting the policy; and an evaluation for the policy was associated with writing the essay. In addition, the conjunctive relations were learned: having the attitude, with low payment, was associated with not writing the essay; having the attitude, with high payment, was associated with writing the essay; having the attitude, under coercion, was associated with writing the essay; and having the attitude, under coercion and with high or low payment, was associated with writing the essay. Testing confirmed that all these associations were learned correctly.

Dissonance Phase and Attitude Change

In the dissonance phase of the simulations, events varied across the four conditions. In the Free Choice, low-payment condition, the attitude and low payment were presented as inputs and the network predicted that not writing the essay would be the output. However, the actual output behavior was writing the essay, leading to dissonance between the predicted behavior and the actual behavior, which should lead to attitude change. In the other three conditions, the behavior predicted by the network and the actual behavior were consistent with one another, which should not lead to attitude change. In the Free Choice, high-payment condition, the attitude and high payment were presented as inputs with writing the essay as the output (both predicted and actual). In the Forced Compliance, low-payment condition, the attitude object, coercion, and low payment were presented as input with writing the essay as output (both predicted and actual). Finally, in the Forced Compliance, high-payment condition, the attitude object, coercion, and high payment were presented as inputs with writing the essay as output (both predicted and actual).

The attitude postmeasure was assessed by activating the attitude object unit and the appropriate additional inputs (i.e., type of payment and coercion) for that condition. (The behavior units were deactivated through lesioning, because only the evaluation is being asked for, so it is inappropriate for the behavior activation to influence the evaluation.) This still allowed the payment and coercion to influence the attitude through their effects on mood.

Results are presented in Figure 10.6a (original study results) and Figure 10.6b (simulation results). The results were consistent with both previous simulations and the experimental data. In the Free Choice condition, the attitude increased the most in the low-payment condition, but in the Forced Compliance condition, the attitude increased the most in the high-payment condition. In the Forced Compliance condition, higher payment was more associated with better mood and a more favorable evaluation of the proposal. However, attitudes were still against the proposal in all conditions, which matches the experimental data.

Simulation 4: Gerard and Mathewson (1966) Severity of Initiation

This experiment was an elaboration of the Aronson and Mills (1959) study that showed that the more severe an initiation to join a group, the more the group was liked. Women who were asked to read a more embarrassing passage aloud (explicit sexual language), as their initiation process, before joining a discussion group, rated the group more positively than women who only had to read a mildly sexually embarrassing passage aloud. In the Gerard and Mathewson (1966) version, to ensure that the effect of the initiation in the original study was due to its aversiveness, and not to sexual arousal, the experimenters used electric shock to operationalize Severity of Initiation. Further, to isolate the effects of the severity of the initiation itself from multiple alternatives, ranging from arousal to extraneous expectation effects, a factor was added to separate the initiation from the act of joining the group. In the noninitiation condition, a shock was administered ostensibly as part of an unrelated experiment. Thus, Gerard and Mathewson's experiment had four conditions: mild shock, no initiation; severe shock, no initiation; mild shock, initiation; and severe shock, initiation. Also, after the shock, all participants listened to a boring discussion by that group. Evaluations of the group were then assessed afterward.

Structure of the Network

The critical features for modeling this experiment were the group, the evaluation of the group, the mild shock and severe shock as inputs, and joining the group as a behavior (see Figure 10.7). A hidden layer was still used, even though it was not necessary to learn any specific conjunctive relations. A positive evaluation would predict joining the group, and shock would predict not joining the group, regardless of the presence of the other feature. This network also contained the path for mood (due to the shock) to affect the evaluation. High shock had a fixed +1 weight to negative mood, and low shock had a fixed +0.1 weight to negative mood. Weights between mood and evaluation were the same as in the Forced Compliance simulation.

Learning Initial Cognitions

The prior learning history was (see Appendix 10.1 for details): the group was mildly associated with the behavior of not joining (because the group discussion turned out to be boring); a positive evaluation of the group was associated with joining and a negative evaluation was associated with not joining; the

FIGURE 10.6. Results for (a) Linder, Cooper, and Jones's (1967) Forced Compliance; and (b) Simulation 3

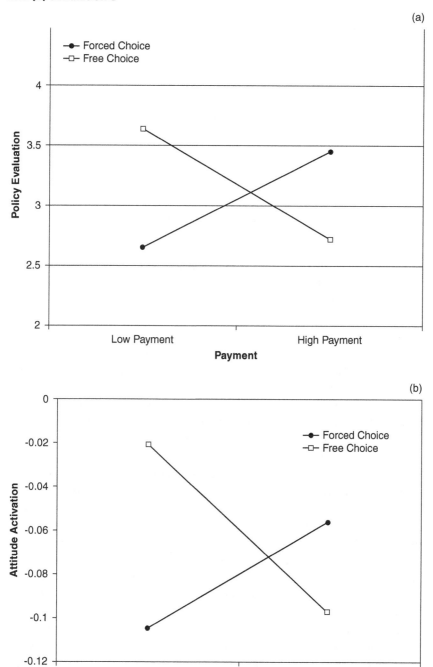

FIGURE 10.7. Network for Simulation 4: Gerard and Mathewson's (1966) Severity of Initiation

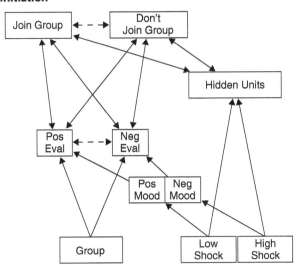

group combined with low shock was associated with mildly not joining; and the group combined with high shock was associated with strongly not joining. Testing confirmed that all associations were learned properly.

Dissonance Phase and Attitude Change

In the dissonance phase of the experiment, the series of events diverged. In the initiation conditions from the actual experiment performed by Gerard and Mathewson (1966), there was a dissonance-producing event, and in the noninitiation conditions there was not—in the noninitiation conditions, the shock and the exposure to the group discussion were presented as separate events in a sequence that had no meaningful connection. Thus, in our simulations, there was a difference in the events presented to the network: in the mild shock, initiation condition, the group and mild shock were presented as inputs, with joining the group as both the predicted output and the actual output. In the severe shock, initiation condition, the group and severe shock were presented as inputs, with not joining the group as the predicted output and joining the group as the actual output. No analogous dissonance-producing events were used for the noninitiation conditions. The attitude change measure was assessed by activating the group and appropriate level of shock as inputs (behavioral units were deactivated through lesioning again, as only evaluation was requested).

Results are presented in Figure 10.8a (original study results) and Figure 10.8b (simulation results). They confirm both the previous simulation results as well as the experimental results. In the initiation condition, severe shock participants liked the group much more than the mild shock participants, while in the noninitiation condition, severe shock participants liked the group slightly less than mild shock participants.

FIGURE 10.8. Results for (a) Gerard and Mathewson's (1966) Severity of Initiation; and (b) Simulation 4

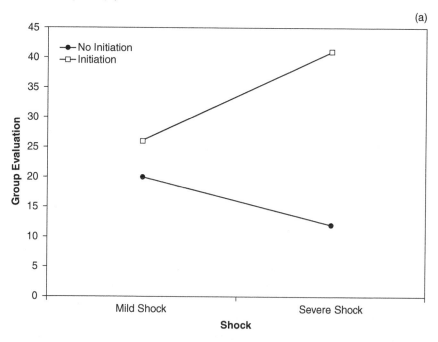

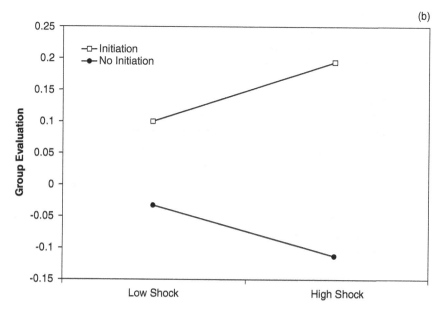

It is worth noting that in order to capture the results in the noninitiation condition, van Overwalle and Jordens had to use an event in the dissonance phase where the person joined the group, even though in the actual experiment participants in these conditions did not join the group. In contrast, we were able to capture the effects in the noninitiation conditions without having to include any event in which participants in the noninitiation condition joined the group.

DISCUSSION

This recurrent neural network model, with CHL, successfully modeled the long-term attitude change that results from reduction of cognitive dissonance, with long-term change represented by changes in the weights among cognitions and evaluations. Further, our multilayer recurrent network used parallel constraint-satisfaction processes to model short-term attitude change, represented by changes in activation.

In all of our simulations, the network first generated an expectation about its behavior (e.g., play with the toy) and then was given feedback about how it actually behaved, which in the dissonant conditions was inconsistent with the expectation generated (e.g., didn't play with the toy). As our network settles, the activations of the other nodes, especially the evaluation nodes, change to become more consistent with each other. For example, because of the recurrent connections, as the activation of the "didn't play with toy" node increases, the activation of the negative evaluation node will tend to increase, and when activation of the "play with toy" node decreases, the activation of the positive evaluation node will also tend to decrease. Then once the network settles the weights will change so that activation of the input nodes is more likely to lead to the same pattern of activation in the future.

In addition to capturing the pattern of results in the studies we simulated, our simulation is more successful than van Overwalle and Jordens' model in capturing the original results from Shultz et al.'s (1999) extension of the choice among alternatives' paradigm (Simulation 1). Van Overwalle and Jordens's (2002) simulation only exhibits spreading apart of choices in the difficult, highly attractive condition, but not in the low-attractiveness condition. In contrast, our simulation captures spreading of alternatives in both high- and low-attractiveness, difficult choice conditions. Also, for the Severity of Initiation simulation (Simulation 4) we were able to successfully simulate the results in the noninitiation conditions without having to introduce the behavior of joining the group, whereas van Overwalle and Jordens had to introduce this behavior, despite the fact that participants in the noninitiation condition did not think that the shock had anything to do with being a part of the boring group.

Theoretical Advantages of a Multilayer, Recurrent Model

A multilayer, recurrent network, with its bidirectional connectivity and constraint-satisfaction processing is much more powerful both in terms of its processing mechanisms and its representational ability than is a two-layer feedforward network and, as a result, it better represents many aspects of human cognitive functioning (e.g., O'Reilly & Munakata, 2000). More specifically, recurrent networks have a number of advantages over two-layer feedforward networks as a model of cognitive dissonance and dissonance reduction processes. Recurrent models can handle a broader range of kinds of inconsistency, they can handle reciprocal influences among different concepts, and they do a better job of representing the difference between stored and constructed attitudes. Further, as we discuss in more detail shortly, the parallel constraint-satisfaction processes that are part of recurrent networks capture the Gestalt-based, inconsistency reducing mechanisms that may underlie cognitive dissonance theory.

Can Handle Wider Array of Types of Inconsistency
First, a model that is multilayered and bidirectionally connected can deal with inconsistency between different kinds of concepts (e.g., attitude vs. belief, affect vs. behavior, belief vs. belief), as well as the inconsistency between an expected and an actual behavior or feeling. In contrast, a feedforward model can only deal with the discrepancy or inconsistency between what is expected and what actually happened for the *same concept* (e.g., expected vs. predicted behavior, expected vs. predicted positive affect). Thus, a recurrent model can deal with a much wider range of types of inconsistency or dissonance. For example, our model simulates the dissonance between two different concepts: an *actual* behavior and an *attitude*. This focus is consistent with many different kinds of dissonance studies, where the main theoretical explanation is in terms of inconsistency between an attitude and an actual behavior.

Can Handle a Wider Array of Influences Among Concepts
Because nodes in a recurrent model are bidirectionally connected, the model can deal with reciprocal influences between concepts. A feedforward network cannot. In a feedforward network, such as the one van Overwalle and Jordens (2002) used, there are only unidirectional links from nodes in the input layer to nodes in the output layer. And there are no links among the nodes within a layer. Thus, in van Overwalle and Jordens's model, because of the absence of links among concepts in the output layer, activation of the behavior node cannot influence the activation of the affect node (or vice versa). Such a claim contradicts considerable data.

Captures the Underlying Theoretical Mechanism Postulated by Cognitive Dissonance Theory
A major characteristic of a recurrent network, because of its bidirectional connectivity, is constraint-satisfaction processes, which implement classic Gestalt-like consistency mechanisms. The original theoretical underpinnings of cognitive dissonance theory owe much to fundamental Gestalt ideas of good form and coherence seeking (see Read & Simon, 2012; Read et al., 1997, for detailed discussions). The central idea is that people have a need for consistency among their cognitions (good form), and that when their cognitions are inconsistent, there

is "tension" in the system that acts to move the set of cognitions in a more consistent or coherent direction. As Read et al. (1997) argued (also see Read & Simon, 2012), parallel constraint-satisfaction mechanisms in a recurrent neural network are one way in which such consistency or coherence seeking can be computationally implemented (either in a computer or in a brain). Then once the network has reached a coherent or consistent state, the links among cognitions can be modified to capture these new relationships among the cognitions and beliefs in the network. Thus, the current model is consistent with the fundamental theoretical assumptions of Cognitive Dissonance Theory, and it provides an account of the mechanisms by which the relevant beliefs change.

In contrast, van Overwalle and Jordens (2002) eschew the standard theoretical underpinnings of cognitive dissonance theory. They do not provide an account of how beliefs might change as the result of a seeking after consistency. Rather, they propose that if relevant beliefs change as a result of direct feedback, that the new attitudes and beliefs are recorded by associative learning processes.

Effects of Mood on Cognitive Dissonance

Our current simulations capture some aspects of mood effects. In Simulation 3 of Linder et al.'s (1967) study on Forced Compliance and writing a counterattitudinal essay, we capture an apparent reward effect of a high payment. Specifically, in the high-coercion condition, participants showed more positive attitudes when they received higher payment for writing the counterattitudinal essay. This occurs because of the mood or affect nodes, which are influenced by reward and punishment, that then feed into the attitude or evaluation nodes. Research demonstrates that people's moods can influence their evaluations of objects (Isen, 2000; Schwarz & Clore, 2007). This network configuration allows us to capture this effect.

And in Simulation 4, Gerard and Mathewson's (1966) Severity of Initiation study, we captured a punishment effect. Participants who were told that receiving the shock was simply part of the experimental procedure showed greater decreases in liking for the group when they received higher levels of shock. Again, we modeled this as a mood effect.

Is This Just Self-Perception Theory?

Given that this model relies on feedback about the actual behavior of an individual, one might ask whether this isn't just self-perception theory (Bem, 1972)? It is true that, just like self-perception theory, our model relies on feedback about its behavior to infer its attitudes? But the same is true of cognitive dissonance theory. And our theoretical mechanisms are quite different from self-perception theory. In our model, the central theoretical mechanisms are parallel constraint-satisfaction processes, which we have argued (e.g., Read et al., 1997) can be viewed as a computational implementation of the Gestalt consistency-seeking processes that were the foundation of cognitive dissonance theory. A constraint-satisfaction process changes the pattern of activation of the nodes in the network, specifically the evaluation nodes, to minimize the inconsistency between the predicted and the actual behavior of the individual. The activation of the mediating evaluation nodes is a result of feedforward activation from the attitude object and feedback activation from the behavior nodes. Over time, the activations of the network settle into a stable state. If this new state differs from the predicted state of the network, learning mechanisms (CHL) act to modify the weights so that in the future the actual state of the network is closer to the predicted state. In contrast, in a self-perception network, there would be no notion of inconsistency and the network would not be trying to minimize inconsistency. Thus, inconsistency and a seeking for coherence would not be driving weight change.

CONCLUSION

Researchers seeking to computationally model cognitive dissonance processes in a connectionist framework have proposed two different types of model: A feedforward model, such as van Overwalle and Jordens (2002), and a recurrent feedback model, such as the one proposed by Shultz and Lepper (1996, 1998) and Read and Miller (1994). Each of these types of models have their limitations. The models proposed by Shultz and Lepper, and by Read and Miller, lacked learning. Although van Overwalle and Jordens's model captured learning, it did not infer its new attitude, but rather it was explicitly instructed. Perhaps more importantly, it could not capture the constraint-satisfaction or Gestalt-like nature of dissonance and dissonance reduction, and thus was unable to represent the process of short-term attitude change, represented by change in activation. The current model integrates the strength of the two approaches, while avoiding some of their important weaknesses. Because it is a multilayer, recurrent, feedback model it can capture the Gestalt-like nature of dissonance and short-term attitude change. And because the model learns, it can also capture long-term attitude change that results from dissonance processes.

APPENDIX 10.1
TRAINING EVENTS FOR EACH SIMULATION

SIMULATION 1: FREE CHOICE

Difficult-High Condition Training (20 Epochs, Learning Rate 0.1):

1. attractive poster +1, positive evaluation +.3, negative evaluation −.3

2. less attractive poster +1, positive evaluation +.25, negative evaluation −.25

3. positive evaluation +1, negative evaluation −1, choose +1, don't choose −1

Easy Condition Training (20 Epochs, Learning Rate 0.1):

1. attractive poster +1, positive evaluation +.3, negative evaluation −.3

2. less attractive poster +1, positive evaluation −.3, negative evaluation +.3

3. positive evaluation +1, negative evaluation −1, choose +1, don't choose −1

Difficult-Low Condition Training (20 Epochs, Learning Rate 0.1):

1. attractive poster +1, positive evaluation −.25, negative evaluation +.25

2. less attractive poster +1, positive evaluation −.3, negative evaluation +.3

3. positive evaluation +1, negative evaluation −1, choose +1, don't choose −1

Dissonance Phase (20 Epochs, Learning Rate 0.1):

1. attractive poster +1, choose +1, don't choose −1

2. less attractive poster +1, choose −1, don't choose +1

SIMULATION 2: FORBIDDEN TOY

Training (100 epochs, learning rate 0.1):

1. Toy +1, play −0.5, don't play +0.5

2. Toy +1, positive evaluation +0.2, negative evaluation −0.2

3. positive evaluation +1, negative evaluation −1, play +0.7, don't play −0.7

4. Toy +1, surveillance +1, play +0.5, don't play −0.5

5. Toy +1, mild threat +1, play +0.5, don't play −0.5

6. Toy +1, severe threat +1, play −0.8, don't play +0.8

7. Toy +1, surveillance +1, mild threat +1, play −0.8, don't play +0.8

8. Toy +1, surveillance +1, severe threat +1, play −1, don't play +1
   Dissonance phase:

No Surveillance, Mild Threat:

Toy +1, mild threat +1, play −1, don't play +1

No Surveillance, Severe Threat:

Toy +1, severe threat +1, play −1, don't play +1

Surveillance, Mild Threat:

Toy +1, surveillance +1, mild threat +1, play −1, don't play +1

Surveillance, Severe Threat:

Toy +1, surveillance +1, severe threat +1, play −1, don't play +1

SIMULATION 3: FORCED COMPLIANCE

Training (100 epochs, learning rate 0.1):

1. Attitude object +1, for proposal −0.5, against proposal +0.5

2. Attitude object +1, write essay −0.5, don't write essay +0.5

3. for proposal +1, against proposal −1, write essay +0.7, don't write essay −0.7

4. Attitude object +1, low payment +1, write essay −0.5, don't write essay +0.5

5. Attitude object +1, high payment +1, write essay +0.8, don't write essay −0.8

6. Attitude object +1, coercion +1, write essay +0.8, don't write essay −0.8

7. Attitude object +1, coercion +1, low payment +1, write essay +0.8, don't write −0.8

8. Attitude object +1, coercion +1, high payment +1, write essay +1, don't write −1
   Dissonance phase:

Free Choice, Low Payment:

Attitude object +1, low payment +1, write essay +1, don't write essay −1

Free Choice, High Payment:

Attitude object +1, high payment +1, write essay +1, don't write essay −1

Forced Compliance, Low Payment:

Attitude object +1, coercion +1, low payment +1, write essay +1, don't write essay −1

Forced Compliance, High Payment:

Attitude object +1, coercion +1, high payment +1, write essay +1, don't write essay −1

SIMULATION 4: SEVERITY OF INITIATION

Training (100 epochs, learning rate 0.1):

1. Group +1, join group −0.2, don't join group +0.2
2. positive evaluation +1, negative evaluation −1, join group +0.7, don't join group −0.7
3. Group +1, low shock +1, join group −0.2, don't join group +0.2
4. Group +1, high shock +1, join group −1, don't join group +1
   Dissonance phase:

Initiation, Low Shock:

Group +1, low shock +1, join group +1, don't join group −1

Initiation, High Shock:

Group +1, high shock +1, join group +1, don't join group −1

No Initiation:

(No events)

REFERENCES

Abelson, R. P., Aronson, E., McGuire, W. J., Newcomb, T. M., Rosenberg, M. J., & Tannenbaum, P. H. (Eds.). (1968). *Theories of cognitive consistency: A sourcebook.* Chicago, IL: Rand McNally.

Aisa, B., Mingus, B., & O'Reilly, R. (2008). The emergent neural modeling system. *Neural Networks, 21,* 1146–1152. http://dx.doi.org/10.1016/j.neunet.2008.06.016

Aronson, E., & Mills, J. (1959). The effect of severity of initiation on liking for a group. *Journal of Abnormal and Social Psychology, 59,* 177–181. http://dx.doi.org/10.1037/h0047195

Bem, D. J. (1972). Self-perception theory. In L. Berkowitz (Ed.), *Advances in experimental social psychology* (Vol. 6, pp. 1–62). New York, NY: Academic Press.

Brehm, J. W. (1956). Postdecision changes in the desirability of alternatives. *Journal of Abnormal and Social Psychology, 52*, 384–389. http://dx.doi.org/10.1037/h0041006

Dawson, C. K., O'Reilly, R. C., & McClelland, J. L. (2003). *The PDP++ Software User's Manual*, version 3.0. Pittsburgh, PA: Carnegie-Mellon University.

Fazio, R. H. (2007). Attitudes as object-evaluation associations of varying strength. *Social Cognition, 25*, 603–637. http://dx.doi.org/10.1521/soco.2007.25.5.603

Festinger, L. (1957). *A theory of cognitive dissonance*. Palo Alto, CA: Stanford University Press.

Festinger, L., & Carlsmith, J. M. (1959). Cognitive consequences of forced compliance. *Journal of Abnormal and Social Psychology, 58*, 203–210. http://dx.doi.org/10.1037/h0041593

Freedman, J. L. (1965). Long-term behavioral effects of cognitive dissonance. *Journal of Experimental Social Psychology, 1*, 145–155. http://dx.doi.org/10.1016/0022-1031(65)90042-9

Gerard, H. B., & Mathewson, G. C. (1966). The effects of severity of initiation on liking for a group: A replication. *Journal of Experimental Social Psychology, 2*, 278–287. http://dx.doi.org/10.1016/0022-1031(66)90084-9

Isen, A. M. (2000). Positive affect and decision making. In M. Lewis & J. M. Haviland-Jones (Eds.), *Handbook of emotions* (2nd ed., pp. 417–435). New York, NY: Guilford Press.

Linder, D. E., Cooper, J., & Jones, E. E. (1967). Decision freedom as a determinant of the role of incentive magnitude in attitude change. *Journal of Personality and Social Psychology, 6*, 245–254. http://dx.doi.org/10.1037/h0021220

O'Reilly, R. C. (1996). Biologically plausible error-driven learning using local activation differences: The generalized recirculation algorithm. *Neural Computation, 8*, 895–938. http://dx.doi.org/10.1162/neco.1996.8.5.895

O'Reilly, R. C., & Munakata, Y. (2000). *Computational explorations in cognitive neuroscience: Understanding the mind by simulating the brain*. Cambridge, MA: The MIT Press.

Read, S. J., & Miller, L. C. (1994). Dissonance and balance in belief systems: The promise of parallel constraint satisfaction processes and connectionist modeling approaches. In R. C. Schank & E. J. Langer (Eds.), *Beliefs, reasoning, and decision making: Psycho-logic in honor of Bob Abelson* (pp. 209–235). Hillsdale, NJ: Erlbaum.

Read, S. J., & Simon, D. (2012). Parallel constraint satisfaction as a mechanism for cognitive consistency. In B. Gawronski & F. Strack (Eds.), *Cognitive consistency: A fundamental principle in social cognition*. New York, NY: Guilford Press.

Read, S. J., Vanman, E. J., & Miller, L. C. (1997). Connectionism, parallel constraint satisfaction processes, and gestalt principles: (Re)introducing cognitive dynamics to social psychology. *Personality and Social Psychology Review, 1*, 26–53. http://dx.doi.org/10.1207/s15327957pspr0101_3

Schwarz, N., & Clore, G. L. (2007). Feelings and phenomenal experiences. In E. T. Higgins & A. Kruglanski (Eds.), *Social psychology. Handbook of basic principles* (2nd ed., pp. 385–407). New York, NY: Guilford Press.

Shultz, T. R., & Lepper, M. R. (1996). Cognitive dissonance reduction as constraint satisfaction. *Psychological Review, 103*, 219–240. http://dx.doi.org/10.1037/0033-295X.103.2.219

Shultz, T. R., & Lepper, M. R. (1998). The consonance model of dissonance reduction. In S. J. Read & L. C. Miller (Eds.), *Connectionist models of social reasoning and social behavior* (pp. 211–244). Hillsdale, NJ: Erlbaum.

Shultz, T. R., & Lepper, M. R. (1999). Computer simulation of cognitive dissonance reduction. In E. Harmon-Jones & J. Mills (Eds.), *Science conference series. Cognitive dissonance: Progress on a pivotal theory in social psychology* (pp. 235–265). Washington, DC: American Psychological Association. http://dx.doi.org/10.1037/10318-010

Shultz, T. R., Léveillé, E., & Lepper, M. R. (1999). Free choice and cognitive dissonance revisited: Choosing "lesser evils" vs. "greater goods." *Personality and Social Psychology Bulletin, 25*, 40–48. http://dx.doi.org/10.1177/0146167299025001004

Simon, D., & Holyoak, K. J. (2002). Structural Dynamics of Cognition: From Consistency Theories to Constraint Satisfaction. *Personality and Social Psychology Review, 6*, 283–294. http://dx.doi.org/10.1207/S15327957PSPR0604_03

Spellman, B. A., Ullman, J. B., & Holyoak, K. J. (1993). A coherence model of cognitive consistency: Dynamics of attitude change during the Persian Gulf War. *Journal of Social Issues, 49*, 147–165. http://dx.doi.org/10.1111/j.1540-4560.1993.tb01185.x

van Overwalle, F., & Jordens, K. (2002). An adaptive connectionist model of cognitive dissonance. *Personality and Social Psychology Review, 6*, 204–231. http://dx.doi.org/10.1207/S15327957PSPR0603_6

11

Neural Basis of Cognitive Dissonance

Keise Izuma and Kou Murayama

More than 6 decades after the original conceptualization of the theory (Festinger, 1957), research on cognitive dissonance has entered a new era; following an emergence of a new interdisciplinary field of social neuroscience in the 1990s, researchers have started investigating the neural basis underlying cognitive dissonance and subsequent attitude change using methods in cognitive neuroscience (Izuma, 2015). Compared with the long history of cognitive dissonance research (Harmon-Jones & Mills, 1999), the endeavor to explore its neural basis is still in its infancy. Nonetheless, social neuroscience studies from the past decade have provided initial findings on brain areas involved in cognitive dissonance and subsequent attitude change.

In this chapter, we first review such past social neuroscience studies that revealed several brain regions involved in cognitive dissonance. Second, we discuss possible neural mechanisms of cognitive dissonance (i.e., functional roles played in the brain regions) based on currently available evidence. Finally, we discuss challenges and difficulties in the field, which need to be carefully addressed in future research. In addition, we briefly discuss how neuroscience methods can not only reveal the neural bases of dissonance, but also has a great potential to advance our *psychological* understandings of cognitive dissonance in a way that would be not possible with traditional behavioral methods.

---

http://dx.doi.org/10.1037/0000135-011
Cognitive Dissonance, Second Edition: Reexamining a Pivotal Theory in Psychology,
E. Harmon-Jones (Editor)
Copyright © 2019 by the American Psychological Association. All rights reserved.

NEURAL CORRELATES OF COGNITIVE DISSONANCE

In 2008, Harmon-Jones and his colleagues applied electroencephalogram (EEG) for the first time in cognitive dissonance research (Harmon-Jones, Gerdjikov, & Harmon-Jones, 2008; Harmon-Jones, Harmon-Jones, Fearn, Sigelman, & Johnson, 2008). A year afterward, van Veen and his colleagues reported the first functional magnetic resonance imaging (fMRI) study that investigated the neural basis of cognitive dissonance (van Veen, Krug, Schooler, & Carter, 2009). Following these seminal papers, a number of social neuroscience studies have been published using both neuroimaging and brain-stimulation methods. These past studies converge to suggest that just like other complex social cognitive processes such as theory of mind and empathy, cognitive dissonance involves different interacting networks of neural structures (Izuma, 2015), which consists of the posterior medial frontal cortex (pMFC), anterior insula, and dorsolateral prefrontal cortex (DLPFC; see Figure 11.1). Although other brain regions have been also implicated, the involvement of these three brain regions seems to be the most consistently observed in past research.

Posterior Medial Frontal Cortex

Among brain regions identified in past dissonance neuroimaging studies, the posterior medial frontal cortex (pMFC) is the most frequently reported (e.g., de Vries, Byrne, & Kehoe, 2015; Izuma et al., 2010; Kitayama, Chua, Tompson, & Han, 2013; van Veen et al., 2009). In 2009, van Veen and his colleagues used the classic "induced compliance" paradigm (Festinger & Carlsmith, 1959); participants were first asked to perform a long (45 minutes), boring task inside an fMRI scanner. Due to the big fMRI scanner noise and the limited freedom to move inside the scanner, performing such a long boring task in the scanner was an unpleasant experience for them. In the second fMRI task, they were asked

FIGURE 11.1. Cognitive Dissonance Network

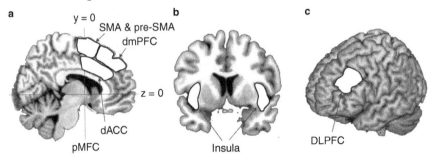

(a) Posterior medial frontal cortex (pMFC), pMFC consists of three sub-regions: (1) dorsal anterior cingulate cortex [dACC], (2) dorso-medial prefrontal cortex [dmPFC], and (3) supplementary motor area (SMA) and pre-supplementary motor area (pre-SMA); (b) insula, and (c) dorsolateral prefrontal cortex (DLPFC). From "Attitude Change and Cognitive Consistency," by K. Izuma, in A. W. Toga (Ed.), *Brain mapping: An encyclopedic reference* (Vol. 3, p. 248). Oxford, England: Elsevier. Adapted with permission.

to rate a number of statements regarding how they felt about the scanner and the task. Participants in the no-dissonance group were asked to respond to each statement as if they really enjoyed the task, and importantly, they were told that they would receive a monetary reward for pretending in this way. Thus, although they were asked to behave inconsistently with their attitudes, they presumably felt no cognitive dissonance because a monetary incentive was provided, which justifies the inconsistency between their attitude and behavior. On the other hand, participants in the dissonance group were also told to respond to each statement as if the task was enjoyable, but no external incentive for doing so was provided. Thus, they were asked to behave inconsistently with their attitude without sufficient justification, a situation known to induce strong cognitive dissonance. In addition to these critical statements recording their attitudes toward the task and scanner experience, participants in both groups were also asked to respond to neutral control statements honestly.

Van Veen et al. (2009) found that when participants in both groups were asked to rate the same statements about the scanner and task again, but this time honestly, participants in the dissonance group reported more positive attitudes compared with those in the no-dissonance group. This behavioral result indicates that when there was not sufficient justification to behave inconsistently with their attitudes, they changed their attitudes in order to make it consistent with their past behavior (i.e., dissonance reduction). Van Veen et al. further found that the pMFC was significantly activated when participants in the dissonance group rated critical statements compared to neutral statements, whereas there was no difference between the two conditions in the no-dissonance group (van Veen et al., 2009). More precisely, their pMFC activations lie in the dorsal anterior cingulate cortex (dACC) and pre-supplementary motor area (pre-SMA; see Figure 11.1a). Among other regions, the bilateral anterior insula also showed similar activation patterns (see below).

Subsequent studies also found activations in the pMFC using another classic dissonance paradigm called the "free-choice" paradigm (Brehm, 1956). Using this paradigm, Izuma and his colleagues (2010) asked participants to perform three different tasks inside an fMRI scanner—(a) first preference rating task, (b) choice task, and (c) second preference rating task. During the first preference rating task, participants rated how much they liked each food item presented on the screen. In the second choice task, pairs of food items were presented, and they were asked to select the one they preferred. Importantly, during the choice task, choice difficulty was systematically manipulated using each participant's preference data obtained in the first rating task, so that two items in a pair were similarly liked by a participant in some trials (the difficult choice condition), while in other trials, one item was highly liked, but the other item was disliked (the easy choice condition).

Following the choice task, participants performed the second preference rating task. This task was the same as the first rating task except that below each food picture, the decision made by a participant during the choice task was presented (e.g., "You chose this item," "You rejected this item") to make inconsistency (or consistency) between their preferences and choices salient. For example, since participants had to pick one of two items during the choice task, they had to give up one of their favorite food items in the difficult choice trials. Thus, when they were presented with an image of a liked-but-rejected food item with "You rejected this item," they perceived a big discrepancy between their behavior (e.g., rejected) and preference (the item was rated highly during the first rating task), a situation that induces high cognitive dissonance.

Their behavioral results showed that participants' preferences for the liked-but-rejected items were significantly reduced. In other words, they justified the choices they made (I rejected it because I didn't like it) (Izuma et al., 2010). When Izuma et al. (2010) analyzed the fMRI data obtained during the second preference rating task, they found that the pMFC (especially dACC and dmPFC; see Figure 11.1a) tracked the degree of discrepancy between their preferences and past choice behaviors on a trial-by-trial basis. Thus, when participants realized that their past behaviors contradicted with their preferences, the pMFC was strongly activated. Among other regions, dorsolateral prefrontal cortex (DLPFC) and posterior cingulate cortex (PCC) also tracked the degree of the discrepancy.

Kitayama and his colleagues (2013) also found the pMFC involvement in cognitive dissonance using the free-choice paradigm and found that the pMFC was activated when participants were making a difficult choice compared with an easy choice. Furthermore, although most past social neuroscience studies on dissonance used classic behavioral paradigms such as "induced compliance" and "free-choice" paradigm, de Vries and his colleagues (2015) took a different approach and also found the pMFC activation. In their fMRI study, participants were presented with an everyday situation that is likely to induce cognitive dissonance (e.g., "Have you ever broken a red light at a pedestrian crossing in front of small children?"). The study found that the pMFC (especially dACC) was significantly activated when participants reflected on their personal experience while reading these dissonance scenarios compared to control scenarios. Moreover, a few studies found that the pMFC activity was related to individual difference in attitude change following cognitive dissonance (Izuma et al., 2010; Qin et al., 2011; van Veen et al., 2009), although the direction of the relation is not consistent across the studies (see Izuma et al., 2010, for more discussion on this point).

Importantly, from these fMRI studies, it still remains unknown whether the pMFC activity simply reflects an epiphenomenon of cognitive dissonance (e.g., emotional reactions to perceived discrepancy between one's attitude and behavior) or it plays an active role in inducing preference change to reduce inconsistency. To tease apart these two possibilities, Izuma and his colleagues (2015) conducted a study using a brain-stimulation method called transcranial magnetic stimulation (TMS) and directly manipulated the activity in the pMFC region. The study used a modified free-choice paradigm, and all participants performed the same three tasks (first preference rating task, choice task, and second preference rating task) as their previous fMRI study (Izuma et al., 2010), and Izuma et al. (2015) down-regulated the activity of the dmPFC using TMS before participants performed the second preference rating task (thus, participants performed the second rating task under the influence of TMS).

If the pMFC plays a role in representing cognitive dissonance and inducing preference change, down-regulating this region would eliminate preference change following difficult choices (participants no longer justify their past choices). Supporting this idea, their results showed that when their pMFC was stimulated by TMS, participants' preference ratings were not influenced by the choices they made, while those who received sham TMS to the pMFC or real TMS to a control region (posterior parietal cortex) still showed typical choice-induced preference change (Izuma et al., 2015). Thus, extending the previous fMRI studies (Izuma et al., 2010; van Veen et al., 2009), this TMS study showed that the relation between the pMFC activity and preference change is not just correlational, but it is the pMFC that causes preference change following the perception of discrepancy between attitude and behavior.

Anterior Insula

The anterior insula is another region frequently reported in neuroimaging studies on cognitive dissonance. The four above-mentioned fMRI studies (de Vries et al., 2015; Izuma et al., 2010; Kitayama et al., 2013; van Veen et al., 2009) found that the anterior insula showed similar activation patterns as the pMFC. Van Veen et al. (2009) found bilateral anterior insula activations when participants were asked to behave inconsistently with their attitudes without sufficient justification. Izuma et al. (2010) also found that left anterior insula activation tracked the degree of discrepancy between behavior and attitude just like the pMFC, although only when the statistical threshold was slightly lowered (Izuma et al., 2010). Kitayama et al. (2013) found significant left anterior insula activation when participants made a difficult choice compared to an easy choice. Finally, de Vries et al. (2015) found left insula activations when participants were reading dissonance scenarios.

Furthermore, another fMRI study (Jarcho, Berkman, & Lieberman, 2011) used the free-choice paradigm and scanned participants' brains only during the choice task (two preference rating tasks were performed outside of the scanner) and found that bilateral anterior insula activations were negatively correlated with preference change on a trial-by-trial bases. Thus, the anterior insula showed reduced activations when confronted with a choice pair for which participants would eventually show greater attitude change (choice justification). Similarly, using the free-choice paradigm, Qin et al. (2011) found that the activity of right anterior insula tracked preference change on an item-by-item basis during the second preference rating task.

Dorsolateral Prefrontal Cortex

A series of EEG studies conducted by Harmon-Jones and his colleagues consistently demonstrated that the DLPFC, especially in the left hemisphere, plays an important role in attitude change following cognitive dissonance (Harmon-Jones, Gerdjikov, et al., 2008; Harmon-Jones, Harmon-Jones, et al., 2008; Harmon-Jones, Harmon-Jones, Serra, & Gable, 2011). The initial study (Harmon-Jones, Gerdjikov, et al., 2008) used the induced-compliance paradigm and asked students (participants) to write a counterattitudinal essay supporting a tuition increase, and their EEG responses were measured while writing the essay. While one group of participants were provided with justification to write a counterattitudinal essay (no-dissonance group), the other group was not provided with such justification (dissonance group). Their behavioral results demonstrated the effect of cognitive dissonance on attitude change; those in the dissonance group showed significantly more positive attitudes toward tuition increase compared to those in the no-dissonance control group. The study further found that left DLPFC activity was higher for the dissonance (no justification) group compared to the no-dissonance group, while there was no difference in other brain regions. A similar finding was also obtained in their follow-up study (Harmon-Jones et al., 2011). The DLPFC activation has been also reported in some of the above-mentioned fMRI studies (e.g., Izuma et al., 2010; Kitayama et al., 2013).

The subsequent EEG study (Harmon-Jones, Harmon-Jones, et al., 2008) extended their initial EEG findings using a neurofeedback technique, which allows one to directly manipulate (not just measure) the activity in the left DLPFC. The study employed the free-choice paradigm, and after participants made a difficult choice between two items that were equally preferred, they were induced to increase or decrease their left DLPFC activity (all participants had undergone neurofeedback training sessions before the main task). The results demonstrated that while those who were induced to increase the left DLPFC activity showed typical patterns of attitude change, those who were induced to decrease the left DLPFC activity didn't show attitude change, indicating that the left DLPFC plays a causal role in choice justification (Harmon-Jones, Harmon-Jones, et al., 2008).

Another piece of evidence supporting the causal role of the left DLPFC in cognitive dissonance comes from a study that used a brain stimulation method called transcranial direct current stimulation (tDCS; Mengarelli, Spoglianti, Avenanti, & di Pellegrino, 2015). Just like TMS, tDCS allows us to temporarily decrease cortical excitability of a target region (note that tDCS can also increase cortical excitability by placing an anodal, as opposed to cathodal, electrode on a target area). Mengarelli and her colleagues (2015) employed the free-choice paradigm and applied cathodal tDCS (which down-regulates the activity of a targeted area) to the left or the right DLPFC for 15 min after participants performed the choice task. Thus, just like the above-mentioned TMS study (Izuma et al., 2015), participants performed the second rating task under the influence of tDCS. The study found that cathodal tDCS over the left DLPFC reduced typical attitude change following difficult choices, while those who received cathodal tDCS to the right DLPFC (and also those who received sham stimulation) showed significant attitude changes (Mengarelli et al., 2015). Taken together with the EEG neurofeedback study (Harmon-Jones, Harmon-Jones, et al., 2008), the two studies consistently demonstrated that when the left DLPFC activity is weakened (through neurofeedback or tDCS), individuals no longer justify their choices, supporting the causal role played by the left DLPFC in attitude change following dissonance.

Other Brain Regions

Posterior Cingulate Cortex

Activation in a posterior part of the cingulate cortex has been reported in some past dissonance neuroimaging studies. For example, Izuma et al. (2010) found that the PCC activity also tracked the degree of discrepancy between attitude and behavior on a trial-by-trial basis just like the pMFC. Kitayama et al. (2013) further reported that PCC activity is correlated with preference change of chosen items during the choice task. A similar finding was also reported in Jarcho et al. (2011), although the activated region is slightly more posterior to PCC (i.e., precuneus). In contrast, although Qin et al. (2011) found that PCC is related to participants' preferences for items, its activity was not related to preference change following choices. Furthermore, Tompson and his colleagues (2016) re-analyzed the fMRI data reported in Kitayama et al. (2013) and found that the connectivity between the medial prefrontal cortex (mPFC) and PCC predicted preference change following choices. Thus, although PCC activation has been reported in some previous neuroimaging studies, the PCC involvement reported in each study is not necessarily consistent with each other, and whether or not the PCC plays a key role (if so, what role) in cognitive dissonance remains unclear.

Ventral Striatum

A few studies reported the involvement of reward-related brain regions, especially ventral striatum (nucleus accumbens), which tracked change in individual's preferences. In a typical free-choice paradigm, individuals increase their preference for a selected item and decrease their preference for a rejected item after making a difficult choice (known as "spreading of alternatives"). Two studies demonstrated that the activity in the ventral striatum showed the same patterns (increased activation for selected items and decreased activation for rejected items; Izuma et al., 2010; Sharot, De Martino, & Dolan, 2009), indicating that dissonance induced preference change can be seen not only at the self-report level, but also at the neural level. Similarly, two different studies showed that the ventral striatum activity during the choice task is related to subsequent changes in preferences (Jarcho et al., 2011; Kitayama et al., 2013).

Hippocampus

Furthermore, although its involvement was not reported in previous studies, it is conceivable that brain regions related to memory, especially hippocampus, also play an important role in cognitive dissonance. One behavioral study (Salti,

El Karoui, Maillet, & Naccache, 2014) demonstrated that in the free-choice paradigm, participants' memory about their past choice is important; if participants didn't remember a choice they had made, they didn't show typical attitude change even after making a difficult choice. Since there is no discrepancy between attitude and behavior (thus no cognitive dissonance), if individuals don't remember their past behaviors, the hippocampus may be necessary for cognitive dissonance.[1]

WHAT ROLES DOES EACH OF THESE REGIONS PLAY?

Although research over the past decade has identified the candidate brain regions (Figure 11.1), which seem to play pivotal roles in cognitive dissonance processes in general, it still remains largely unclear what functional role each of these regions play. For the pMFC, there are currently two ideas about the role of the pMFC in cognitive dissonance, namely conflict detection hypothesis and reinforcement learning hypothesis.

First, some researchers (e.g., Harmon-Jones, Harmon-Jones, et al., 2008; Kitayama et al., 2013; van Veen et al., 2009) have argued that the reason that the pMFC, especially the dACC, is activated by cognitive dissonance is because of its well-known conflict monitoring function. Using a variety of different tasks such as the Stroop task and Flanker task, past cognitive neuroscience studies have consistently demonstrated that the dACC is activated when there is a conflict at motor response level (i.e., two different motor responses are activated at the same time; Botvinick, Braver, Barch, Carter, & Cohen, 2001; Carter & van Veen, 2007; Mansouri, Tanaka, & Buckley, 2009). In addition to the dACC, the DLPFC is also often implicated in such tasks that require cognitive control (e.g., Kerns et al., 2004). According to cognitive control theory of dACC function (Botvinick et al., 2001; Carter & van Veen, 2007), the dACC monitors the presence of response conflict and sends conflict-related information to the DLPFC that adjusts the level of cognitive control accordingly to resolve the conflict (behavioral adjustment). As argued by Harmon-Jones, Harmon-Jones, et al. (2008), this general framework that the dACC and DLPFC play roles in conflict detection and conflict resolution, respectively, seems to fit well with possible neural processes underlying attitude change following cognitive dissonance such that the dACC monitors the presence of a cognitive type of conflict (cognitive dissonance), and the DLPFC exerts cognitive control to resolve the dissonance (attitude adjustment). However, although the close match between the neural mechanisms of response conflict vs. cognitive dissonance

---

[1] It should be noted that a previous study (Lieberman, Ochsner, Gilbert, & Schacter, 2001) demonstrated that amnesic patients also showed attitude change following a difficult choice, indicating that memory is not necessary for cognitive dissonance. However, this study didn't address the artifact pointed out by Chen & Risen (2010; see below), and accordingly, it is unclear if the result holds after controlling for the artifact (see Izuma & Murayama, 2013).

processing seems appealing, there is currently no direct evidence showing the link between them.

The other idea is that the reason why the dACC is activated by cognitive dissonance is because it is processed as a negative outcome, and attitude change following dissonance shares the same neural mechanisms as reinforcement learning (Izuma, 2013). Thus, just like we try to avoid choosing the same option after receiving negative monetary outcome in a simple decision-making task (behavioral adjustment), we try to avoid a negative emotional state of cognitive dissonance by adjusting our attitudes. For example, a monkey single-cell recording study showed that monkey dACC neurons respond to negative outcome (reduced reward), which induces behavioral adjustment (Shima & Tanji, 1998). In this study, monkeys were trained to perform a simple cue-response task. In each trial, following a visual cue, monkeys either pushed or turned a handle. Importantly, monkeys could freely choose which action to take based on the amount of reward (fruit juice) they received at the end of each trial. Monkeys usually kept selecting the same action as long as the action was rewarded and changed their action when the amount of reward was reduced. The study found that neurons in the dACC responded only when monkeys received reduced reward that subsequently led monkeys to alter their action in the next trial. Similar findings were also replicated in a human fMRI study (Bush et al., 2002). Furthermore, using a variety of reward-based learning or decision-making tasks, past neuroscience research has shown that the dACC responds to negative outcomes and plays a pivotal role in subsequent behavioral adjustment (e.g., Hayden, Heilbronner, Pearson, & Platt, 2011; Matsumoto, Matsumoto, Abe, & Tanaka, 2007).

Currently, only one study has directly tested the two competing hypotheses. Izuma and Adolphs (2013) investigated the neural bases of cognitive inconsistency as defined by balance theory (Heider, 1958). Balance theory and cognitive dissonance theory share the same basic cognitive consistency principle; we prefer incoming information to be consistent with existing cognitions, beliefs and attitudes, and if there is inconsistency, people are motivated to reduce it (Abelson et al., 1968; Gawronski & Strack, 2012). Thus, just like cognitive dissonance theory, balance theory predicts that we change our attitudes following cognitive inconsistency (imbalance). While cognitive dissonance theory focuses on inconsistency between attitude and behavior, balance theory focuses on inconsistency among three attitudes; (a) one's attitude toward another person, (b) one's attitude toward an object, and (c) another person's attitude toward the same object (Heider, 1958).

In Izuma and Adolphs's study (2013), participants were first presented with a T-shirt design and asked to rate how much they liked each design. After giving their rating, they were presented with how students from the same university (liked group) or sex offenders (disliked group) rated the same item. In the second rating task, they were asked to rate the same T-shirt designs one more time, but this time no others' rating was presented. Consistent with the balance theory, Izuma and Adolphs found that participants' ratings were positively influenced by their fellow students' opinions (the higher the other students' rating for a T-shirt, the more participants increased their preference rating for the same T-shirt), while their ratings were negatively influenced by sex offenders' opinions (the higher the sex offenders' rating for a T-shirt, the more participants decreased their preference rating for the same T-shirt).

In addition to the T-shirt rating task, Izuma and Adolphs (2013) asked the same participants to perform two additional tasks; one is a simple reward task (the monetary incentive delay task; Knutson, Westdorp, Kaiser, & Hommer, 2000), which was intended to localize areas within the pMFC that are the most sensitive to negative outcome, and the other is a cognitive control task (the multi-source interference task; Bush & Shin, 2006), which was intended to localize pMFC areas that are the most sensitive to response conflict. The study found that just like the previous cognitive dissonance study (Izuma et al., 2010), the pMFC (especially dmPFC) tracked the degree of cognitive imbalance on a trial-by-trial basis (Izuma & Adolphs, 2013). Furthermore, interestingly, the pMFC region activated by cognitive imbalance overlapped with the area activated by negative outcome (posterior dmPFC), but not with the area activated by response conflict (pre-SMA; Izuma & Adolphs, 2013). Thus, although the activation overlap does not necessarily mean the same neural mechanisms (i.e., only indirect support for the reinforcement learning hypothesis), the study provided clear evidence against the response conflict hypothesis. Within the pMFC, the area activated by cognitive inconsistency is distinct from the area activated by response conflict.

Similarly, several studies (e.g., Jarcho et al., 2011; Kitayama et al., 2013; Qin et al., 2011; van Veen et al., 2009) interpreted the anterior insula activation in response to cognitive dissonance as reflecting the insula's known role in representing negative emotion and physiological arousal (Calder et al., 2007; Chang, Gianaros, Manuck, Krishnan, & Wager, 2015; Damasio et al., 2000). However, at this point, this is a speculation based entirely on reverse inference (Poldrack, 2006), and the exact role played by the anterior insula in cognitive dissonance is yet to be discovered.

Finally, some researchers (Kitayama et al., 2013; Tompson et al., 2016) argued that the reason why the PCC activation is found in dissonance studies is because of its involvement in self-reference processing (Northoff et al., 2006). Although the idea that the PCC activation indexes self-relevance is interesting, there is currently no direct evidence supporting the idea (e.g., we don't know whether the same PCC region is activated by cognitive dissonance and self-referential processing), and it is yet to be empirically tested.

To summarize, while the involvements of the brain regions (pMFC, DLPFC, anterior insula, and PCC) have been frequently reported in the past neuroimaging studies, at this point, their functional interpretations are based almost entirely on reverse inference (Poldrack, 2006), and thus remain highly speculative. As discussed in the next section, reverse inference based on the pMFC and anterior insula are especially problematic. Thus, there still remains much to be done to unveil neural mechanisms underlying cognitive dissonance and subsequent attitude change, and there are a few important avenues for future research as discussed below.

LIMITATION, CHALLENGE, AND HOPE

A Methodological Artifact in the Free-Choice Paradigm

As reviewed above, the majority of past social neuroscience studies on cognitive dissonance used the free-choice paradigm (Brehm, 1956). In fact, out of 13 neuroimaging and brain-stimulation studies discussed above, only three studies (Harmon-Jones, Gerdjikov, et al., 2008; Harmon-Jones et al., 2011; van Veen et al., 2009) used paradigms other than the free-choice.[2] A main reason why most of the studies used the free-choice paradigm is probably because it allows researchers to manipulate cognitive dissonance on a within-subject basis (i.e., within-subject design), which is often preferred for a neuroimaging study due to large individual difference in brain activation (another practical reason is because an fMRI study is more costly than a behavioral study, so less participants [less scan time] are preferred).

However, importantly, a serious methodological flaw in the free-choice paradigm has been pointed out (Chen & Risen, 2010). Chen and Risen (2010) argued that the free-choice paradigm could measure attitude changes even in the complete absence of cognitive dissonance. The critical point is that, even if a participant gave the same ratings to two items in the first rating task, his/her preferences for the items are likely to differ at least slightly. Thus, it is likely that participant's choice between the two items reflects this subtle difference in his/her preference. Thus, the higher preference ratings in the second rating task do not necessarily mean that the act of making a choice changed the true preference—the higher preference ratings in the second rating task may simply reflect the pre-existing preference, which was not evident in the first rating task (see Izuma & Murayama, 2013, for more detailed discussions on this issue). Thus, attitude changes measured in the free-choice paradigm could be entirely due to the statistical artifact. Chen and Risen's claim has been empirically tested by several studies (e.g., Izuma et al., 2010; Koster, Duzel, & Dolan, 2015; Salti et al., 2014; Sharot, Fleming, Yu, Koster, & Dolan, 2012), and they demonstrated that significant attitude changes could be observed even in the condition where cognitive dissonance can never influence an individual's attitude.[3] The finding indicates that the effect of the methodological artifact is not negligible. Furthermore, while a few recent studies have demonstrated the effect of

---

[2] In addition to these three studies, de Vries et al. (2015) used scenarios to induce cognitive dissonance. Although the approach is interesting, there was no behavioral evidence suggesting that cognitive dissonance was actually induced, which makes interpretation of their fMRI results difficult.

[3] While the typical free-choice paradigm follows the rate-choose-rate procedure, these studies also employed a condition where participants follow the rate-rate-choose procedure (see Izuma & Murayama, 2013). In this control condition, since choices are made at the end of the experiment, choices can never affect preference change, while the effect of the statistical artifact is still present. Thus, it is possible to test the effect of the artifact using this rate-rate-choose condition, and the five studies consistently found the significant preference change even in this rate-rate-choose condition.

cognitive dissonance on attitude change even after controlling for the artifact (Izuma et al., 2010, 2015; Koster et al., 2015; Salti et al., 2014; Sharot et al., 2012), the meta-analysis by Izuma and Murayama (2013) showed that the magnitude of the effect is substantially smaller than what was previously reported ($d = 0.61$ vs. 0.26).

Despite its importance, most of the past social neuroscience studies that used the free-choice paradigm failed to address the problem (Harmon-Jones, Harmon-Jones, et al., 2008; Jarcho et al., 2011; Kitayama et al., 2013; Mengarelli, Spoglianti, Avenanti, & di Pellegrino, 2015; Qin et al., 2011; Sharot et al., 2009; Tompson et al., 2016). For example, although a few studies (Jarcho et al., 2011; Kitayama et al., 2013; Qin et al., 2011; Tompson et al., 2016) found that preference changes were correlated with activities in the dissonance network (Figure 11.1) and other regions, since the effect of cognitive dissonance is confounded with the effect purely explained by the artifact, it remains unclear whether the results reported in these studies hold after controlling for the artifact (see Izuma & Murayama, 2013). Recently, Tompson et al. (2016) argued that based on their finding that the mPFC–PCC connectivity was significantly correlated with attitude change, the attitude change they observed in the conventional free-choice paradigm is unlikely to be explained by the artifact. Although the idea of testing the validity of the paradigm using neuroimaging data is interesting, their claim is based on circular logic (a single analysis is used for testing the link between the mPFC–PCC connectivity and attitude change as well as the validity of the free-choice paradigm; see Amodio, 2010), and this idea needs to be tested in an independent study (i.e., after independently establishing the construct validity of the neural data). Thus, findings reported in those studies that didn't address the artifact need to be interpreted with caution, and the artifact should be addressed in any future studies that use the free-choice paradigm (see Izuma & Murayama, 2013, for more discussion on how to control the artifact).

Reverse Inference Problem

In addition to the statistical artifact inherent in the free-choice paradigm, another major challenge that applies to all studies regardless of experimental paradigms is how we can go beyond reverse inference to better understand an exact functional role played by each region in the dissonance network (Figure 11.1) and other regions in cognitive dissonance. This is especially important because two regions in the network, namely the pMFC and anterior insula, are known to be two of the most functionally heterogeneous regions in the brain, and thus functional interpretations of these regions based on reverse inference tend to be unreliable (see Poldrack, 2006). Yarkoni, Poldrack, Nichols, Van Essen, and Wager (2011) analyzed the large dataset that include a total of 3,489 past neuroimaging studies and found that the pMFC and anterior insula (and DLPFC) are the most frequently activated regions across all studies (regardless of tasks; Yarkoni et al., 2011), and two meta-analyses showed that the pMFC is involved in a variety of cognitive and emotional processes (Shackman et al., 2011; Torta & Cauda, 2011). For example, although Kitayama et al. (2013) showed that the pMFC is activated in the difficult choice condition compared to the easy choice condition, the pMFC is known to play a role in a value comparison process during a simple binary choice (Hare, Schultz, Camerer, O'Doherty, & Rangel, 2011) and processing conflict at the decision level (so-called decision conflict; Izuma et al., 2013; Pochon, Riis, Sanfey, Nystrom, & Cohen, 2008; Shenhav, Straccia, Cohen, & Botvinick, 2014), and both accounts predicted and observed higher pMFC activity during difficult choices rather than easy choices. Thus, it is unclear if the dACC activity while making difficult choices is related to cognitive dissonance. Similarly, the functional specificity of the insula, PCC and DLPFC are also limited (Cieslik et al., 2013; Craig, 2009; Leech & Sharp, 2014). For example, although insula activity was often interpreted as reflecting negative emotion in past studies (Jarcho et al., 2011; Kitayama et al., 2013; Qin et al., 2011; van Veen et al., 2009), the insula is also consistently activated by reward (Sescousse, Caldú, Segura, & Dreher, 2013). Thus, given the highly limited functional specificity of these regions, the conclusions based on reverse inference (e.g., pMFC = conflict, anterior insula = negative affect, DLPFC = cognitive control [or approach motivation], and PCC = self-reference) are at best suggestive and need to be rigorously tested in future research.

The first step toward this goal may be to use functional localizer tasks just like Izuma and Adolphs's (2013) study mentioned above. By asking the same sample of individuals to perform a cognitive dissonance task as well as localizer tasks such as a self-reference task (PCC) and a task that induces negative affect (insula), we are able to test whether areas activated by the cognitive dissonance task actually overlap with areas activated by the localizer tasks within each of the PCC and insula regions. Since a functional dissociation within each of the dissonance-related brain regions (pMFC, anterior insula, DLPFC, and PCC) are demonstrated by previous research (e.g., Cieslik et al., 2013; de la Vega, Chang, Banich, Wager, & Yarkoni, 2016; Deen, Pitskel, & Pelphrey, 2011; Leech & Sharp, 2014), it may be that areas activated by dissonance are different from areas activated by a localizer task within each anatomical region. It should be noted that, although meta-analyses of neuroimaging studies provide us with information about which brain regions are consistently activated by a certain psychological or cognitive process, and the comparison between a cognitive dissonance neuroimaging study and a meta-analysis can give us a useful insight into the functional role of a specific brain region, spatial information from a meta-analysis tends to be limited because different studies use different participants, different normalization algorithms, etc. Thus, simply comparing results from an fMRI study with a past meta-analysis might lead us to a spurious conclusion (see Deen, Koldewyn, Kanwisher, & Saxe, 2015, for an fMRI study that highlights the importance of asking the same sample of individuals to perform multiple tasks).

Importantly, even if activation overlaps are found, the overlaps between two different tasks cannot be taken as strong evidence for the shared neural mechanism. It is still possible that the same area is activated for different reasons. It may be that distinct populations of neurons specialized for different cognitive processes are located in close proximity within the same region. Recently, a neuroimaging data analysis technique called multi-voxel pattern analysis (MVPA) has been proven to be useful to interpret activation overlaps (Peelen & Downing, 2007). For example, although it was previously observed that physical pain and social pain (rejection) activated the same area within the dACC (Kross, Berman, Mischel, Smith, & Wager, 2011), a recent MPVA study showed that neural representations within the dACC are distinct (Woo et al., 2014), suggesting that largely distinct populations of neurons encode physical and social pain (see Iannetti, Salomons, Moayedi, Mouraux, & Davis, 2013). Thus, the use of functional localizer tasks and MVPA (when overlapping activations were found) will provide much stronger evidence for the neural mechanisms underlying cognitive dissonance.

How Can Neuroscience Methods Contribute to the Psychological Understanding of Cognitive Dissonance?

As we gain more knowledge about the neural basis of cognitive dissonance, or social cognition in general, it may be possible to use neuroscience methods to gain unique insights into psychological mechanisms underlying cognitive dissonance in a way that would never be possible with currently existing behavioral methods. For example, works by Izuma and his colleagues (Izuma & Adolphs, 2013; Izuma et al., 2010) demonstrated that the same pMFC region tracks the degree of cognitive dissonance and cognitive imbalance on a trial-by-trial basis (see Izuma, 2013, 2015). Thus, it may be possible to use the activity in the pMFC as a neural index of cognitive dissonance (although the construct validity of such a neural measure need to be established first with a carefully designed experimental paradigm). In past behavioral studies, the existence of cognitive dissonance was only inferred from attitude change. While it is known that skin conductance response (SCR) increases when dissonance is aroused (Croyle & Cooper, 1983; Harmon-Jones, Brehm, Greenberg, Simon, & Nelson, 1996), the sensitivity of SCR to cognitive dissonance is likely to be limited (e.g., SCR is affected by factors other than cognitive dissonance such as general arousal and fear). In contrast, pMFC activity seems to be sensitive to the degree of cognitive dissonance as demonstrated by the two fMRI studies (Izuma & Adolphs, 2013; Izuma et al., 2010). Thus, an independent and accurate neural measure of cognitive dissonance has a great potential to advance our psychological understanding of cognitive dissonance.

Another possible future contribution of neuroscience methods is the controversy between cognitive dissonance theory and self-perception theory (Bem, 1967). Self-perception theory posits that individuals come to know their internal state (e.g., attitude) by observing their own behavior just like we infer other's internal state by observing their behavior. The theory has posed an important and serious challenge to cognitive dissonance theory; typical behavioral findings demonstrated in the past cognitive dissonance research could be explained by this self-perception process rather than cognitive dissonance (e.g., since I rejected an item, I must not like it). Despite the long history of dissonance research, the controversy has not been fully resolved (Greenwald, 2012; Harmon-Jones, Amodio, & Harmon-Jones, 2009; Olson & Stone, 2005). In all the experimental paradigms used in previous cognitive dissonance research, the two theories predict the same pattern of behavior (attitude change). Thus, it has been a major challenge to design an experimental paradigm that crucially tests the predictions from the theories. However, although the two theories predict the same behavior, underlying psychological processes are quite different between the theories, and if so, neural responses are likely to be differ as well. Thus, we may be able to distinguish these two theories from brain activations. The attempt to distinguish two different psychological processes (e.g., motivations) which lead to the same observed behavior from neural signals has already started in research on prosocial behavior. For example, individuals help others because of a purely altruistic motivation (e.g., empathy-based altruism) or a selfish motivation (e.g., reciprocity concern). Two recent fMRI MVPA studies demonstrated that we could distinguish different motivations for altruistic behaviors based on neural signals (Hein, Morishima, Leiberg, Sul, & Fehr, 2016; Tusche, Böckler, Kanske, Trautwein, & Singer, 2016). Since the brain has rich information on psychological processes underlying a behavior, psychological studies on dissonance (or any psychological topics) can be greatly benefitted by using neuroscience methods.

CONCLUSION

More than a half-century after the original conceptualization of cognitive dissonance theory in the 1950s, dissonance researchers have finally started looking at brain activations while an individual experiences cognitive dissonance. Although neuroimaging and brain-stimulation studies provided initial evidence for candidate brain regions and their possible functional roles, the endeavor is still very much in progress, and our understanding of the neural mechanisms underlying cognitive dissonance is still limited. Nonetheless, although there are important methodological and conceptual challenges we have to overcome, there is a good reason to believe that future studies will bring a lot of interesting findings. Furthermore, neuroscience methods have a great potential to help us test psychological hypotheses and further refine and advance the theory of cognitive dissonance in a way that was never even imagined by early researchers.

REFERENCES

Abelson, R. P., Aronson, E., McGuire, W. J., Newcomb, T. M., Rosenberg, M. J., & Tannenbaum, P. H. (1968). *Theories of cognitive consistency: A sourcebook.* Chicago, IL: Rand McNally.

Amodio, D. M. (2010). Can neuroscience advance social psychological theory? Social neuroscience for the behavioral social psychologist. *Social Cognition, 28,* 695–716. http://dx.doi.org/10.1521/soco.2010.28.6.695

Bem, D. J. (1967). Self-perception: An alternative interpretation of cognitive dissonance phenomena. *Psychological Review, 74*, 183–200. http://dx.doi.org/10.1037/h0024835

Botvinick, M. M., Braver, T. S., Barch, D. M., Carter, C. S., & Cohen, J. D. (2001). Conflict monitoring and cognitive control. *Psychological Review, 108*, 624–652. http://dx.doi.org/10.1037/0033-295X.108.3.624

Brehm, J. W. (1956). Postdecision changes in the desirability of alternatives. *Journal of Abnormal and Social Psychology, 52*, 384–389. http://dx.doi.org/10.1037/h0041006

Bush, G., & Shin, L. M. (2006). The Multi-Source Interference Task: An fMRI task that reliably activates the cingulo-frontal-parietal cognitive/attention network. *Nature Protocols, 1*, 308–313. http://dx.doi.org/10.1038/nprot.2006.48

Bush, G., Vogt, B. A., Holmes, J., Dale, A. M., Greve, D., Jenike, M. A., & Rosen, B. R. (2002). Dorsal anterior cingulate cortex: A role in reward-based decision making. *Proceedings of the National Academy of Sciences of the United States of America, 99*, 523–528. http://dx.doi.org/10.1073/pnas.012470999

Calder, A. J., Beaver, J. D., Davis, M. H., van Ditzhuijzen, J., Keane, J., & Lawrence, A. D. (2007). Disgust sensitivity predicts the insula and pallidal response to pictures of disgusting foods. *The European Journal of Neuroscience, 25*, 3422–3428. http://dx.doi.org/10.1111/j.1460-9568.2007.05604.x

Carter, C. S., & van Veen, V. (2007). Anterior cingulate cortex and conflict detection: An update of theory and data. *Cognitive, Affective & Behavioral Neuroscience, 7*, 367–379. http://dx.doi.org/10.3758/CABN.7.4.367

Chang, L. J., Gianaros, P. J., Manuck, S. B., Krishnan, A., & Wager, T. D. (2015). A sensitive and specific neural signature for picture-induced negative affect. *PLoS Biology, 13*, e1002180. http://dx.doi.org/10.1371/journal.pbio.1002180

Chen, M. K., & Risen, J. L. (2010). How choice affects and reflects preferences: Revisiting the free-choice paradigm. *Journal of Personality and Social Psychology, 99*, 573–594. http://dx.doi.org/10.1037/a0020217

Cieslik, E. C., Zilles, K., Caspers, S., Roski, C., Kellermann, T. S., Jakobs, O., . . . Eickhoff, S. B. (2013). Is there "one" DLPFC in cognitive action control? Evidence for heterogeneity from co-activation-based parcellation. *Cerebral Cortex, 23*, 2677–2689. http://dx.doi.org/10.1093/cercor/bhs256

Craig, A. D. (2009). How do you feel—now? The anterior insula and human awareness. *Nature Reviews Neuroscience, 10*, 59–70. http://dx.doi.org/10.1038/nrn2555

Croyle, R. T., & Cooper, J. (1983). Dissonance arousal: Physiological evidence. *Journal of Personality and Social Psychology, 45*, 782–791. http://dx.doi.org/10.1037/0022-3514.45.4.782

Damasio, A. R., Grabowski, T. J., Bechara, A., Damasio, H., Ponto, L. L., Parvizi, J., & Hichwa, R. D. (2000). Subcortical and cortical brain activity during the feeling of self-generated emotions. *Nature Neuroscience, 3*, 1049–1056. http://dx.doi.org/10.1038/79871

de la Vega, A., Chang, L. J., Banich, M. T., Wager, T. D., & Yarkoni, T. (2016). Large-scale meta-analysis of human medial frontal cortex reveals tripartite functional organization. *The Journal of Neuroscience, 36*, 6553–6562. http://dx.doi.org/10.1523/JNEUROSCI.4402-15.2016

de Vries, J., Byrne, M., & Kehoe, E. (2015). Cognitive dissonance induction in everyday life: An fMRI study. *Social Neuroscience, 10*, 268–281. http://dx.doi.org/10.1080/17470919.2014.990990

Deen, B., Koldewyn, K., Kanwisher, N., & Saxe, R. (2015). Functional organization of social perception and cognition in the superior temporal sulcus. *Cerebral Cortex, 25*, 4596–4609. http://dx.doi.org/10.1093/cercor/bhv111

Deen, B., Pitskel, N. B., & Pelphrey, K. A. (2011). Three systems of insular functional connectivity identified with cluster analysis. *Cerebral Cortex, 21*, 1498–1506. http://dx.doi.org/10.1093/cercor/bhq186

Festinger, L. (1957). *A Theory of Cognitive Dissonance*. Palo Alto, CA: Stanford University Press.

Festinger, L., & Carlsmith, J. M. (1959). Cognitive consequences of forced compliance. *Journal of Abnormal Psychology, 58,* 203–210.

Gawronski, B., & Strack, F. (Eds.). (2012). *Cognitive consistency: A fundamental principle in social cognition.* New York, NY: Guilford Press.

Greenwald, A. G. (2012). There Is nothing so theoretical as a good method. *Perspectives on Psychological Science, 7,* 99–108. http://dx.doi.org/10.1177/1745691611434210

Hare, T. A., Schultz, W., Camerer, C. F., O'Doherty, J. P., & Rangel, A. (2011). Transformation of stimulus value signals into motor commands during simple choice. *Proceedings of the National Academy of Sciences of the United States of America, 108,* 18120–18125. http://dx.doi.org/10.1073/pnas.1109322108

Harmon-Jones, E., Amodio, D. M., & Harmon-Jones, C. (2009). Action-based model of dissonance: A review, integration, and expansion of conceptions of cognitive conflict. *Advances in Experimental Social Psychology, 41,* 119–166.

Harmon-Jones, E., Brehm, J. W., Greenberg, J., Simon, L., & Nelson, D. E. (1996). Evidence that the production of aversive consequences is not necessary to create cognitive dissonance. *Journal of Personality and Social Psychology, 70,* 5–16. http://dx.doi.org/10.1037/0022-3514.70.1.5

Harmon-Jones, E., Gerdjikov, T., & Harmon-Jones, C. (2008). The effect of induced compliance on relative left frontal cortical activity: A test of the action-based model of dissonance. *European Journal of Social Psychology, 38,* 35–45. http://dx.doi.org/10.1002/ejsp.399

Harmon-Jones, E., Harmon-Jones, C., Fearn, M., Sigelman, J. D., & Johnson, P. (2008). Left frontal cortical activation and spreading of alternatives: Tests of the action-based model of dissonance. *Journal of Personality and Social Psychology, 94,* 1–15. http://dx.doi.org/10.1037/0022-3514.94.1.1

Harmon-Jones, E., Harmon-Jones, C., Serra, R., & Gable, P. A. (2011). The effect of commitment on relative left frontal cortical activity: Tests of the action-based model of dissonance. *Personality and Social Psychology Bulletin, 37,* 395–408. http://dx.doi.org/10.1177/0146167210397059

Harmon-Jones, E., & Mills, J. (Eds.). (1999). *Cognitive dissonance: Progress on a pivotal theory in social psychology.* Washington, DC: Braum-Brumfield. http://dx.doi.org/10.1037/10318-000

Hayden, B. Y., Heilbronner, S. R., Pearson, J. M., & Platt, M. L. (2011). Surprise signals in anterior cingulate cortex: Neuronal encoding of unsigned reward prediction errors driving adjustment in behavior. *The Journal of Neuroscience, 31,* 4178–4187. http://dx.doi.org/10.1523/JNEUROSCI.4652-10.2011

Heider, F. (1958). *The psychology of interpersonal relations.* New York, NY: Wiley. http://dx.doi.org/10.1037/10628-000

Hein, G., Morishima, Y., Leiberg, S., Sul, S., & Fehr, E. (2016). The brain's functional network architecture reveals human motives. *Science, 351,* 1074–1078. http://dx.doi.org/10.1126/science.aac7992

Iannetti, G. D., Salomons, T. V., Moayedi, M., Mouraux, A., & Davis, K. D. (2013). Beyond metaphor: Contrasting mechanisms of social and physical pain. *Trends in Cognitive Sciences, 17,* 371–378. http://dx.doi.org/10.1016/j.tics.2013.06.002

Izuma, K. (2013). The neural basis of social influence and attitude change. *Current Opinion in Neurobiology, 23,* 456–462. http://dx.doi.org/10.1016/j.conb.2013.03.009

Izuma, K. (2015). Attitude change and cognitive consistency. In A. W. Toga (Ed.), *Brain mapping: An encyclopedic reference* (Vol. 3, pp. 247–250). Oxford, England: Elsevier. http://dx.doi.org/10.1016/B978-0-12-397025-1.00188-3

Izuma, K., & Adolphs, R. (2013). Social manipulation of preference in the human brain. *Neuron, 78,* 563–573. http://dx.doi.org/10.1016/j.neuron.2013.03.023

Izuma, K., Akula, S., Murayama, K., Wu, D. A., Iacoboni, M., & Adolphs, R. (2015). A causal role for posterior medial frontal cortex in choice-induced preference change. *The Journal of Neuroscience, 35,* 3598–3606. http://dx.doi.org/10.1523/JNEUROSCI.4591-14.2015

Izuma, K., Matsumoto, M., Murayama, K., Samejima, K., Norihiro, S., & Matsumoto, K. (2013). Neural correlates of cognitive dissonance and decision conflict. In T. Omori, Y. Yamaguchi, Y. Sakaguchi, N. Sato, and I. Tsuda (Eds.), *Advances in Cognitive Neurodynamics (III): Proceedings of the Third International Conference on Cognitive Neurodynamics—2011* (pp. 623–628). Dordrecht, the Netherlands: Springer. http://dx.doi.org/10.1007/978-94-007-4792-0_83

Izuma, K., Matsumoto, M., Murayama, K., Samejima, K., Sadato, N., & Matsumoto, K. (2010). Neural correlates of cognitive dissonance and choice-induced preference change. *Proceedings of the National Academy of Sciences of the United States of America, 107*, 22014–22019. http://dx.doi.org/10.1073/pnas.1011879108

Izuma, K., & Murayama, K. (2013). Choice-induced preference change in the free-choice paradigm: A critical methodological review. *Frontiers in Psychology, 4*, 41. http://dx.doi.org/10.3389/fpsyg.2013.00041

Jarcho, J. M., Berkman, E. T., & Lieberman, M. D. (2011). The neural basis of rationalization: Cognitive dissonance reduction during decision-making. *Social Cognitive and Affective Neuroscience, 6*, 460–467. http://dx.doi.org/10.1093/scan/nsq054

Kerns, J. G., Cohen, J. D., MacDonald, A. W., III, Cho, R. Y., Stenger, V. A., & Carter, C. S. (2004). Anterior cingulate conflict monitoring and adjustments in control. *Science, 303*, 1023–1026. http://dx.doi.org/10.1126/science.1089910

Kitayama, S., Chua, H. F., Tompson, S., & Han, S. (2013). Neural mechanisms of dissonance: An fMRI investigation of choice justification. *NeuroImage, 69*, 206–212. http://dx.doi.org/10.1016/j.neuroimage.2012.11.034

Knutson, B., Westdorp, A., Kaiser, E., & Hommer, D. (2000). FMRI visualization of brain activity during a monetary incentive delay task. *NeuroImage, 12*, 20–27. http://dx.doi.org/10.1006/nimg.2000.0593

Koster, R., Duzel, E., & Dolan, R. J. (2015). Action and valence modulate choice and choice-induced preference change. *PLoS One, 10*, e0119682. http://dx.doi.org/10.1371/journal.pone.0119682

Kross, E., Berman, M. G., Mischel, W., Smith, E. E., & Wager, T. D. (2011). Social rejection shares somatosensory representations with physical pain. *Proceedings of the National Academy of Sciences of the United States of America, 108*, 6270–6275. http://dx.doi.org/10.1073/pnas.1102693108

Leech, R., & Sharp, D. J. (2014). The role of the posterior cingulate cortex in cognition and disease. *Brain: A Journal of Neurology, 137*, 12–32. http://dx.doi.org/10.1093/brain/awt162

Lieberman, M. D., Ochsner, K. N., Gilbert, D. T., & Schacter, D. L. (2001). Do amnesics exhibit cognitive dissonance reduction? The role of explicit memory and attention in attitude change. *Psychological Science, 12*, 135–140. http://dx.doi.org/10.1111/1467-9280.00323

Mansouri, F. A., Tanaka, K., & Buckley, M. J. (2009). Conflict-induced behavioural adjustment: A clue to the executive functions of the prefrontal cortex. *Nature Reviews Neuroscience, 10*, 141–152. http://dx.doi.org/10.1038/nrn2538

Matsumoto, M., Matsumoto, K., Abe, H., & Tanaka, K. (2007). Medial prefrontal cell activity signaling prediction errors of action values. *Nature Neuroscience, 10*, 647–656. http://dx.doi.org/10.1038/nn1890

Mengarelli, F., Spoglianti, S., Avenanti, A., & di Pellegrino, G. (2015). Cathodal tDCS over the left prefrontal cortex diminishes choice-induced preference change. *Cerebral Cortex, 25*, 1219–1227. http://dx.doi.org/10.1093/cercor/bht314

Northoff, G., Heinzel, A., de Greck, M., Bermpohl, F., Dobrowolny, H., & Panksepp, J. (2006). Self-referential processing in our brain—A meta-analysis of imaging studies on the self. *NeuroImage, 31*, 440–457. http://dx.doi.org/10.1016/j.neuroimage.2005.12.002

Olson, J. M., & Stone, J. (2005). The influence of behavior on attitudes. In D. Albarracin, B. T. Johnson, & M. P. Zanna (Eds.), *The handbook of attitudes* (pp. 223–271). Mahwah, NJ: Erlbaum.

Peelen, M. V., & Downing, P. E. (2007). Using multi-voxel pattern analysis of fMRI data to interpret overlapping functional activations. *Trends in Cognitive Sciences, 11*, 4–5. http://dx.doi.org/10.1016/j.tics.2006.10.009

Pochon, J. B., Riis, J., Sanfey, A. G., Nystrom, L. E., & Cohen, J. D. (2008). Functional imaging of decision conflict. *The Journal of Neuroscience, 28*, 3468–3473. http://dx.doi.org/10.1523/JNEUROSCI.4195-07.2008

Poldrack, R. A. (2006). Can cognitive processes be inferred from neuroimaging data? *Trends in Cognitive Sciences, 10*, 59–63. http://dx.doi.org/10.1016/j.tics.2005.12.004

Qin, J., Kimel, S., Kitayama, S., Wang, X., Yang, X., & Han, S. (2011). How choice modifies preference: Neural correlates of choice justification. *NeuroImage, 55*, 240–246. http://dx.doi.org/10.1016/j.neuroimage.2010.11.076

Salti, M., El Karoui, I., Maillet, M., & Naccache, L. (2014). Cognitive dissonance resolution is related to episodic memory. *PLoS One, 9*, e108579. http://dx.doi.org/10.1371/journal.pone.0108579

Sescousse, G., Caldú, X., Segura, B., & Dreher, J.-C. (2013). Processing of primary and secondary rewards: A quantitative meta-analysis and review of human functional neuroimaging studies. *Neuroscience and Biobehavioral Reviews, 37*, 681–696. http://dx.doi.org/10.1016/j.neubiorev.2013.02.002

Shackman, A. J., Salomons, T. V., Slagter, H. A., Fox, A. S., Winter, J. J., & Davidson, R. J. (2011). The integration of negative affect, pain and cognitive control in the cingulate cortex. *Nature Reviews Neuroscience, 12*, 154–167. http://dx.doi.org/10.1038/nrn2994

Sharot, T., De Martino, B., & Dolan, R. J. (2009). How choice reveals and shapes expected hedonic outcome. *The Journal of Neuroscience, 29*, 3760–3765. http://dx.doi.org/10.1523/JNEUROSCI.4972-08.2009

Sharot, T., Fleming, S. M., Yu, X., Koster, R., & Dolan, R. J. (2012). Is choice-induced preference change long lasting? *Psychological Science, 23*, 1123–1129. http://dx.doi.org/10.1177/0956797612438733

Shenhav, A., Straccia, M. A., Cohen, J. D., & Botvinick, M. M. (2014). Anterior cingulate engagement in a foraging context reflects choice difficulty, not foraging value. *Nature Neuroscience, 17*, 1249–1254. http://dx.doi.org/10.1038/nn.3771

Shima, K., & Tanji, J. (1998). Role for cingulate motor area cells in voluntary movement selection based on reward. *Science, 282*, 1335–1338. http://dx.doi.org/10.1126/science.282.5392.1335

Tompson, S., Chua, H. F., & Kitayama, S. (2016). Connectivity between mPFC and PCC predicts post-choice attitude change: The self-referential processing hypothesis of choice justification. *Human Brain Mapping, 37*, 3810–3820. http://dx.doi.org/10.1002/hbm.23277

Torta, D. M., & Cauda, F. (2011). Different functions in the cingulate cortex, a meta-analytic connectivity modeling study. *NeuroImage, 56*, 2157–2172. http://dx.doi.org/10.1016/j.neuroimage.2011.03.066

Tusche, A., Böckler, A., Kanske, P., Trautwein, F.-M., & Singer, T. (2016). Decoding the charitable brain: Empathy, perspective taking, and attention shifts differentially predict altruistic giving. *The Journal of Neuroscience, 36*, 4719–4732. http://dx.doi.org/10.1523/JNEUROSCI.3392-15.2016

van Veen, V., Krug, M. K., Schooler, J. W., & Carter, C. S. (2009). Neural activity predicts attitude change in cognitive dissonance. *Nature Neuroscience, 12*, 1469–1474. http://dx.doi.org/10.1038/nn.2413

Woo, C. W., Koban, L., Kross, E., Lindquist, M. A., Banich, M. T., Ruzic, L., . . . Wager, T. D. (2014). Separate neural representations for physical pain and social rejection. *Nature Communications, 5*, 5380. http://dx.doi.org/10.1038/ncomms6380

Yarkoni, T., Poldrack, R. A., Nichols, T. E., Van Essen, D. C., & Wager, T. D. (2011). Large-scale automated synthesis of human functional neuroimaging data. *Nature Methods, 8*, 665–670. http://dx.doi.org/10.1038/nmeth.1635

12

Moving Beyond Attitude Change in the Study of Dissonance-Related Processes

An Update on the Role of Discomfort

Patricia G. Devine, John M. Tauer, Kenneth E. Barron, Andrew J. Elliot, Kristen M. Vance, and Eddie Harmon-Jones

In 1957, Leon Festinger outlined a straightforward set of assumptions concerning the motivational underpinnings of cognitive dissonance. Festinger posited that (a) an inconsistency between cognitions created an uncomfortable psychological tension state, and (b) people would be motivated to reduce the tension by implementing some change that would restore consonance among the inconsistent elements. Festinger's theory is essentially a process model, as represented in Figure 12.1. In Festinger's model, inconsistency between cognitions (A) leads to dissonance (B), an uncomfortable psychological tension and arousal state that the person will be motivated to reduce. According to the model, the motivational properties of dissonance will lead to a dissonance-reduction strategy (C), which, if effective, will alleviate dissonance (D).

Much of the imaginative work of dissonance researchers has been devoted to documenting the motivational properties of dissonance, and an enormous amount of evidence consistent with the predictions of dissonance theory has been obtained. For example, hundreds of studies have shown that, when people engage in counterattitudinal behaviors (A), ostensibly effective dissonance-reduction strategies, such as attitude change, are implemented (C) (see Cooper

http://dx.doi.org/10.1037/0000135-012
Cognitive Dissonance, Second Edition: Reexamining a Pivotal Theory in Psychology,
E. Harmon-Jones (Editor)
Copyright © 2019 by the American Psychological Association. All rights reserved.

FIGURE 12.1. Schematic of Festinger's (1957) Process Model of Dissonance

A	B	C	D
Inconsistency Between Cognitions	Dissonance Created	Reduction Strategy Implemented	Dissonance Alleviated

& Fazio, 1984, for a review).[1] However, direct evidence regarding the arousal (B) and reduction (D) of dissonance has been more elusive. Given the extant evidence, the reasoning about dissonance arousal and its reduction has been necessarily indirect. The logic is as follows: Because dissonance-reduction strategies (e.g., attitude change) are implemented after a procedure designed to create inconsistencies between attitudes and behavior, it has been assumed that (a) dissonance was created, (b) dissonance motivated the use of the reduction strategy, and (c) the reduction strategy was successful in alleviating the dissonance. Although the well-established attitude-change findings are clearly consistent with theory-derived predictions, they do not provide direct tests of the process assumptions of dissonance theory. In short, the part of dissonance theory that has proven rather elusive has been the core assumption that the tension created is psychologically distressing, and that this distress is alleviated after the implementation of a dissonance-reduction strategy.

In this chapter, we argue that outcome measures such as attitude change or other ostensibly effective dissonance-reduction strategies (e.g., bolstering, self-affirmation, trivialization) cannot provide this type of evidence because such measures are silent regarding underlying processes. Thus, the methods most commonly used to test dissonance assumptions are limited in what they can reveal about the nature of the dissonance and whether dissonance-reduction strategies are effective in alleviating dissonance-related distress. Our position is that dissonance theorists have asked too much of attitude change (and other outcome measures). We suggest that more thorough and complete testing of dissonance theory may be possible if we expand our methodological tools in the assessment of dissonance. To this end, we offer one such tool and provide evidence supporting the efficacy of it as a measure that is sensitive to

---

[1] Throughout the chapter, we focus on induced-compliance paradigms that have traditionally used attitude change as the indicator of dissonance. We should be clear, however, that the induced-compliance paradigm is not the only one that suffers from an overreliance on the use of attitude measures as the indicator of dissonance. For example, the free-choice paradigm relies on the spreading of alternatives, and the selective-exposure paradigm relies on preference for attitude-consistent information. We suggest that these paradigms, with their emphasis on outcome measures to indicate dissonance arousal and reduction, are also limited in what they can reveal about the nature of the dissonance experience or the process of dissonance induction and reduction. Over the years, the induced-compliance paradigm, however, has been the most frequently used paradigm in dissonance research. Therefore, we use this paradigm to illustrate our concerns regarding the overreliance on such outcome measures as indicators of both dissonance arousal and reduction.

both dissonance induction (B) and reduction (D). Before introducing the measure, however, we review the historical approaches in which attitude change plays a central role.

ATTITUDE CHANGE AS THE INDICATOR OF DISSONANCE: THE GOOD, THE BAD, AND THE UGLY

Historically, the induced-compliance paradigm has been the most frequently used paradigm for studying dissonance hypotheses (see Cooper & Fazio, 1984). In this paradigm, participants are induced to freely choose to advocate a counterattitudinal position, which theoretically sets the stage for creating dissonance (commonly referred to as the *high-choice* condition). As a comparison condition, other participants are assigned to advocate a counterattitudinal position (commonly referred to as the *low-choice* condition); these participants theoretically do not experience dissonance, because they had no choice regarding the position they would advocate. After the counterattitudinal behavior, attitudes are assessed for participants in both choice conditions. In keeping with dissonance theory predictions, studies have repeatedly shown that high-choice participants show greater attitude change than their low-choice counterparts. Such findings have been interpreted to suggest that the dissonance experience is unpleasant and that it motivates attitude change that presumably alleviates dissonance-related distress. In addition, it has often been assumed that these attempts to reduce dissonance are successful. There are clearly some strengths to this empirical strategy.

The Good

Attitude change as the operational definition of dissonance reduction has served dissonance researchers well and yielded key insights regarding many aspects of cognitive dissonance. In the absence of any direct indicators of dissonance, testing outcomes that are consistent with the theory (e.g., attitude change among only high-choice participants after a counterattitudinal behavior) is a sensible and useful empirical strategy. Indeed, we are not suggesting that examining attitude change is in any way wrong or naive. Rather, we are suggesting that our overall understanding of the dynamics of dissonance processes may be improved by developing measures that can be used in conjunction with attitude change (and other outcome measures) to more fully reveal dissonance-related processes.

One of the primary goals early in the history of dissonance research was to demonstrate that the dominant theoretical paradigm in psychology at the time, reinforcement theory, could not account for the provocative findings generated in the tradition of dissonance experiments (see Aronson, 1992, for more detail). As such, the focus was on producing outcomes that were not readily interpretable from a reinforcement perspective. As an illustrative example, consider Festinger and Carlsmith's (1959) classic study in which participants who chose to convince an unsuspecting participant (actually a confederate) that a boring task was actually interesting came to like the task more if they were offered low ($1) compared with high ($20) compensation for their efforts. Thus, early on, the goal of the research was to produce outcomes that were consistent with dissonance theory and not easily handled by alternative theoretical accounts. It was assumed, rather than tested, that the processes outlined by Festinger (1957) were responsible for the outcomes.

As dissonance research moved forward, however, issues arose concerning whether the motivational assumptions outlined by Festinger (1957) were responsible for the observed outcomes (Bem, 1967; Chapanis & Chapanis, 1964; Tedeschi, Schlenker, & Bonoma, 1971) that highlighted the need for evidence beyond attitude change to support dissonance interpretations for these outcomes. In the absence of direct measures of dissonance, these issues were, to say the least, challenging for dissonance theorists. Such theoretical and empirical challenges, however, ultimately served to showcase the cleverness and ingenuity of a generation of dissonance researchers, who developed compelling ways to circumvent the fact that there were no good direct ways to measure dissonance. This was perhaps the most positive by-product of the need to rely on indirect assessment of dissonance. The creativity of these dissonance theorists served to inspire, and continues to inspire, subsequent generations of social psychologists both within and beyond dissonance research.

Consider, as just one of many possible examples, the creative solution to the problem of having no direct measure of dissonance evidenced in Zanna and Cooper's (1974) work on the arousal component of dissonance. Although they could not measure arousal directly, their theoretical resourcefulness led them to adopt a misattribution approach, which drew heavily on Schachter and Singer's (1962) two-factor theory of emotion in characterizing dissonance as an arousal state open to various cognitive labels. Zanna and Cooper reasoned that participants who freely chose to advocate a counterattitudinal position would not change their attitude if given the opportunity to misattribute their arousal.[2] In keeping with their predictions, high-choice participants given a placebo that would ostensibly make them feel tense changed their attitudes less than their high-choice counterparts, who had ingested a drug that supposedly would make them feel relaxed. Zanna and Cooper's study, along with a variety of conceptual replications (see review by Fazio & Cooper, 1983), makes a strong case for the position that dissonance has arousal properties. The key point to be emphasized here is that in the absence of any direct way to assess

---

[2] It is of interest to note that Zanna and Cooper (1974) collected a measure of felt tension with a single item, ranging from *calm* (1) to *tense* (31). In general, participants who were expected to feel tension (e.g., standard high-choice condition and participants in the "drug"-creating arousal conditions) reported higher levels of felt tension. Although these findings were reported, Zanna and Cooper's primary focus was to provide evidence that dissonance had arousal properties. Very few others have attempted to measure the felt discomfort created by dissonance tasks, and studies that did typically suffered from shortcomings that limited the informativeness of the measures (see Elliot & Devine, 1994, for a discussion).

the arousal component of dissonance, Zanna and Cooper used their theoretical resourcefulness and empirical imaginativeness to circumvent the problem. However, there are also some limitations to the emphasis on arousal that have created interpretational difficulties, if not theory-damning concerns, for dissonance theorists through the years.

The Bad

Although the field got around the fact that there was not a direct indicator of dissonance (i.e., unpleasant tension and arousal) and progress was made, we argue that the field asked too much of attitude change for informing the conceptual analysis of dissonance. That is, attitude change was the indicator that dissonance was induced *and* reduced. Thus, the fact that high-choice participants changed their attitudes more than low-choice participants was taken as evidence that dissonance was experienced among the high-choice participants. Attitude change also served the function of telling researchers, by its absence, that dissonance was no longer present (although, as will become clear later, this may not always be a valid inference). For example, when people implement an ostensibly effective dissonance-reduction strategy, such as bolstering (Sherman & Gorkin, 1980), self-affirmation (Steele & Liu, 1983), or trivialization (Simon, Greenberg, & Brehm, 1995) and then attitudes do not change, it is assumed that dissonance motivation is no longer present. In short, attitude change has been the primary indicator that dissonance was created and that it was reduced.

We suggest that attitude change is at best an indirect indicator of whether dissonance has been induced or reduced. This observation is, of course, not novel. Overreliance on attitude change as an indicator of dissonance induction and reduction has created interpretational difficulties in many studies in which results did not conform with expected dissonance outcomes. For example, when attitude change is not observed in the induced-compliance paradigm, what can be concluded? Was dissonance not successfully created (e.g., perhaps one's procedure was flawed)? Did participants find alternative ways to alleviate their discomfort before attitudes were assessed? Was attitude change not a viable strategy for all participants? Did attitude change reduce dissonance for those who used this strategy? These are crucial questions and ones that attitude change cannot answer.

To illustrate the conceptual ambiguities associated with the use of attitude change as the sole indicator of dissonance, consider a classic study by Cooper and Worchel (1970). The goal of the study was to demonstrate that advocating a counterattitudinal position does not lead to the arousal of cognitive dissonance unless that advocacy results in undesirable consequences. In this study, participants were asked to perform an extremely dull task (cf. Festinger & Carlsmith, 1959) and were offered varying incentives for telling a waiting participant (actually a confederate) that the task was interesting and enjoyable. Before reporting their attitudes toward the task, half of the participants learned that they had successfully convinced the waiting participant that the task was interesting. The other half learned that the participant still believed that the task would be dull.

Cooper and Worchel's (1970) findings revealed that only those participants who believed that they had succeeded in convincing the waiting participant and complied for a small incentive came to believe the task was interesting (e.g., showed the classic dissonance-induced attitude shift). Cooper and Worchel suggested that those who were unsuccessful in convincing the participant (as well as those who received a sufficient incentive) did not change their attitudes because dissonance was not aroused in these participants. We would argue, however, that sole reliance on attitude change in this paradigm cannot reveal whether these participants experienced dissonance. It is at least conceptually possible that dissonance *was* created for the low-incentive participants who learned that their efforts to deceive the waiting participant failed but was reduced before participants' attitudes were assessed. Simply agreeing to the counterattitudinal behavior (i.e., to deceive the waiting participant) would be sufficient to induce dissonance (e.g., Elliot & Devine, 1994; Rabbi, Brehm, & Cohen, 1959). Indeed, learning that they had been unsuccessful in their deception efforts may have been sufficient to alleviate any dissonance-related distress that the deception caused them.

Similar ambiguities arise in other paradigms (with other theoretical agendas) as well. For example, Steele (1988; Steele & Liu, 1983) suggested that classic dissonance manipulations, such as the induced-compliance paradigm, serve to threaten people's global sense of self-integrity. He argued that to alleviate the discomfort, one need not make adjustments (e.g., attitude change) to the cognitions directly involved in the inconsistency but instead could engage in some activity that might restore (or reaffirm) one's global sense of self-integrity. To support this logic, Steele and Liu had participants write a counterattitudinal essay. Then, before reporting their attitudes, participants filled out a value-affirming scale on a dimension that was either important or unimportant to their self-identities. In keeping with Steele's theory, attitude change was observed only among participants for whom the self-affirmation opportunity was not important to their self-identities. However, Steele noted a couple of alternative explanations for the attitude data in Steele and Liu's studies, which suggest that attitude change may not be an adequate measure to demonstrate that dissonance was alleviated. He suggested that the important self-affirmations may have bolstered or frozen participants' initial attitudes, resulting in little attitude change. Thus, it appears that in the dissonance literature, the absence of a more direct measure of dissonance makes it difficult to make strong inferences about the presence or absence of dissonance.

Note that the studies reviewed in this section are not the only studies challenged by interpretational ambiguities that derive from having to reason indirectly about the arousal and reduction of dissonance. These studies were selected to illustrate the interpretational difficulties that arise under such circumstances. The ambiguities are clearly evident in other dissonance research as well. Consider, for example, the difficulties that could arise in a study if some participants' responses fit the classic dissonance attitude-change pattern, but other participants' responses did not. What is the researcher to make of such variability? Was dissonance successfully created for only some of the participants? Or is it possible that attitude change was not a dissonance-reduction option for some people (e.g., people who are highly committed to their attitudes; Hardyck & Kardush, 1968)? Similarly, inconsistent findings (e.g., failure to reliably obtain preference for attitude-consistent information in the selective-exposure literature) proved difficult to resolve in the absence of some indicator that provided independent evidence that dissonance was successfully induced (Cialdini, Petty, & Cacioppo, 1981).

In short, although attitude change can be informative and has been useful in providing support for dissonance theory, it simply cannot rule out alternative explanations (i.e., dissonance was never created; dissonance was created, but not reduced; dissonance was reduced through some other strategy besides attitude change). And, finally, virtually no evidence exists to suggest that if attitude change occurred, participants felt better—that any discomfort that had been created by the dissonance-induction procedure was alleviated. This is perhaps the issue that has received the least empirical attention in the dissonance literature and one that, as illustrated below, raises some questions about the effectiveness of attitude change in explaining the mechanisms underlying the dissonance process.

The Ugly

According to dissonance theory, attitude change was the outcome of a presumed motivational state. The field generally, and dissonance researchers more specifically, was ultimately dissatisfied with having to rely exclusively on indirect evidence for the motivational state. In response to this set of circumstances, an exciting line of research ensued, the goal of which was to provide evidence that dissonance was at least arousing, if not directly psychologically unpleasant. Several studies attempted to show the arousal properties of dissonance by using indirect research techniques, such as incidental retention, response competition, and misattribution of arousal (e.g., Kiesler & Pallak, 1976; Pallak & Pittman, 1972; Zanna & Cooper, 1974).

Other investigators attempted to provide direct evidence regarding the arousal component of dissonance by measuring physiological changes that theoretically would accompany the dissonance. Studies provided evidence supporting the dissonance-as-physiological-arousal hypothesis (Elkin & Leippe, 1986; Harmon-Jones, Brehm, Greenberg, Simon, & Nelson, 1996; Losch & Cacioppo, 1990). For example, in a set of induced-compliance experiments, Elkin and Leippe's (1986) participants displayed elevated galvanic skin responses (GSRs), as well as attitude change, after freely choosing to advocate a counter-attitudinal position. Losch and Cacioppo (1990) obtained a similar pattern of results by means of a misattribution paradigm and frequency of nonspecific skin conductance responses (NS-SCRs) as the physiological indicator of dissonance arousal. Most recently, Harmon-Jones et al. (1996, Experiment 3) showed increased NS-SCRs in high- but not low-choice conditions. Taken together, these studies provide compelling evidence that there is a physiological component to the dissonance state. See also Chapters 4 and 11, this volume, for further evidence of physiological responses associated with cognitive dissonance processes.

With such strong evidence in hand for the arousal component of dissonance, Elkin and Leippe (1986; see also Harmon-Jones et al., 1996) also attempted to test the hypothesis that attitude change would lead to the reduction in the indicator of the presumed motivational state. Specifically, they tested the assumption that implementing a dissonance-reduction strategy, in this case attitude change, would lead to a reduction in dissonance. Elkin and Leippe argued that support for this assumption was critical to the contention that dissonance is a motivational state. Indeed, such studies provided the first opportunity to test the process assumptions suggested by Festinger's (1957) model. However, these efforts to directly support the hypothesis that dissonance reduction occurs after attitude change were foiled. That is, although Elkin and Leippe were able to show that GSR increased reliably when participants freely chose to advocate a counterattitudinal position (A → B) and that these participants changed their attitudes in the direction of the position they advocated (B → C), they failed to show dissonance reduction in the form of a significant decrease in GSRs in the post-attitude-change period (C did not lead to D).

Such findings were ultimately troublesome for the theory and led Elkin and Leippe (1986) to call into question the veracity of Festinger's (1957) assumptions regarding the motivational nature of dissonance arousal: "It is only though the arousal's subsequent reduction that motivation can be implied, and we found no evidence that explicit attitude change reduced arousal. . . . Cognitive dissonance, then, may or may not be a motivational state" (p. 64). This type of statement was damning for the theory. Echoing these types of concerns, Wilder (1992) observed the following: "Questions of the reality of dissonance as a measurable tension or aversive state have always dogged the theory" (p. 352). In the wake of such disappointing findings regarding Festinger's dissonance-reduction postulate as well as the need to rely on indirect reasoning regarding dissonance-related processing, empirical progress regarding dissonance-related hypotheses was largely stalled. However, more recent findings using an alternative measure of dissonance have paved the way to directly test Festinger's assumptions regarding dissonance arousal and reduction. This measure serves as a "dissonance thermometer" of sorts and is sensitive to both the induction and reduction of dissonance-related distress.[3] Used in conjunction with outcome measures such as attitude change, a measure of dissonance affect may yield insights concerning the dynamics of dissonance induction and reduction that would be impossible to obtain through outcome measures alone.

---

[3] We thank Mark Zanna for the suggestion of the label *dissonance thermometer*. We think this label is intuitive and captures the essence of the measure.

MEASURING DISSONANCE AS PSYCHOLOGICAL DISCOMFORT: A DISSONANCE THERMOMETER

Both indirect (e.g., attitude change) and direct (e.g., arousal) indicators of dissonance have created difficulties for testing core assumptions of dissonance theory. A close reading of Festinger's (1957) classic monograph, however, reveals that Festinger conceptualized dissonance in two distinguishable ways. He explicitly delineated psychological discomfort as a component of dissonance, and he alluded to dissonance as a bodily condition analogous to a tension or drive state like hunger (Croyle & Cooper, 1983). In Brehm and Cohen's (1962) restatement of dissonance theory, they distinctly characterized dissonance as a state of arousal and focused extensively on its drivelike properties. As previously suggested, most research investigating the nature of dissonance, whether indirectly or directly, has primarily focused on Brehm and Cohen's derived arousal component of dissonance rather than the psychological discomfort component identified by Festinger. Indeed, the discomfort component of dissonance has most often been assumed rather than measured directly.

We believe the field has been too narrowly focused on arousal as the motivational component of dissonance. Elliot and Devine (1994) argued that for a variety of reasons psychological discomfort may be the preferred component of dissonance to consider when exploring the dissonance-reduction process. First, physiological measures are imperfect measures of psychological processes, which may place limits on their use for tracking dissonance-reduction processes (Harmon-Jones & Beer, 2009). Second, Cooper and Fazio (1984) suggested that arousal plays only a distal role in dissonance reduction. That is, although arousal is posited to instigate attributional interpretation, Cooper and Fazio argued that it is the phenomenological experience of discomfort created by the attributional judgment that is the proximal motivational force encouraging the implementation of a dissonance-reduction strategy. Third, even if both arousal and discomfort serve proximal functions in the dissonance process, the time course of dissonance reduction may be different for arousal and psychological discomfort. For example, the dissonance-reduction experience may be marked by immediate psychological relief after the implementation of a dissonance-reduction strategy, followed by more gradual reduction of dissonance-based arousal. Under these circumstances, it may be more feasible to empirically demonstrate the alleviation of the psychological discomfort component of dissonance than a reduction of the arousal component, which may require a time sequence of unknown length. Empirical work (Elliot & Devine, 1994) designed specifically to assess the psychological component of dissonance suggests that efforts to assess the psychological component of dissonance may be revealing regarding both the nature of the dissonance experience and the motivational properties of the dissonance state.

Elliot and Devine (1994) argued that to the extent that dissonance is experienced as psychological discomfort (Festinger, 1957), it should be revealed as elevated feelings of discomfort (e.g., uncomfortable, uneasy, bothered) after a counterattitudinal advocacy (see also Devine, Monteith, Zuwerink, & Elliot,

1991). While acknowledging the potential limitations of self-report measures (Nisbett & Wilson, 1977), Elliot and Devine argued that feelings of discomfort could be sensitively assessed with a self-report measure of affect. To the extent that this self-report measure of discomfort was successful, it could serve as a dissonance thermometer sensitive to increases and decreases in psychological discomfort. Elliot and Devine argued further that in the induced-compliance paradigm, if attitude change was truly motivated by an effort to alleviate dissonance, discomfort feelings would be alleviated after the implementation of this reduction strategy. Thus, in an attempt to directly measure psychological discomfort after a counterattitudinal advocacy and its presumed alleviation following attitude change, Elliot and Devine varied the order of the placement of measures of affect and attitude in two induced-compliance studies. To the extent that such a pattern could be shown, it would provide the first direct evidence to support Festinger's (1957) assertion that dissonance is fundamentally a motivational state. The minimum conditions needed to explore these issues are conditions that provide the opportunity to show that discomfort increases in the theoretically predicted circumstances (e.g., counterattitudinal advocacy), and that after an ostensibly effective dissonance-reduction strategy, the discomfort dissipates.

Initial Evidence for Dissonance as Psychological Discomfort

The utility of the affect measure for assessing dissonance is well illustrated in Elliot and Devine's (1994) second study. In this study, all participants wrote a counterattitudinal essay arguing for a 10% tuition increase. The study had three conditions. The low-choice control provided baseline affect and attitude scores. The two high-choice conditions differed only in the order in which participants reported affect and attitude.

That is, after freely choosing to write and prepare the counterattitudinal essay, half of the high-choice participants immediately reported their attitude and then their affect. In the other high-choice condition, the affect measure preceded reports of attitude.[4]

Replicating the standard induced-compliance effect, participants in the high-choice conditions reported more attitude change than their counterparts in the low-choice condition (see Table 12.1). However, in keeping with Festinger's (1957) theorizing about dissonance induction and reduction, discomfort feelings were elevated only in the condition in which affect was reported before attitudes were assessed. These data suggest that preparing the counterattitudinal essay led to feelings of discomfort. Of critical importance for supporting Festinger's dissonance-reduction postulate, the level of discomfort feelings reported after participants were provided with an attitude-change opportunity dropped to baseline levels and did not differ from the affect reported by low-choice participants, who reported affect before preparing their

---

[4] In all of our studies reviewed, choice manipulation checks indicated the effectiveness of the choice manipulation.

TABLE 12.1. Mean Attitude Change and Discomfort Ratings as a Function of Experimental Condition

	Experimental condition		
Measure	High-choice affect–attitude	High-choice attitude–affect	Low choice
Attitude change	5.29$_a$	5.50$_a$	2.92$_b$
Discomfort	3.71$_a$	2.61$_b$	2.33$_b$

Note. Attitude-change values greater than 1 represent change in the direction favoring the proposed tuition increase. Discomfort values had a possible range of 1 to 7, with 7 representing the highest level of dissonance affect. Within each dependent measure, means with different subscripts differ significantly at $p < .01$ by the Fisher least significant difference test. Data from Elliot and Devine (1994, Study 2).

counterattitudinal essays. Thus, it appears that feelings of discomfort dissipate after a dissonance-reduction strategy is implemented. Moreover, the affect findings are unique to discomfort feelings. The affect measure in Elliot and Devine's (1994) research included items that would tap other forms of psychological distress (e.g., guilt or depressed affect) as well as positive affect. None of these other affect measures were influenced by the experimental manipulations.

These findings are important in a number of respects. By focusing on and measuring the psychological discomfort component of dissonance, these data both clarify the nature of the dissonance experience and directly demonstrate the alleviation of dissonance on the implementation of an ostensibly effective dissonance-reduction strategy. Moreover, dissonance appears to be a distinct aversive feeling and not an undifferentiated arousal state. Perhaps most important, by demonstrating that attitude change was in the service of reducing the discomfort created by the counterattitudinal advocacy, Elliot and Devine (1994) obtained the first direct support for both dissonance induction and reduction.

Using the dissonance thermometer, Matz and Wood (2005) extended this research to test whether the social group could be a source of cognitive dissonance, as Festinger (1957) had predicted. That is, in a group, disagreement from others causes dissonance, and cognitive changes within the group toward consensus may reduce this dissonance discomfort. They found that individuals in a group with others who ostensibly disagreed with them reported feeling more dissonance discomfort than individuals in a group with others who agreed with them. Follow-up studies revealed that standard moderators of dissonance—lack of choice and opportunity to self-affirm—decreased the dissonance discomfort caused by group disagreement. Finally, a third study revealed that the dissonance created by group disagreement was reduced via several routes to achieve group consensus; these included persuading others in the group, changing one's own position, and joining a different group that possessed similar attitudes (see Matz, Hofstedt, & Wood, 2008, for a replication and extension).

Dowsett, Semmler, Bray, Ankeny, and Chur-Hansen (2018) used a version of the dissonance thermometer to examine dissonance discomfort after individuals were exposed to either information about the life of a meat lamb or information about the nutritional benefits of meat. They predicted that being exposed to the information about the meat lamb would evoke dissonance because of the "meat paradox" (Loughnan, Haslam, & Bastian, 2010). That is, individuals often experience dissonance over eating meat (animals) because they also love animals. Results revealed that individuals (who were meat eaters) exposed to the information about the life of a meat lamb reported significantly more dissonance discomfort than individuals exposed to the information about the nutritional benefits of meat. Illustrating the complexity of dissonance reduction strategies, men in this condition had more favorable attitudes toward eating meat, whereas women had less favorable toward meat eating, compared with men and women in the condition exposed to information about the nutritional benefits of meat.

Levy, Harmon-Jones, and Harmon-Jones (2018) found evidence of psychological discomfort in response to a very simple cognitive inconsistency, in line with Festinger's (1957) idea that dissonance occurs in a wide range of situations. In this research, participants simply read sentences that ended with expected words or unexpected words (e.g., "She couldn't start her car without the right teeth"). And implicit, self-report (single item valence rating), and psychophysiological measures of negative affect were collected after exposure to these words. Results revealed that the dissonance-arousing unexpected words, as compared with the expected words, evoked more dissonance discomfort across all three types of measures.

Attitude Importance, Resistance to Change, and the Dissonance Thermometer

We have argued that in dissonance research, there has been an overreliance on attitude change as the key dissonance-reduction strategy (see also Simon et al., 1995; Steele, 1988). We believe that this strategy is, in part, responsible for a relative lack of attention to the study of dissonance-related processes involving important attitudes, which by definition may be more resistant to change than relatively unimportant attitudes (Boninger, Krosnick, Berent, & Fabrigar, 1995; Zuwerink & Devine, 1996). In the induced-compliance literature, when participants freely choose to advocate a counterattitudinal position, the cognition about this behavior, partly because of its immediate salience, is highly resistant to change (hence attitudes are changed to restore consonance). When a counterattitudinal behavior conflicts with a personally important attitude, both the attitude and the cognition about one's behavior are likely to be highly resistant to change. When attitude change is not an option, other strategies for reducing dissonance-related distress would be required. A by-product of studying relatively unimportant attitudes is that there has been comparatively little focus on alternative dissonance-reduction strategies.

The issue of attitude importance did not escape the attention and theorizing of Festinger (1957) or the early dissonance researchers. Although it has long been assumed that attitude change may not be a viable dissonance-reduction strategy when the dissonance is associated with important attitudes, empirical attempts to explicate the role of attitude importance are scant. Theorists have articulated some of the challenges associated with studying

TABLE 12.2. Mean Attitude Change and Discomfort Ratings as a Function of Experimental Condition and Importance Level

	Experimental condition					
	High-choice affect–attitude		High-choice attitude–affect		Low choice	
Measure	Low imp	High imp	Low imp	High imp	Low imp	High imp
Attitude change	3.75_a	1.86_c	5.30_b	2.57_c	2.83_c	1.42_c
Discomfort	3.60_a	3.70_a	2.10_c	3.84_a	2.67_b	2.44_{bc}

Note. Imp = importance. Attitude-change values greater than 1 represent change in the direction favoring reduction of recycling efforts. Discomfort values had a possible range of 1 to 7, with 7 representing the highest level of dissonance affect. Within each dependent measure, means with different subscripts differ significantly at $p < .01$ by the Fisher least significant difference test.

important attitudes within the dissonance framework (e.g., Cooper & Mackie, 1983; Hardyck & Kardush, 1968; Pilisuk, 1968; Sherman & Gorkin, 1980). As noted by Sherman and Gorkin (1980), "when the original attitude is an especially strong and central one, involving a large degree of relevance and prior commitment, attitude change is unlikely" (p. 389). In response, Sherman and Gorkin examined a form of attitude bolstering, arguing that neither attitude change nor denying the behavior was possible.

In our work, we have sought to document the role of attitude importance in the dissonance process. Specifically, we have begun to investigate how attitude importance influences the nature of the dissonance experience and the types of dissonance-reduction strategies that may prove effective (or ineffective) in alleviating distress. In one study, using a counterattitudinal advocacy paradigm with recycling as the issue, we replicated the essential design of Elliot and Devine (1994) but included participants who varied in the self-reported importance of their recycling attitudes (Devine, Froning, & Elliot, 1995). That is, some of the participants reported that their recycling attitudes were highly personally important, whereas others, although equally in favor of recycling, indicated that their attitudes were less personally important. Low- and high-importance participants were then randomly assigned to one of three conditions. Following Elliot and Devine (1994), this study included a low-choice condition, to establish baseline affect and attitude scores, and two high-choice conditions that differed only in the order in which participants reported their affect and their attitude.

Under low choice, as can be seen in Table 12.2, both low- and high-importance participants reported little discomfort or attitude change.[5] Under

---

[5] In this study, all measures were taken after the essay was prepared. In Elliot and Devine (1994), low-choice participants reported affect before the essay task was introduced. Although this provided a nice baseline affect measure, it did not directly address whether the low-choice instructions were dissonance inducing. The data from the Devine et al. (1995) study suggest that the low-choice instructions did not lead to elevated levels of discomfort for high- or low-importance participants. Assessing affect after rather than before the essay task is, we think, generally a preferred strategy.

high choice, the effects were moderated by attitude importance. For low-importance participants, both the attitude change and the discomfort data replicated the findings of Elliot and Devine (1994). Specifically, attitude change for low-importance participants was elevated under both high-choice conditions; however, discomfort feelings were elevated only for low-importance, high-choice participants when affect was reported before attitudes were assessed. For high-importance participants, however, attitude change was not a viable dissonance-reduction strategy. In neither high-choice condition did high-importance participants change their attitudes against campus recycling. Moreover, their discomfort was elevated whether they reported attitude or affect first.

When attitude change is not viable, are there strategies that can be effective for alleviating dissonance-related distress? Two recent lines of research suggest an affirmative answer to this question. One line of work follows directly from the Devine et al. (1995) study examining dissonance and attitude change in people of varying levels of attitude importance. Because high-importance people continue to experience discomfort after the attitude-change opportunity, they will still be motivated to reduce their distress. Thus, in a follow-up study, Tauer and Devine (1998) replicated Devine et al.'s (1995) basic design, but they provided all participants with a subsequent alternative dissonance-reduction opportunity, in this case, altering the perception of the strength of their essay (cf. Scheier & Carver, 1980; Simon et al., 1995). Theoretically, individuals with attitudes of low importance, who are likely to change their attitudes and therefore be free from dissonance motivation, would not take advantage of this subsequent opportunity. However, individuals with attitudes of high importance would alter the perception of the strength of their essay because they continued to experience high levels of discomfort and thus dissonance motivation. To the extent that altering the perception of essay strength was an effective dissonance-reduction strategy for these individuals, they would experience a reduction of discomfort. This line of work is important because it will help to shed light on the effectiveness of different strategies and the conditions under which alternative strategies are most optimal.

In another study, Tauer, Devine, and Elliot (1998) garnered evidence that self-affirmations are effective at reducing dissonance for people low and high in attitude importance. Once again using the recycling issue, half of the low- and high-importance participants completed a self-affirmation task before reporting their affect; for the other half of the participants, the order of these tasks was reversed. The self-affirmation task involved generating four examples of times when they had demonstrated their most cherished characteristics (see Vance, Devine, & Barron, 1997). When the affect measure preceded the self-affirmation task, feelings of discomfort were elevated for both high- ($M = 3.83$) and low- ($M = 2.94$) importance participants. When the affect measure followed the self-affirmation task, feelings of discomfort for both high- ($M = 3.09$) and low- ($M = 2.22$) importance participants were reduced, although discomfort was still somewhat elevated for high-importance participants. It is also of interest to note that there was no evidence of attitude change for either high- or low-importance participants in this study. In all conditions, attitudes were assessed after the affect and self-affirmation opportunities. High-importance participants, of course, were not expected to show evidence of attitude change (cf. Devine et al., 1995). Of particular interest, however, was that low-importance participants, after having completed a self-affirmation task, did not change their attitudes.

In other research, Galinsky, Stone, and Cooper (2000) replicated the results of Elliot and Devine (1994) and also found evidence that suggested that self-affirmations decrease attitude change because they also decrease the negative affect associated with dissonance. Additionally, Holland, Meertens, and Van Vugt (2002, Study 2) induced dissonance by providing participants information that indicated they were prejudiced toward groups with whom that they do not want to be prejudiced (i.e., Dutch participants and Turkish and Moroccan groups). This information increased dissonance discomfort among participants low in self-esteem but not among participants high in self-esteem. These results are consistent with the self-affirmation theory prediction that high self-esteem serves as a resource or buffer against threatening, dissonance-arousing information. Taken together, these studies suggest that self-affirmation alleviates dissonance discomfort and, thus, reduces the motivational force that produces attitude change (Elliot & Devine, 1994; Festinger, 1957).

METHODOLOGICAL AND THEORETICAL BENEFITS OF USING THE DISSONANCE THERMOMETER

Several methodological and theoretical benefits accrue from having a measure that is both easy to implement and sensitive to dissonance induction as well as reduction. First, and most obviously, the measure can serve as a manipulation check for both dissonance induction and reduction. As noted previously, the absence of a manipulation check created interpretational difficulties for dissonance researchers when results did not conform to theoretical predictions. It was not possible to determine whether the experimental procedures had failed to evoke dissonance or whether the dissonance that had been created was reduced through the implementation of an alternative reduction strategy. Cialdini et al. (1981) suggested that research on selective exposure and dissonance was (temporarily) abandoned against a backdrop of seemingly inconsistent results. These inconsistencies proved difficult to interpret, in part due to the absence of an effective dissonance manipulation check. Use of the dissonance thermometer may facilitate progress in such areas.

Having an effective dissonance manipulation check may also provide efficient ways for validating new procedures for instilling dissonance, such as the hypocrisy procedure developed by Aronson and colleagues (see Aronson, 1992; Stone, Aronson, Crain, Winslow, & Fried, 1994). The goal of the hypocrisy manipulation is to show that dissonance can be created and can lead to dissonance-related cognitive and behavioral changes even when participants advocate a proattitudinal position (e.g., in favor of safe sex). In developing the technique, Stone et al. (1994), in the long tradition of dissonance research, relied on producing theory-consistent changes in behavior or attitudes to validate the hypocrisy procedure. We suggest that more efficient and potentially more informative progress can be made by using a measure like the dissonance thermometer during the validation process. For example, it would be immediately apparent if new procedures were effective if they led to increases in psychological discomfort.

In a similar fashion, the dissonance thermometer can be used to assess the efficacy of alternative dissonance-reduction strategies without relying exclusively on attitude change (see Tauer & Devine, 1998). The most often used strategy for validating the efficacy of alternative dissonance-reduction strategies (e.g., trivialization, self-affirmation) is to show that after implementing an ostensibly effective strategy, attitudes do not change (e.g., Simon et al., 1995; Steele & Liu, 1983, respectively). The dissonance thermometer can provide information on the efficacy of dissonance-reduction strategies much more directly (i.e., discomfort decreases) and may, as a result, enable new progress to be made in exploring alternative strategies for alleviating dissonance-related discomfort. Along these lines, Gosling, Denizeau, and Oberlé (2006) investigated denial of responsibility as a mode of dissonance reduction, and found that following counterattitudinal behavior, participants used the mode of discrepancy reduction that was first presented to them, regardless of whether it was attitude change, trivialization, or denial of responsibility. In a subsequent experiment, they found that the denial of responsibility reduced dissonance discomfort.

Finally, use of a dissonance manipulation check may ultimately permit the use of more efficient experimental designs. Historically, the dissonance literature has included low-choice conditions primarily to validate that little attitude change occurs when theoretically it should not. A direct measure of dissonance may obviate the need for such control conditions, at least in some circumstances.

Although the benefits of a dissonance manipulation check are considerable, some of the potentially more powerful benefits of a more direct dissonance measure may come in the form of improved theory testing and elaboration. As stated in the beginning of this chapter, Festinger (1957) proposed essentially a process model: A (inconsistency between cognitions) → B (dissonance) → C (some dissonance-reduction strategy) → D (alleviation of dissonance). However, empirical strategies to date have been largely limited to investigations in which A is created and C is observed. Although research investigating the arousal component of dissonance has attempted to explore the mediational processes suggested by the model, complications arise when arousal does not appear to dissipate after an ostensibly effective dissonance-reduction strategy is implemented (e.g., Elkin & Leippe, 1986). A measure of the psychological component of dissonance, which has been shown to be sensitive to dissonance induction and reduction, provides an additional tool for directly testing the process assumptions as they unfold over time. Specifically, a complete understanding of dissonance theory requires testing whether dissonance is created, whether a reduction opportunity is used, and whether dissonance reduction follows the implementation of an ostensibly effective dissonance-reduction strategy. Exploring these ideas calls for a mediational analysis that will allow researchers to directly test the process of dissonance induction and reduction.

Having a more direct measure of dissonance may ultimately help in addressing the long-standing debate concerning the necessary and sufficient conditions for dissonance arousal. Cooper and Fazio (1984) maintained that taking responsibility for the production of aversive consequences is necessary for the arousal of dissonance. However, in using a discomfort measure of dissonance, Harmon-Jones (2000) showed that the production of aversive consequences is not necessary to create dissonance-related discomfort. That is, when participants advocated a counterattitudinal position for which there could be no aversive consequences (i.e., the evidence of their counterattitudinal behavior is literally thrown away), discomfort feelings were elevated. Thus, although the production of aversive consequences may heighten the dissonance experience, Harmon-Jones's research suggests that aversive consequences are not necessary. As these findings suggest, when used in conjunction with other measures, the dissonance thermometer may enable more precise evaluation of the plausibility of the core assumptions of the various revisions of dissonance theory proposed over the years.

A final set of issues that may be fruitful to explore with the dissonance thermometer concerns the qualitative nature of the affect associated with different types of cognitive inconsistencies and the possibility that not all dissonances are created equal. Because the affect measure was designed to be sensitive to both global and more specific forms of affective distress, it may play a role in elucidating theory and enable the field to address issues that have long proved vexing for dissonance theorists. These include assessing the magnitude of dissonance experienced and how people resolve dissonance when inconsistencies involve important, central, or self-defining attitudes.

For example, following in the tradition of Aronson's (1968) reconceptualization of dissonance, Elliot and Devine (1994) suggested that the self may be implicated to varying degrees in the dissonance process. Specifically, the self-relevance of the threatened cognition may be critical in determining the qualitative nature of the affect experienced as a result of dissonance. Similarly, Aronson (1992) argued that dissonance-induction procedures, such as the hypocrisy manipulation, were likely to lead to feelings of guilt and not just global discomfort. The typical strategies used to validate hypocrisy-induced dissonance reduction (e.g., cognitive or behavioral change) are silent on the qualitative nature of the affect created by the manipulation. To the extent that the quality of affect experienced is important in determining whether particular strategies are likely to be effective in reducing dissonance-related distress, it will be important to establish precisely what type of affect is evoked by alternative procedures (see Vance et al., 1997). Our measure, which was developed with the goal of assessing various qualities of affect elicited in response to cognitive inconsistencies, is well suited to these tasks (see Devine et al., 1991).

For example, our work on the affective consequences of prejudice-related discrepancies (i.e., actual responses revealing more prejudice than is permitted by one's nonprejudiced standards) has shown that violations of well-internalized, self-defining standards generate general negative affect (i.e., discomfort) and a more specific negative self-directed affect (i.e., guilt; see Devine et al., 1991). Violations of less internalized standards simply elicit more global negative affect. The dissonance thermometer was essential for detecting this difference in the experience of dissonance for attitudes that are more, compared with less, self-defining. Moreover, Vance and Devine (1997) used the dissonance thermometer after a hypocrisy manipulation relevant to nonprejudiced standards and behavior. Participants advocated the importance of treating Blacks in a nonprejudiced manner, then recalled times they had responded with prejudice. The combination of these experiences resulted in increased global discomfort, as well as elevated feelings of guilt and self-criticism. Similarly, Son Hing, Li, and Zanna (2002) found that when individuals who scored high in aversive racism were induced to experience hypocrisy about their prejudice, they felt more guilt and discomfort than a comparison condition. Moreover, after these individuals acted in a nonprejudiced manner, they felt less guilt and discomfort. These findings support Aronson's (1992) general proposal about the consequences of hypocrisy but, perhaps more important, when combined with our previous findings, suggest that it may be prudent to think more completely about the specific qualities of affect associated with alternative dissonance manipulations.

Along these lines, research has found that individuals experiencing dissonance report feeling tense (induced compliance; Zanna & Cooper, 1974), mental discomfort and frustration (effort justification; Shaffer & Hendrick, 1974; induced compliance; Shaffer, 1975), bashful (induced compliance; Kidd & Berkowitz, 1976), and distressed, threatened, angry, and frustrated (belief disconfirmation; Burris, Harmon-Jones, & Tarpley, 1997). Thus, the words associated with the feeling state of dissonance may depend on the type of cognitive discrepancy aroused, as well as the emotion word vocabularies of the individuals investigated. For instance, individuals may report feeling more distressed when exposed to belief disconfirming information, but more regret after making difficult decisions. In addition, the topic of the counterattitudinal essay or belief disconfirmation may also influence the emotion words individuals feel most strongly. Consequently, it is not surprising that factor analyses of the negative affect reported in dissonance experiments (e.g., Gosling et al., 2006) do not always converge with the ones reported by Elliot and Devine (1994). As this evidence suggests, it appears that not all dissonances are created or resolved equally. The use of a direct measure of affect makes it possible to more fully explore these issues.

QUESTIONS ABOUT THE DISSONANCE THERMOMETER

Are individuals always aware of their dissonance discomfort? Theory and research have suggested that individuals are not always consciously aware of their affective states (e.g., Winkielman & Berridge, 2004). Moreover, research using the misattribution paradigm (e.g., Zanna & Cooper, 1974) suggests that the source of the dissonance discomfort is not very well known to participants, because if the source were well known, they would not be able to misattribute their discomfort to another source. The misattribution paradigm relies on the individuals being less than perfectly aware of the source of their emotion. If individuals are not very aware of the source of their dissonance discomfort (e.g., their counterattitudinal essay), they may not be very aware of their discomfort. In other words, the dissonance discomfort (evoked in the lab) may be a subtle or vague feeling, and consequently at least some individuals may be unable to accurately report feeling it. If so, some situations or individuals may not provide evidence of dissonance discomfort on self-report measures.

Might the measurement of self-reported discomfort or negative affect influence the process of dissonance reduction? Yes, according to some research. For instance, Pyszczynski, Greenberg, Solomon, Sideris, and Stubing (1993) posited that the expression of negative affect may reduce the motivation to engage in discrepancy reduction (e.g., attitude change). They based this prediction on the idea that discrepancy reduction functions to protect individuals from the negative affective state of dissonance. If, however, individuals acknowledge and express their dissonance discomfort, they would be less motivated to engage in discrepancy reduction. In one high-choice condition of the Pyszczynski et al. (1993) experiment, participants were instructed, prior to writing the counterattitudinal essay, to express any subtle feelings of anxiety or tension they experienced. Results revealed that this condition had less attitude change than a standard high-choice condition and a high-choice condition in which participants were instructed to suppress negative feelings. In a similar manner, Stice (1992) found that individuals induced to express their feelings about their counterattitudinal behavior to the experimenter had less attitude change, compared to individuals who engaged in the same counterattitudinal behavior but did not express their feelings. These experiments suggest that expressing the negative affect associated with dissonance following the evocation of cognitive discrepancy may reduce the motivation to engage in discrepancy reductions such as attitude change. Although these experiments used fairly strong inductions to have participants express their dissonance discomfort, it is possible that having individuals express their dissonance discomfort by completing a self-report measure of negative affect could have a similar effect of reducing the motivation to engage in discrepancy reduction. Indeed, Galinsky et al. (2000) conducted an induced compliance experiment in which dissonance discomfort was measured. Their results revealed that participants who wrote a counterattitudinal essay (under high choice) reported more dissonance discomfort, but did not show evidence of attitude change. Along the lines suggested above, Galinsky et al. (2000) posited that "the expression of dissonance-produced negative affect may have reduced participants' dissonance motivation and their need to engage in attitude change" (p.137). Thus, use of measures of self-reported negative affect in dissonance experiments may have the unfortunate consequence of eliminating effects on measures of cognitive discrepancy. However, if the self-report measures are presented to participants in a manner that avoids a full expression of negative affect, this unfortunate consequence may be eliminated.

CONCLUSION

Overreliance on attitude change has limited our ability to test core assumptions of dissonance theory. In response, we have offered an additional methodological tool and have reviewed evidence supporting its use. We have reviewed evidence from traditional dissonance paradigms that supports the efficacy of the dissonance thermometer and encourages dissonance researchers to revisit conceptual and theoretical issues that have been difficult to explore in the absence of a direct measure of dissonance. The use of an affect measure is not a panacea for the dissonance literature. Our purpose has been to illustrate how an affect measure can be used and may facilitate progress on central questions in the dissonance literature. Through its use, this research provides direct evidence to support the theoretical process outlined by Festinger (1957). Indeed, we expect that the most important developments afforded by the dissonance thermometer lie ahead and look forward to the next 60 years of dissonance-related theory and research.

REFERENCES

Aronson, E. (1968). Dissonance theory: Progress and problems. In R. Abelson, E. Aronson, W. McGuire, T. Newcomb, M. Rosenberg, & P. Tannenbaum (Eds.), *The cognitive consistency theories: A sourcebook* (pp. 5–27). Chicago, IL: Rand McNally.

Aronson, E. (1992). The return of the repressed: Dissonance theory makes a comeback. *Psychological Inquiry, 3*, 303–311. http://dx.doi.org/10.1207/s15327965pli0304_1

Bem, D. J. (1967). Self-perception: An alternative interpretation of cognitive dissonance phenomena. *Psychological Review, 74*, 183–200. http://dx.doi.org/10.1037/h0024835

Boninger, D. S., Krosnick, J. A., Berent, M. K., & Fabrigar, L. R. (1995). The causes and consequences of attitude importance. In R. E. Petty & J. A. Krosnick (Eds.), *Attitude strength: Antecedents and consequences* (pp. 159–189). Hillsdale, NJ: Erlbaum.

Brehm, J., & Cohen, A. (1962). *Explorations in cognitive dissonance*. New York, NY: Wiley. http://dx.doi.org/10.1037/11622-000

Burris, C. T., Harmon-Jones, E., & Tarpley, W. R. (1997). "By faith alone": Religious agitation and cognitive dissonance. *Basic and Applied Social Psychology, 19*, 17–31.

Chapanis, N. P., & Chapanis, A. (1964). Cognitive dissonance: Five years later. *Psychological Bulletin, 61*, 1–22. http://dx.doi.org/10.1037/h0043457

Cialdini, R., Petty, R., & Cacioppo, J. (1981). Attitude and attitude change. *Annual Review of Psychology, 32*, 357–404. http://dx.doi.org/10.1146/annurev.ps.32.020181.002041

Cooper, J., & Fazio, R. (1984). A new look at dissonance theory. In L. Berkowitz (Ed.), *Advances in experimental social psychology* (Vol. 17, pp. 229–266). San Diego, CA: Academic Press.

Cooper, J., & Mackie, D. (1983). Cognitive dissonance in an intergroup context. *Journal of Personality and Social Psychology, 44*, 536–544. http://dx.doi.org/10.1037/0022-3514.44.3.536

Cooper, J., & Worchel, S. (1970). Role of undesired consequences in arousing cognitive dissonance. *Journal of Personality and Social Psychology, 16*, 199–206. http://dx.doi.org/10.1037/h0029830

Croyle, R. T., & Cooper, J. (1983). Dissonance arousal: Physiological evidence. *Journal of Personality and Social Psychology, 45*, 782–791. http://dx.doi.org/10.1037/0022-3514.45.4.782

Devine, P., Froning, D., & Elliot, A. (1995). [Attitude importance, dissonance, and resistance to attitude change]. Unpublished raw data.

Devine, P. G., Monteith, M. J., Zuwerink, J. R., & Elliot, A. J. (1991). Prejudice with and without compunction. *Journal of Personality and Social Psychology, 60*, 817–830. http://dx.doi.org/10.1037/0022-3514.60.6.817

Dowsett, E., Semmler, C., Bray, H., Ankeny, R. A., & Chur-Hansen, A. (2018). Neutralising the meat paradox: Cognitive dissonance, gender, and eating animals. *Appetite, 123*, 280–288. http://dx.doi.org/10.1016/j.appet.2018.01.005

Elkin, R. A., & Leippe, M. R. (1986). Physiological arousal, dissonance, and attitude change: Evidence for a dissonance-arousal link and a "don't remind me" effect. *Journal of Personality and Social Psychology, 51*, 55–65. http://dx.doi.org/10.1037/0022-3514.51.1.55

Elliot, A. J., & Devine, P. G. (1994). On the motivational nature of cognitive dissonance: Dissonance as psychological discomfort. *Journal of Personality and Social Psychology, 67*, 382–394. http://dx.doi.org/10.1037/0022-3514.67.3.382

Fazio, R. F. I., & Cooper, J. (1983). Arousal in the dissonance process. In J. Cacioppo & R. Petty (Eds.), *Social psychophysiology* (pp. 122–152). New York, NY: Guilford Press.

Festinger, L. (1957). *A theory of cognitive dissonance*. Palo Alto, CA: Stanford University Press.

Festinger, L., & Carlsmith, J. M. (1959). Cognitive consequences of forced compliance. *Journal of Abnormal and Social Psychology, 58*, 203–210. http://dx.doi.org/10.1037/h0041593

Galinsky, A. D., Stone, J., & Cooper, J. (2000). The reinstatement of dissonance and psychological discomfort following failed affirmations. *European Journal of Social Psychology, 30*, 123–147. http://dx.doi.org/10.1002/(SICI)1099-0992(200001/02)30:1<123::AID-EJSP981>3.0.CO;2-T

Gosling, P., Denizeau, M., & Oberlé, D. (2006). Denial of responsibility: A new mode of dissonance reduction. *Journal of Personality and Social Psychology, 90*, 722–733. http://dx.doi.org/10.1037/0022-3514.90.5.722

Hardyck, J., & Kardush, M. (1968). A modest modish model for dissonance reduction. In R. Abelson, E. Aronson, W. McGuire, T. Newcomb, M. Rosenberg, & P. Tannenbaum (Eds.), *Theories of cognitive consistency: A sourcebook* (pp. 684–692). Chicago, IL: Rand McNally.

Harmon-Jones, E. (2000). Cognitive dissonance and experienced negative affect: Evidence that dissonance increases experienced negative affect even in the absence of aversive consequences. *Personality and Social Psychology Bulletin, 26*, 1490–1501. http://dx.doi.org/10.1177/01461672002612004

Harmon-Jones, E., & Beer, J. S. (2009). *Methods in social neuroscience*. New York, NY: Guilford Press.

Harmon-Jones, E., Brehm, J., Greenberg, J., Simon, L., & Nelson, D. (1996). Evidence that the production of aversive consequences is not necessary to create cognitive dissonance. *Journal of Personality and Social Psychology, 70*, 5–16. http://dx.doi.org/10.1037/0022-3514.70.1.5

Holland, R. W., Meertens, R. M., & Van Vugt, M. (2002). Dissonance on the road: Self-esteem as a moderator of internal and external self-justification strategies.

Personality and Social Psychology Bulletin, 28, 1713–1724. http://dx.doi.org/10.1177/014616702237652

Kidd, R. F., & Berkowitz, L. (1976). Effect of dissonance arousal on helpfulness. *Journal of Personality and Social Psychology, 33*, 613–622. http://dx.doi.org/10.1037/0022-3514.33.5.613

Kiesler, C. A., & Pallak, M. S. (1976). Arousal properties of dissonance manipulations. *Psychological Bulletin, 83*, 1014–1025. http://dx.doi.org/10.1037/0033-2909.83.6.1014

Levy, N., Harmon-Jones, C., & Harmon-Jones, E. (2018). Dissonance and discomfort: Does a simple cognitive inconsistency evoke a negative affective state? *Motivation Science, 4*, 95–108. http://dx.doi.org/10.1037/mot0000079

Losch, M., & Cacioppo, J. (1990). Cognitive dissonance may enhance sympathetic tonus, but attitudes are changed to reduce negative affect rather than arousal. *Journal of Experimental Social Psychology, 26*, 289–304. http://dx.doi.org/10.1016/0022-1031(90)90040-S

Loughnan, S., Haslam, N., & Bastian, B. (2010). The role of meat consumption in the denial of moral status and mind to meat animals. *Appetite, 55*, 156–159.

Matz, D. C., Hofstedt, P. M., & Wood, W. (2008). Extraversion as a moderator of the cognitive dissonance associated with disagreement. *Personality and Individual Differences, 45*, 401–405. http://dx.doi.org/10.1016/j.paid.2008.05.014

Matz, D. C., & Wood, W. (2005). Cognitive dissonance in groups: The consequences of disagreement. *Journal of Personality and Social Psychology, 88*, 22–37. http://dx.doi.org/10.1037/0022-3514.88.1.22

Nisbett, R., & Wilson, T. (1977). Telling more than we can know: Verbal reports on mental processes. *Psychological Review, 84*, 231–259. http://dx.doi.org/10.1037/0033-295X.84.3.231

Pallak, M. S., & Pittman, T. S. (1972). General motivational effects of dissonance arousal. *Journal of Personality and Social Psychology, 21*, 349–358. http://dx.doi.org/10.1037/h0032266

Pilisuk, M. (1968). Depth, centrality, and tolerance in cognitive consistency. In R. Abelson, E. Aronson, W. McGuire, T. Newcomb, M. Rosenberg, & P. Tannenbaum (Eds.), *The cognitive consistency theories: A sourcebook* (pp. 693–699). Chicago, IL: Rand McNally.

Pyszczynski, T., Greenberg, J., Solomon, S., Sideris, J., & Stubing, M. J. (1993). Emotional expression and the reduction of motivated cognitive bias: Evidence from cognitive dissonance and distancing from victims' paradigms. *Journal of Personality and Social Psychology, 64*, 177–186. http://dx.doi.org/10.1037/0022-3514.64.2.177

Rabbi, J. M., Brehm, J. W., & Cohen, A. R. (1959). Verbalization and reactions to cognitive dissonance. *Journal of Personality, 27*, 407–417. http://dx.doi.org/10.1111/j.1467-6494.1959.tb02363.x

Schachter, S., & Singer, J. E. (1962). Cognitive, social, and physiological determinants of emotional state. *Psychological Review, 69*, 379–399. http://dx.doi.org/10.1037/h0046234

Scheier, M., & Carver, C. (1980). Private and public self-attention, resistance to change, and dissonance reduction. *Journal of Personality and Social Psychology, 39*, 390–405. http://dx.doi.org/10.1037/0022-3514.39.3.390

Shaffer, D. R. (1975). Some effects of consonant and dissonant attitudinal advocacy on initial attitude salience and attitude change. *Journal of Personality and Social Psychology, 32*, 160–168. http://dx.doi.org/10.1037/h0076854

Shaffer, D. R., & Hendrick, C. (1974). Dogmatism and tolerance for ambiguity as determinants of differential reactions to cognitive inconsistency. *Journal of Personality and Social Psychology, 29*, 601–608. http://dx.doi.org/10.1037/h0036678

Sherman, S., & Gorkin, L. (1980). Attitude bolstering when behavior is inconsistent with central attitudes. *Journal of Experimental Social Psychology, 16*, 388–403. http://dx.doi.org/10.1016/0022-1031(80)90030-X

Simon, L., Greenberg, J., & Brehm, J. (1995). Trivialization: The forgotten mode of dissonance reduction. *Journal of Personality and Social Psychology, 68,* 247–260. http://dx.doi.org/10.1037/0022-3514.68.2.247

Son Hing, L. S., Li, W., & Zanna, M. P. (2002). Inducing hypocrisy to reduce prejudicial responses among aversive racists. *Journal of Experimental Social Psychology, 38,* 71–78. http://dx.doi.org/10.1006/jesp.2001.1484

Steele, C. M. (1988). The psychology of self-affirmation: Sustaining the integrity of the self. In L. Berkowitz (Ed.), *Advances in experimental social psychology* (Vol. 21, pp. 261–302). New York, NY: Academic Press. http://dx.doi.org/10.1016/S0065-2601(08)60229-4

Steele, C. M., & Liu, T. J. (1983). Dissonance processes as self-affirmation. *Journal of Personality and Social Psychology, 45,* 5–19. http://dx.doi.org/10.1037/0022-3514.45.1.5

Stice, E. (1992). The similarities between cognitive dissonance and guilt: Confessions as a relief of dissonance. *Current Psychological Research & Reviews, 11,* 69–77. http://dx.doi.org/10.1007/BF02686829

Stone, J., Aronson, E., Crain, A., Winslow, M., & Fried, C. (1994). Inducing hypocrisy as a means of encouraging young adults to use condoms. *Personality and Social Psychology Bulletin, 20,* 116–128. http://dx.doi.org/10.1177/0146167294201012

Tauer, J., & Devine, P. (1998). [Attitude importance and the efficacy of alternative dissonance reduction strategies]. Unpublished raw data.

Tauer, J., Devine, P., & Elliot, A. (1998, May). *Attitude importance, dissonance, and resistance to attitude change reduction.* Paper presented at the 7th annual meeting of the Midwestern Psychological Association, Chicago, IL.

Tedeschi, J. T., Schlenker, B. R., & Bonoma, T. V. (1971). Cognitive dissonance: Private ratiocination or public spectacle? *American Psychologist, 26,* 685–695. http://dx.doi.org/10.1037/h0032110

Vance, K., & Devine, P. (1997). [How self-affirmations influence the motivation and behaviors associated with prejudice reduction]. Unpublished raw data.

Vance, K., Devine, P., & Barron, K. (1997, May). *The effects of self-affirmation on the prejudice reduction process.* Paper presented at the Midwestern Psychological Association Meeting, Chicago, IL.

Wilder, D. (1992). Yes, Elliot, there is dissonance. *Psychological Inquiry, 3,* 351–352. http://dx.doi.org/10.1207/s15327965pli0304_17

Winkielman, P., & Berridge, K. C. (2004). Unconscious emotion. *Current Directions in Psychological Science, 13,* 120–123. http://dx.doi.org/10.1111/j.0963-7214.2004.00288.x

Zanna, M. P., & Cooper, J. (1974). Dissonance and the pill: An attribution approach to studying the arousal properties of dissonance. *Journal of Personality and Social Psychology, 29,* 703–709. http://dx.doi.org/10.1037/h0036651

Zuwerink, J., & Devine, P. (1996). Attitude importance and resistance to persuasion: It's not just the thought that counts. *Journal of Personality and Social Psychology, 70,* 931–944. http://dx.doi.org/10.1037/0022-3514.70.5.931

APPENDIX A

Social Communication and Cognition

A Very Preliminary and Highly Tentative Draft

Leon Festinger

In order to understand and explain communication behavior in persons, it is necessary to separate various kinds of communication since the whole area of communication is probably as all inclusive as human behavior. We shall here concern ourselves with one conceptually defined subarea under the rubric of communication, which seems to be important. Specifically, we shall present a theory, together with some supporting data, to explain communication oriented toward acquiring or supporting one's cognition. We shall state the theory in a series of hypotheses along with derivations which can be made from them.

HYPOTHESES CONCERNING THE RELATION BETWEEN COMMUNICATION AND COGNITION

Here we will deal with the ways in which persons acquire cognition. Much of what we say under this heading may seem trivial and well known, but it is necessary to state these things as precisely as possible in order to develop our theory coherently.

Hypothesis 1

There are two major sources of cognition, namely, own experience and communication from others.

Acquiring cognition through one's own experience is, of course, the most direct way. We can think of the other source, that is, communication from others, as being an indirect way of acquiring cognition.

From *Social Communication and Cognition: A Very Preliminary and Highly Tentative Draft* (Unpublished manuscript), by L. Festinger, 1954. Copyright 1954 by Leon Festinger. Reprinted with permission.

Frequently, cognition is acquired by a combination of both. Thus, for example, a child may learn from his mother that fire is dangerous and will hurt if touched. This cognition will undoubtedly be reinforced the first time the child gets burnt. One can raise the question of where, in this denotation of two sources of cognition, one would place such things as reading a newspaper, listening to a radio, hearing a political speech, or seeing a sign along a road that says "15 miles to Peoria." These are all sources of cognition, none of them direct, but there seems to be a big difference among them. On logical grounds, according to our division, we would have to say that in each case the cognition that was acquired about the environment was acquired indirectly, through communication from others. Practically no one, however, will react to the traffic sign as anything other than fact, while many will react to what the politician tells them as quite different from fact. (We will ignore here the cognition acquired about the politician himself from listening to him. This particular cognition is of course acquired directly through experience.) We see then, that in the case of acquiring cognition indirectly, there are factors which will affect the impact which the communication has on the cognition of the recipient. We will deal with this more in detail later.

Hypothesis 2

The impact of direct experience will exert pressure on the cognition to conform to the experience.

In other words, there will be forces acting on the person to have his cognition correspond to reality as he experiences it. The result of this will be that, in general, persons will have a correct picture of the world around them in which they live. This is, of course, not surprising since the organism would have a hard time surviving if this were not the case.

Hypothesis 3

The strength of the impact of indirect experience (communication) to make the cognition conform will vary with the relationship between the communicator and recipient.

To make this hypothesis specific enough to be useful we must specify something more about the dimensions of relationship between the communicator and recipient which are relevant and the direction of the effect on impact of the communication. We will do this by stating two subsidiary hypotheses.

Hypothesis 3.1
The greater the "trustworthiness" of the communicator, the greater will be the impact on the cognition.

Trustworthiness here means a complex of things which, in the future, might better be separated. We will, however, spell out some of the things which affect it. To the extent that the communicator is seen as in the same situation as the recipient and consequently likely to experience things from the same point of view, he will be seen as trustworthy. Also, to the extent that the communicator is seen as performing an impartial service for the recipient, he will be seen as trustworthy. A road sign, for example, is seen as a communication emanating from an impartial servant and is hence regarded as trustworthy. A union member will regard a statement of fact or of opinion or of interpretation as more trustworthy if it comes from another union member (a person in similar circumstances) than if it comes from an executive of the company.

Hypothesis 3.2

The stronger the attraction on the recipient toward association with the communicator, the greater will be the impact of the communication on cognition.

This hypothesis is related closely to others which will be stated later, and so no detailed explanation will be given at this point.

THE RELATION BETWEEN COGNITION AND BEHAVIOR

It has frequently been stated that cognition steers behavior. This is quite true and is important for an understanding of the directedness of behavior in an organism. For an understanding of cognition formation and the communication processes which determine and result from cognition formation, it is also important to understand that behavior steers cognition. In the following hypotheses we will state our theory of how this takes place.

Hypothesis 4

There exists a tendency to make one's cognition and one's behavior consonant.

In order to explain this hypothesis, which is basic to the theory, we must spend some time in giving definitions of the terms we have used. First of all, although it may seem obvious, let us state more specifically the distinction between cognition and behavior. By cognition we wish to designate opinions, beliefs, values, knowledges, and the like about one's environment, including oneself in this environment. By behavior we wish to designate actions of the person and reactions which he has. Actions would include driving a car, reading a book, being a man, residing in a certain place, and the like. Reactions would include things like being afraid, being hopeful, being anxious, and others.

It is also necessary to define consonance and the lack of consonance which we will call dissonance. There are three possible relations which can exist between items of behavior and items of cognition, namely, consonance, dissonance, and irrelevance. (These same three relations may also exist among items of cognition or among items of behavior. To avoid confusion we shall not deal with these at this point but shall return to them later.) A relationship of irrelevance exists if a particular item of cognition has absolutely nothing to do with a particular item of behavior. Thus, for example, an irrelevant relation exists between having the opinion that elementary schools are overcrowded and the behavior of playing golf on a nice sunny Saturday morning. Such irrelevant relations produce no pressures on persons and we may, for the rest of the paper, ignore them.

A relationship of consonance exists between a particular item of cognition and some item of behavior if, holding the motivation the same, this behavior would follow upon this cognition in the absence of other cognitions and in the absence of restraints. Thus, for example, the knowledge that construction crews are working on a certain street would be consonant with the behavior of taking an alternate route in driving to work. The opinion that it is going to rain would be consonant with the behavior of carrying a raincoat. The belief that thieves are around would be consonant with feeling afraid when walking home alone on a dark night.

A relationship of dissonance exists between an item of cognition and an item of behavior if, under the same conditions described in the paragraph above, a different behavior would follow upon this cognition. Thus, for example, the belief that it is going to rain is dissonant with the behavior of going on a picnic. The opinion that some other person is a very excellent and very careful driver would be dissonant with having a fear reaction while driving with him in the ordinary course of events.

One may, of course, raise the question as to why dissonances ever arise. There are many circumstances in which dissonances are almost unavoidable, and it will help our discussion later to list now the various ways in which dissonances can occur.

1. A change occurs in the situation. A given behavior may have been consonant with cognition before a change occurred in the situation. This new set of circumstances impinges upon the person's cognition either directly or indirectly, and the new cognition is, at least momentarily, dissonant with the existing behavior.

2. Initial direct contact with a situation. A person's cognition may have been formed from communication with others. The first direct experience may impinge on the cognition so as to produce dissonance with the existing behavior at least temporarily.

3. New communication from others. This can function in the same way as the above two to introduce a new cognitive item which is dissonant with existing behavior.

4. Simultaneous existence of various cognitive elements. It is probably a usual state of affairs that there are several relevant cognitive items, some of which are consonant with a given behavior and others of which are dissonant with that same behavior. Under such circumstances, it may not be possible for the person to find a behavior which eliminates all dissonances.

We can now return to an elaboration of Hypothesis 4. This hypothesis states then that, if a state of consonance exists it is an equilibrium, that is, no forces to change the relation are acting. If a dissonance exists, there will be forces set up to eliminate the dissonance and produce consonance. We will list the various ways in which these forces can act as subsidiary hypotheses.

Hypothesis 4.1
Given a dissonance between an item of cognition and an item of behavior, there will be a tendency to change the behavior so as to make it consonant with the cognition.

When this tendency is strong enough to produce actual changes in behavior, we will observe the kinds of things which have generally been treated as problems of learning or adaptation. For our present focus of interest, we will not elaborate on these problem areas but will rather concern ourselves with those situations where the tendency to change one's behavior is not strong enough so that the existing behavior persists.

Hypothesis 4.2
Given a dissonance between an item of cognition and an item of behavior there will be a tendency to change the cognition so as to make it consonant with the behavior.

In general there are two ways in which the cognition can be changed, assuming we are dealing with persons who are in sufficient contact with reality, so that Hypotheses 1, 2, and 3 hold. One of these is to actually act on the environment so as to produce a situation where the veridical cognition will be consonant with the behavior in question. Of course, such action would only be successful in producing consonance in circumstances where the person has control over the environment. We will leave this without further elaboration since, again, it is not our main focus of interest.

Probably the major way in which cognition is changed so as to make it consonant with behavior is by selective exposure to either direct or indirect impact from the environment and actively seeking communications which will change the cognition in the desired manner. Thus, for example, a person who is afraid of riding in airplanes may avidly read and remember every account of an airplane disaster which he comes across and may avoid hearing about or reading about safety records and the like. Or let us imagine a person who has bought a new car just prior to the introduction of some new improvement. He may very actively try to persuade his friends that this new improvement is useless and will not work and adds unnecessarily to the expense of the car. If he succeeds in persuading them, he will then have support for a cognition consonant with his possession of a car which does not have this new improvement.

Hypothesis 5

If a consonance exists there will be resistance to changes in behavior or cognition which would introduce dissonance.

Hypothesis 6

If a dissonance exists there will be resistance to changes in behavior or cognition which would increase the magnitude of the dissonance.

To summarize the statements involved in Hypotheses 4 through 6, we may say that tendencies operate to avoid increases and produce decreases of dissonance. These tendencies, when equilibrium does not exist, will manifest themselves either in changes of behavior or in changes of cognition. In order to make the theory more usable, it is necessary to state some of the conditions which will determine whether the behavior or the cognition changes.

Hypothesis 7

Behavior or cognition will change in the presence of a dissonance, if the strength of the dissonance is greater than the resistance to change of either the behavior or the cognition in question.

Hypothesis 8

Whether the behavior or the cognition changes will be determined by which has the weakest resistance to change.

The last two hypotheses will have meaning only to the extent that we can specify resistance to change and the determinants of the strength of resistance to change of both behavior and cognition. We shall consequently proceed to do this.

RESISTANCE TO CHANGE OF BEHAVIOR AND COGNITION

We will state two hypotheses which are in essence an attempt to state some of the sources of resistance to change.

Hypothesis 9

The resistance to changing behavior which is dissonant with cognition will be directly related to the strength of the motivation which this behavior satisfies, the amount of effort or pain or loss involved in changing the behavior, and the number of cognitive elements which are consonant with the behavior.

Thus, for example, a person who has strong motivation toward having status and power might behave as if he had them, even though his cognition was dissonant with this behavior. The stronger the motivation, the more resistant would the behavior be to change. Under these circumstances, provided the cognition is less resistant to change, the person will find ways to change his cognition rather than change his behavior.

An example of another source of resistance might be a person who has recently bought a new car and later knowledge tends to make his cognition dissonant with this behavior. Changing the behavior, that is, selling the car and getting another, might involve financial loss and might also involve admitting that he had been foolish to have made the original purchase. There will, consequently, be a certain resistance to changing the behavior.

The last factor mentioned in the hypothesis is, of course, clear. If the behavior in question is already consonant with many cognitive elements, it will be much more resistant to change than if there are no consonances between cognitive elements and this item of behavior.

Hypothesis 10

The resistance to changing an element of cognition which is dissonant with some behavior will vary directly with the number of behavior items with which this cognitive element is consonant, with the importance of those behavior items, and with the strength of the impact of the environment, directly or indirectly, which supports this cognition.

The last of the factors listed in the above hypothesis is relatively clear. If the paper on which I am writing this is white, and I continue to see it as white, it will be difficult to change this cognition. Or if someone believes that modern art is decadent and all his associates tell him that this opinion is correct, it will be rather resistant to change.

Also, if an element of cognition is consonant with many items of behavior in which the person engages, it will be more resistant to change than an element of cognition which is not consonant with any behavior. The more important a particular behavior, the more resistance will there be to changing an element of cognition which is consonant with it. Importance of the behavior would depend upon the strength of the motivation which the behavior satisfies.

At this point we would like to digress slightly to deal with a concept which has been used frequently by others but which we have not mentioned, namely, consistency among cognitive elements. Thus, for example, various persons have maintained, and it seems plausible, that new cognitions are absorbed by persons so that they are consistent with what already exists in the cognition. This has been maintained about opinions, attitudes, perceptions, and the like. We have, however, not defined anything so far about relations among cognitive elements. Such definition is necessary, however. We will maintain here that any two or more cognitive elements which are consonant with the same behavior items and dissonant with the same behavior items are consonant with each other. Such a set of cognitive elements, which are consonant with one another, in this sense is a consistent cognitive system. The first part of Hypothesis 10, in light of this definition, could be stated as follows:

> *Corollary 10.* The resistance to changing an element of cognition which is dissonant with some behavior will vary directly with the number and importance of the cognitive elements in the consistent system of which this particular element is a part.

THE RELATION OF COGNITION TO CHOICE

Thus far we have dealt only with the relation of cognition to behavior which already exists. There are many situations in which a person has decided or is forced to do something, but there are still alternatives which are available to him. We will here state a number of hypotheses dealing with the relationship between cognition and, at the moment, nonexistent behavior.

For the purposes of the following discussion let us distinguish three kinds of situations with respect to behavior in which a person might find himself.

1. A given realm of behavior may be entirely irrelevant for a person. This would mean that he does not engage in any of these behaviors nor is there a likelihood that he may. Thus, for example, the whole realm of behavior related to cars may be completely irrelevant to a poor farm worker in India. We will refer to this as an irrelevant realm of behavior.

2. A person may not engage in any number of possible specific behaviors, but there is the possibility, likelihood, or even certainty that at some time in the future he will engage in at least one of them. Thus, for example, a person may have accepted a job in a different city from the one in which he now lives. This means that he is going to have to select a neighborhood in which to live, find a house to buy or an apartment to rent, and the like. All of these behaviors are ones in which, at some future time, he will engage in. We will refer to this as relevant future behavior.

3. The person engages in some behavior or has committed himself to some specific course of action. This is the kind of situation which we have been discussing above, and we will not dwell on it again. It is clear that this situation, which we will call relevant present behavior, and the situation of relevant future behavior may exist simultaneously. The person in the example above is in both of these situations. His decision to accept the new job has committed him to a specific course of action and is, hence, present relevant behavior. At the same time, it has involved him in a situation of relevant future behavior.

Hypothesis 11

There will be no active seeking out or active avoidance of cognition related to an irrelevant realm of behavior.

A person in this situation may be a passive recipient of such cognition, but there will be no initiative on his part. Thus, for example, most persons do not exert effort to find out or to avoid finding out how far from the earth the moon is.

Hypotheses 12

In the situation of relevant future behavior there will be active seeking out of cognition relevant to each of the possible future behaviors.

If there are a variety of possible behavior items, one or more of which the person may engage in in the future, this person will actively seek cognition relevant to each of them. Thus, for example, if a person has decided to buy a new car, but has not yet decided what kind to buy, he will actively seek information about each of those which he regards as possible purchases. Of course, once a decision has been made, this type of cognition seeking stops. From then on, the person will seek information consonant with his behavior and avoid information which is dissonant with it, as stated in Hypothesis 4. This partial reversal of information seeking behavior and the result of acquiring mainly consonant cognition after the decision results in what Lewin has called "freezing of decisions."

DERIVATIONS AND DATA

There is surprising little data extant in the literature which is relevant to the above set of hypotheses. The data which we have been able to find is not always such as to be completely trustworthy. We will present it for what it is worth along with the statement of the major derivations from the hypotheses.

Derivation A

If a person's action or reaction with respect to some event is dissonant with his cognition, he will communicate with others, the content of the communication being consonant with his action or reaction.

Derivation B

Such communications (the specific content) will be widespread if many persons have the same initial cognition and the same dissonant action or reaction.

There are data of a sort relevant to these derivations from two studies of rumors in India. Prasad (1950) systematically recorded rumors which were widely current immediately after the earthquake in the province of Bihar in India on January 15, 1934. The quake itself was a strong and prolonged one, felt over a wide geographical area. Actual damage was quite localized, and for a period of time communication with the damaged area was poor. We are, then, dealing with communication among persons who felt the shock of the quake but did not see any actual damage or destruction. While the study does not report anything about the specific reactions of these persons to the quake, it is probably plausible to assume that these persons, who knew nothing about earthquakes or their causes, had a very strong reaction of fear to the violent and prolonged quake which they felt. We will also assume that this reaction of being afraid persisted in them for some time after the shock was over. While the shock was going on, this fear reaction would be consonant with their cognition. But when the shock was over—the next day or even the day after that—when they could see no difference in anything around them, no destruction, no further threatening things, their cognition became dissonant with this reaction of fear which persisted. If this interpretation of the reactions of these persons is correct, then Derivation A would lead us to expect communication which would be consonant with fear reduction, namely communication, which would make it "appropriate" to be afraid. According to Derivation B, we would expect these communications to be widespread since many of the persons would have had the same fear reaction.

Actually, the vast majority of the rumors which Prasad recorded were what one might call "fear provoking" rumors. The following are a fair sample of these rumors as illustrations.

- The water of the River Ganges disappeared at the time of the earthquake, and people bathing were imbedded in the sand.

- There will be a severe cyclone at Patna between 18 and 19 January. (The earthquake was on January 15.)

- There will be a severe earthquake on the lunar eclipse day.

- A flood was rushing from the Nepal borders to Madhubani.

- 23 January 1934 will be a fatal day. Unforeseeable calamities will arise.

- There will be a *Pralaya* (total deluge and destruction) on 26 February 1934.

It is clear that a goodly number of rumors arose which predicted that more disasters were shortly to come. This cognition is, of course, consonant with the reaction of being afraid. The data, interpreted in this way, tend to support our derivations. This support is, however, weak because so much has to be read into the situation to make an assumption about the reaction of persons, and because there are many possible other explanations of why these particular kinds of rumors arose in such a situation. It is fortunate, however, that there is another study which can serve as sort of a control to compare with the one just discussed.

Sinha (1952) reports a careful collection of reports and rumors following a terrible disaster in Darjeeling, India. The author states, "There had been landslides before but nothing like this had ever happened. Loss of life and damage to property were heavy and extensive.... In the town itself houses collapsed and victims lay buried under the debris.... Over a hundred and fifty persons lost their lives in the district, about thirty of them in the town itself. Over a hundred were injured. More than 200 houses were damaged and over 2000 people were rendered homeless." In other words, it was a disaster easily comparable to that of an earthquake. The author states, "There was a feeling of instability and uncertainty similar to that which followed the Great Indian Earthquake of 1934," (p. 200).

We may then regard this aspect of the situation to be sufficiently comparable to allow us to compare the rumors which arose in this situation with those which arose following the 1934 earthquake. There is, however, one important difference which enables us to regard this study as a control. While the rumors following the earthquake were collected from persons who had no direct experience with the destruction, the rumors which Sinha reports were collected from persons in Darjeeling who did experience and see the destruction. In other words, we may again assume that the persons in this area had a strong fear reaction to the landslide all around them. However, there was evidence of the destruction, and consequently, their cognition was consonant with this fear reaction. In this situation then, we would *not* expect any rumors which predicted further disasters.

Actually there was a complete absence of rumors predicting further disasters. Some of the rumors represented slight exaggeration of the actual damage, and some rumors are even of the hopeful variety. The following is a selection of rumors to illustrate the general kind that existed.

- "Many houses have come down on the A-road." (p. 201; Only one house had actually collapsed on this particular road.)
- Widespread belief that there had been a slight earthquake, which had helped in producing the damage. (There had been no earthquake.)
- "It has been announced that the water supply will be restored in a week." (p. 203)
- "It will take months before the water supply is resumed." (p. 203)
- "There are extensive floods in the plains. . . . Many bridges have been washed away." (p. 204)

The remarkable thing about these rumors is the lack of serious exaggeration and even the presence of a few which are hopeful. The contrast with the rumors following the earthquake reported by Prasad is quite dramatic.

Since it seems that the two studies are comparable except for the fact that, in one instance, rumors were collected which circulated among persons not on the scene of destruction, and, in the other instance, the rumors circulated among persons on the scene of destruction, this difference in the nature of the rumors tends to give further support to the derivation.

Derivation C

If cognition is consonant with behavior, and events occur which would tend to make the cognition dissonant with the behavior, there will be communication whose content reaffirms the consonant cognition and denies the dissonant cognition.

There are data relevant to this derivation from a study by Sady (1948) of rumors among the Japanese in the relocation centers during the second World War. The data are not ideal for our purposes since, just as in the case with the previous studies cited, there is relatively little information given as to the actions and reactions of the people in the various specific situations in which the rumors arose. The result is that, in order to interpret the data with reference to this derivation, we are forced to make various guesses about the reactions of the persons involved. These data are, however, the best that we have been able to discover.

Because of this problem of guessing the reaction of the residents of the relocation centers, we shall deal only with rumors that circulated near the beginning of the establishment of the camps or just prior to the closing of the camps. In both of these instances we can be reasonably sure about some of the reactions of the residents. When they were first sent to the camp, they were very upset and anxious. They had been uprooted suddenly, and the major reaction, which persisted for some time, was fear and anxiety. Once in the camps, however, there was a tendency for cognition to become dissonant with the reaction of fear and anxiety. There were consequently many rumors which would tend to prevent this dissonance from arising. Rumors that many people were dying because of the heat and that their bodies were taken away secretly at night, or that the site for the relocation center had been deliberately chosen so that as many as possible of the evacuees would die, and many others of the same type were widely current. The following specific instance will illustrate the process.

During the first summer at the Poston Camp, temporary clinics operated before the regular hospital was ready. When the hospital was opened, these temporary clinics were closed, and a 24-hour home call service for emergencies was instituted. The change was, of course, an improvement in the medical services offered in the camp. This, according to our interpretation, would tend to introduce cognitions dissonant with the persisting reactions of fear and anxiety. In spite of (or perhaps to counteract) the fact of the introduction of the 24-hour home call service, the story circulated widely and was widely accepted that doctors would *not* make any more home calls. No matter how serious the case, the patient, they said, would have to go to the hospital before seeing a doctor. Thus, the change in medical services, through the rumor, was accepted into the cognition as a change for the worse and thus was consonant with their fear and anxiety.

Toward the end, when persons started to be resettled, the prevalent reactions, according to Sady, were again fear and anxiety, but this time about the problems of resettlement. There was apparently a considerable fear of how they would be treated by the communities on the outside. There were again quite a number of rumors which provided cognition consonant with this fear and which counteracted events which tended to produce dissonant cognitions. The following specific example will illustrate this.

The father and son of a family in one of the camps left to inspect their farm and to make arrangements for returning the entire family to their original home. A few hours after they left, the rumor spread that they had been beaten up on the way and that one of them had been taken to the hospital. Administration personnel from the camp contacted the father and son and discovered the story was false, that they had been given an excellent reception. This was made public but the rumor persisted. The father and son then returned to camp, and the whole family left for their farm. Several letters were received from them telling about the good treatment they were receiving. Nevertheless, rumors continued to circulate, such as that they were having difficulty shopping and had become discouraged about staying on their farm. Again the rumors served to counteract dissonant cognition and preserve the consonance with their reactions of fear.

There is one other, rather dramatic, illustration of this process of avoiding dissonance from this same study. During the war, some Nisei and some Issei requested repatriation to Japan, the Nisei renouncing their citizenship. While the majority of the Issei in the relocation centers believed and hoped that the war would end in a negotiated peace, most of those who had requested repatriation firmly believed that Japan would win the war and explained news of Japanese reverses as American propaganda. The renunciation of citizenship and the request for repatriation were rather irrevocable decisions, and at the time these decisions were made, the cognition of these persons was consonant with their decision. This group who had requested repatriation continued to believe that Japan had won the war even after the surrender. After having seen the newspapers and photographs attesting to the surrender of Japan, the great majority of the Japanese in the camps accepted the evidence. Those who had requested repatriation, however, held fast to their belief that Japan had won and continued to dismiss the evidence as American propaganda. This belief persisted all the way back to Japan on the boat. It was not until after landing in Japan that this belief was finally dispelled. The following Associated Press news story describes the situation.

> *Nippon Times*, December 2, 1945
> "Bitter Disappointment Marks Return Home of Nisei Who Wished They Had Stayed in U.S."
> Why 95% of those who came back to Japan on the ship with me thought that Japan had won the war: They thought it just a bunch of American propaganda that Japan surrendered and they believed that they were being brought back to Japan because Japanese had won the war and were compelling the Americans to transport them.

We will now discuss some data relevant to Hypotheses 11 and 12. Baxter (1951) reports a study in which a number of persons were interviewed periodically during the election campaign of 1948. Particular attention was paid to the collection of data concerning discussions with others about the election. The panel of respondents was interviewed in June 1948 for the first time. Among other things, they were asked whether they were doing anything for their party in the present election, how interested they were in that election and whether or not they had talked politics with anyone that month. Table A.1 presents the data based on these three questions.

An examination of the figures makes it clear that those who are doing something for their party talk more about politics than those who are not doing

TABLE A.1. Percentage of Respondents Who Talked Politics in June

	% talked politics	Total #
Doing something for party		
High interest in election	65%	40
Low interest in election	68%	19
Doing nothing for party		
High interest in election	38%	487
Low interest in election	14%	217

anything. If doing something for the party in the election campaign can be viewed as a behavioral commitment, then the interpretation would seem indicated that, having committed themselves behaviorally, there are pressures to talk politics and so make their cognition consonant with this behavior. Those who have not committed themselves behaviorally, with the election still so far in the future, show much lower incidence of seeking or giving opinions concerning politics. The possible interpretation that those who are doing something for the party are simply more interested in the election is ruled out by the fact that there are very similar proportions of interested and uninterested persons in both classifications.

This interpretation is supported more strongly if we examine this data more closely. To the extent that high interest in the election can be interpreted as indicating how important the person thinks the election is for himself, we would expect that the highly interested persons would talk politics more frequently than the less interested persons. This is indeed true for those who are not doing anything for the party, in other words, those not behaviorally committed. For those who are behaviorally committed, however, there is no difference at all in the frequency with which the highly and less interested persons discuss politics. In fact there is a slight difference in the opposite direction. It is possible that those who are behaviorally committed, and yet have low interest in the election, talk as much or even more than the others in order to make their cognition consonant with their behavior of working for the party.

Table A.2 shows the percentage among those who did talk politics in June who talked frequently. It is clear that all the differences are in the same direction even to the reversal between the high and low interest groups who are committed to working for the party.

According to Hypotheses 11 and 12 we would, of course, explain the low percentages of persons talking politics in June among those highly interested but not working for the party by the fact that any decision (as to voting) was still a long way off. We would then expect that these percentages would increase enormously as the election drew near and the future implied behavior became salient. Table A.3 shows the data for the percent in the various classifications who talked politics in October, just prior to the election.

Again, all of the differences are in the same direction as they were in the previous tabulations, including the reversal between the interest groups who

TABLE A.2. Percents of Those Talking Politics in June Who Talked Often

	% talking often	Total #
Doing something for the party		
High interest	77%	26
Low interest	85%	13
Doing nothing for the party		
High interest	56%	183
Low interest	36%	31

TABLE A.3. Percents Talking Politics in October

	% talking often	Total #
Doing something for the party		
High interest	94%	46
Low interest	100%	6
Doing nothing for the party		
High interest	90%	418
Low interest	78%	152

were working for the party. The only difference now is that the two high interest groups talk almost as much. In other words, the immediacy of the election has had the anticipated effect.

In the preceding three tables which we have discussed, we cannot, because of the small numbers of cases in the group who are not very interested in the election and are working for the party, be very confident about the tendency for them to talk even more than those who are highly interested in the election. We can, however, be quite confident that among those committed to working for the party, the factor of interest in the election makes no difference in their tendency to talk politics.

Let us now turn our attention to the kind of data which is more usually obtained in studies of public opinion and mass media. The hypotheses and derivations which we have stated should be relevant to this type of material. Unfortunately, once more, we run up against the obstacle that there are practically no studies in which sufficient data were gathered to make a test of these hypotheses unequivocal. Typically, the elements of data which are missing are those concerning the behavior and reactions of the persons, the degree of commitment to the specific behavior or reaction which exists. We will discuss below a selection of material where plausible assumptions can be made regarding these missing items of data and see to what extent the results fit the theory we have presented.

There are many instances in the literature of reported relationships between information about or awareness of some item and some other variable which can usually be called "interest in the matter." Interest in something is, of course, a very vague term and does not usually refer to anything unambiguous. To the extent that interest is a measure of how important the problem is to the person, we would expect this relationship from our theory. That is, the more important an implied future behavior was, the stronger would be the tendency to acquire information relevant to it. Sometimes, however, the variable of "interest" seems to be interpretable as a reaction or behavior, and in such cases, the data should conform to the predictions from the theory. We will give a few examples of such instances. It must be remembered that in most cases the data simply relate two variables with no indication of the direction of causality. That is, it is possible that a relationship between interest and amount of information could be found because once the person acquires the information, for whatever reason this may have occurred, it stimulates his

286   Appendix A

TABLE A.4. Relation of Awareness of Cancer Campaign to Choice of Cancer as a "Most Dangerous" Disease

Awareness	Cancer named	Cancer not named
Very high	**11%**	3%
High	34%	15%
Medium	37%	25%
Low	9%	28%
Very low	8%	27%
Not ascertained	1%	2%
	100%	**100%**

interest in the problem. Probably this kind of thing always happens to some extent. In our interpretation, however, we will not dwell on this direction of causality but shall explore how the data can be interpreted from the other causal direction.

We will first examine a number of items of data from a report by the Survey Research Center, University of Michigan (1948) of a survey concerning awareness of a recent Cancer Society campaign and attitudes toward cancer.

Respondents in this survey were asked which diseases they considered "most dangerous." Table A.4 shows the relationship obtained between whether or not cancer was named as a "most dangerous disease" and the awareness of the cancer campaign.

Before interpreting this relationship let us speculate briefly about the meaning it has for a person to name cancer as one of the "most dangerous diseases." It will help in this speculation, of course, to know something about the reasons persons gave for feeling it was so dangerous. Actually, 74% of those who named cancer as one of the most dangerous diseases gave as a reason that it is incurable or that it is fatal. Let us imagine, then, that naming cancer as a most dangerous disease indicates some fear of cancer, or at least indicates the presence of an implied future behavior, namely, something must be done to avoid it. If this is true, then the relationship obtained with awareness of the campaign would be consistent with our theory. A campaign by a cancer society may be expected to provide information about things to do to prevent cancer and may also be expected to provide cognition consonant with a "fear of cancer." We would then expect persons who are afraid of the disease or who have an implied future behavior to expose themselves to the campaign and hence be more highly aware of it than persons who are not afraid of it or have no implied future behavior. It can readily be seen that, interpreted in this way, such data support the theory. It can also readily be seen that an enormous amount of interpretation and conjecture is necessary in order to interpret the data at all. This, unfortunately, is true of almost all of the data in the literature.

Those data which we have had to infer or conjecture are precisely the ones that would have to be supplied to make a test of the theory rigorous. There is much material of this type which we could present and discuss, but there is little point in doing this since in all cases the same problems will obtain.

VOLUNTARY AUDIENCES

The theory which we have developed in the preceding pages has direct implications concerning who exposes himself to what. In other words, the theory predicts certain things about the composition of voluntary audiences. Specifically, it states the following things:

1. People with no present behavior or implied future behavior relevant to a given topic should not be found among purely voluntary audiences.

2. People who would expect to obtain cognition dissonant with present behavior should not be found in purely voluntary audiences.

3. Persons who expect to obtain cognition consonant with present behavior should be in voluntary audiences.

4. People with implied future behavior should expose themselves voluntarily irrespective of the bias of the communication.

Let us make clear, of course, that this does not refer to exposure for purposes of amusement or pleasure such as listening to a play or a dance band on the radio. That part of such a program that deals with propaganda, advertising, or educational material is communicating to an involuntary audience, that is, an audience that was lured there for some other purpose. By a purely voluntary audience, we mean one which exposed itself voluntarily to the particular material in question.

One can find frequent remarks in the literature that tend to confirm these implications of the theory. It is often stated by persons writing on the subject that people listen to things they already agree with and do not expose themselves to things they disagree with. However, in going through the literature one begins to wonder where they reached this conclusion because there is almost a complete absence of data concerning it. For example, Klapper (1949) states, "this phenomenon of self-selection might well be called the most basic process thus far established by research on the effects of mass media. Operative in regard to intellectual or aesthetic level of material, its political tenor, or any of a dozen other aspects, the process of self-selection works toward two manifestations of the same end: every product of mass media (1) attracts an audience which already prefers that particular type of material, and (2) fails to attract any significant number of persons who are either of contrary inclination or who have been hitherto uninterested." He presents no data in support of this, however, except to quote Lazarsfeld (1942) as follows: "even so called educational programs are not free from this tendency. Some time ago there was a program on the air which showed in different installments how all the nationalities in this country have contributed to American culture. The purpose was to teach tolerance of other nationalities. The indications were, however, that the audience for each program consisted mainly of the national group which was currently being praised. There was little chance for the program to teach tolerance, because . . . self-selection . . . produced a body of listeners who heard only about the contributions of a country which they already approved."

Lazarsfeld, in turn, presents no data to support this impression. The one instance he mentions does, of course, support our derivations. Certainly being a member of a specific nationality group in America is an irrevocable behavior. Cognitions that this nationality group is important in American culture would be consonant with being a member of the group. Consequently they listen to a broadcast which provides this consonant cognition.[1]

REFERENCES

Baxter, D. (1951). *Interpersonal contact and exposure to mass media during a presidential campaign* (Unpublished doctoral dissertation). Columbia University, New York, NY.

Klapper, J. (1949, August). *Effects of the mass media* (A report to the director of the Public Library Inquiry). New York, NY: Columbia University, Bureau of Applied Social Research.

Lazarsfeld, P. (1942). Effects of radio on public opinion. In D. Waples (Ed.), *Print, radio, and film in a democracy* (pp. 114–158). Chicago, IL: University of Chicago Press.

Prasad, J. (1950). A comparative study of rumours and reports in earthquakes. *British Journal of Psychology, 41*, 129–144.

Sady, R. R. (1948). *The function of rumors in relocation centers* (Unpublished doctoral dissertation). University of Chicago, Chicago, IL.

Sinha, D. (1952). Behaviour in a catastrophic situation: A psychological study of reports and rumors. *British Journal of Psychology, 43*, 200–209.

Survey Research Center, University of Michigan. (1948, December). *The American public discuss cancer and the American Cancer Society campaign: A national survey.* Ann Arbor, MI: Author.

---

[1] Festinger reported the results of a study by Childs in the original version of this paper. Because the editors could not find the study to which he referred, the discussion of this study was eliminated from the present version.

APPENDIX B

Reflections on Cognitive Dissonance
30 Years Later

Leon Festinger

Let me try to touch a little on various things that have been mentioned, going back to history. I will try to be as amusing as I can be. Actually this isn't the 30th anniversary, it's perhaps the 31st or something like that. The manuscript of the book was finished in early 1956. I had signed a contract with Row, Peterson, who were very enthusiastic about publishing it. But by the time the manuscript was finished, the enthusiastic part of Row, Peterson had left that company, and Row, Peterson's enthusiasm diminished incredibly. After about eight months had gone by since they had the manuscript, I phoned them, expressed a bit of displeasure, and I was told in a very sympathetic terms that they had to put off production because a more important book had come in that they had to get out. Then the book appeared with a very flimsy cover and no slipcover at all, and when I complained about that, I was assured that was the new style in books. Then, after two years they let it go out of print, and there were no plans to reprint it. Fortunately, there was a captive press, that is, Stanford University Press. I was on the faculty committee, and they were persuaded to reprint it. So it came to life and continued living as a book.

I have never really thoroughly understood the early reactions to the theory of cognitive dissonance. The first thing I realized was the great wisdom of the decision of American Psychological Association to have a journal called *Contemporary Psychology*. Before *Contemporary Psychology* appeared, almost every APA journal carried reviews, and it is true that some books never got reviewed and some books got two or three reviews, but with the journal *Contemporary Psychology*, you were assured that there would be one and only one review of a book. The editors in their wisdom chose as their reviewer a gentleman called Solomon Asch, a great believer of human rationality, and he wrote a marvelous review. He approached the thing as a moral dilemma, and after considerable discussion,

---

This is a transcript of remarks Leon Festinger made as a discussant in the symposium Reflections on Cognitive Dissonance: 30 Years Later at the 95th Annual Convention of the American Psychology Association. The other members of the symposium were Elliot Aronson, Jack Brehm, Joel Cooper, and Judson Mills.

From *Reflections on Cognitive Dissonance: 30 Years Later* (Unpublished manuscript), by L. Festinger, 1987. Copyright 1987 by Leon Festinger. Reprinted with permission.

he came out with the Scottish verdict not proven, implying that the alternatives were guilty or not guilty. But the reaction to it was more general than that. He was not alone. Others also went to great pains to try to demonstrate that the theory was incorrect. Which is OK. At least that was a more scientific approach. At that time at least, and I don't know whether it still exists today, there was a bit of an illness in social psychology, because people took more delight in countering rather than in exploring and questioning and conceivably supporting. I hope social psychology isn't that way any longer.

Other theories were also proposed, and there were a whole slew of inconsistency theories. For example, balance theory attempted a very, very elegant mathematical formulation of inconsistency at least among triads; you know, if A likes B and B likes C and A doesn't like C, that was imbalanced. I well remember several times protesting that it was demonstrably wrong because, for example, I like chicken, chickens like chicken food and I don't like chicken food. But everyone treated it as a joke, and nobody took it seriously. It's a rather serious criticism.

As I say, I never really understood the emotionality of the controversy. One result of that was that experiment after experiment on the part of the dissonance movement was oriented toward proving again and again and again that there is a process of dissonance reduction that occurs under certain conditions. They showed that it occurs here and it occurs there and perhaps, undoubtedly, it was very necessary at the time, but it was also a huge waste of effort of a lot of talented people who should have been devoting their efforts to clarifying the concepts, improving the definitions and changing it. No theory is going to be inviolate. Let me put it clearly. The only kind of theory that can be proposed and ever will be proposed that absolutely will remain inviolate for decades, certainly centuries, is a theory that is not testable. If a theory is at all testable, it will not remain unchanged. It has to change. All theories are wrong. One doesn't ask about theories, can I show that they are wrong or can I show that they are right, but rather one asks, how much of the empirical realm can it handle and how must it be modified and changed as it matures?

As a lot of people know, I ended up leaving social psychology, meaning dissonance theory, and I want to clarify that. Lack of activity is not the same as lack of interest. Lack of activity is not desertion. I left and stopped doing research on the theory of dissonance because I was in a total rut. The only thing I could think about was how correct the original statement had been. Let me give you an example. When Jack Brehm and Bob Cohen produced their excellent book, *Explorations in Cognitive Dissonance,* one of the things they highlighted was the necessity of choice. I've never said this to Jack before. If you're eavesdropping you'll hear it now. I said to myself, what kind of a contribution is this? It says in the original book that in order for dissonance to be large enough to exist there has to be minimal pressure on the person to do what the person does. If there is too much pressure, there is too much justification for having done it and it is all consonant with having done it, there is no dissonance. Doesn't that encompass the idea of choice? Isn't choice one part of that? I said to myself, these wonderful people whom I like and respect are taking one operation and elevating it to the status of a construct and it's terrible. I may have been right, I may have been wrong. But that is to illustrate to you how every word in that book was perfect. So to me, I did a good thing for cognitive dissonance by leaving it. I think if I had stayed in it, I might have retarded progress for cognitive dissonance for at least a decade.

It seems to me that all of that controversy is documented and today there is a much more normal course of events. I think the talk by Joel Cooper is a very fine illustration of what ought to be and what should have been going on for decades and decades. Trying to explicate, trying to pin down boundary conditions and not just in a way that says, well if this condition is fulfilled you get dissonance reduction and if this condition isn't fulfilled you don't get it, but to understand why and broaden the theory and elaborate it. In addition, the demonstration that there is some physiological evidence for arousal I think is an extremely important finding and needs more research done. Recent stuff that has started exploring alternative modes of dissonance reduction is perhaps some of the most encouraging work I think that is going on. The early experiments emphasizing predictions from the theory that were counterintuitive generally blocked off every conceivable avenue of dissonance reduction that we could block off, so that whatever effect there was would show itself in attitude change. But in the ordinary world and if the experimenter is not very careful, a little bit sloppy, there are lots and lots of avenues of dissonance reduction, and those have never been explored. I still think that one of the major avenues of dissonance reduction is to change your behavior. When I think of examples, I even go back to examples that are in the book. If somebody is in a room, wants to leave the room, and just walks straight into a wall where there is no door, I would think there was considerable dissonance. And the usual way in which that dissonance is reduced is the person looks around and says, O my God, the door is there, and he walks out the door. And that's not very remarkable. But there are also many other avenues of cognitive dissonance reduction aside from attitude change. There is intricate restructuring of whole kinds of networks and relations among cognitions. Somebody can remember what his grandmother told him when he was two years old which solves everything, et cetera. Exploration of that kind of thing is very, very important. I'm glad it's going on.

I am quite sure that there is enough validity to the theory, and as changes are made, emendations are made, there will be even more validity to the theory, that research on it will continue, and a lot will get clarified. One thing that I think has to be done is for more research to go on on dissonance producing situations and dissonance reduction processes as they occur in the "real world." I put it "real world" because Elliot is quite correct. In the good old days when you did laboratory experiments, we created a real world in the laboratory. I don't know how we would have gotten anything through ethics committees. One of the things about laboratory experiments is that you can only get out the stuff that you put into it and any good experimenter who is concerned in testing a part of the hypothesis is going to try to eliminate from that laboratory experiment all of the unwanted stuff that generally floats around, and dissonance arousing and dissonance reducing processes are not the only things that affect man, using man in the generic sense. I think we need to find out about how dissonance processes and dissonance reducing processes interact in the presence of other things that are powerful influences of human behavior and human cognition, and the only way to do that is to do studies in the real world. They're messy and difficult. You don't expect the precision out of those studies that you can get in the laboratory. But out of them will emerge more ideas which we can then bring into the laboratory to clarify and help to broaden and enrich the work.

APPENDIX C

Historical Note on Festinger's Tests of Dissonance Theory

Judson Mills

Leon Festinger is a famous figure in social psychology. Festinger was, according to Jones (1985), "the dominant figure in social psychology for a period roughly spanning the two decades from 1950 to 1970" (p. 68). His theory of cognitive dissonance "is generally recognized as Festinger's greatest creative contribution, and research related to dissonance dominated the journals of social psychology from the late 1950's to the early 1970's" (Jones, 1985, p. 69).

Stories of the foibles of famous figures hold a fascination, which leads them to be told and retold. When such a story about a famous figure in social psychology appears in the *Journal of Personality and Social Psychology*, which is considered to be archival, it takes on an appearance of authenticity and may be presumed accurate by scholars of the field. A statement in the *Journal of Personality and Social Psychology* about Festinger's tests of dissonance theory will be regarded as factual unless corrected.

In a recent article in the *Journal of Personality and Social Psychology*, Anderson and Anderson (1996) stated that "Festinger is reported to have tried a number of ways to experimentally test dissonance theory, with limited success. Finally, Festinger and Carlsmith (1959) succeeded in getting the various parameters set in the range necessary for replicable dissonance results to be obtained" (pp. 741–742). That statement cannot be commented on by Festinger, who is no longer living. However, I was in position to know about Festinger's tests of dissonance theory up to and including Festinger and Carlsmith (1959) and can attest, on the basis of personal knowledge, that the report in the *Journal of Personality and Social Psychology* about Festinger's tests of dissonance theory is inaccurate.

Festinger presented the first version of dissonance theory in January of 1954, in a graduate seminar at the University of Minnesota, which I attended, and I was Festinger's research assistant from the fall of 1954 through the spring of 1957. In September 1956 at Stanford, Festinger showed a written description of the procedure that was to be used in Festinger and Carlsmith (1959) to Leonard Hommel, who was then also a research assistant to Festinger, and me, and he asked us to find some boring tasks and to devise measures. At the start of that study in the fall of 1956, Hommel was the first experimenter and I was the second experimenter who collected the ratings of the boring tasks, a role later shared with Robert Terwilliger, who interviewed half the participants in the published study. J. Merrill Carlsmith replaced Hommel in January 1957.

Except for the change in the first experimenter, the only substantial change in the procedure in Festinger and Carlsmith (1959) from the original design given by Festinger to Hommel and myself was inclusion of the mention of being on call in the future in the $1 and $20 conditions (which I believe was done to reduce refusals to accept the money). Festinger did not, before devising the procedure in Festinger and Carlsmith, try a number of ways to experimentally test dissonance theory with limited success. The procedure of Festinger and Carlsmith was not developed by altering various parameters until finally succeeding in getting them set in the range necessary.

REFERENCES

Anderson, C. A., & Anderson, K. B. (1996). Violent crime rate studies in philosophical context: A destructive testing approach to heat and Southern culture of violence effects. *Journal of Personality and Social Psychology, 70*, 740–756.

Festinger, L., & Carlsmith, J. M. (1959). Cognitive consequences of forced compliance. *Journal of Abnormal and Social Psychology, 58*, 203–210.

Jones, E. E. (1985). Major developments in social psychology during the past five decades. In G. Lindzey & E. Aronson (Eds.), *Handbook of social psychology* (Vol. 1, 3rd ed., pp. 47–107). New York, NY: Random House.

INDEX

A

Abelson, R. P., 36, 119, 122
Abstract cognitions, 17–18
Academic underperformance, of Black students, 168–170
ACC (anterior cingulate cortex), 81–82, 130
Accessible conflict, 128–132
Accessible discrepancies, 117–132
   and accessible conflict, 128–132
   in ambivalence research, 119–121, 124–126
   and simultaneous accessibility, 121–128
Action-based model, 16–17, 77–83
Action orientation, 80
Act rationalization, 56–59
Adolphs, R., 235–236
Affirmation(s), 164
   and confronting people with, 185–187
   relevant, avoidance of, 182–185
Alcohol, 127–128
Allport, G. W., 74
Alternatives, spreading of, 5, 14, 32
Ambivalence
   felt, 120, 124–125
   potential, 124–125
   research on, 119–121
American Psychologist, 28
Animals, dissonance reduction in, 83
Ankeny, R. A., 257–258
Anterior cingulate cortex (ACC), 81–82, 130
Anterior insula, 231, 236, 239
Approach motivation, 80, 83

Argumentation, 44–45
Aronson, E., 7, 144, 151–152
   on consonant cognitions, 162
   on discomfort, 119
   on failure expectancies in experiments, 76
   on hypocrisy, 264
   on self, 263
   on self-consistency, 179
   on self-esteem, 154
Aronson, J., 164, 167, 170, 182–185
Asch, S. E., 142, 289–290
Attention, enhanced, 103
Attitude change, 44–45
   absence of, 65–68
   and ambivalence research, 120
   and aversive consequences, 72
   and cognitive inconsistency, 100
   and discomfort, 249–254
   and dissonance reduction, 182–190
   in feedforward models, 199–200
   in forced compliance study, 203–204, 212–213
   as indicator of dissonance, 249–254
   and simultaneous accessibility, 122
Aversive consequences, 48, 65–77, 153
   and inconsistency, 176–179
   and self-affirmation, 185
Aversive events, 35
Aversive feelings, from cognitive inconsistency, 99

B

Balance theory, 235
Balloun, J. L., 73
BAS (behavioral approach system), 129, 130
Bassili, J., 124
Batson, C. D., 73
Baumeister, R. E., 154
Baxter, D., 283
Beauvois, J.-L., 44, 50, 72
Becker, A. P., 107
Behavior
   and dissonance reduction, 81
   effective, 78
   in feedforward models, 199–200
   Leon Festinger on relationship between cognition and, 273–276
   in forced compliance study, 212–213
   in free choice simulation, 206
   normative/ideographics standards of, 178–179
   rationalization, 43–46
Behavioral approach system (BAS), 129, 130
Behavioral conflicts, 81–82
Behavioral element(s), 29, 35
Behavioral inhibition system (BIS), 128–130
Belief(s)
   (un)falsifiable, 102
   propositional, 93, 104–105
   system, 95, 98
Belief affirmation experiment, 75–76
Belief-disconfirmation paradigm, 6, 72–76
Belief updating, 101–103
Bem, D. J., 118
Benthin, A. C., 163
Berry, A., 154
Beverage experiment, 68–70
BIS (behavioral inhibition system), 128–130
Blanton, H., 163, 182–187
Blind-choice paradigm, 83
Bodenhausen, G. V., 107
Boring passages experiment, 70
Brain regions, 234–236
Brannon, S. M., 108–109
Bray, H., 257–258
Brehm, J. W., 14
   on attitude change, 44
   on dissonance arousal, 36
   on dissonance ratio, 41–42
   on free choice, 5, 120, 204
   on inconsistent cognitions, 48
   on self-affirmation, 37
   on trivialization, 126
Brock, T. C., 73, 122, 123
Burris, C. T., 76
"But only," 176

C

Cacioppo, J., 253
Calculation, radical, 54–55
Cancer, 286
Carlsmith, J. M., 293–294
   on attitude change, 10, 44
   on counterattitudinal behavior, 54
   on failure expectancies in experiments, 76
   on forbidden-toy paradigm, 123
   on inconsistency, 177
   on induced compliance, 7, 64
   on self-persuasion, 147
   on truth telling experiment, 46–48
Central processing unit (CPU), 165
Change, resistance to, 4, 78–79, 276–277
Cheating, 34
Chen, M. K., 13–14, 237
CHL (Contrastive Hebbian Learning), 200–202, 221
Choice certainty theory, 31, 32
Chua, H. F., 14
Chur-Hansen, A., 257–258
Cialdini, R., 261
Cognition(s)
   Leon Festinger on social communication and, 271–288
   and resistance to change, 4
   social, 124
   types of, 55–56
Cognitive consistency, 91–111
   and belief updating, 101–103
   defined, 92
   and dissonance elicitation, 98–99
   elements of, 92–95
   and expectancy violation, 103–104
   future research, areas for, 108–109
   and implicit vs. explicit evaluations, 104–108
   importance of, 95–96
   and inconsistency identification, 96–98
   and inconsistency resolution, 99–100
   three-stage model of, 96–100
   universality of need for, 109–111
Cognitive discrepancy, 71, 74, 76–79
Cognitive dissonance
   defined, 92
   Leon Festinger's reflections on, 289–292
   and neural correlates, 240–241
   social factors of, 119
   Western phenomenon of, 110
Cognitive rationalization, 58
Cohen, A. R., 36, 41–42, 44, 46, 48
Cohen, G. L., 167
Commitment, 46, 78–79
Commitment cognitions, 55–56
Commitment compliance, 48–53
Concrete cognitions, 17–18
Conflict, accessible, 128–132

Conflict, Decision, and Dissonance (Festinger), 32
Conflict-related distress, 131
Consequences, 15–16
 aversive. *See* Aversive consequences
 of behavioral elements, 35
 desired, 33–38
Consonance, 273–274
Consonant cognition, 3, 66, 79–80
Consonant information, 30
Constraint-satisfaction module (cs++), 201, 219–220
Contemporary Psychology, 289
Contrastive Hebbian Learning (CHL), 200–202, 221
Cooper, J., 291
 on affirmation, 164
 on attitude change, 10–11
 on aversive consequences, 35, 65
 on aversive-consequences revision, 73, 152–153, 263
 on behavior, 178–179
 on counterattitudinal behavior, 8
 and "dissonance and pill" study, 99, 250
 on dissonance arousal, 151
 on dissonance reduction, 255
 and forced compliance study, 202
 on inconsistency, 177
 and new look revision, 119, 121
 on self-affirmation, 261, 291
 task incentivizing study, 251–252
Cornell, D. P., 154
Counterattitudinal advocacy paradigm, 182, 259
Counterattitudinal-attitude paradigm, 149
Counterattitudinal behavior, 7–8, 54
 and ambivalence research, 120
 and attitude change, 44–45
 in aversive-consequences revision, 66–72
 in induced-compliance experimental results, 64, 107
 and trivialization, 126
CPU (central processing unit), 165
Critchlow, B., 127
Cs++ (constraint-satisfaction module), 201, 219–220
Culture, dissonance reduction and, 12–13
dACC (dorsal anterior cingulate cortex), 234–235

D

dACC (dorsal anterior cingulate cortex), 234–235
Decision making, 5
De Houwer, J., 103
Deliberative mind-set, 128, 129
Delta-rule learning, 198
Denizeau, M., 262

Devine, P. G., 120, 255–257, 260, 263, 264
De Vries, J., 230, 231
Discomfort, 119, 247–266
 and attitude change, 249–254, 258–261
 dissonance thermometer as tool for measuring, 255–266
 measuring dissonance as, 255–261
 relief, from alcohol, 127
Disconfirming information, 102
Discrepancy reduction, 80, 81
Disidentification, 170
Dissonance
 defined, 92
 measuring, as discomfort, 255–261
Dissonance arousal, 81–82, 176–177, 255
Dissonance effects, 63–84
 in action-based model, 77–83
 in aversive-consequences revision, 65–77
 in belief-disconfirmation paradigm, 72–76
 in induced-compliance experimental results, 64, 68–72
 in 1957 model, 64
Dissonance elicitation, 98–100
Dissonance motivation, 176
Dissonance ratio, 4, 41–43, 54–55
Dissonance reduction, 119, 175–191
 and approach motivation, 80
 and aversive consequences, 176–179
 and avoidance of relevant affirmations, 182–185
 and behavior, 81
 and confronting people with affirmation, 185–187
 and culture, 12–13
 and discomfort, 248, 255
 and double forced compliance, 56–58
 future research, areas for, 190–191
 inconsistent cognitions in, 176–177
 in nonhuman animals, 83
 and prefrontal cortex, 82–83
 self-role in, 179–180
 and temporary positive feeling of self-affirmation, 187–189
Dissonance theory, 3–4. *See also* Radical dissonance theory
 desired consequences in, 33–38
 historical notes on Festinger's tests of, 293–294
 impact of, 145
 improving the 1957 version of, 27–38
 magnitude of avoidance of dissonance in, 29–31
 prospective choices in, 31–33
 revisions of, 15–18
Dissonance thermometer, 255–266
Dissonant cognition, 3, 79–80
Dissonant information, 30

Distal motivation, 79, 99, 100
Dorsal anterior cingulate cortex (dACC), 234–235
Dorsolateral prefrontal cortex (DLPFC), 228, 230, 231–234
Double compliance, 46–47
Double forced compliance, 56–59
Dowsett, E., 257–258
Dual relationships, 47

E

EEG (electroencephalogram), 82, 228, 231–232, 233
Effective behavior, 78
Effort-justification, 6–7, 20, 80, 83, 264
Eggleston, T. J., 163
Ego theory, 42
Electrodermal activity experiment, 70
Electroencephalogram (EEG), 228, 231–232
Elkin, R. A., 253–254
Elliot, A. J., 120, 255–257, 260, 263
Emergent, 201
Expectancy violation, 103–104, 108
Experimental reality, 145
Explicit evaluations, vs. implicit, 104–108
Explorations in Cognitive Dissonance (Brehm and Cohen), 290
External commitment theory, 42

F

Falsifiable beliefs, 102
Fazio, R. H., 35, 121
  on aversive-consequences revision, 73, 152–153, 263
  on dissonance reduction, 255
  on inconsistency, 176
  and new look, 119, 121
Feedforward models, 198–201
Fein, S., 166–167
Felt ambivalence, 120, 124
Festinger, Leon, 293–294
  on attitude change, 44
  on belief-disconfirmation paradigm, 6
  on belief intensification, 73
  on belief updating, 101
  on cognitive consistency, 95
  on cognitive dissonance (1987 paper), 289–292
  on counterattitudinal behavior, 54
  on culture, 12
  on dissonance theory, 3–4, 27–28
  on inconsistency, 177
  on inconsistent cognitions, 92, 96
  on induced compliance, 64
  on induced-compliance paradigm, 7–8
  on negative-incentive effect, 10
  obituary of, 28
  on postdecision dissonance, 32
  and preconception performance experiment, 143
  on role of desired consequences, 33
  on social communication and cognition (1954 draft), 271–288
  on truth telling experiment, 46–48
fMRI (functional magnetic resonance imaging), 82–83, 228–231–233, 235, 237, 239–241
Forbidden-toy, 8, 122–124, 165, 198
Forbidden toy simulation, 199–200, 202, 208–212, 222–223
Forced compliance, 7, 43, 48–53, 152, 160, 198
Forced compliance simulation, 202–203, 212–214, 220, 223–224
Fragile self-esteem, 154–155
Free-choice paradigm, 5–6, 13, 100, 110
  in anterior insula, 231
  in argumentation/attitude change, 44–45
  in commitment, 49–53
  in dorsolateral prefrontal cortex, 232
  Leon Festinger on relationship of cognition and, 277–279
  and neural correlates, 237–238
  in posterior medial frontal cortex, 228, 230
  simulation of, 204–208, 213
  training events in, simulation of, 222
Freedman, J. L., 208–212
Fried, C., 151–152
Functional magnetic resonance imaging (fMRI), 82–83, 228–231

G

Galinsky, A. D., 164, 261, 265–266
Galvanic skin responses (GSRs), 253–254
Gawronski, B., 95, 103–104, 107–109
Generative cognition, 43–46, 54, 72
Gerard, H. B., 214–218
Ghiglione, R., 44
Gibbons, F. X., 163
Girandola, F., 46–48
Girotto, V., 94
Glass, D. C., 154–155
Gosling, P., 262
Greenberg, J., 36, 37, 120, 126, 265
Greenwald, A. G., 96
Griffin, D. W., 120
Group behavior, 214, 216
GSRs (galvanic skin responses), 253–254

H

Hardyck, J. A., 122
Harlow, T., 154
Harmon-Jones, C., 258

Harmon-Jones, E., 36
  on ambivalence research, 120
  on aversive-consequences revision, 263
  on discomfort, 258
  on inconsistency, 99
  on neural correlates, 228, 231–232
  on simultaneous-accessibility, 121
Health, and self-affirmation, 167
Heider, F., 43, 94
Heine, S. J., 12
Hershey's Kiss experiment, 70–71
High choice, 8, 69–70, 189
High justification, 64–65
Hippocampus, 233–234
Holland, R. W., 261
Hommel, Leonard, 293–294
Hovland, C. I., 142
Hyper-accessibility, 121
Hypocrisy, 126–127, 148–153, 261–263
Hypocrisy paradigm, 20, 97–98, 127, 261–262

I

Implicit evaluations, vs. explicit, 104–108
Impression-management theory, 11
Inconsistency, 119, 176–177. *See also* Cognitive consistency
  of identification, 96–98
  native, 120
  in recurrent neural network model of cognitive dissonance, 219
  of resolution, 99–100
Induced-compliance paradigm, 7–8, 10, 64–66, 81–82, 107, 166, 177, 183, 188, 232, 248, 251–253, 256, 258, 264–265
  and attitude change, 100, 165–166, 249
  and aversive-consequences revision, 68–72
  in posterior medial frontal cortex, 228, 230
Information
  consonant, 30
  disconfirming, 102
  dissonant, 30
  expectancy violation, 103–104
  exposure, 31
  useful, 77–78
Insko, C. A., 35
Izuma, K., 228–231, 233, 235–236, 238

J

Jamieson, D. W., 120
Japan, 283
Jarcho, J. M., 232
Johnson-Laird, P. N., 94
Jones, E. E., 8, 202
Jordens, K., 198–200

Josephs, R. A., 127
Joule, R.-V., 44–48, 72
Journal of Personality and Social Psychology, 293
Justification, 64–65

K

Kaplan, K. J., 120
Kardush, M., 122
Kelly, K., 164
Keough, K. A., 167
Kernis, M., 154
Kiesler, C. A., 42, 46, 49, 123
Kitayama, S., 14, 230, 232, 239

L

Legrenzi, P., 94
Lehman, D. R., 12
Leippe, M. R., 253–254
Lepper, M. R., 198, 204–208
Léveillé, E., 204–208
Levèque, L., 44–45
Levy, N., 258
Li, W., 264
Linder, D. E., 8, 202, 212–214
Liu, T. J., 37, 121–122, 160–161, 180, 252
Logic, 94–95, 108
Losch, M., 253
Low choice, 8, 69–70, 189
Low justification, 64–65

M

Magnitude of avoidance, 29–31
Mathewson, G. C., 214–218
Matz, D. C., 257
Measurement error, 13–14
"meat paradox," 257–258
Meertens, R. M., 261
Mengarelli, F., 232
Mere-ownership effects, 108
Metee, D. R., 154
Mills, J., 7, 9, 30, 144
Misattribution paradigm, 10
Modeling, neural network. *See* Recurrent neural network model of cognitive dissonance
Models, feedforward, 198–201
Monkey single-cell recoding study, 235
Mood, 220
Morality salience, 130
Morally good self, 46, 53
Motivation
  approach, 80–81
  distal, 79, 99, 100
  proximal, 79, 99, 100
  trait approach, 81

Multi-voxel pattern analysis (MVPA), 240
Murayama, K., 238

N

Nash, K., 129
Native inconsistency, 120
Negative affective reaction, 109
Negative-incentive effect, 7–8, 10
Negotiation biases, 167–168
Nelson, D. E., 36, 120
Neural correlates, 81–83, 227–241
  anterior cingulate cortex, 81–82
  anterior insula, 231
  dorsolateral prefrontal cortex, 231–233
  and free choice, 237–238
  hippocampus, 233–234
  posterior cingulate cortex, 233
  posterior medial frontal cortex, 228–231
  prefrontal cortex, 82–83
  and reverse inference problem, 238–239
  roles played by various brain regions, 234–236
  and understanding of cognitive dissonance, 240–241
  ventral striatum, 233
Neural network model. *See* Recurrent neural network model of cognitive dissonance
New look, 15–16, 48, 119, 121
Nichols, T. E., 238
Nonhuman animals, dissonance reduction in, 83
Nonspecific skin conductance responses (NS-SCRs), 253–254
Noordewier, M. K., 109
No-paradigmatic-sequence condition, 51–52
Nude Olympics, 187–188

O

Oberlé, D., 262
Object evaluation, in free choice simulation, 204, 206

P

Pallak, M. S., 123
Paradigmatic-sequence condition, 50–51
Parallel constant-satisfaction network, 197–198, 218, 220
PCC (posterior cingulate cortex), 233, 236, 239
Personal responsibility, 66, 73
Persuasion biases, 167–168
PFC (preference for consistency), 125–126
PMFC. *See* Posterior medial frontal cortex

Poldrack, R. A., 238
Political discussions, 283–285
Posterior cingulate cortex (PCC), 233, 236, 239
Posterior medial frontal cortex (pMFC), 228–231, 234, 236, 239, 240
Potential ambivalence, 124–125
Prasad, J., 279–280
Precision, of theory building, 148
Preference for consistency (PFC), 125–126
Prefrontal cortex, 82–83
Prejudice, 166–167
Princeton University, 187
Propositional beliefs, 93, 104–105
Prospective choices, 31–33
Proulx, T., 101
Proximal motivation, 79, 99, 100
Public evaluation of alternatives, 32
Pyszczynski, T., 265

Q

Qin, J., 231, 232

R

Rabbie, J. M., 44
Radical dissonance theory, 41–59
  commitment to compliance in, 48–53
  and double forced compliance/act rationalization, 56–59
  generative cognition and behavior rationalization in, 43–46
  1957 version of dissonance theory vs., 53–57
  truth telling in, 46–48
Rationalization, 118
Reactive approach motivation (RAM), 129–132
Read, S. J., 198, 220
Recall experiment, 68–70
Recurrent neural network model of cognitive dissonance, 197–224
  constraint-satisfaction module in, 219
  and feedforward models, 198–201
  forbidden toy simulation, 208–212
  forced compliance simulation, 212–214
  free choice simulation, 204–208
  inconsistency in, 219
  mood in, 220
  overview, 201–202
  and self-perception theory, 220–221
  severity of initiation simulation, 214–218
  simulation procedure overview, 202–204
  simulation training events, 222–224
  theoretical advantages, 218–220
Reduction, dissonance. *See* Dissonance reduction

Reflections on Cognitive Dissonance (Festinger), 27
Reinforcement
  effect, 49
  theory, 142
Relationships, dual, 47
Religious experiments. *See* Belief-disconfirmation paradigm
Religious zeal, 131
Research paradigms, 5–9
  belief-disconfirmation paradigm, 6
  effort-justification paradigm, 6–7
  forbidden-toy paradigm, 8
  free-choice paradigm, 5–6, 13
  induced-compliance paradigm, 7–8
  misattribution paradigm, 10
Resistance to change, 4, 78–79, 276–277
Reverse inference problem, 238–239
Reward, 54–55
Riecken, H. W., 6, 73, 101
Risen, J. L., 13–14, 237
Rohan, M. J., 154
Role models, effect of, 169
Ronis, D. L., 96
Rosenberg, M. J., 36, 122
Row, Peterson, 289
Rydell, R. J., 103–104

S

Sacchi, D. L. M., 108–109
Sady, R. R., 281
Scalise, C. J., 179
Schachter, S., 6, 73, 101
Scher, S. J., 177
Schopenhauer, A., 118
Schumann, K., 132
Scope, of theory building, 148
Scott, W. A., 120
SCR (skin conductance response), 240
Self, 36–37
  and dissonance reduction, 83
  and implicit evaluation, 107
  morally good, 46, 53
Self-affirmation theory, 16, 98–99, 119, 121, 159–171
  academic underperformance of Black students according to, 168–170
  and discomfort, 260–261
  disidentification in, 170
  dispositional self-esteem in, 163–165
  and dissonance reduction, 180–189
  effect of positive role models in, 169
  health considerations in, 167
  and need for a new theory, 162
  persuasion/negotiation biases in, 167–168
  prejudice in, 166–167
  resources model, 163

  summary of, 160–161
  synthetic approach of, 171
  temporary positive feeling of, 187–189
Self-concept, 15, 141–155
  and hypocrisy, 148–153
  and inconsistent cognitions, 119
  and self-affirmation theory, 161
  and self-justification, 153–155
  and self-persuasion, 145–147
  and theory building, 147–148
Self-consistency, 15, 161, 163, 179
Self-esteem, 71, 154, 163–165
Self-integrity, 252
Self-justification, 147, 153–155
Self-perception theory, 9–11, 45, 118–119, 220–221, 240–241
Self-persuasion, 145–147
Self-reference effect, 121
Self-relevance, 96, 98
Self-role, in dissonance reduction, 179–180
Semmler, C., 257–258
Severity of initiation simulation, 214–218, 220, 224
Shultz, T. R., 198, 204–208
Sideris, J., 265
Simon, L., 36, 37, 120, 126, 162
Simulation procedure, of recurrent neural network model of cognitive dissonance, 202–204
Simulation training events, of recurrent neural network model of cognitive dissonance, 222–224
Simultaneous accessibility, 97, 121–128
Simultaneous activation, 93
Sinha, D., 280
Skin conductance, 70, 120, 240
Smoking, 34
Social cognition, 124
Social communication, 271–288
Social influence, 141–142
Solomon, S., 265
Son Hing, L. S., 264
Southwick, L. L., 127
Spencer, S. J., 166–167
Spreading of alternatives, 5, 12–15, 32, 80, 81, 83, 100, 107–108, 110, 208, 218, 233, 248
State Self-Esteem Scale, 71
Steele, C. M., 37, 119, 121–122, 127, 160–162, 167, 180, 252
Stereotype threat, 168
Stice, E., 265
Stone, J., 164, 178–180, 261
Strack, F., 107
Stubing, M. J., 265
Subjective importance, 98
Sullivan, H. S., 191
Sun, C.-R., 154

T

Task-relevance, 98
Tauer, J., 260
tDCS (transcranial direct current stimulation), 232
Terwilliger, Robert, 294
Theoretical advantages, of recurrent neural network model of cognitive dissonance, 218–220
Theory building, 147–148
A Theory of Cognitive Dissonance (Festinger), 3
Thibodeau, R., 162
Thompson, M. M., 120
Threat conditions, 123
"Throwing oneself into one's work," 123
TMS (transcranial magnetic stimulation), 230–231
Tompson, S., 14, 232, 238
Topolinski, S., 109
Trait approach motivation, 81
Transcendence experiment, 74–75
Transcranial direct current stimulation (tDCS), 232
Transcranial magnetic stimulation (TMS), 230–231
Trivialization, 126
Trustworthiness, 272–273
Truth telling, 46–48

U

Unfalsifiable beliefs, 102
University of Provence, 47

V

Vance, K., 264
Van Dijk, E., 109
Van Essen, D. C., 238
Van Overwalle, F., 198–200
Van Veen, V., 228–229, 231
Van Vugt, M., 261
Ventral striatum, 83, 233
Voluntary audiences, 287–288

W

Wager, T. D., 238
Waschull, S., 154
Weiss, W., 142
Well-grounded self-esteem, 154–155
When prophecy fails study, 101
Within-subjects design difficult decision paradigm, 82
Wood, W., 257
Worchel, S., 65, 177, 251–252
Worldview defense, 130

Y

Yarkoni, T., 238
Ye, Y., 103

Z

Zajonc, R. B., 28
Zanna, M. P., 10–11, 99, 120, 151, 250, 264
Zentall, T. R., 83

ABOUT THE EDITOR

Eddie Harmon-Jones, PhD, is a professor of psychology at The University of New South Wales. His research focuses on emotions and motivations, their implications for social and cognitive processes, and their underlying physiological substrates. His research has been supported by the National Institute of Mental Health, the National Science Foundation, and the Australian Research Council. In 2002, he received the Award for Distinguished Early Career Contribution to Psychophysiology from the Society for Psychophysiological Research. In 2012, he received the Career Trajectory Award from the Society of Experimental Social Psychology. He has authored over 200 articles and book chapters, and has edited six scholarly books. He has served as an associate editor of the *Journal of Personality and Social Psychology*, the *International Journal of Psychophysiology*, and *Emotion*. He is currently an associate editor of the journal *Psychological Science*.